Yuto Tsukuda

This year's resolution—wake up in the morning.

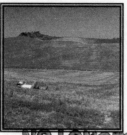

Shun Saeki

It's been over a year since my first ferret crossed over the rainbow bridge. It always hurts to lose a family member, but I was glad for the time we had together.

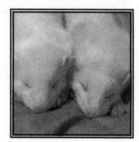

About the authors

Yuto Tsukuda won the 34th Jump Juniketsu Newcomers' Manga Award for his one-shot story *Kiba ni Naru*. He made his *Weekly Shonen Jump* debut in 2010 with the series *Shonen Shikku*. His follow-up series, *Food Wars!: Shokugeki no Soma*, is his first English-language release.

Shun Saeki made his *Jump NEXT!* debut in 2011 with the one-shot story *Kimi to Watashi no Renai Soudan. Food Wars!: Shokugeki no Soma* is his first *Shonen Jump* series.

Food Wars!
SHOKUGEKI NO SOMA

Volume 16
Shonen Jump Advanced Manga Edition
Story by Yuto Tsukuda, Art by Shun Saeki
Contributor Yuki Morisaki

Translation: Adrienne Beck
Touch-Up Art & Lettering: Stephen Dutro
Design: Izumi Evers
Editor: Jennifer LeBlanc

Printed in the U.S.A.

Published by VIZ Media, LLC
P.O. Box 77010
San Francisco, CA 94107

10 9 8 7 6 5 4 3 2 1
First printing, February 2017

www.viz.com

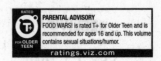

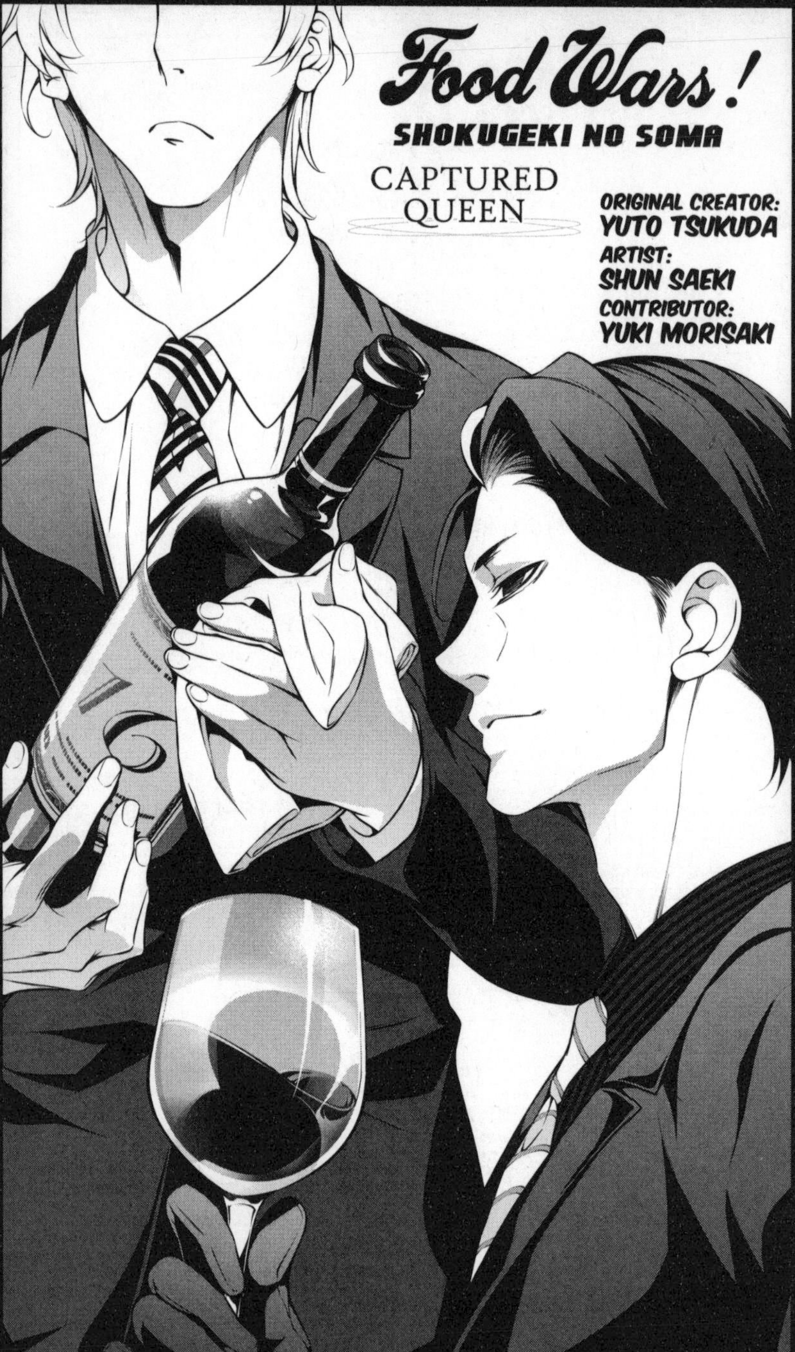
Food Wars!
SHOKUGEKI NO SOMA
CAPTURED QUEEN
ORIGINAL CREATOR:
YUTO TSUKUDA
ARTIST:
SHUN SAEKI
CONTRIBUTOR:
YUKI MORISAKI

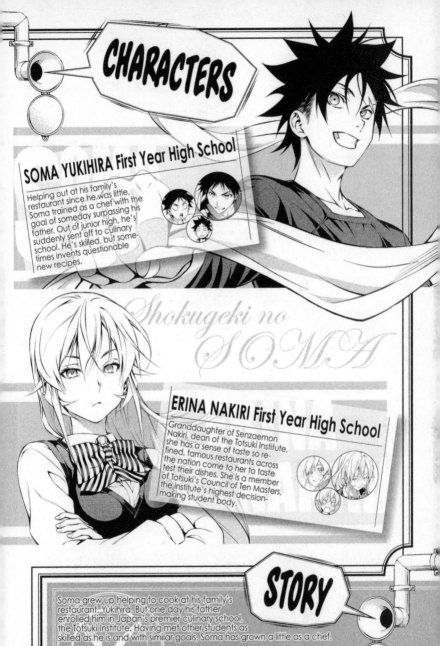

CHARACTERS

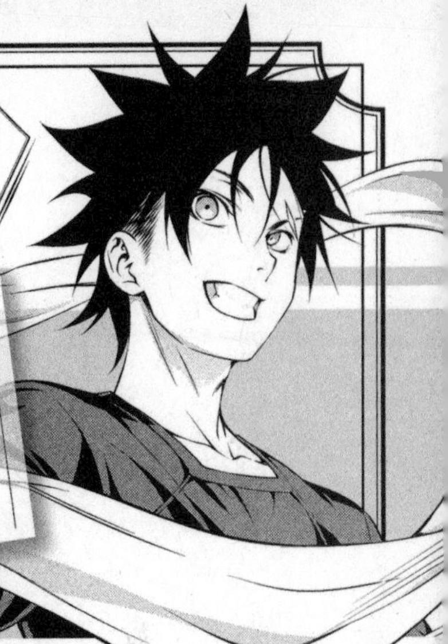

SOMA YUKIHIRA First Year High School

Helping out at his family's restaurant since he was little, Soma trained as a chef with the goal of someday surpassing his father. Out of junior high, he's suddenly sent off to culinary school. He's skilled, but sometimes invents questionable new recipes.

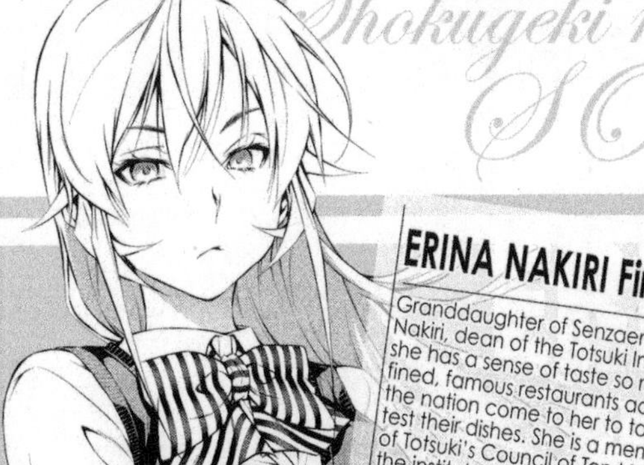
Shokugeki no SOMA

ERINA NAKIRI First Year High School

Granddaughter of Senzaemon Nakiri, dean of the Totsuki Institute, she has a sense of taste so refined, famous restaurants across the nation come to her to taste test their dishes. She is a member of Totsuki's Council of Ten Masters, the institute's highest decision-making student body.

STORY

Soma grew up helping to cook at his family's restaurant, Yukihira. But one day his father enrolled him in Japan's premier culinary school, the Totsuki Institute. Having met other students as skilled as he is and with similar goals, Soma has grown a little as a chef.

The curtain rises on the last major fall event at the Totsuki Institute, the Moon Festival! Looking for a chance to take on a Council of Ten member in a shokugeki, Soma challenges eighth seat Terunori Kuga's massive restaurant with a tiny food cart. His type of cuisine? Kuga's specialty, of course—Chinese! Things get off to a rocky start for Soma, and after two days, he's deep in the red. What's his plan for getting out of not only the red but also imminent expulsion?!

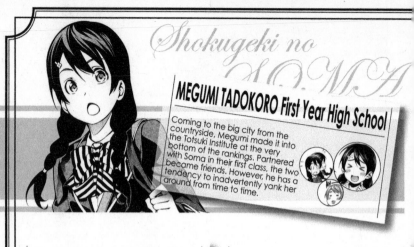

Shokugeki no SOMA

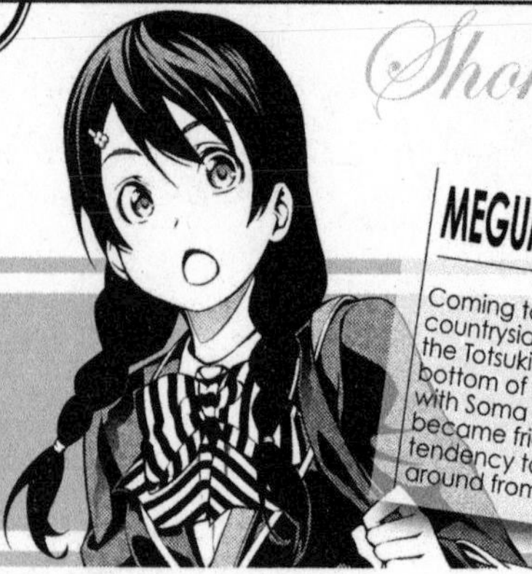

MEGUMI TADOKORO First Year High School

Coming to the big city from the countryside, Megumi made it into the Totsuki Institute at the very bottom of the rankings. Partnered with Soma in their first class, the two became friends. However, he has a tendency to inadvertently yank her around from time to time.

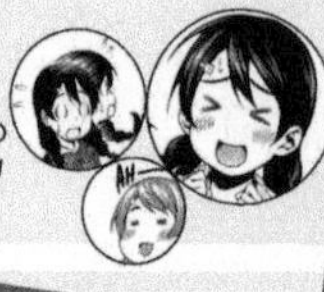
AH

TAKUMI ALDINI First Year High School

Working at his family's trattoria in Italy from a young age, he transferred into the Totsuki Institute in junior high. Isami is his younger twin brother.

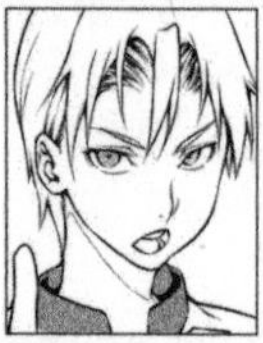

IKUMI MITO First Year High School

Specializing in meat dishes, she is defeated by Soma in a shokugeki and forced to join the Donburi Bowl Society. Her nickname is "Nikumi" (which she hates).

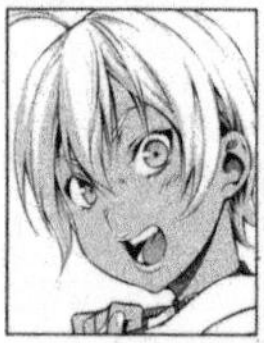

ALICE NAKIRI First Year High School

Erina's cousin, she has spent much of her life overseas with her parents learning cooking from a scientific perspective through molecular gastronomy.

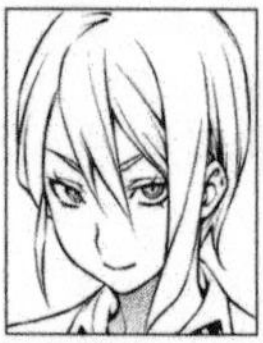

AKIRA HAYAMA First Year High School

A master of spices and the winner of the Fall Classic, Hayama grew up as an orphan in a Southeast Asian slum, where Jun Shiomi found and adopted him.

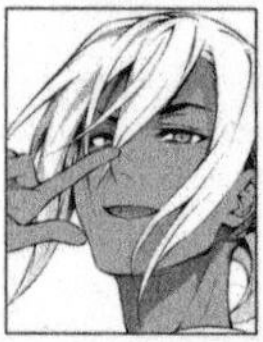

HISAKO ARATO First Year High School

Erina's exceptionally loyal and devoted aide, she is skilled in medicinal cooking. Her current worry is the proliferation of her nickname, Secretary Girl.

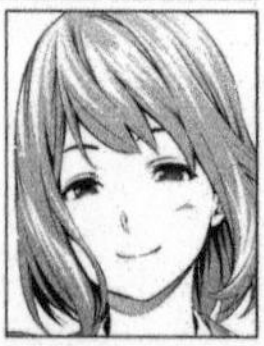

TERUNORI KUGA Second Year High School

Council of Ten eighth seat and captain of the Chinese-Food Research Society, he's cheerful and upbeat, but not satisfied with his current council seat position.

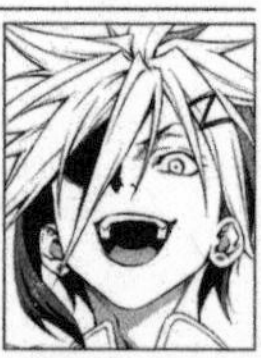

Food Wars! SHOKUGEKI NO SOMA

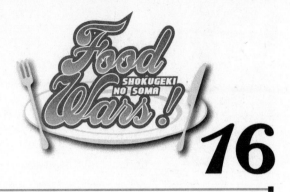

16

Table of Contents

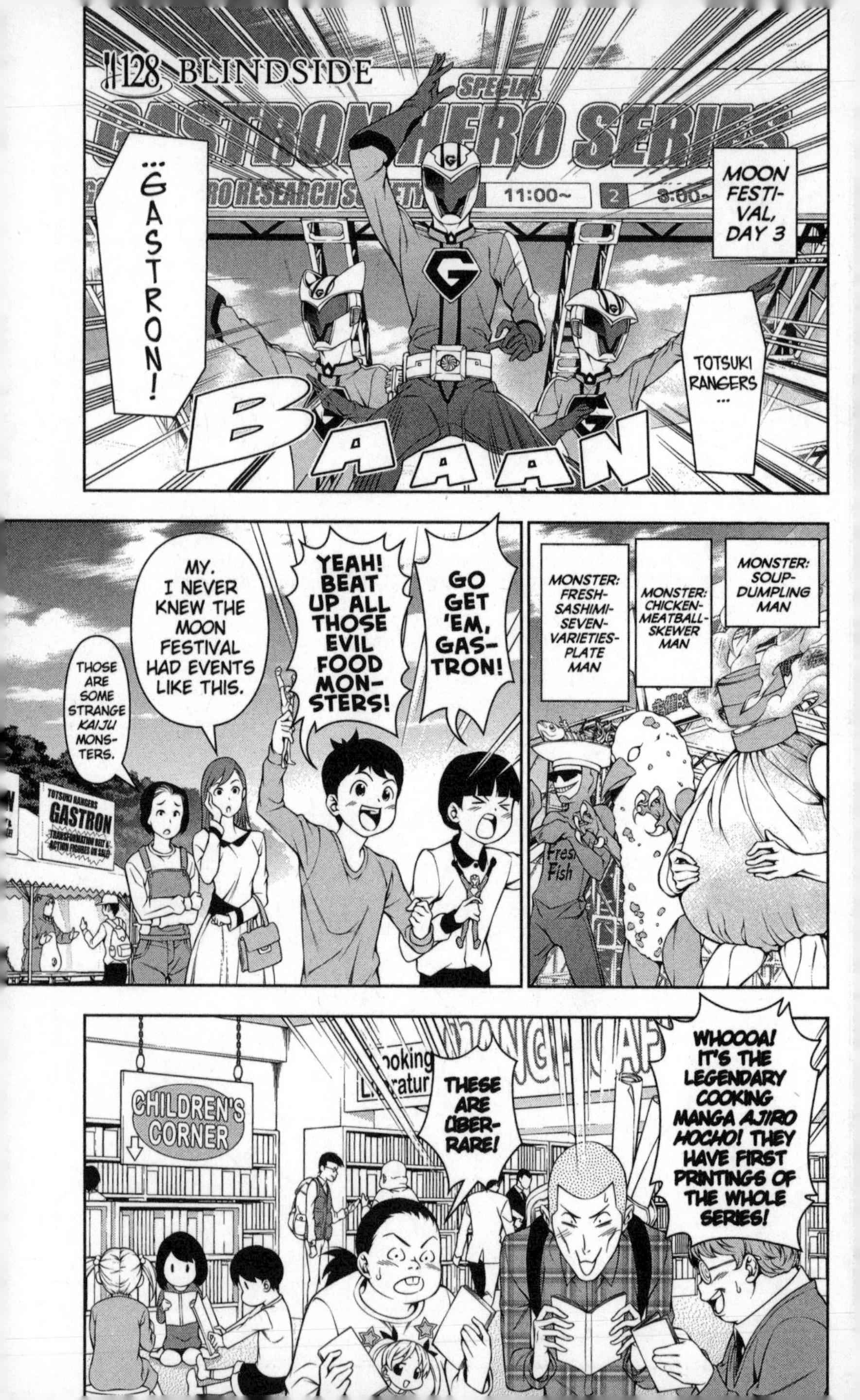

#128 BLINDSIDE
SPECIAL
11:00~
MOON FESTIVAL, DAY 3
TOTSUKI RANGERS...
...GASTRON!
BAAAN
MONSTER: SOUP-DUMPLING MAN
MONSTER: CHICKEN-MEATBALL-SKEWER MAN
MONSTER: FRESH-SASHIMI-SEVEN-VARIETIES-PLATE MAN
Fresh Fish
GO GET 'EM, GASTRON!
YEAH! BEAT UP ALL THOSE EVIL FOOD MONSTERS!
MY. I NEVER KNEW THE MOON FESTIVAL HAD EVENTS LIKE THIS.
THOSE ARE SOME STRANGE *KAIJU* MONSTERS.
TOTSUKI RANGERS GASTRON
TRANSFORMATION BELT & ACTION FIGURES ON SALE!
WHOOOA! IT'S THE LEGENDARY COOKING MANGA AJIRO HOCHO! THEY HAVE FIRST PRINTINGS OF THE WHOLE SERIES!
THESE ARE ÜBER-RARE!
Cooking Literatur
CHILDREN'S CORNER

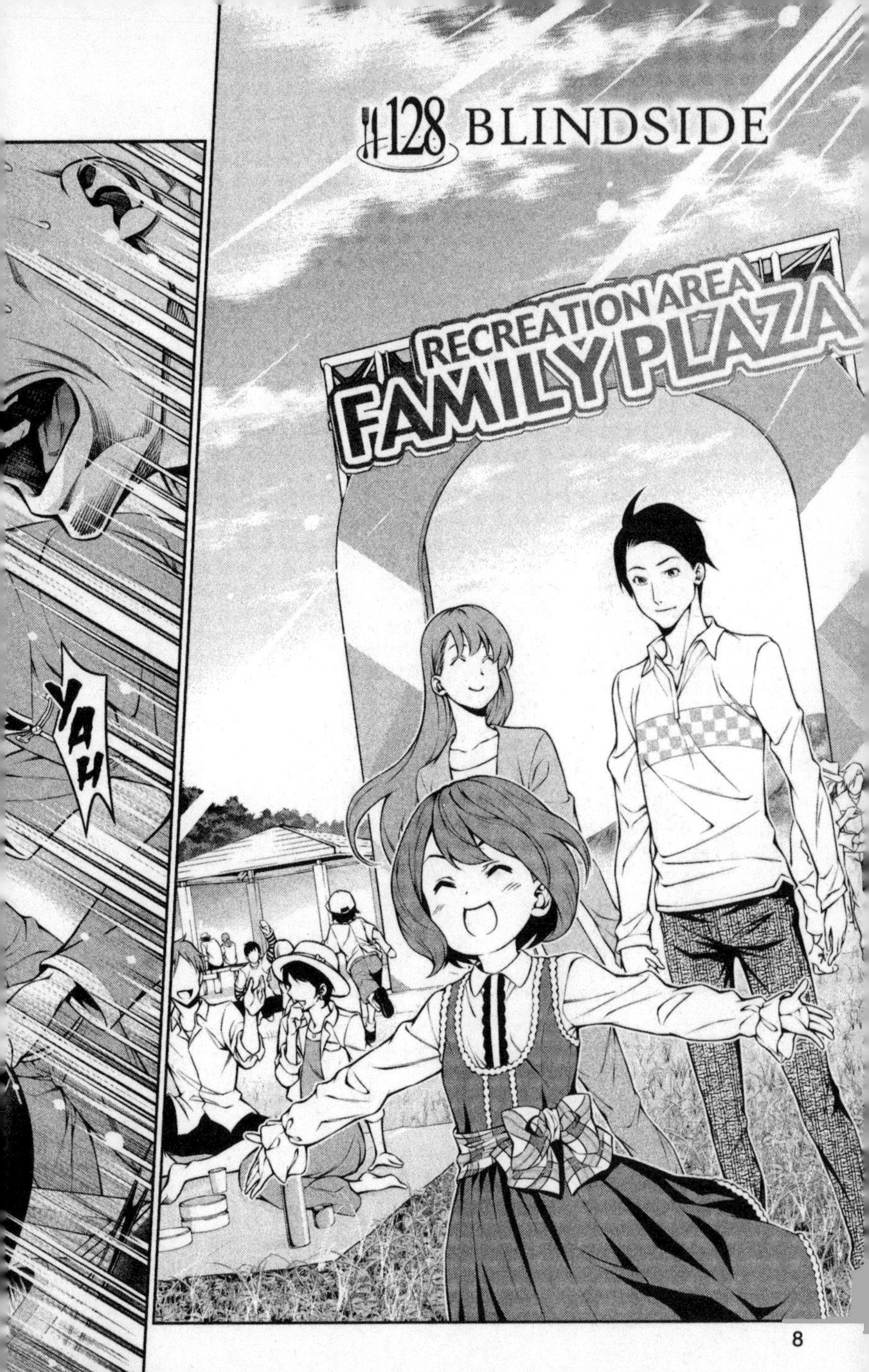

128 BLINDSIDE
RECREATION AREA
FAMILY PLAZA
YAH

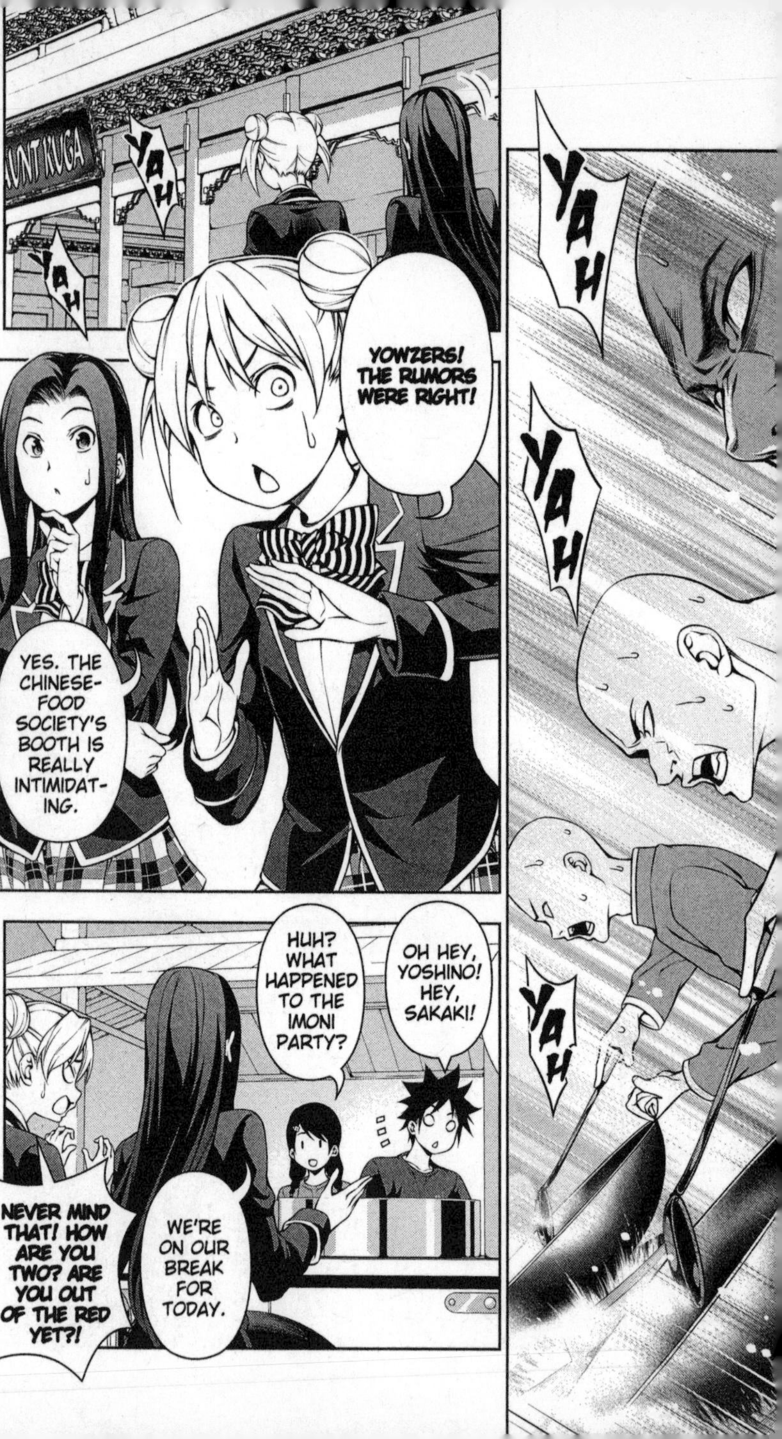
YAH
YAH
YAH
AUNT KUGA
YAH
YAH
YOWZERS! THE RUMORS WERE RIGHT!
YES. THE CHINESE-FOOD SOCIETY'S BOOTH IS REALLY INTIMIDATING.
OH HEY, YOSHINO! HEY, SAKAKI!
HUH? WHAT HAPPENED TO THE IMONI PARTY?
WE'RE ON OUR BREAK FOR TODAY.
NEVER MIND THAT! HOW ARE YOU TWO? ARE YOU OUT OF THE RED YET?!

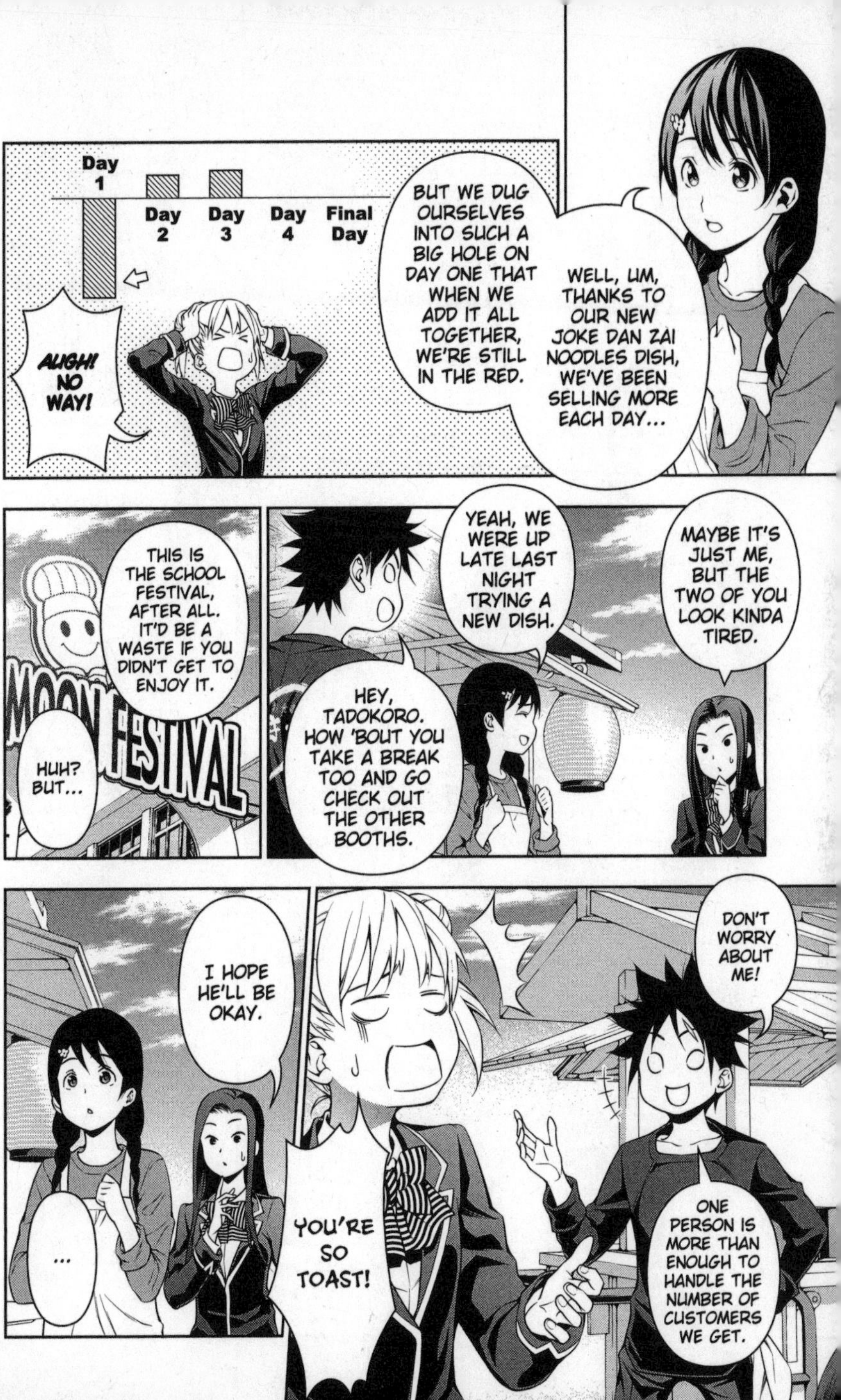
WELL, UM, THANKS TO OUR NEW JOKE DAN ZAI NOODLES DISH, WE'VE BEEN SELLING MORE EACH DAY...
BUT WE DUG OURSELVES INTO SUCH A BIG HOLE ON DAY ONE THAT WHEN WE ADD IT ALL TOGETHER, WE'RE STILL IN THE RED.
Day 1
Day 2
Day 3
Day 4
Final Day
AUGH! NO WAY!
MAYBE IT'S JUST ME, BUT THE TWO OF YOU LOOK KINDA TIRED.
YEAH, WE WERE UP LATE LAST NIGHT TRYING A NEW DISH.
HEY, TADOKORO. HOW 'BOUT YOU TAKE A BREAK TOO AND GO CHECK OUT THE OTHER BOOTHS.
THIS IS THE SCHOOL FESTIVAL, AFTER ALL. IT'D BE A WASTE IF YOU DIDN'T GET TO ENJOY IT.
MOON FESTIVAL
HUH? BUT...
DON'T WORRY ABOUT ME!
ONE PERSON IS MORE THAN ENOUGH TO HANDLE THE NUMBER OF CUSTOMERS WE GET.
YOU'RE SO TOAST!
I HOPE HE'LL BE OKAY.
...

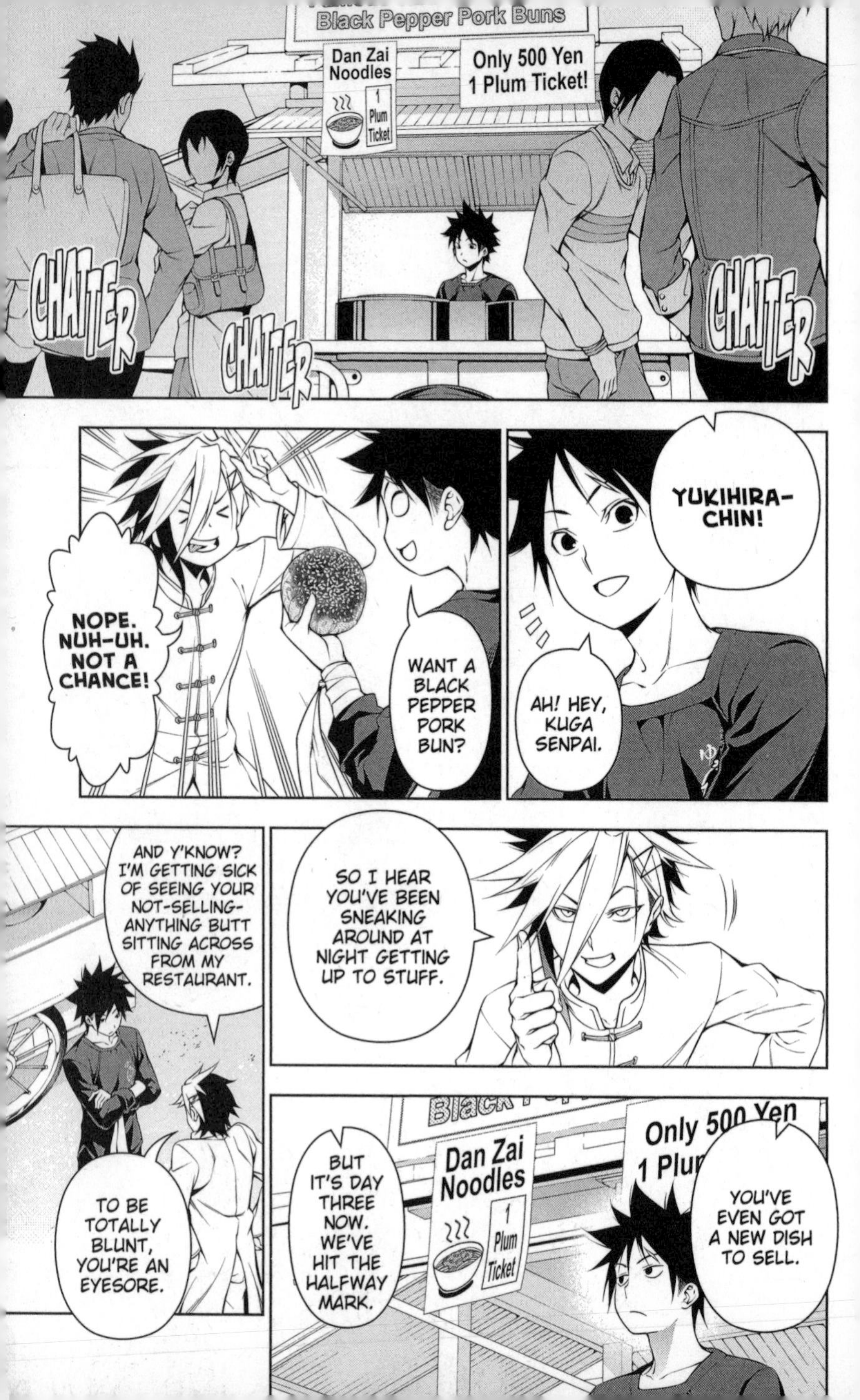
Black Pepper Pork Buns
Only 500 Yen 1 Plum Ticket!
Dan Zai Noodles
1 Plum Ticket
CHATTER
CHATTER
CHATTER
YUKIHIRA-CHIN!
AH! HEY, KUGA SENPAI.
WANT A BLACK PEPPER PORK BUN?
NOPE. NUH-UH. NOT A CHANCE!
SO I HEAR YOU'VE BEEN SNEAKING AROUND AT NIGHT GETTING UP TO STUFF.
Only 500 Yen
Dan Zai Noodles
1 Plum Ticket
YOU'VE EVEN GOT A NEW DISH TO SELL.
BUT IT'S DAY THREE NOW. WE'VE HIT THE HALFWAY MARK.
AND Y'KNOW? I'M GETTING SICK OF SEEING YOUR NOT-SELLING-ANYTHING BUTT SITTING ACROSS FROM MY RESTAURANT.
TO BE TOTALLY BLUNT, YOU'RE AN EYESORE.

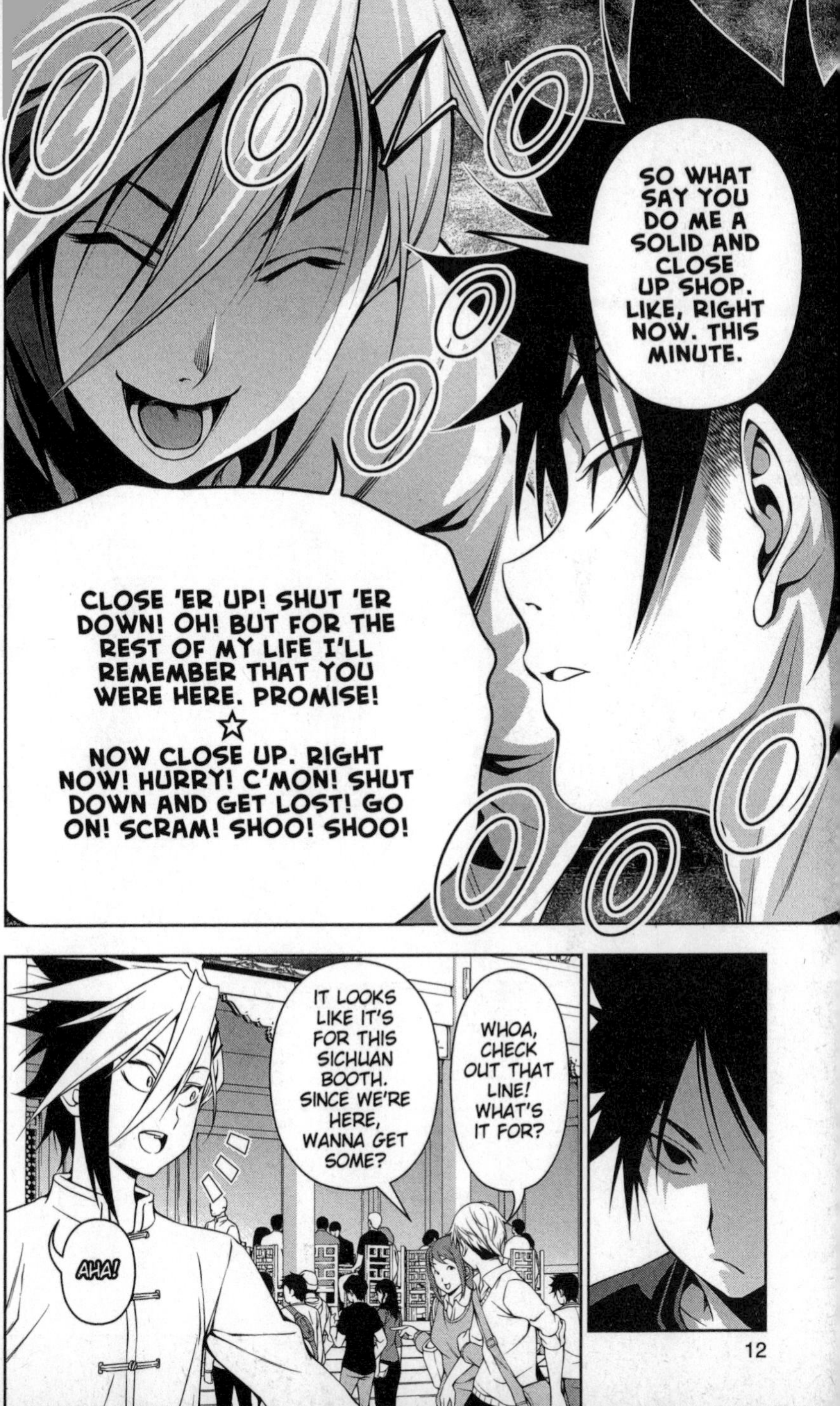
SO WHAT SAY YOU DO ME A SOLID AND CLOSE UP SHOP. LIKE, RIGHT NOW. THIS MINUTE.
CLOSE 'ER UP! SHUT 'ER DOWN! OH! BUT FOR THE REST OF MY LIFE I'LL REMEMBER THAT YOU WERE HERE. PROMISE! ☆ NOW CLOSE UP. RIGHT NOW! HURRY! C'MON! SHUT DOWN AND GET LOST! GO ON! SCRAM! SHOO! SHOO!
WHOA, CHECK OUT THAT LINE! WHAT'S IT FOR?
IT LOOKS LIKE IT'S FOR THIS SICHUAN BOOTH. SINCE WE'RE HERE, WANNA GET SOME?
AHA!

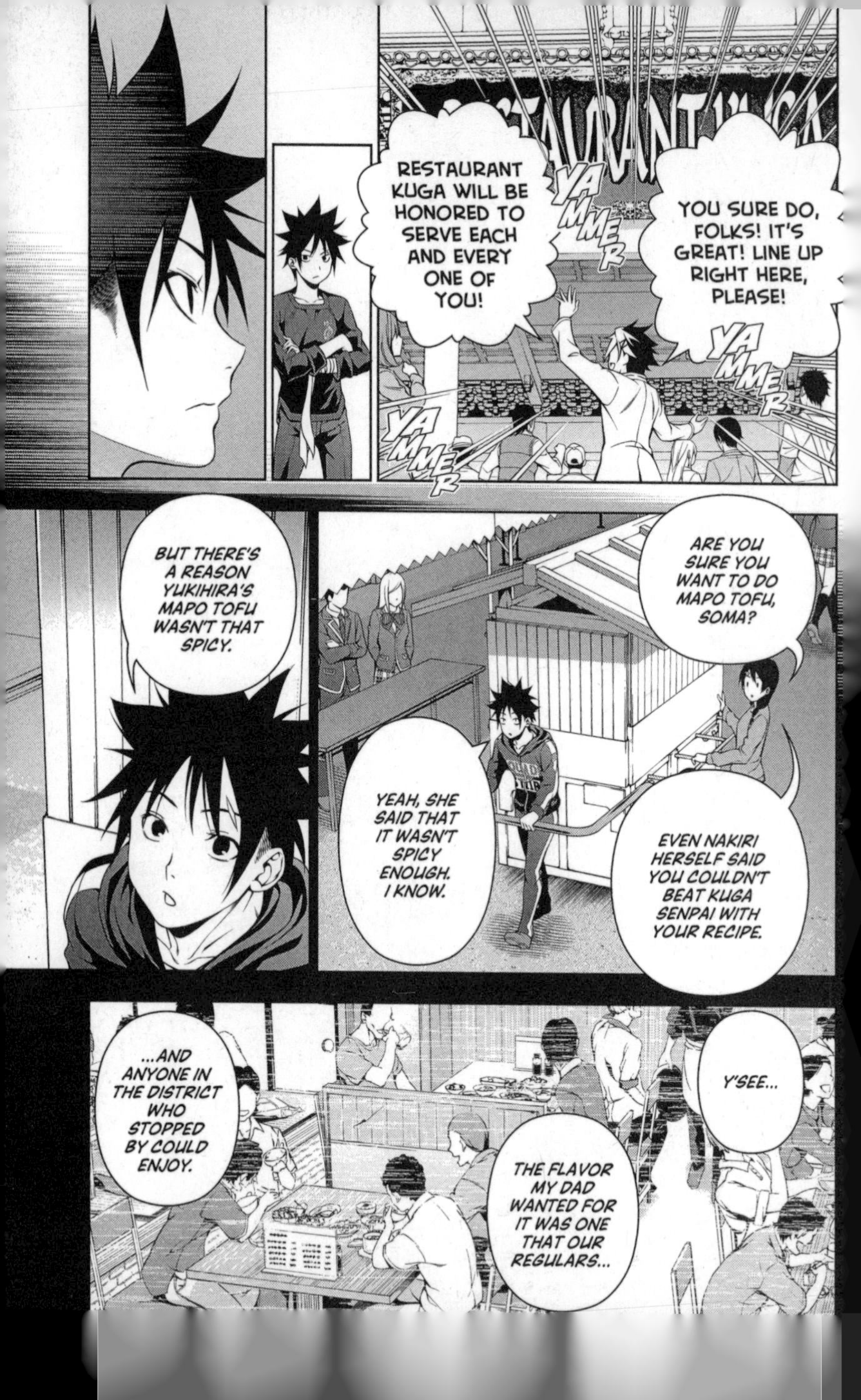
YOU SURE DO, FOLKS! IT'S GREAT! LINE UP RIGHT HERE, PLEASE!
RESTAURANT KUGA WILL BE HONORED TO SERVE EACH AND EVERY ONE OF YOU!
YAMMER
YAMMER
YAMMER
ARE YOU SURE YOU WANT TO DO MAPO TOFU, SOMA?
EVEN NAKIRI HERSELF SAID YOU COULDN'T BEAT KUGA SENPAI WITH YOUR RECIPE.
YEAH, SHE SAID THAT IT WASN'T SPICY ENOUGH. I KNOW.
BUT THERE'S A REASON YUKIHIRA'S MAPO TOFU WASN'T THAT SPICY.
Y'SEE...
THE FLAVOR MY DAD WANTED FOR IT WAS ONE THAT OUR REGULARS...
...AND ANYONE IN THE DISTRICT WHO STOPPED BY COULD ENJOY.

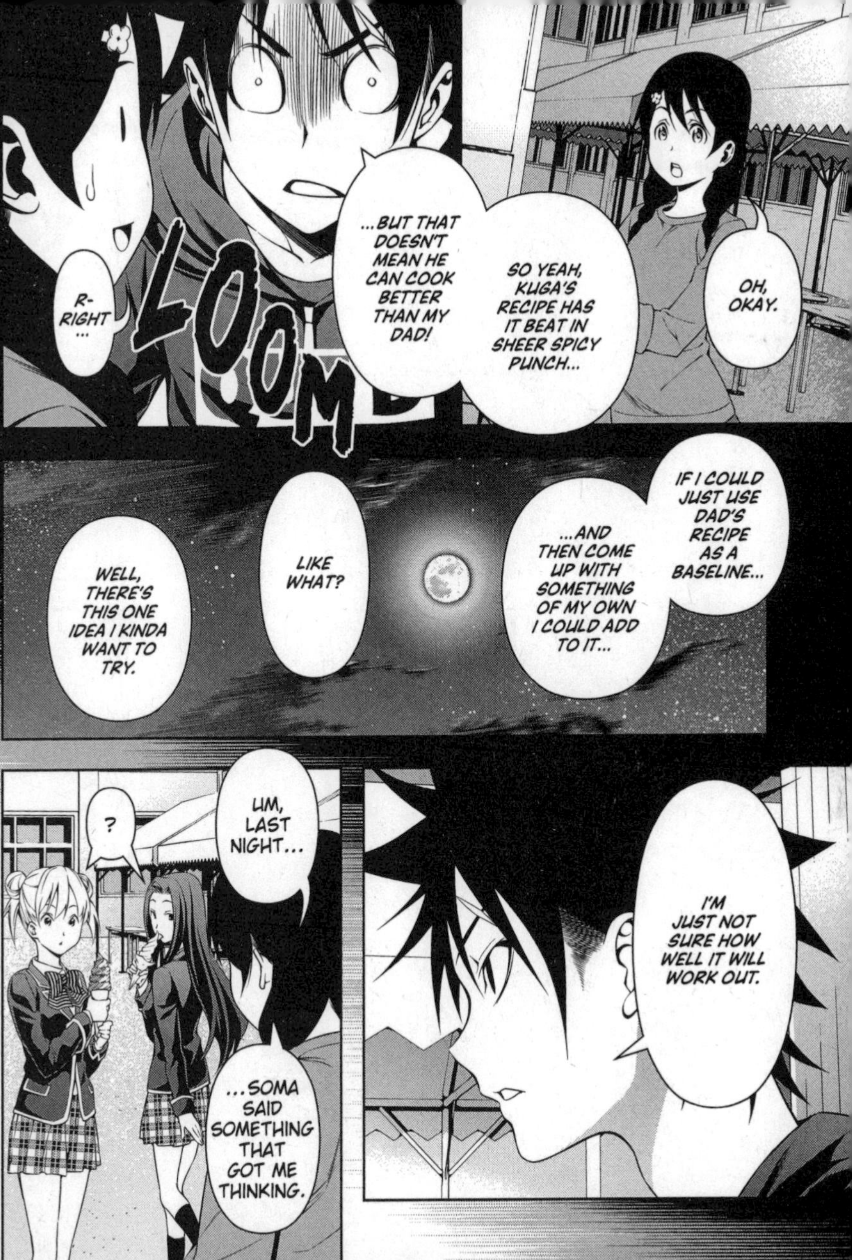
OH, OKAY.
SO YEAH, KUGA'S RECIPE HAS IT BEAT IN SHEER SPICY PUNCH...
...BUT THAT DOESN'T MEAN HE CAN COOK BETTER THAN MY DAD!
LOOM
R-RIGHT...
IF I COULD JUST USE DAD'S RECIPE AS A BASELINE...
...AND THEN COME UP WITH SOMETHING OF MY OWN I COULD ADD TO IT...
LIKE WHAT?
WELL, THERE'S THIS ONE IDEA I KINDA WANT TO TRY.
I'M JUST NOT SURE HOW WELL IT WILL WORK OUT.
UM, LAST NIGHT...
?
...SOMA SAID SOMETHING THAT GOT ME THINKING.

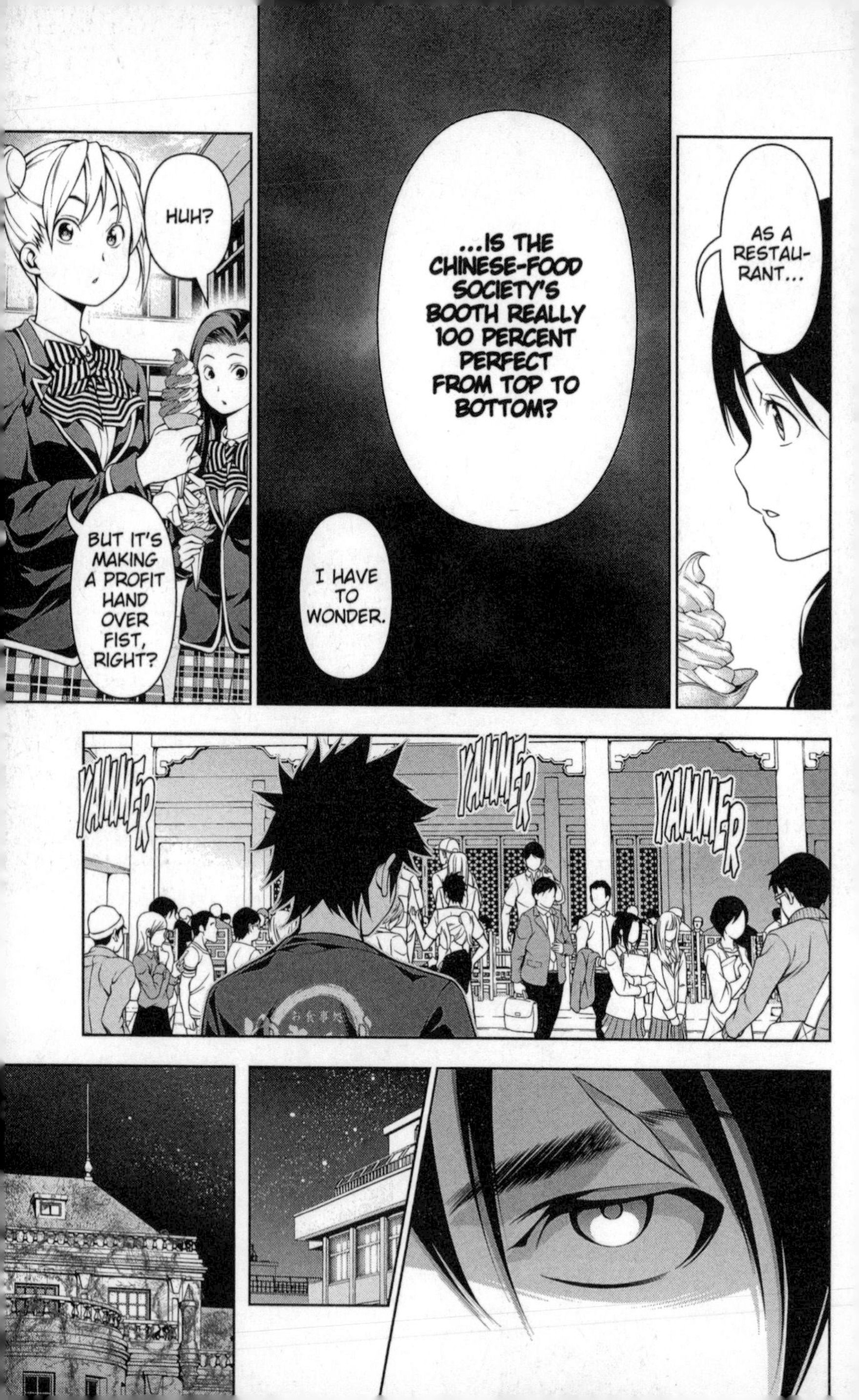
AS A RESTAURANT...
...IS THE CHINESE-FOOD SOCIETY'S BOOTH REALLY 100 PERCENT PERFECT FROM TOP TO BOTTOM?
I HAVE TO WONDER.
HUH?
BUT IT'S MAKING A PROFIT HAND OVER FIST, RIGHT?
YAMMER
YAMMER
YAMMER

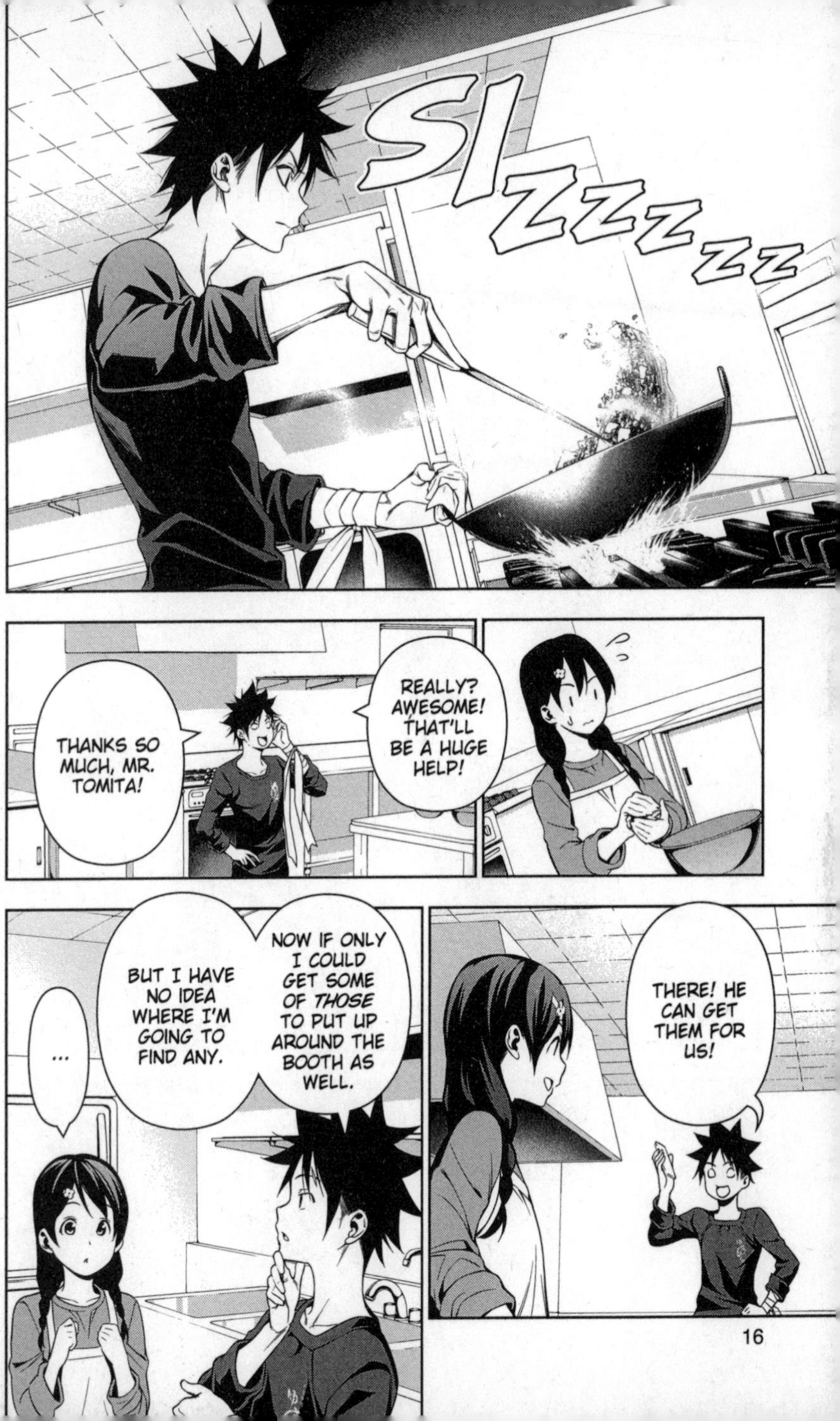
SIZZZZZZ
REALLY? AWESOME! THAT'LL BE A HUGE HELP!
THANKS SO MUCH, MR. TOMITA!
THERE! HE CAN GET THEM FOR US!
NOW IF ONLY I COULD GET SOME OF *THOSE* TO PUT UP AROUND THE BOOTH AS WELL.
BUT I HAVE NO IDEA WHERE I'M GOING TO FIND ANY.
...

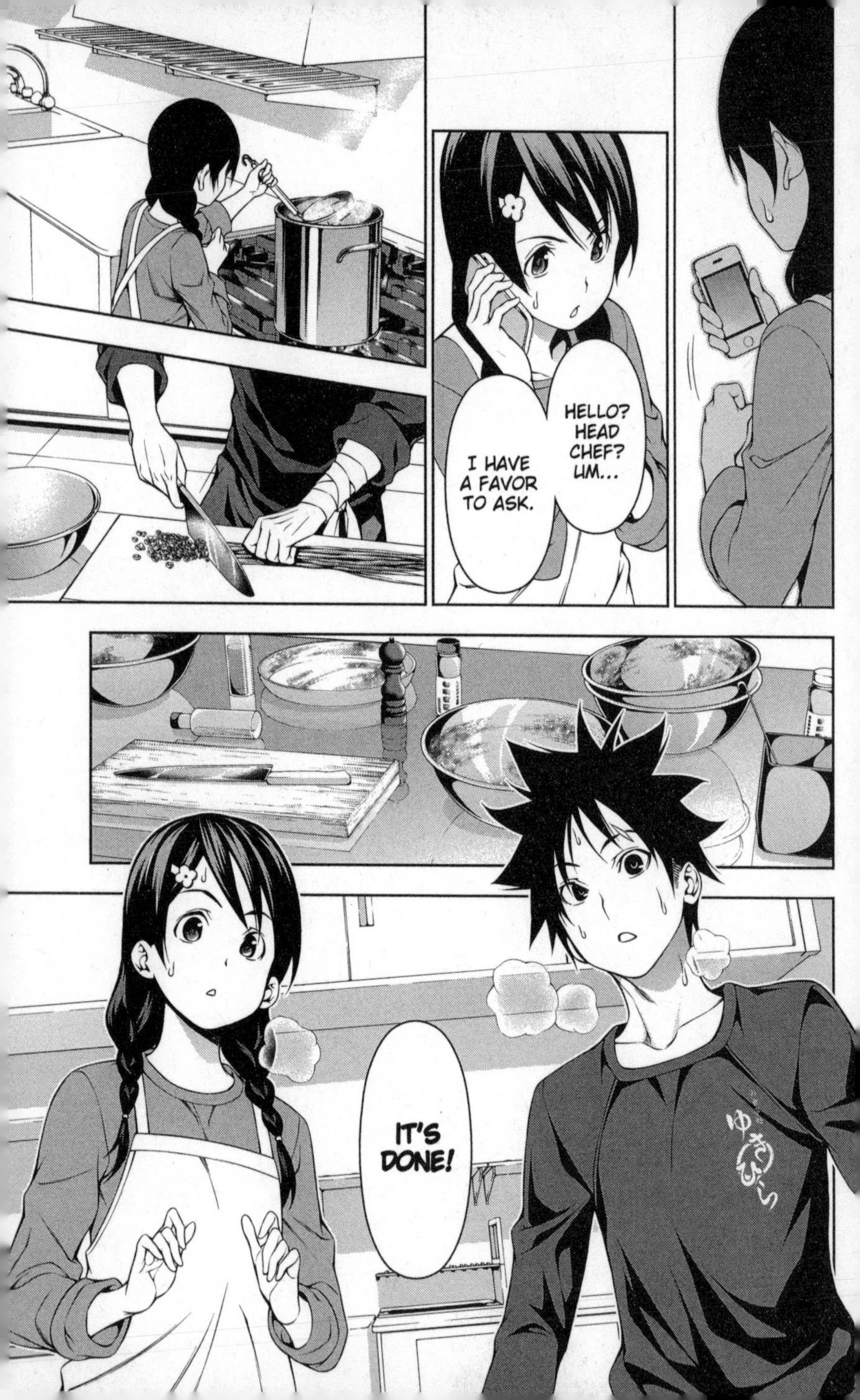
HELLO? HEAD CHEF? UM...
I HAVE A FAVOR TO ASK.
IT'S DONE!

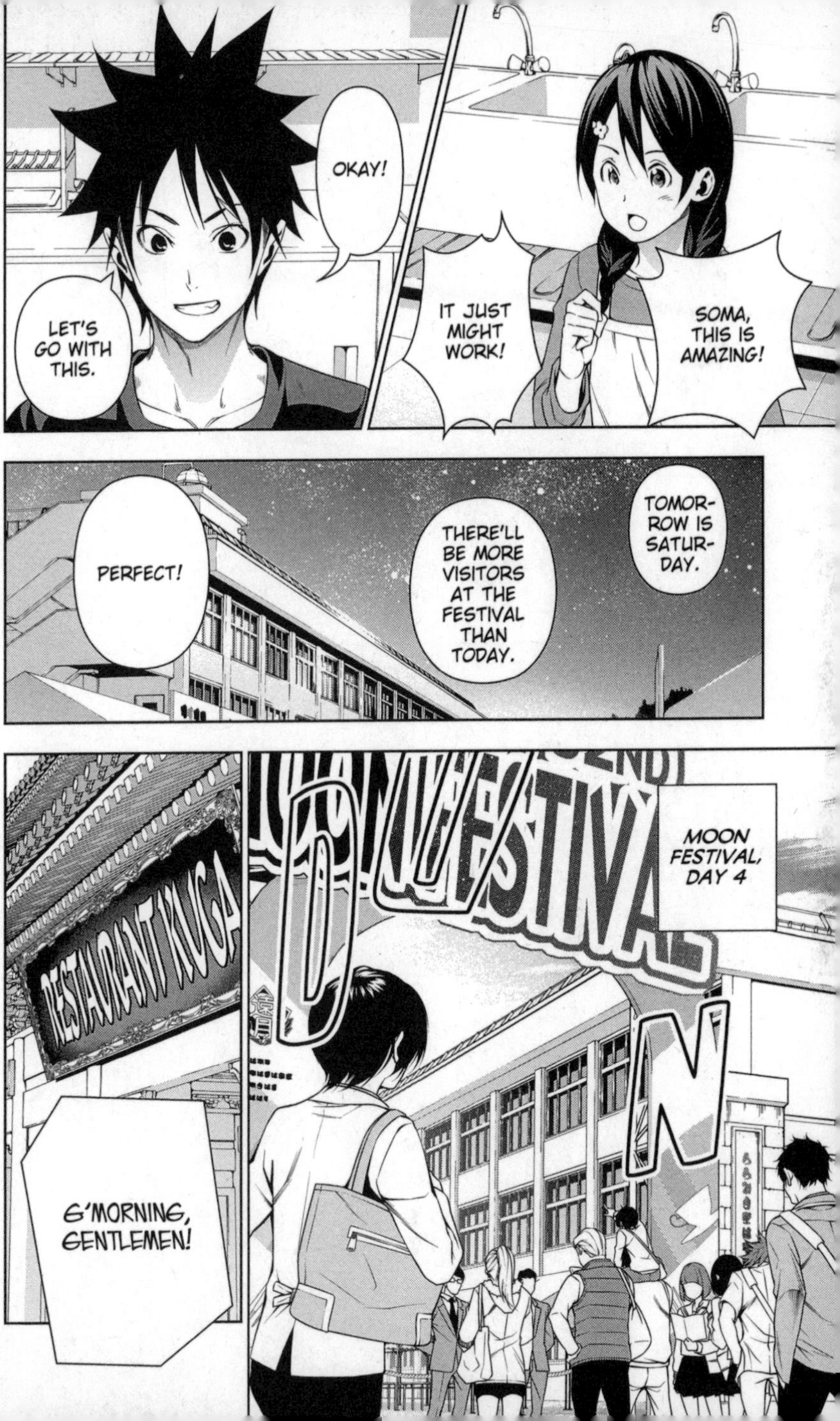
SOMA, THIS IS AMAZING!
IT JUST MIGHT WORK!
OKAY!
LET'S GO WITH THIS.
TOMORROW IS SATURDAY.
THERE'LL BE MORE VISITORS AT THE FESTIVAL THAN TODAY.
PERFECT!
MOON FESTIVAL, DAY 4
RESTAURANT KUGA
G'MORNING, GENTLEMEN!

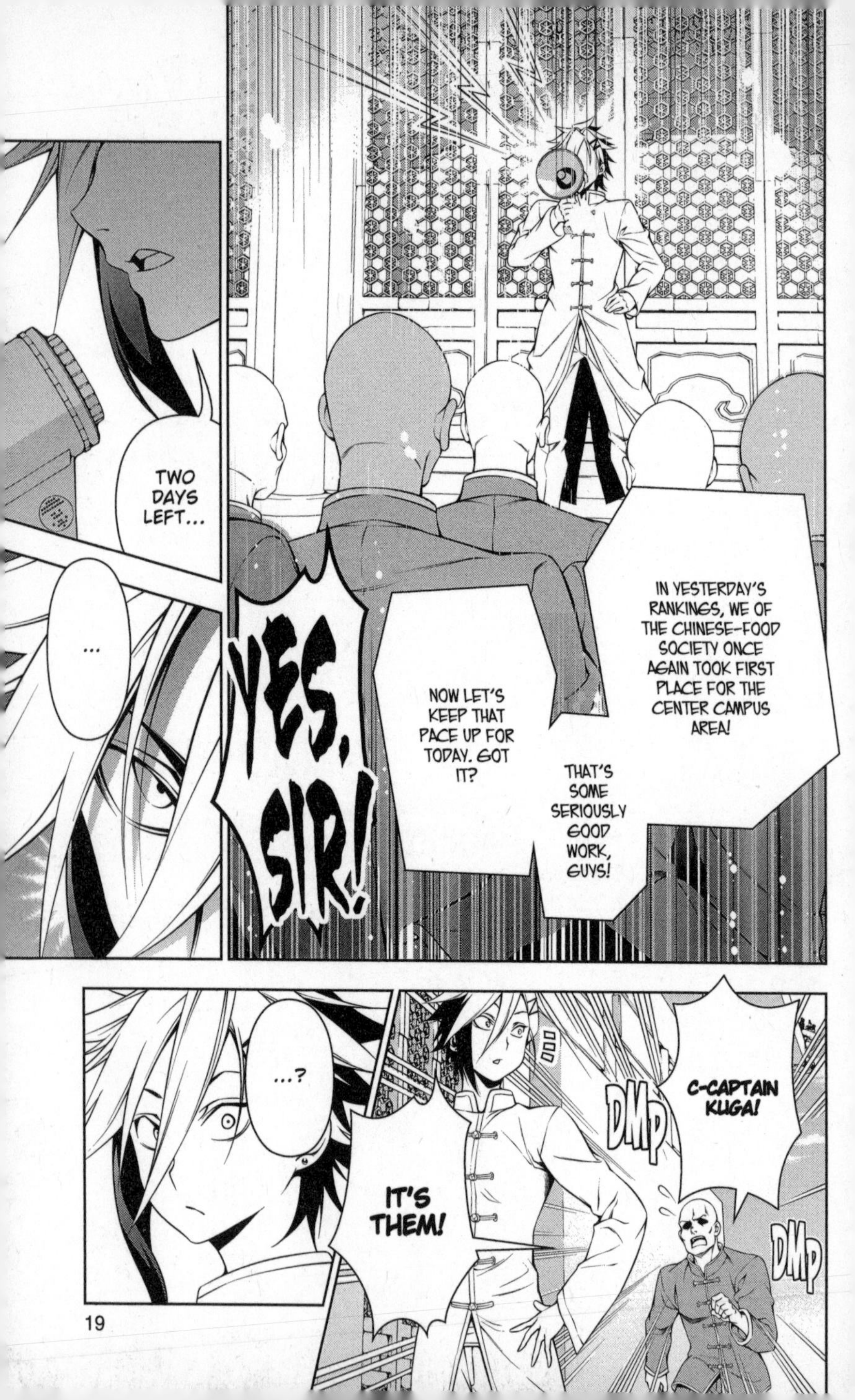
IN YESTERDAY'S RANKINGS, WE OF THE CHINESE-FOOD SOCIETY ONCE AGAIN TOOK FIRST PLACE FOR THE CENTER CAMPUS AREA!
THAT'S SOME SERIOUSLY GOOD WORK, GUYS!
NOW LET'S KEEP THAT PACE UP FOR TODAY. GOT IT?
YES, SIR!
TWO DAYS LEFT...
...
C-CAPTAIN KUGA!
DMP
DMP
IT'S THEM!
...?

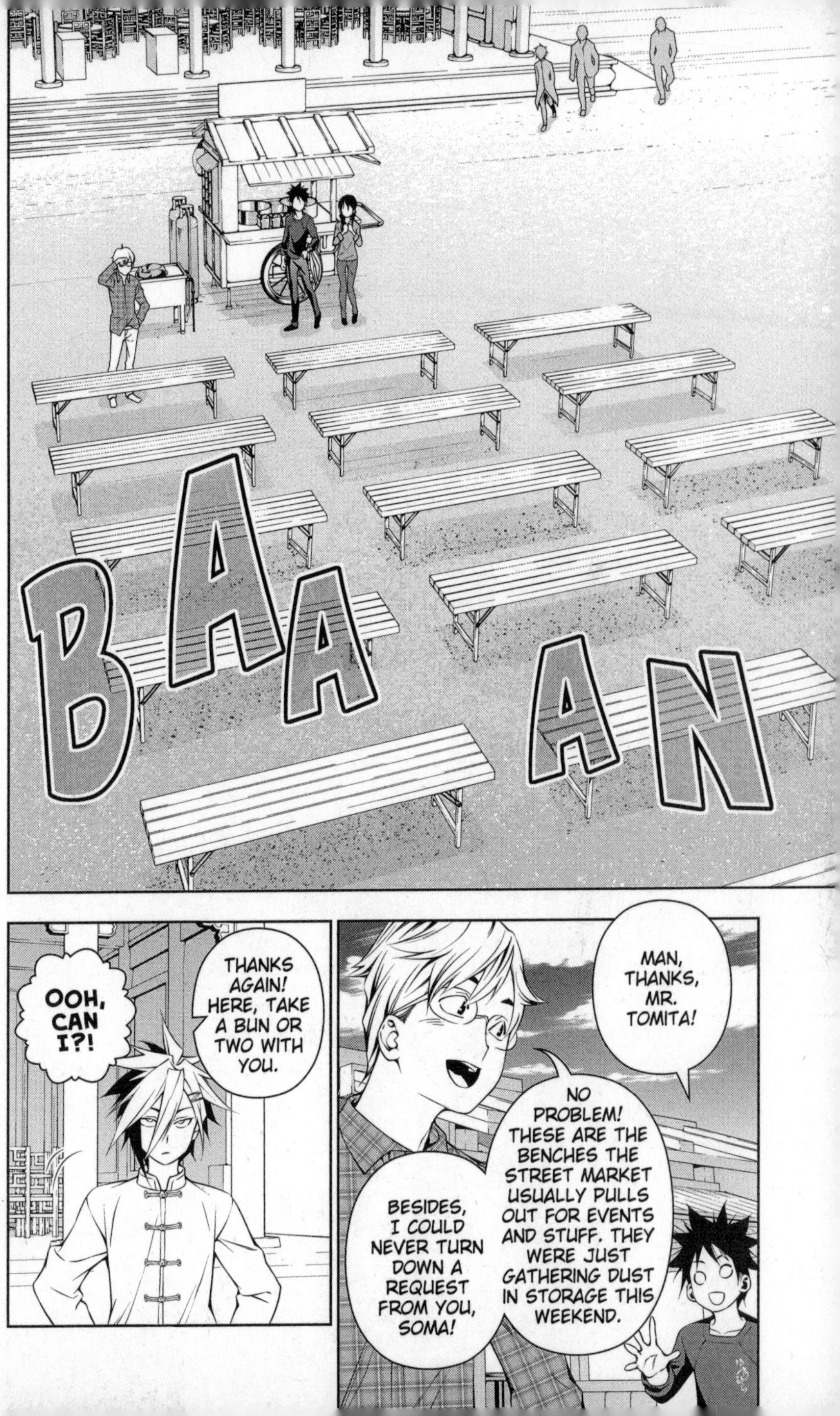
BAAAAN
MAN, THANKS, MR. TOMITA!
NO PROBLEM! THESE ARE THE BENCHES THE STREET MARKET USUALLY PULLS OUT FOR EVENTS AND STUFF. THEY WERE JUST GATHERING DUST IN STORAGE THIS WEEKEND.
BESIDES, I COULD NEVER TURN DOWN A REQUEST FROM YOU, SOMA!
THANKS AGAIN! HERE, TAKE A BUN OR TWO WITH YOU.
OOH, CAN I?!

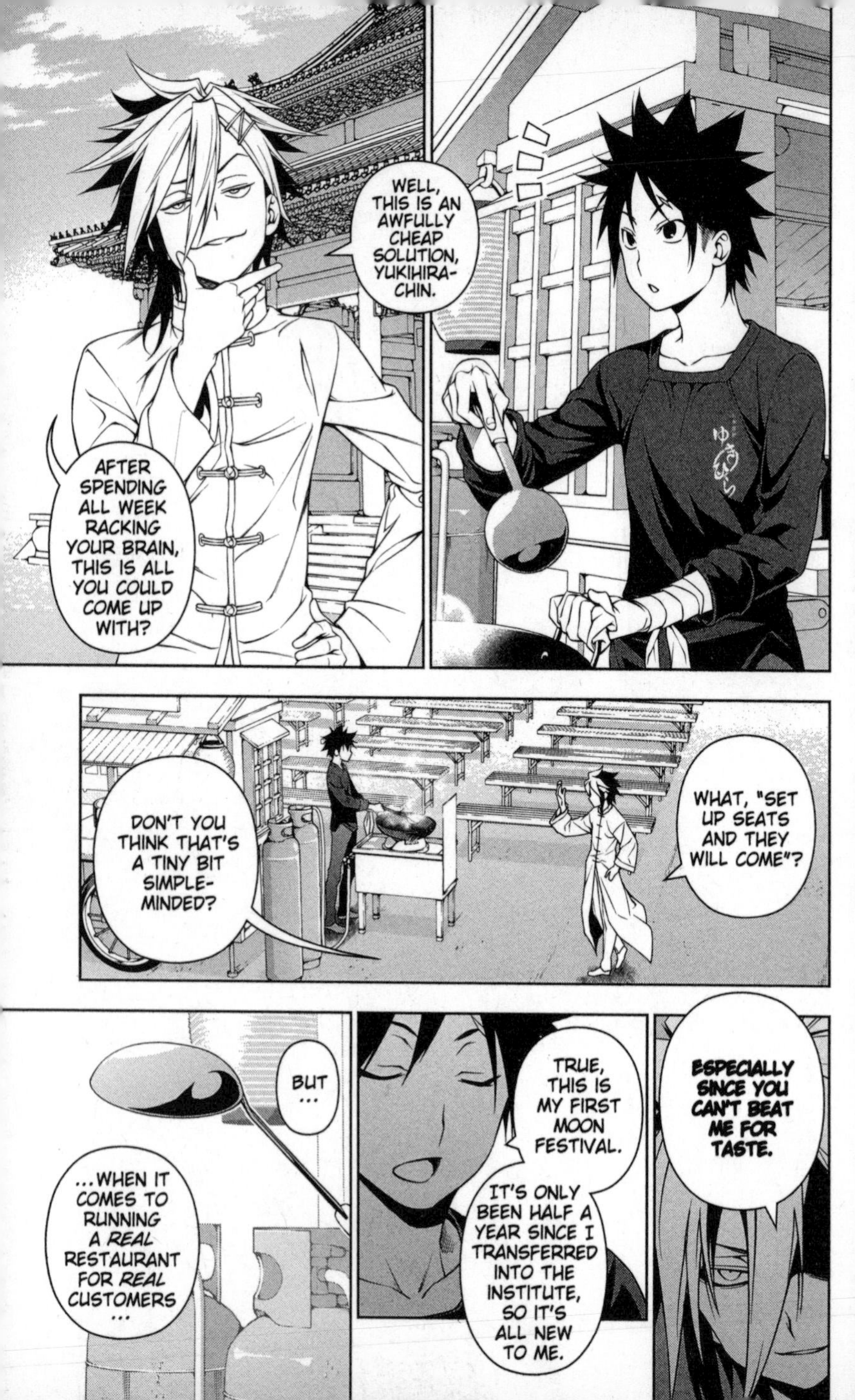
WELL, THIS IS AN AWFULLY CHEAP SOLUTION, YUKIHIRA-CHIN.
AFTER SPENDING ALL WEEK RACKING YOUR BRAIN, THIS IS ALL YOU COULD COME UP WITH?
WHAT, "SET UP SEATS AND THEY WILL COME"?
DON'T YOU THINK THAT'S A TINY BIT SIMPLE-MINDED?
ESPECIALLY SINCE YOU CAN'T BEAT ME FOR TASTE.
TRUE, THIS IS MY FIRST MOON FESTIVAL.
IT'S ONLY BEEN HALF A YEAR SINCE I TRANSFERRED INTO THE INSTITUTE, SO IT'S ALL NEW TO ME.
BUT...
...WHEN IT COMES TO RUNNING A *REAL* RESTAURANT FOR *REAL* CUSTOMERS...

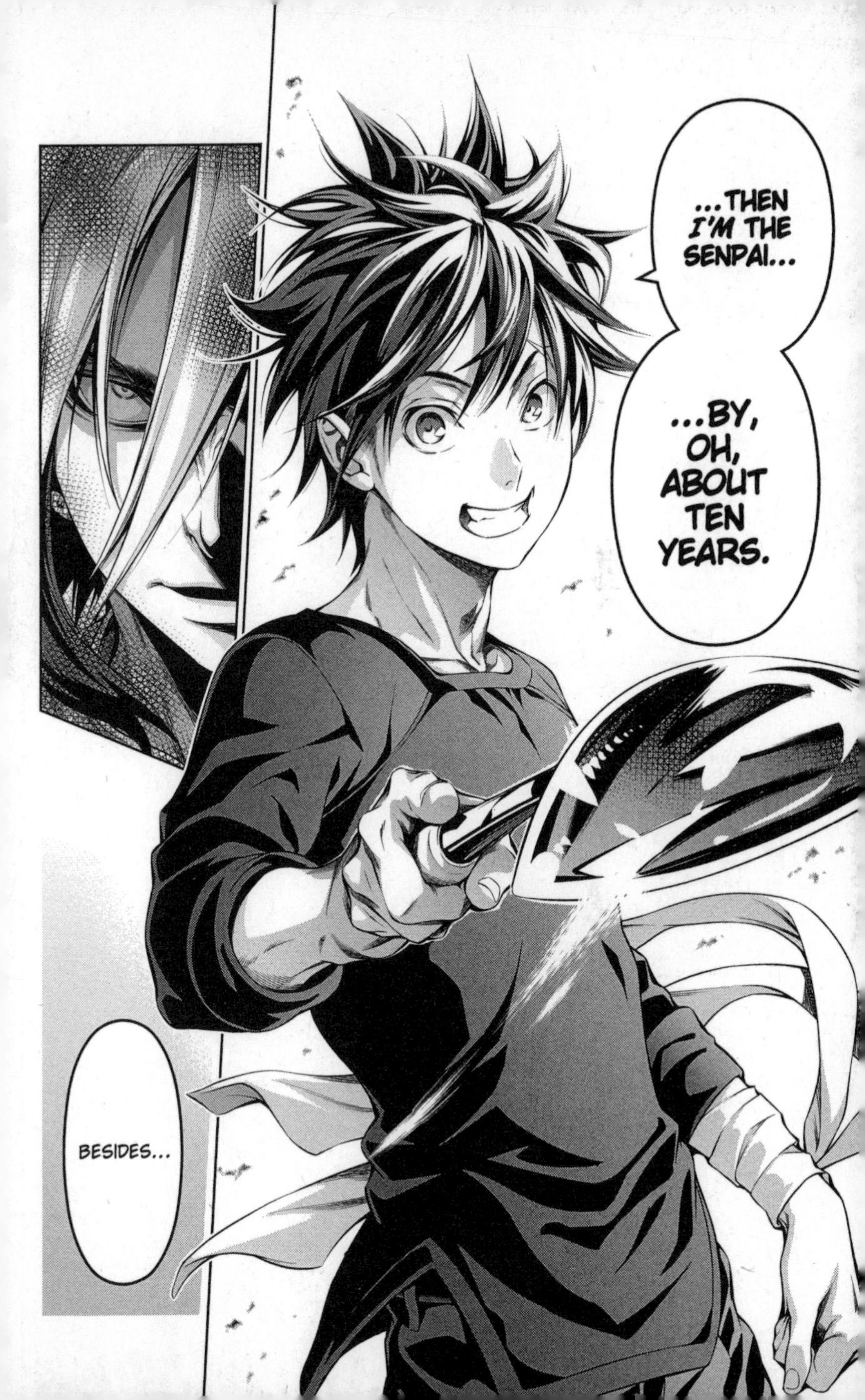
...THEN I'M THE SENPAI...
...BY, OH, ABOUT TEN YEARS.
BESIDES...

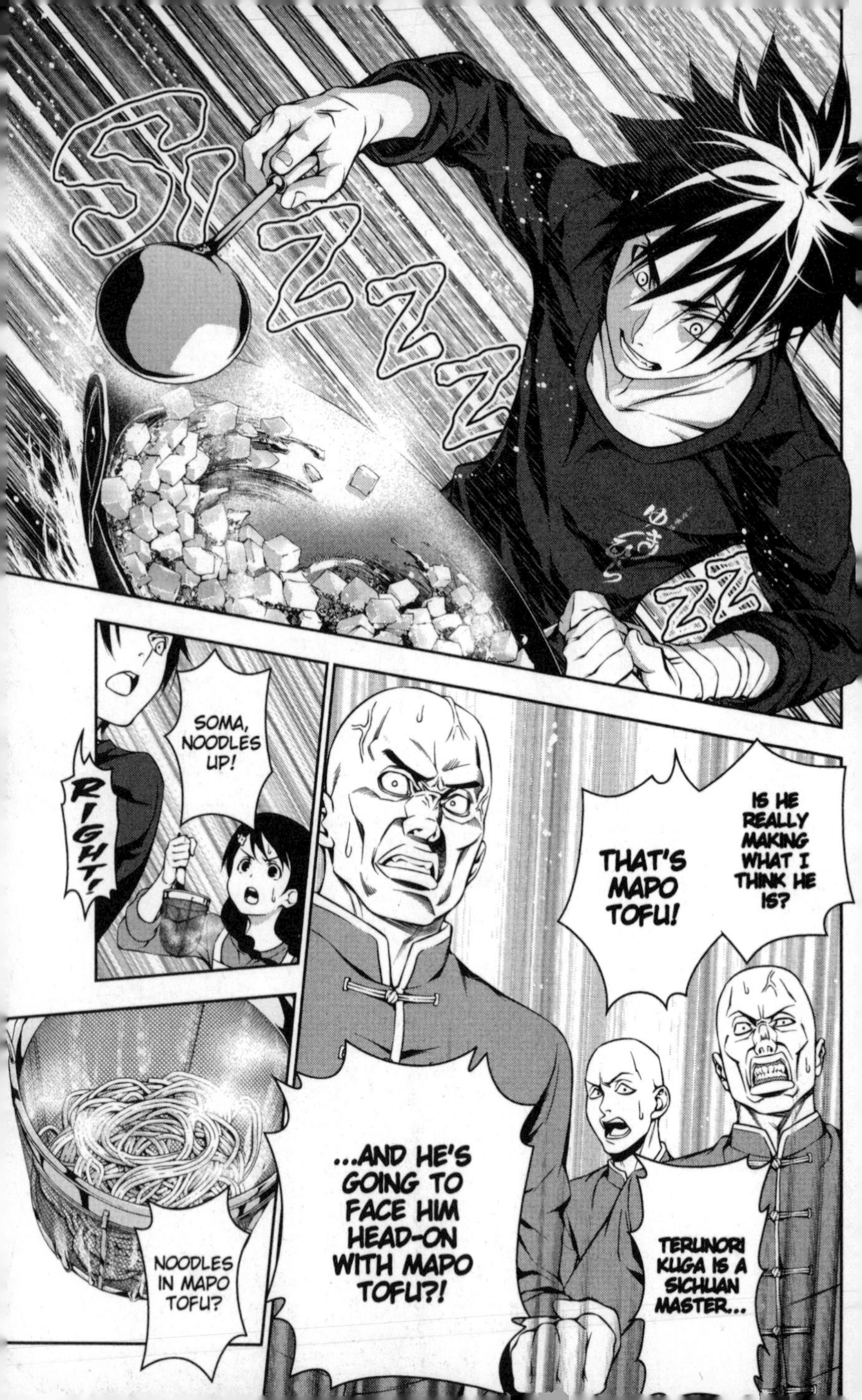
SIZZZZ
ZZ
IS HE REALLY MAKING WHAT I THINK HE IS?
THAT'S MAPO TOFU!
SOMA, NOODLES UP!
RIGHT!
TERUNORI KUGA IS A SICHUAN MASTER...
...AND HE'S GOING TO FACE HIM HEAD-ON WITH MAPO TOFU?!
NOODLES IN MAPO TOFU?

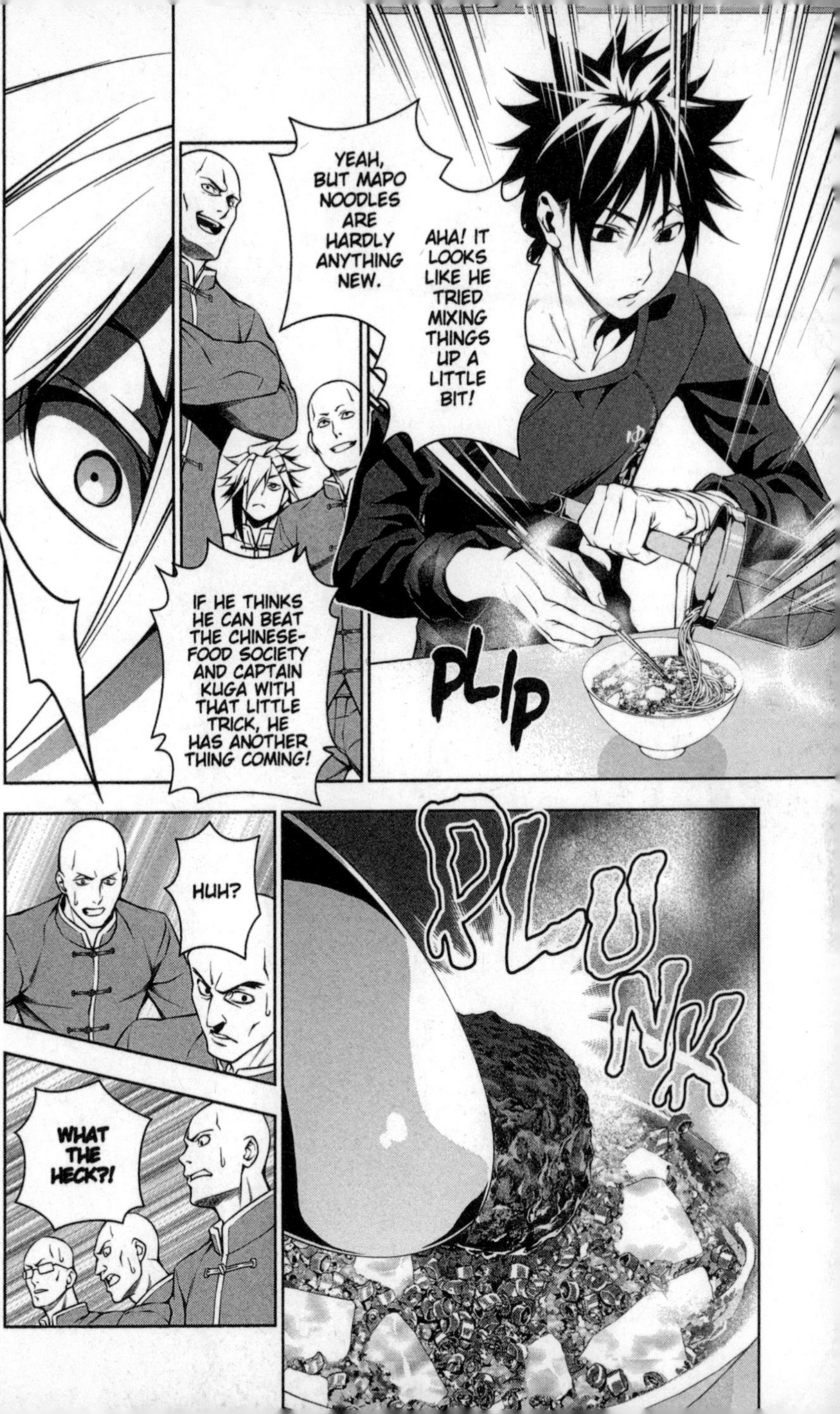
AHA! IT LOOKS LIKE HE TRIED MIXING THINGS UP A LITTLE BIT!
YEAH, BUT MAPO NOODLES ARE HARDLY ANYTHING NEW.
PLIP
IF HE THINKS HE CAN BEAT THE CHINESE-FOOD SOCIETY AND CAPTAIN KUGA WITH THAT LITTLE TRICK, HE HAS ANOTHER THING COMING!
PLUNK
HUH?
WHAT THE HECK?!

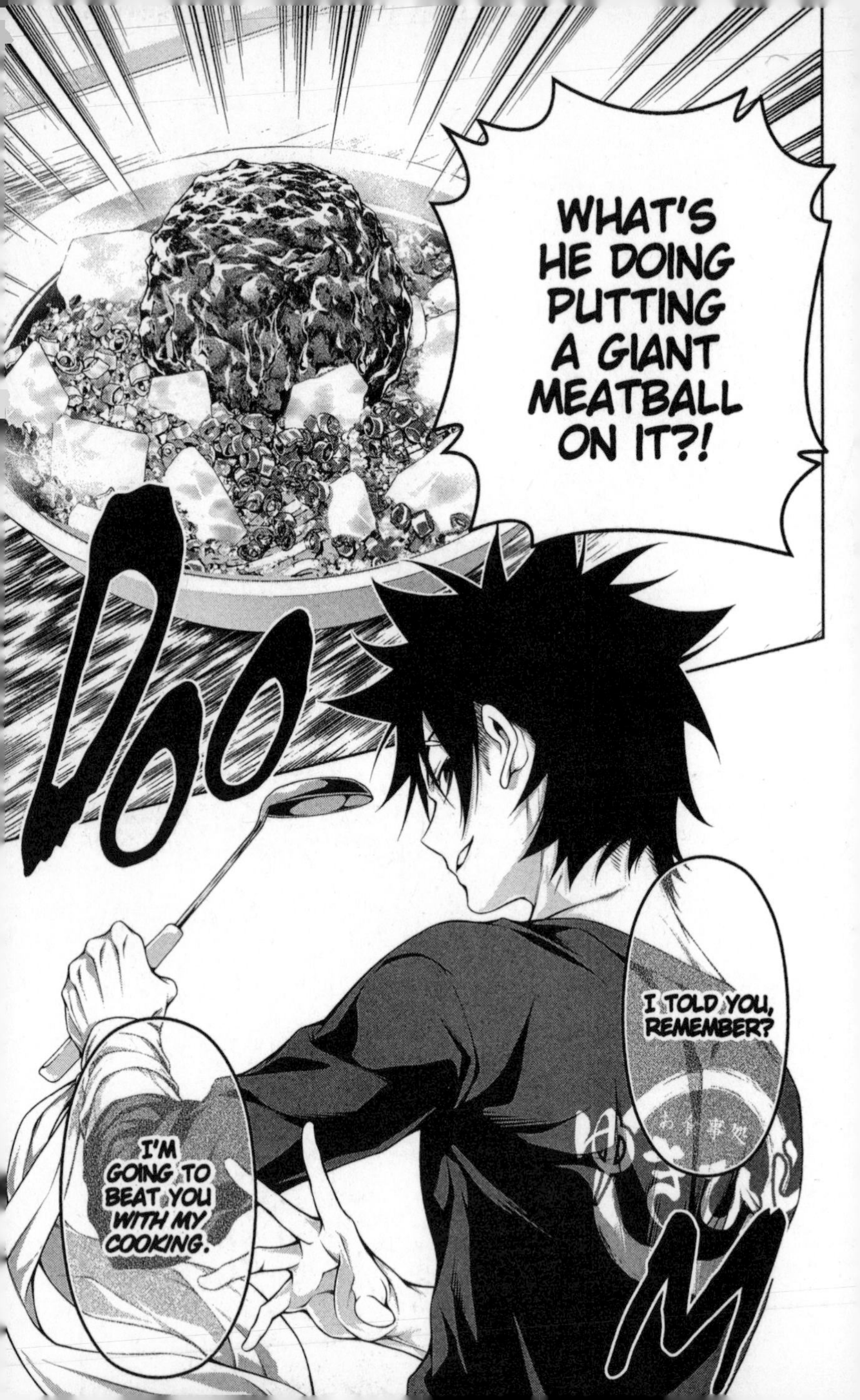
WHAT'S HE DOING PUTTING A GIANT MEATBALL ON IT?!
DOO
I TOLD YOU, REMEMBER?
I'M GOING TO BEAT YOU WITH MY COOKING.

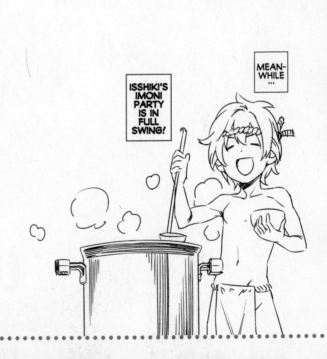

MEAN-
WHILE
...

ISSHIKI'S
IMONI
PARTY
IS IN
FULL
SWING!

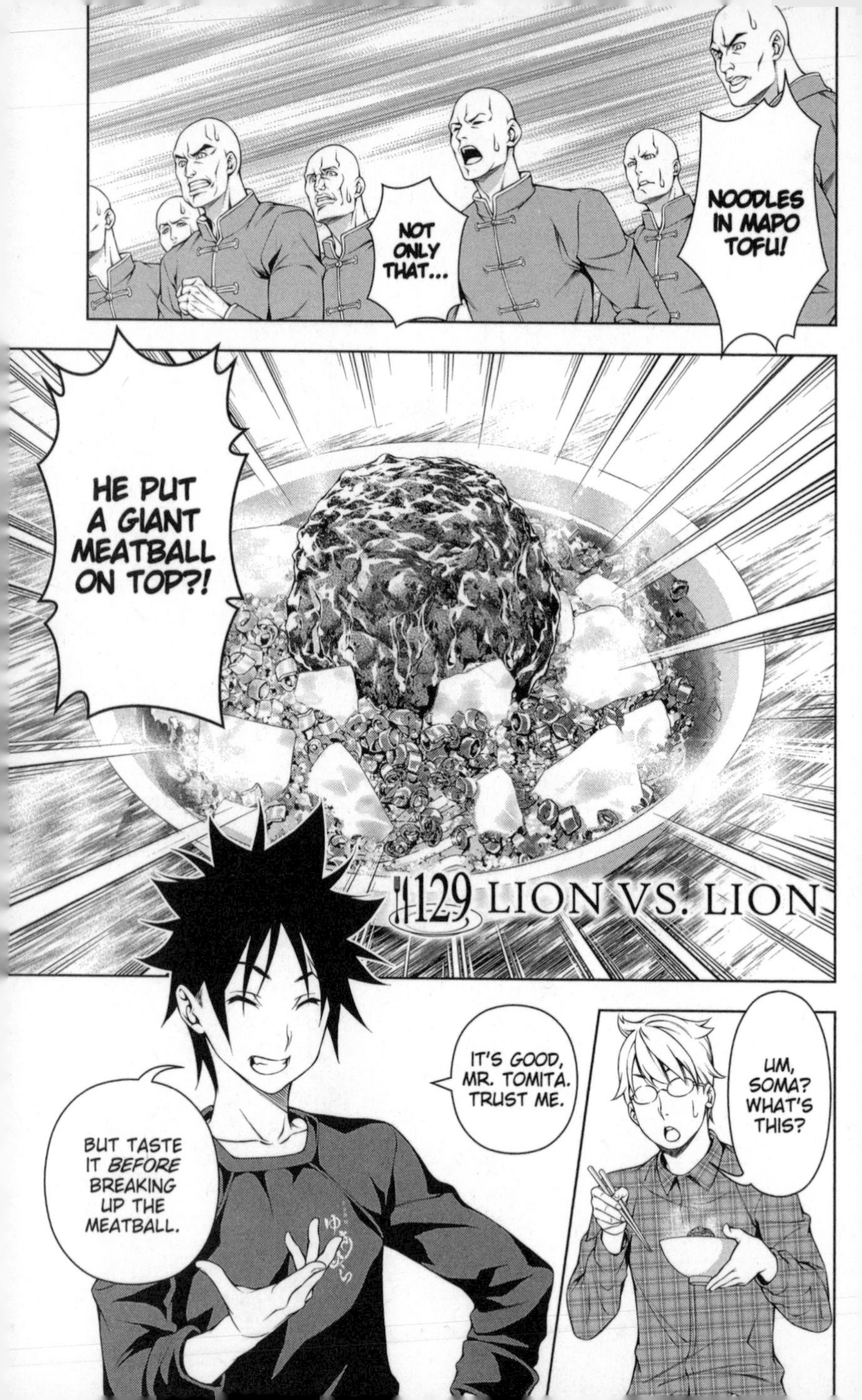
NOODLES IN MAPO TOFU!
NOT ONLY THAT...
HE PUT A GIANT MEATBALL ON TOP?!
129 LION VS. LION
UM, SOMA? WHAT'S THIS?
IT'S GOOD, MR. TOMITA. TRUST ME.
BUT TASTE IT *BEFORE* BREAKING UP THE MEATBALL.

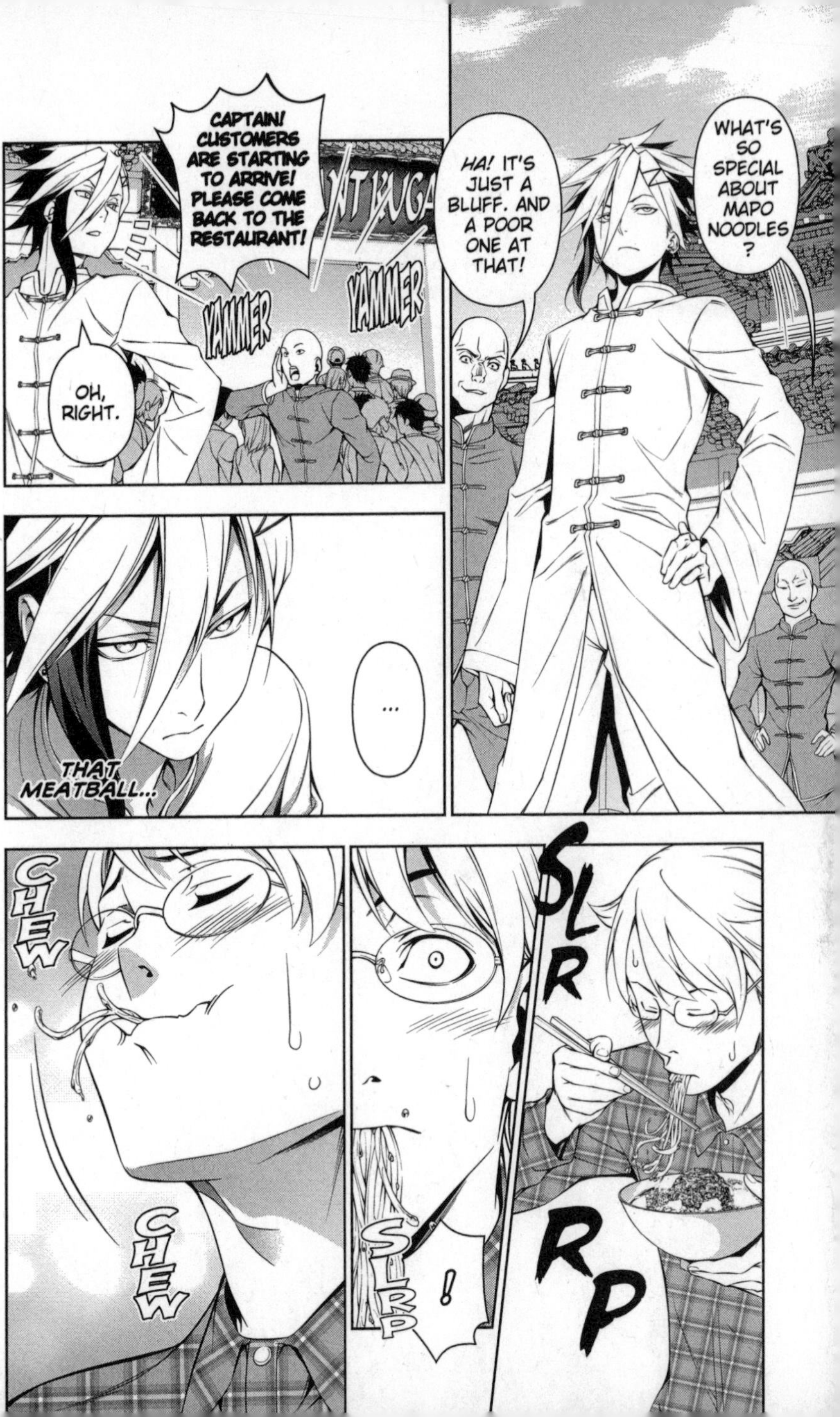
WHAT'S SO SPECIAL ABOUT MAPO NOODLES?
HA! IT'S JUST A BLUFF. AND A POOR ONE AT THAT!
CAPTAIN! CUSTOMERS ARE STARTING TO ARRIVE! PLEASE COME BACK TO THE RESTAURANT!
YAMMER
YAMMER
OH, RIGHT.
...
THAT MEATBALL...
SLRRP
!
SLRP
CHEW
CHEW

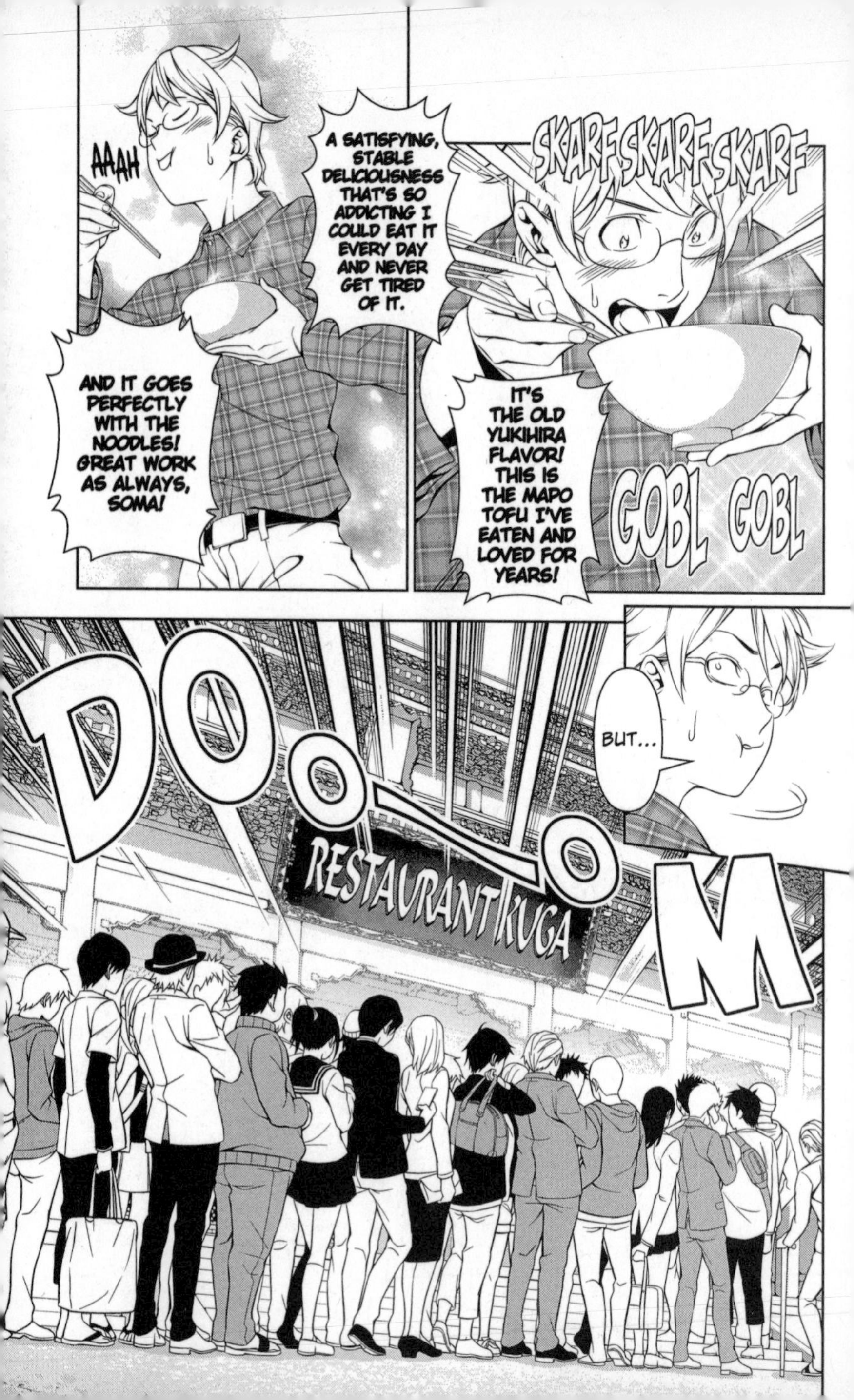
SKARF SKARF SKARF
GOBL GOBL
IT'S THE OLD YUKIHIRA FLAVOR! THIS IS THE MAPO TOFU I'VE EATEN AND LOVED FOR YEARS!
AAAH
A SATISFYING, STABLE DELICIOUSNESS THAT'S SO ADDICTING I COULD EAT IT EVERY DAY AND NEVER GET TIRED OF IT.
AND IT GOES PERFECTLY WITH THE NOODLES! GREAT WORK AS ALWAYS, SOMA!
BUT...
DOOOM
RESTAURANT KUGA

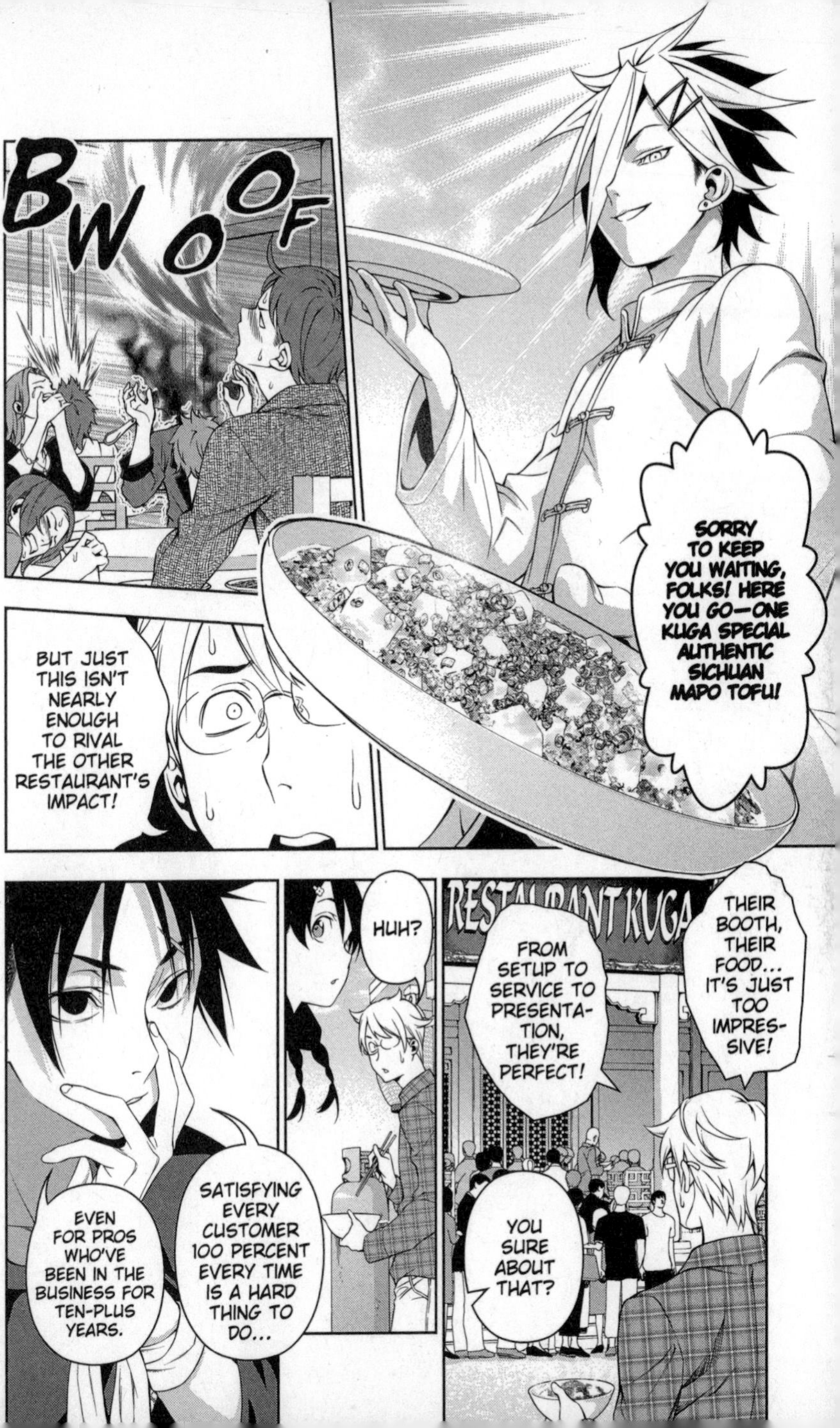
SORRY TO KEEP YOU WAITING, FOLKS! HERE YOU GO—ONE KUGA SPECIAL AUTHENTIC SICHUAN MAPO TOFU!
BWOOF
BUT JUST THIS ISN'T NEARLY ENOUGH TO RIVAL THE OTHER RESTAURANT'S IMPACT!
THEIR BOOTH, THEIR FOOD... IT'S JUST TOO IMPRES-SIVE!
FROM SETUP TO SERVICE TO PRESENTA-TION, THEY'RE PERFECT!
YOU SURE ABOUT THAT?
HUH?
SATISFYING EVERY CUSTOMER 100 PERCENT EVERY TIME IS A HARD THING TO DO...
EVEN FOR PROS WHO'VE BEEN IN THE BUSINESS FOR TEN-PLUS YEARS.

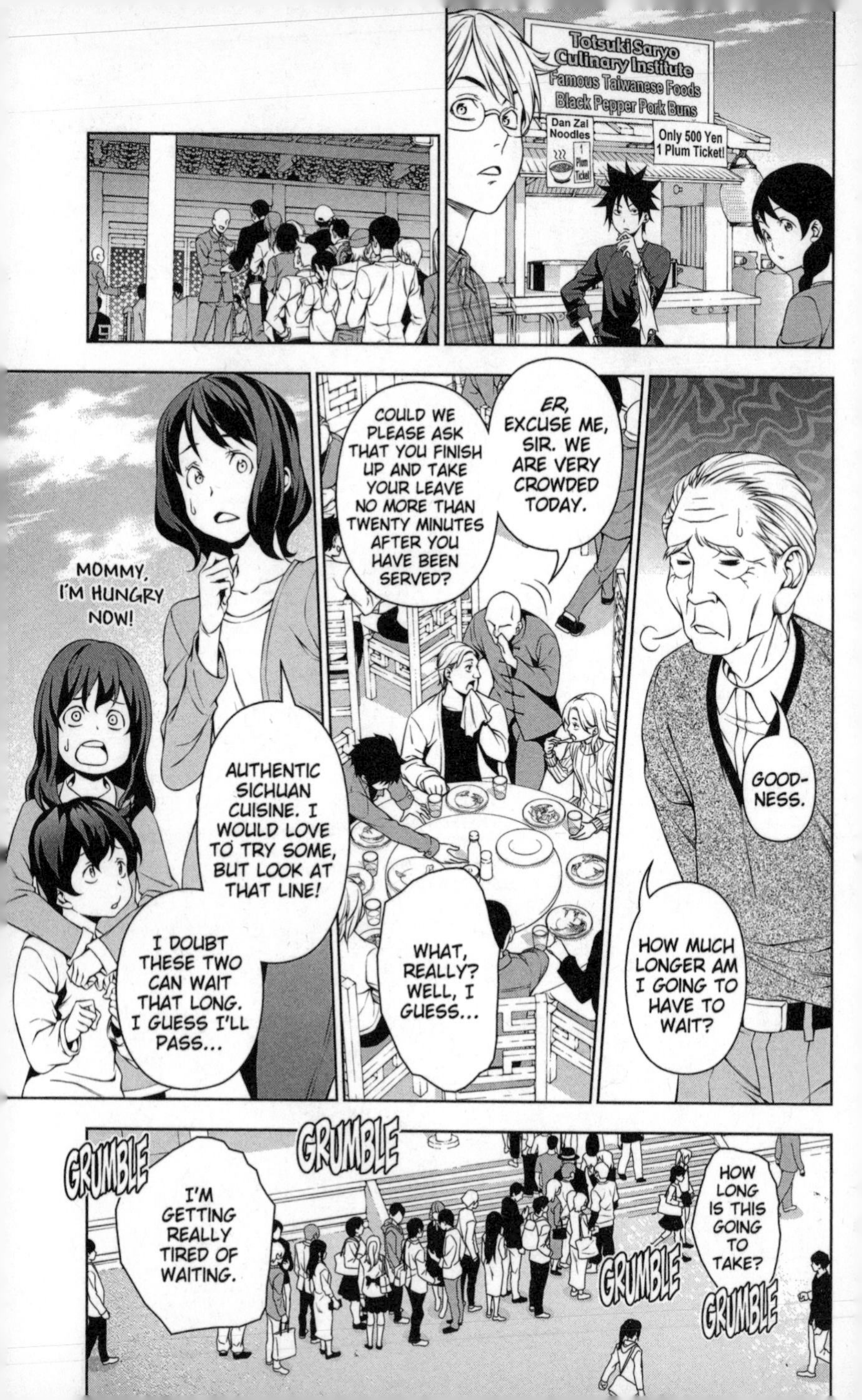
Totsuki Saryo Culinary Institute
Famous Taiwanese Foods
Black Pepper Pork Buns
Dan Zai Noodles
1 Plum Ticket
Only 500 Yen 1 Plum Ticket!
GOODNESS.
HOW MUCH LONGER AM I GOING TO HAVE TO WAIT?
ER, EXCUSE ME, SIR. WE ARE VERY CROWDED TODAY.
COULD WE PLEASE ASK THAT YOU FINISH UP AND TAKE YOUR LEAVE NO MORE THAN TWENTY MINUTES AFTER YOU HAVE BEEN SERVED?
WHAT, REALLY? WELL, I GUESS...
MOMMY, I'M HUNGRY NOW!
AUTHENTIC SICHUAN CUISINE. I WOULD LOVE TO TRY SOME, BUT LOOK AT THAT LINE!
I DOUBT THESE TWO CAN WAIT THAT LONG. I GUESS I'LL PASS...
GRUMBLE
HOW LONG IS THIS GOING TO TAKE?
GRUMBLE
GRUMBLE
I'M GETTING REALLY TIRED OF WAITING.
GRUMBLE

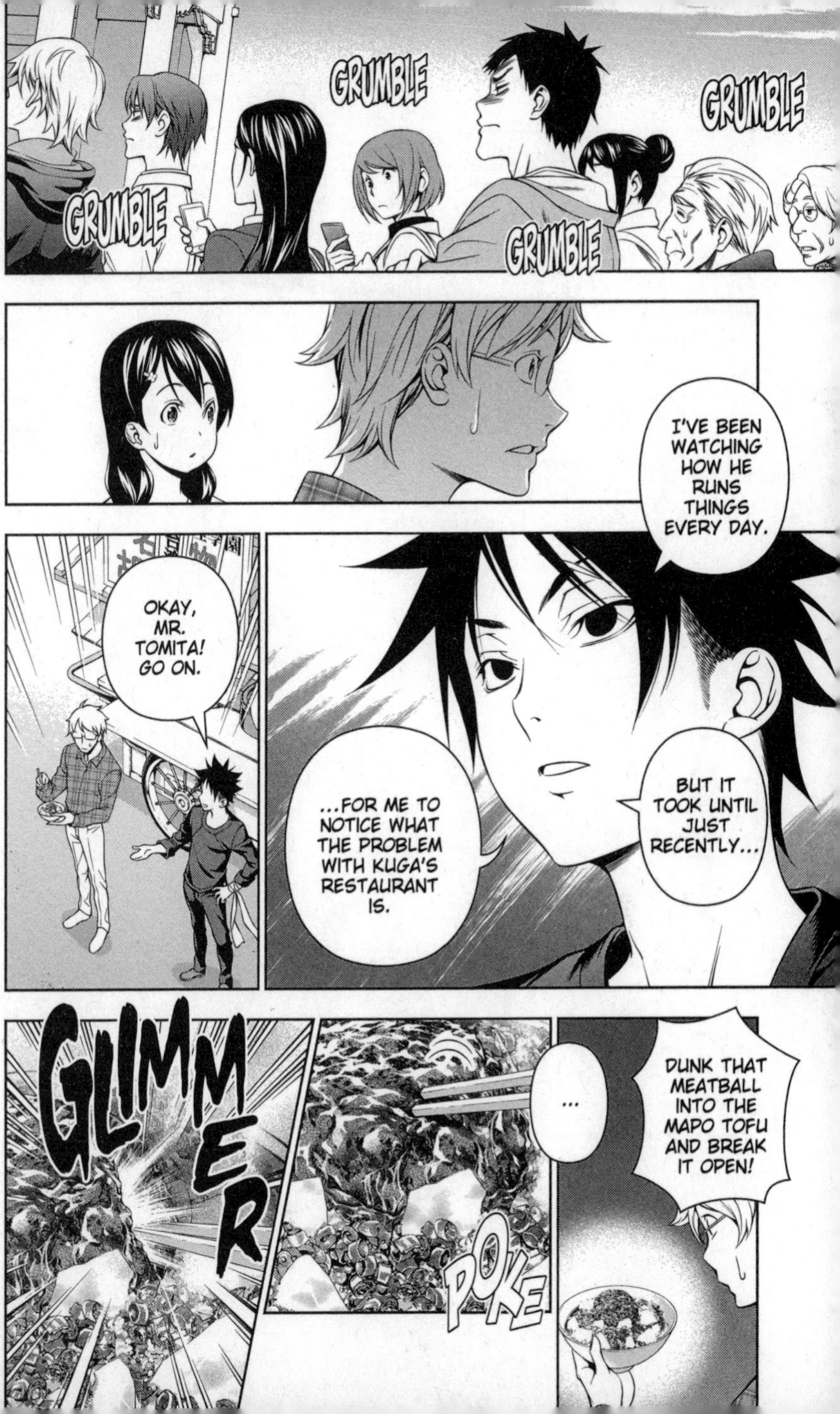
GRUMBLE
GRUMBLE
GRUMBLE
GRUMBLE
I'VE BEEN WATCHING HOW HE RUNS THINGS EVERY DAY.
BUT IT TOOK UNTIL JUST RECENTLY...
...FOR ME TO NOTICE WHAT THE PROBLEM WITH KUGA'S RESTAURANT IS.
OKAY, MR. TOMITA! GO ON.
DUNK THAT MEATBALL INTO THE MAPO TOFU AND BREAK IT OPEN!
...
POKE
GLIMMER

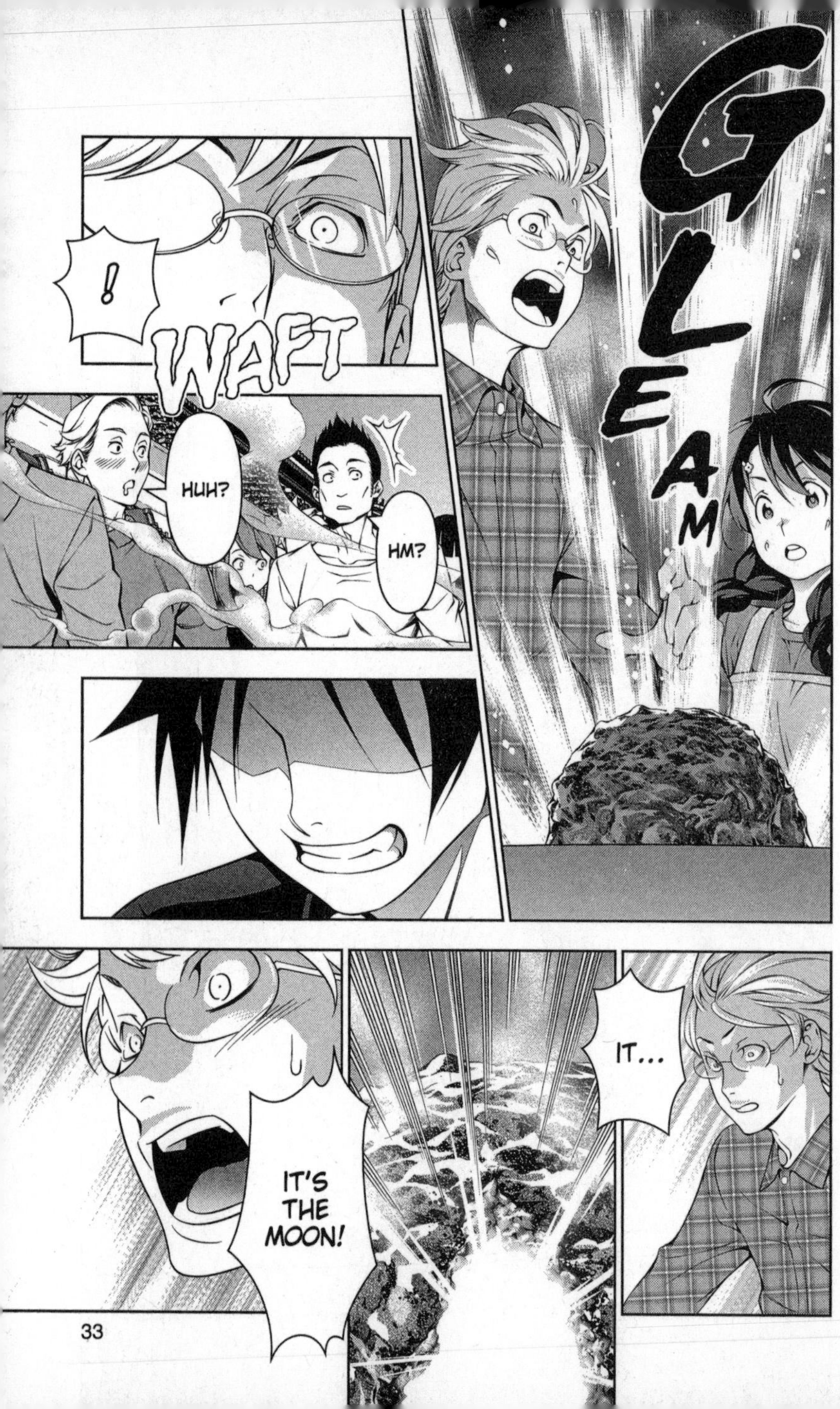
GLEAM
!
WAFT
HM?
HUH?
IT...
IT'S THE MOON!

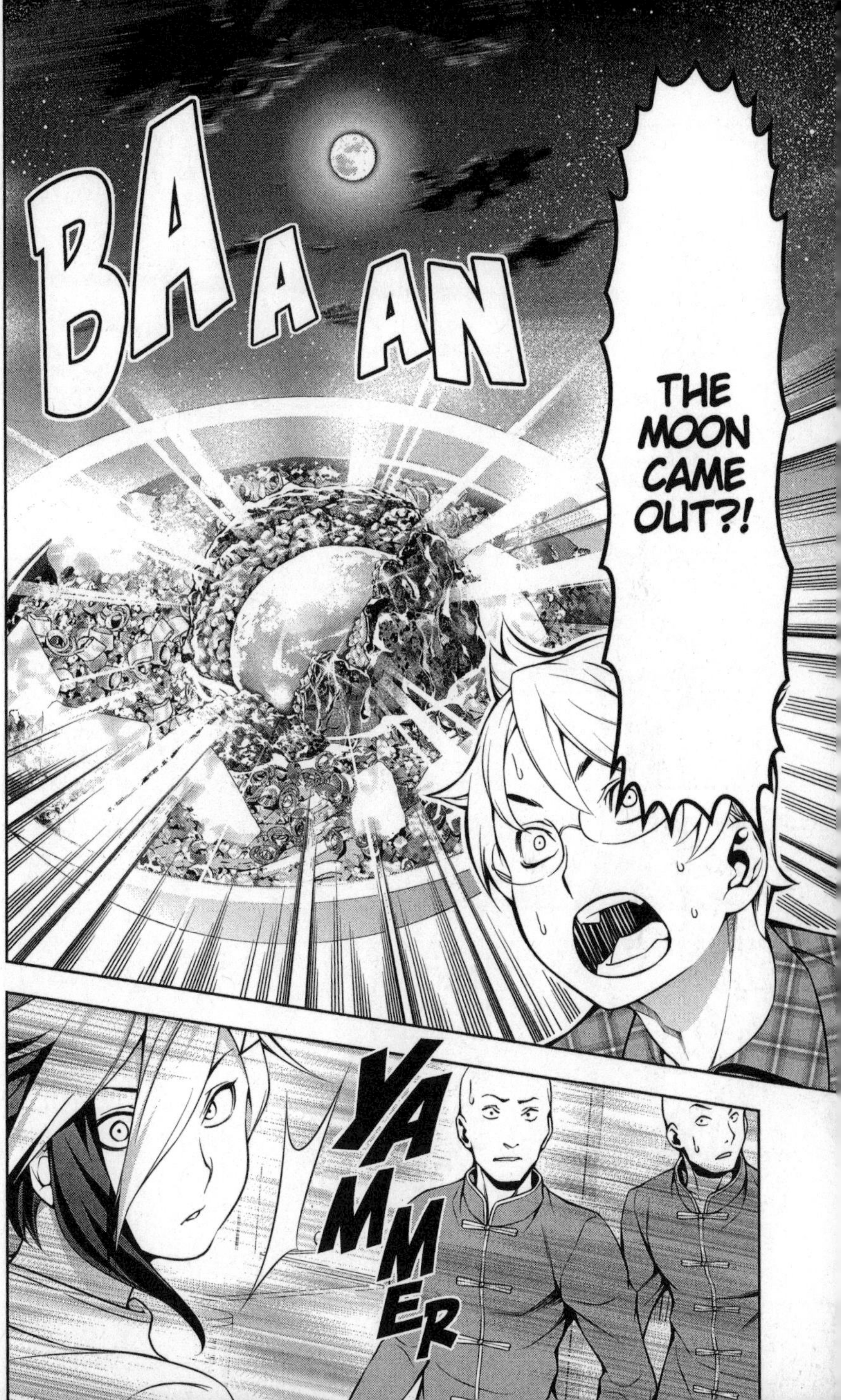
THE MOON CAME OUT?!
BAAAAN
YAMMMER

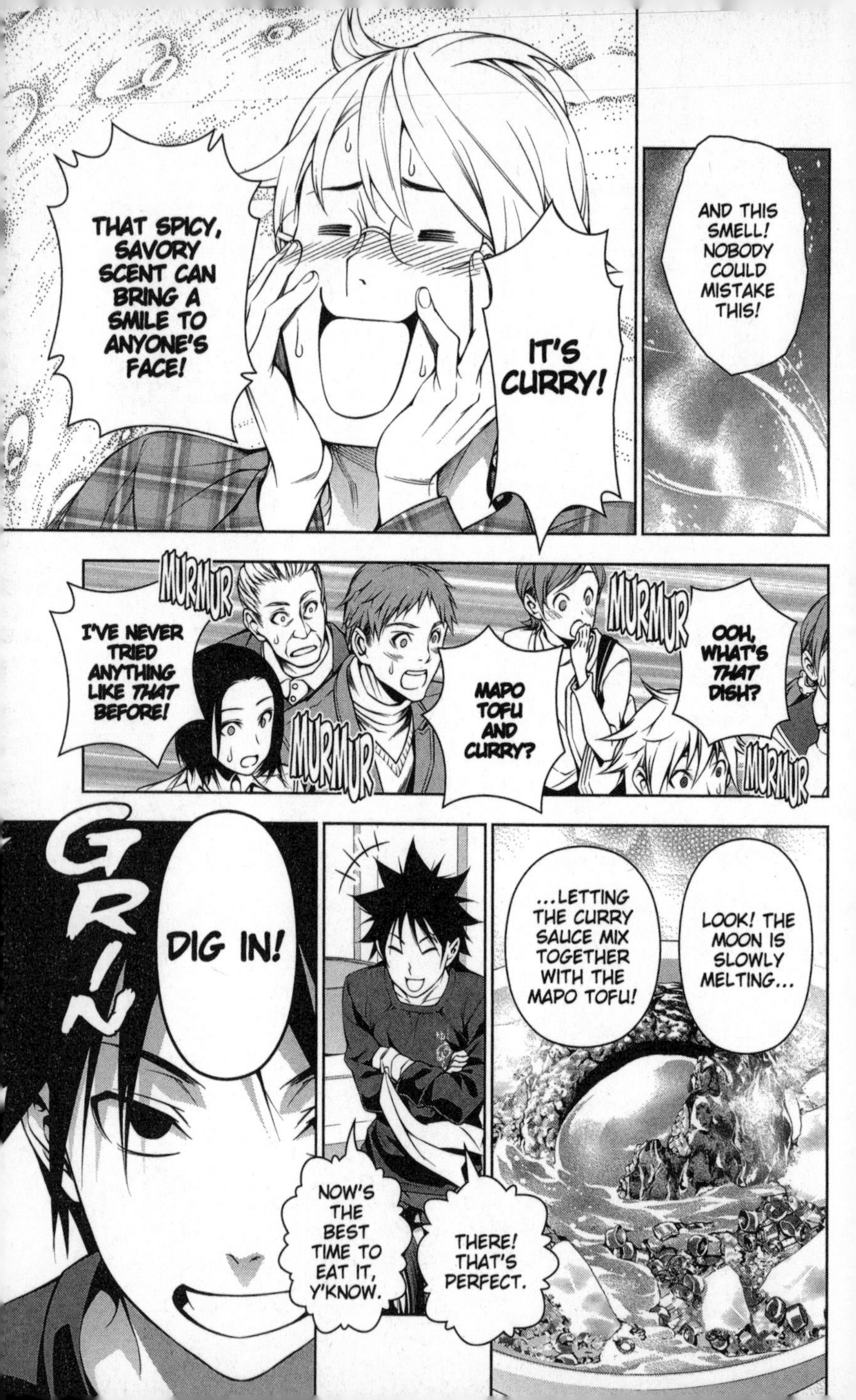
AND THIS SMELL! NOBODY COULD MISTAKE THIS!
IT'S CURRY!
THAT SPICY, SAVORY SCENT CAN BRING A SMILE TO ANYONE'S FACE!
MURMUR
OOH, WHAT'S *THAT* DISH?
MURMUR
MAPO TOFU AND CURRY?
MURMUR
I'VE NEVER TRIED ANYTHING LIKE *THAT* BEFORE!
MURMUR
LOOK! THE MOON IS SLOWLY MELTING...
...LETTING THE CURRY SAUCE MIX TOGETHER WITH THE MAPO TOFU!
THERE! THAT'S PERFECT.
NOW'S THE BEST TIME TO EAT IT, Y'KNOW.
GRIN
DIG IN!

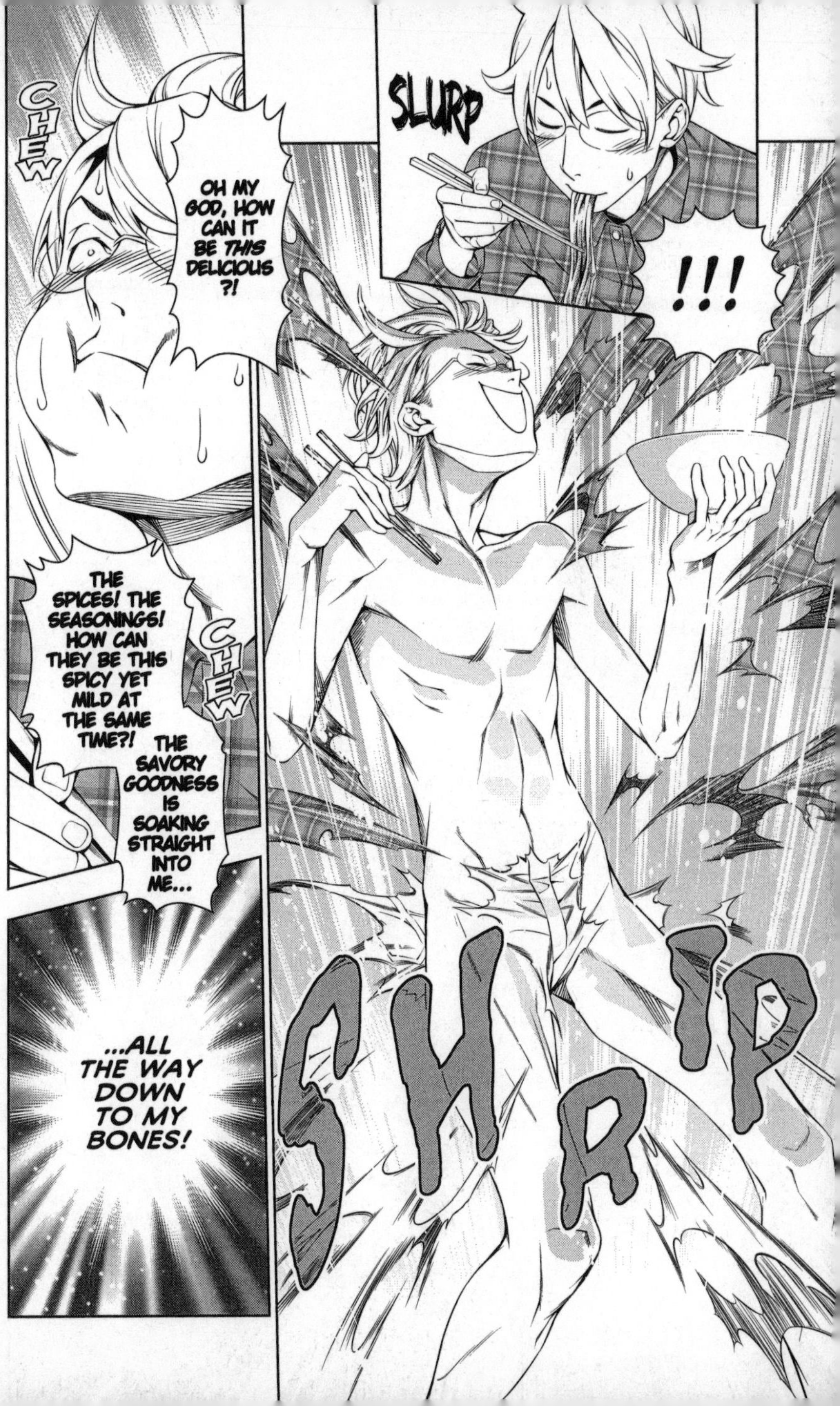
SLURP
!!!
SHRIP
CHEW
OH MY GOD, HOW CAN IT BE *THIS* DELICIOUS ?!
THE SPICES! THE SEASONINGS! HOW CAN THEY BE THIS SPICY YET MILD AT THE SAME TIME?!
CHEW
THE SAVORY GOODNESS IS SOAKING STRAIGHT INTO ME...
...ALL THE WAY DOWN TO MY BONES!

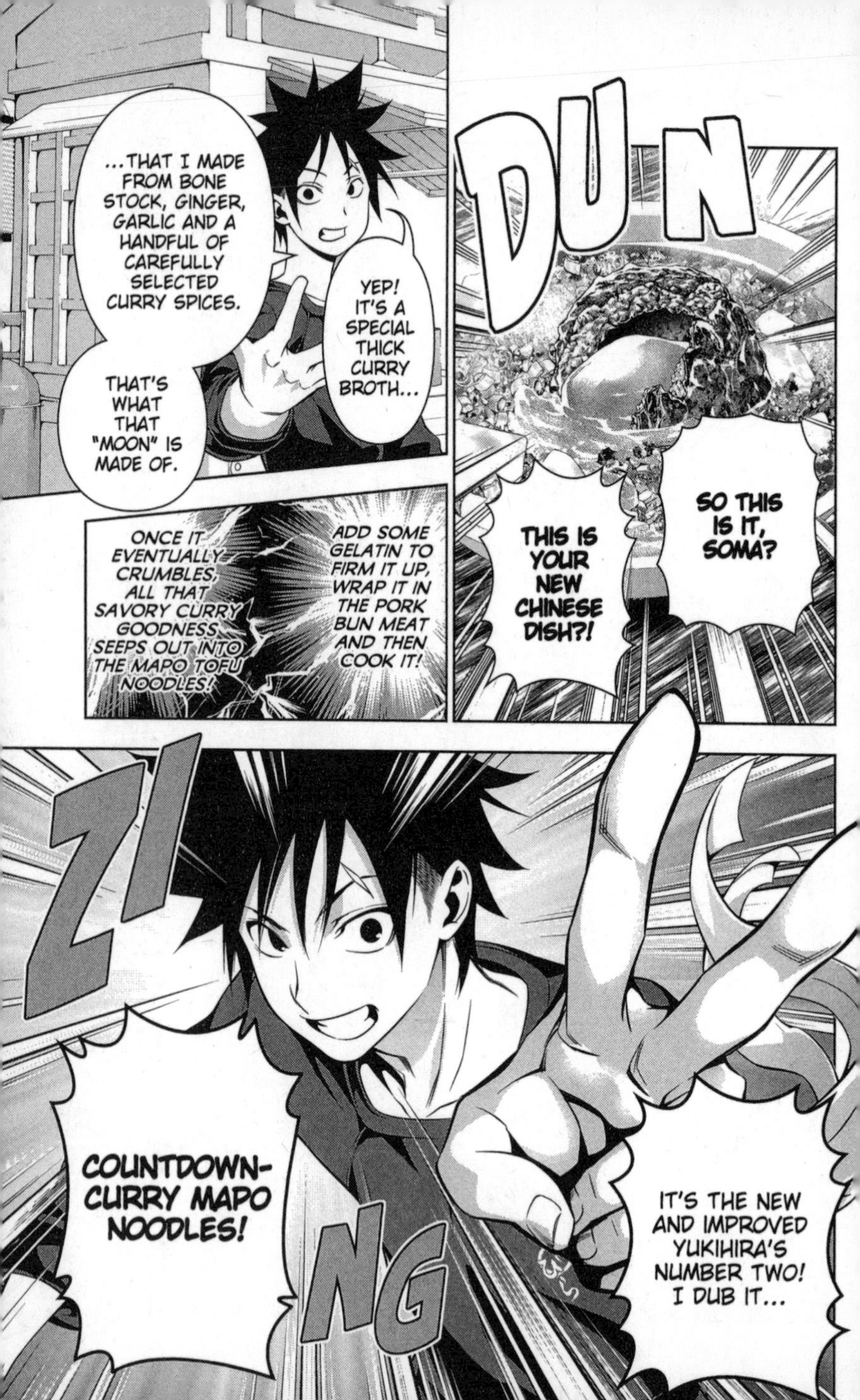
DUN
SO THIS IS IT, SOMA?
THIS IS YOUR NEW CHINESE DISH?!
YEP! IT'S A SPECIAL THICK CURRY BROTH...
...THAT I MADE FROM BONE STOCK, GINGER, GARLIC AND A HANDFUL OF CAREFULLY SELECTED CURRY SPICES.
THAT'S WHAT THAT "MOON" IS MADE OF.
ADD SOME GELATIN TO FIRM IT UP, WRAP IT IN THE PORK BUN MEAT AND THEN COOK IT!
ONCE IT EVENTUALLY CRUMBLES, ALL THAT SAVORY CURRY GOODNESS SEEPS OUT INTO THE MAPO TOFU NOODLES!
ZI
NG
IT'S THE NEW AND IMPROVED YUKIHIRA'S NUMBER TWO! I DUB IT...
COUNTDOWN-CURRY MAPO NOODLES!

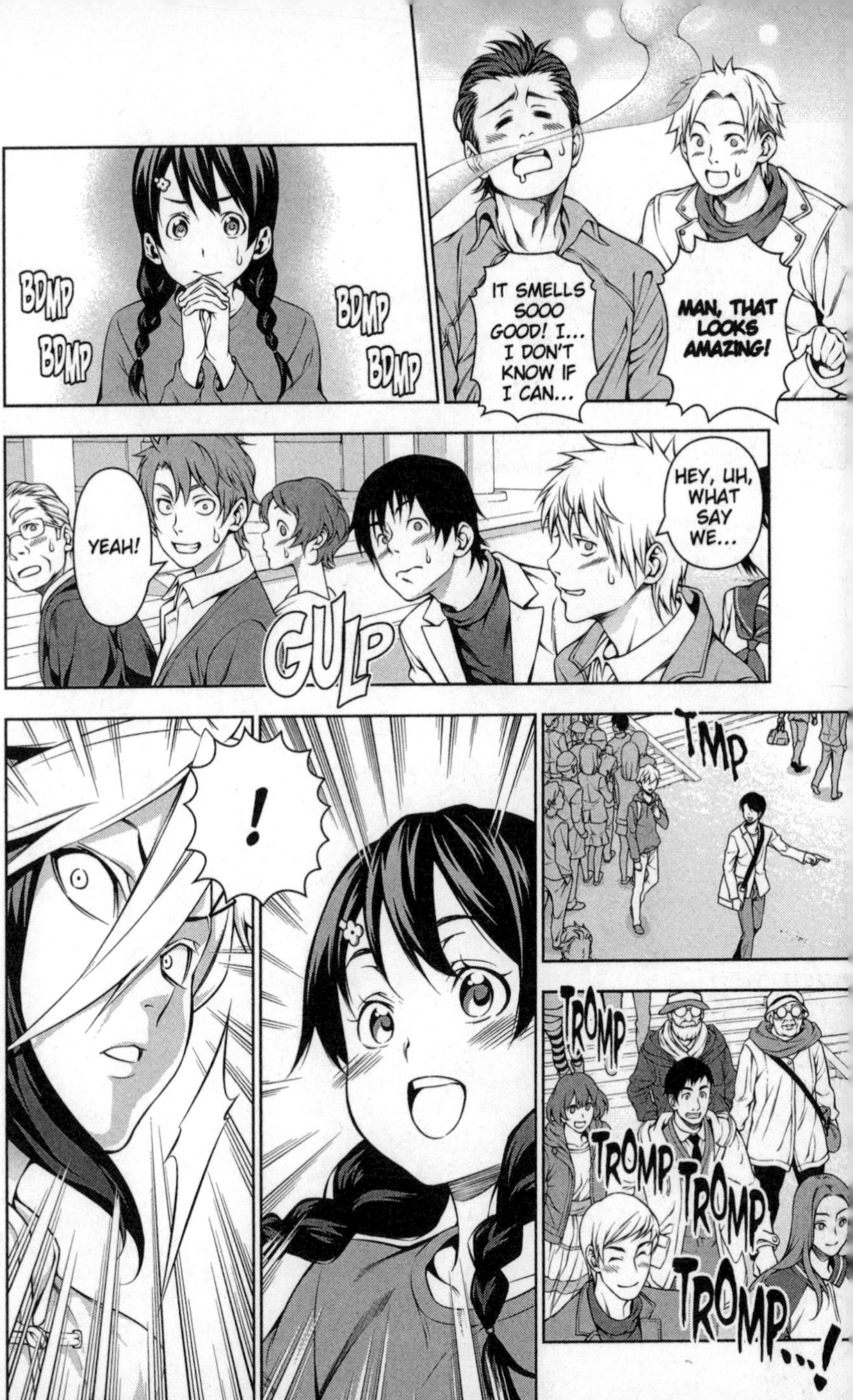
MAN, THAT LOOKS AMAZING!
IT SMELLS SOOO GOOD! I... I DON'T KNOW IF I CAN...
BDMP
BDMP
BDMP
BDMP
HEY, UH, WHAT SAY WE...
GULP
YEAH!
TMP
TROMP
TROMP
TROMP
TROMP...!
!

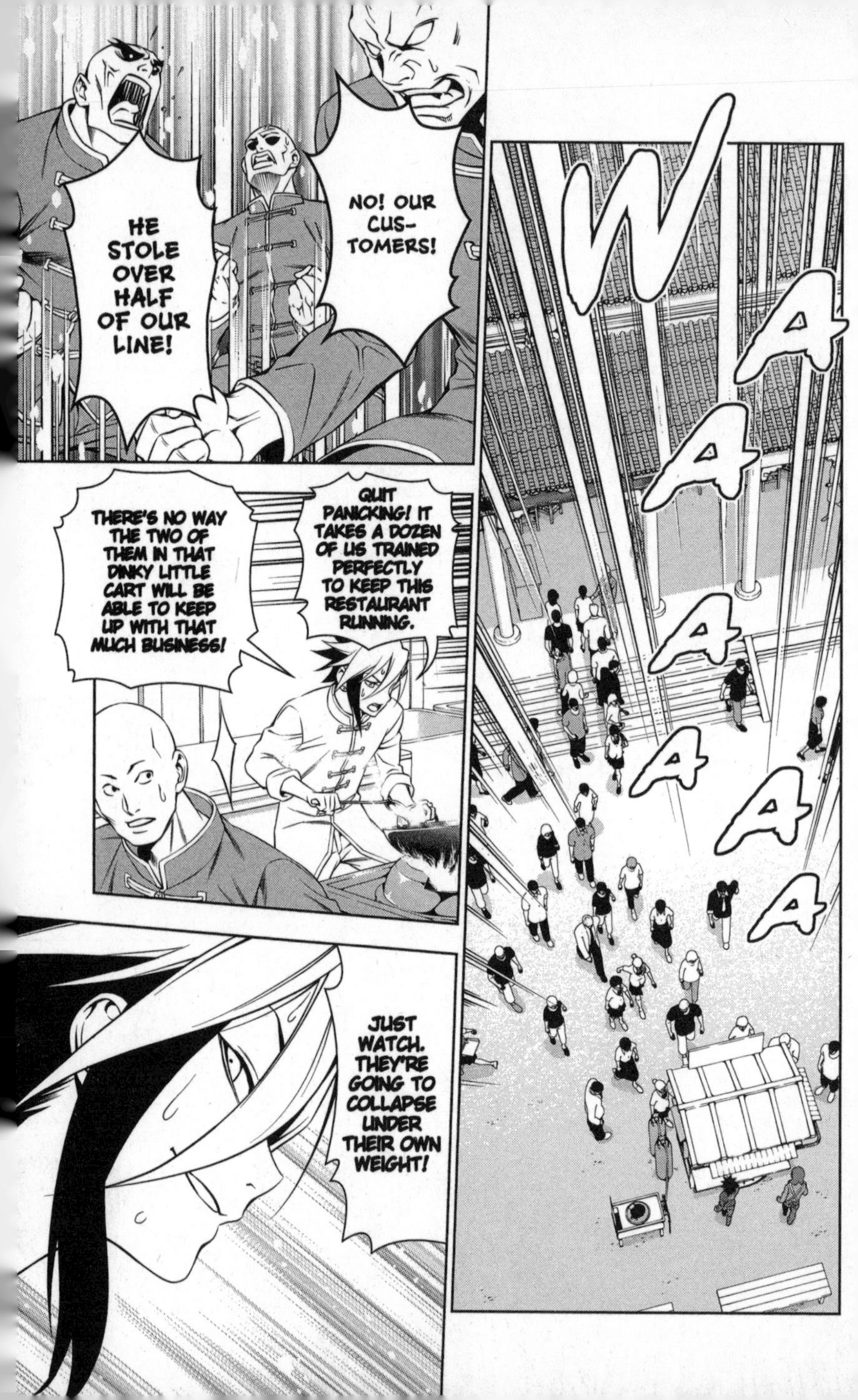
WAAAAAA
NO! OUR CUS-TOMERS!
HE STOLE OVER HALF OF OUR LINE!
QUIT PANICKING! IT TAKES A DOZEN OF US TRAINED PERFECTLY TO KEEP THIS RESTAURANT RUNNING.
THERE'S NO WAY THE TWO OF THEM IN THAT DINKY LITTLE CART WILL BE ABLE TO KEEP UP WITH THAT MUCH BUSINESS!
JUST WATCH. THEY'RE GOING TO COLLAPSE UNDER THEIR OWN WEIGHT!

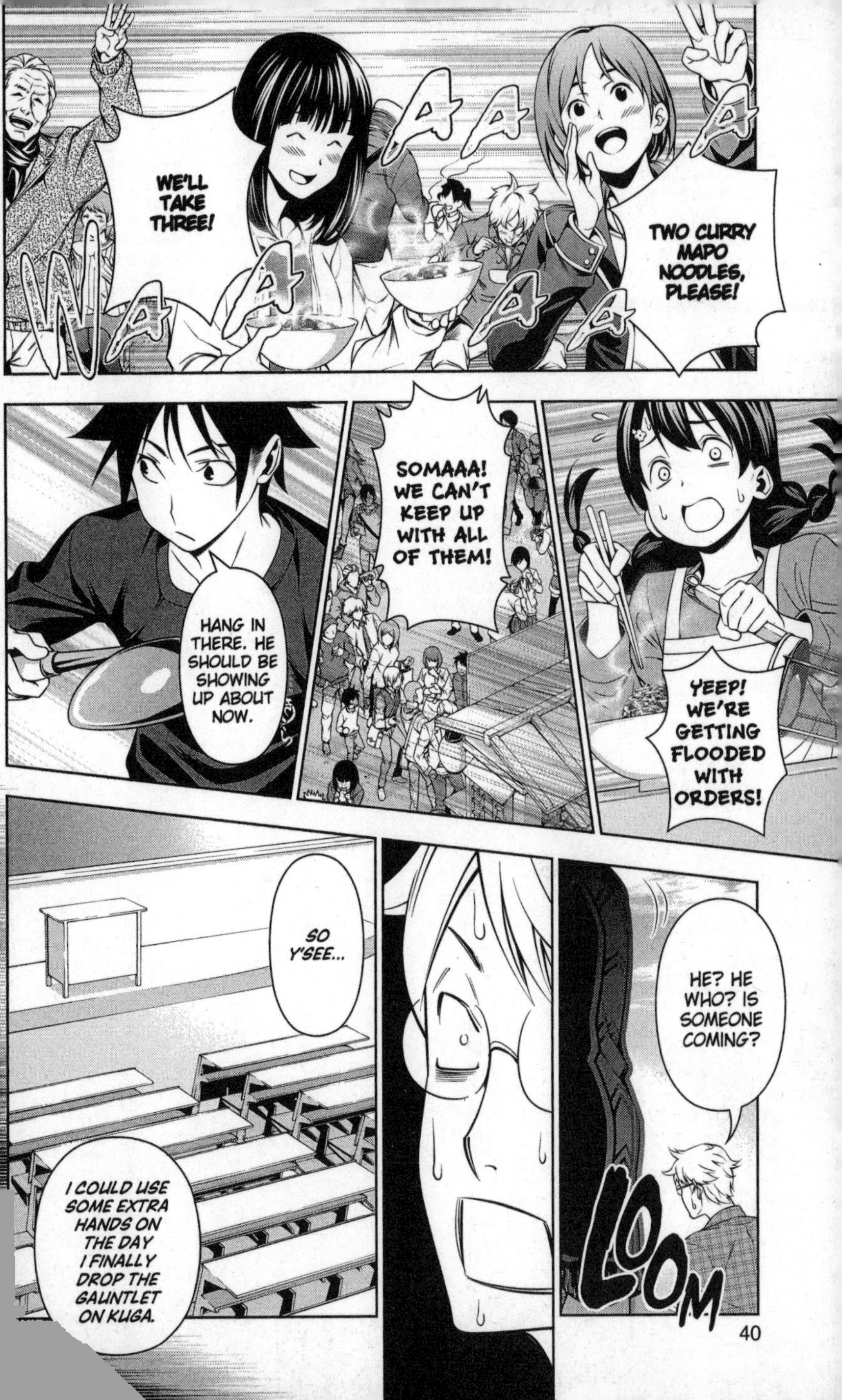
TWO CURRY MAPO NOODLES, PLEASE!
WE'LL TAKE THREE!
WAAAAAAA
YEEP! WE'RE GETTING FLOODED WITH ORDERS!
SOMAAA! WE CAN'T KEEP UP WITH ALL OF THEM!
HANG IN THERE. HE SHOULD BE SHOWING UP ABOUT NOW.
HE? HE WHO? IS SOMEONE COMING?
LOOM
SO Y'SEE...
I COULD USE SOME EXTRA HANDS ON THE DAY I FINALLY DROP THE GAUNTLET ON KUGA.

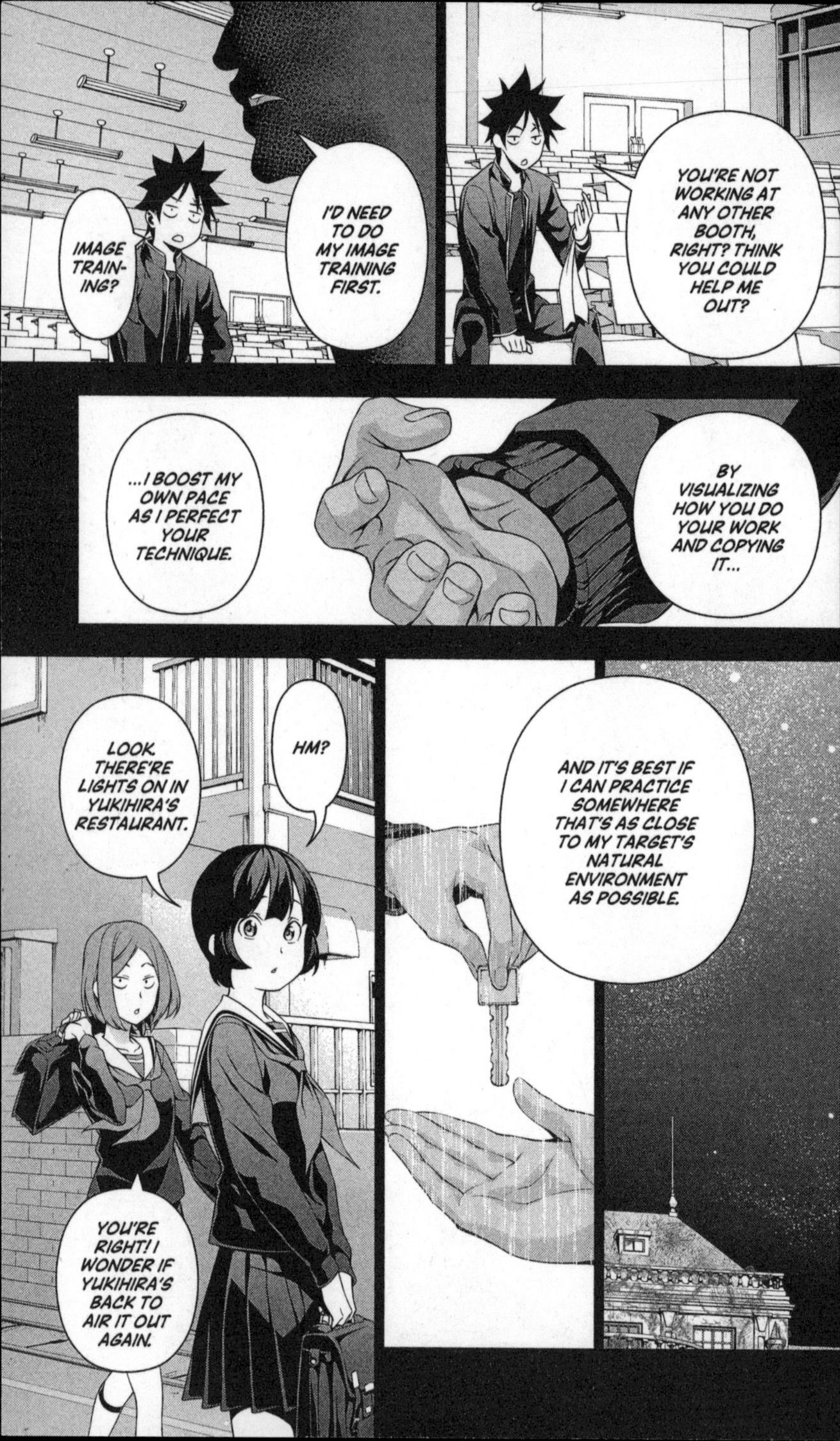
YOU'RE NOT WORKING AT ANY OTHER BOOTH, RIGHT? THINK YOU COULD HELP ME OUT?
I'D NEED TO DO MY IMAGE TRAINING FIRST.
IMAGE TRAIN-ING?
BY VISUALIZING HOW YOU DO YOUR WORK AND COPYING IT...
...I BOOST MY OWN PACE AS I PERFECT YOUR TECHNIQUE.
AND IT'S BEST IF I CAN PRACTICE SOMEWHERE THAT'S AS CLOSE TO MY TARGET'S NATURAL ENVIRONMENT AS POSSIBLE.
LOOK. THERE'RE LIGHTS ON IN YUKIHIRA'S RESTAURANT.
HM?
YOU'RE RIGHT! I WONDER IF YUKIHIRA'S BACK TO AIR IT OUT AGAIN.

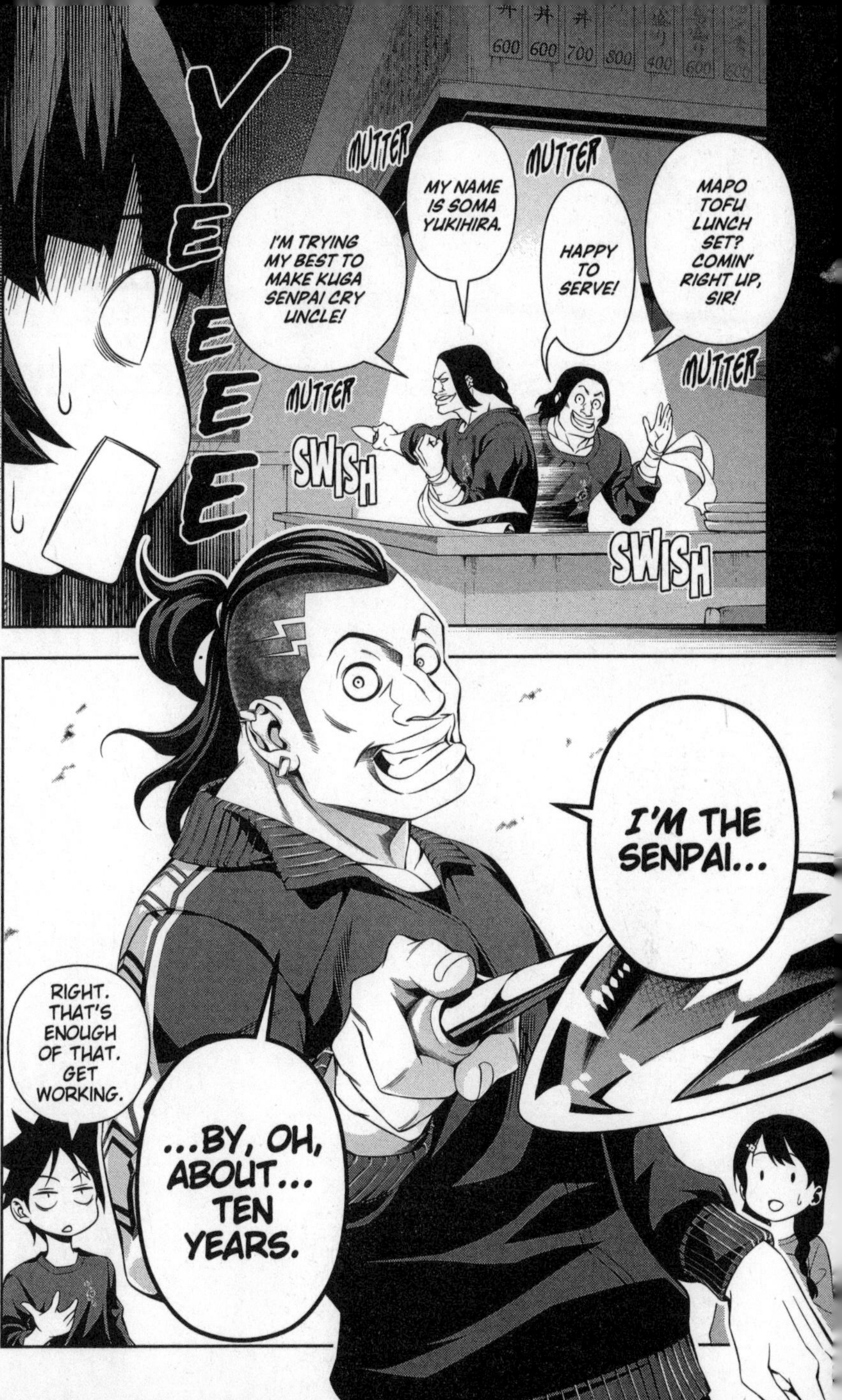
MAPO TOFU LUNCH SET? COMIN' RIGHT UP, SIR!
MUTTER
HAPPY TO SERVE!
MUTTER
MY NAME IS SOMA YUKIHIRA.
MUTTER
I'M TRYING MY BEST TO MAKE KUGA SENPAI CRY UNCLE!
MUTTER
SWISH
SWISH
YEEEEE
I'M THE SENPAI...
...BY, OH, ABOUT... TEN YEARS.
RIGHT. THAT'S ENOUGH OF THAT. GET WORKING.

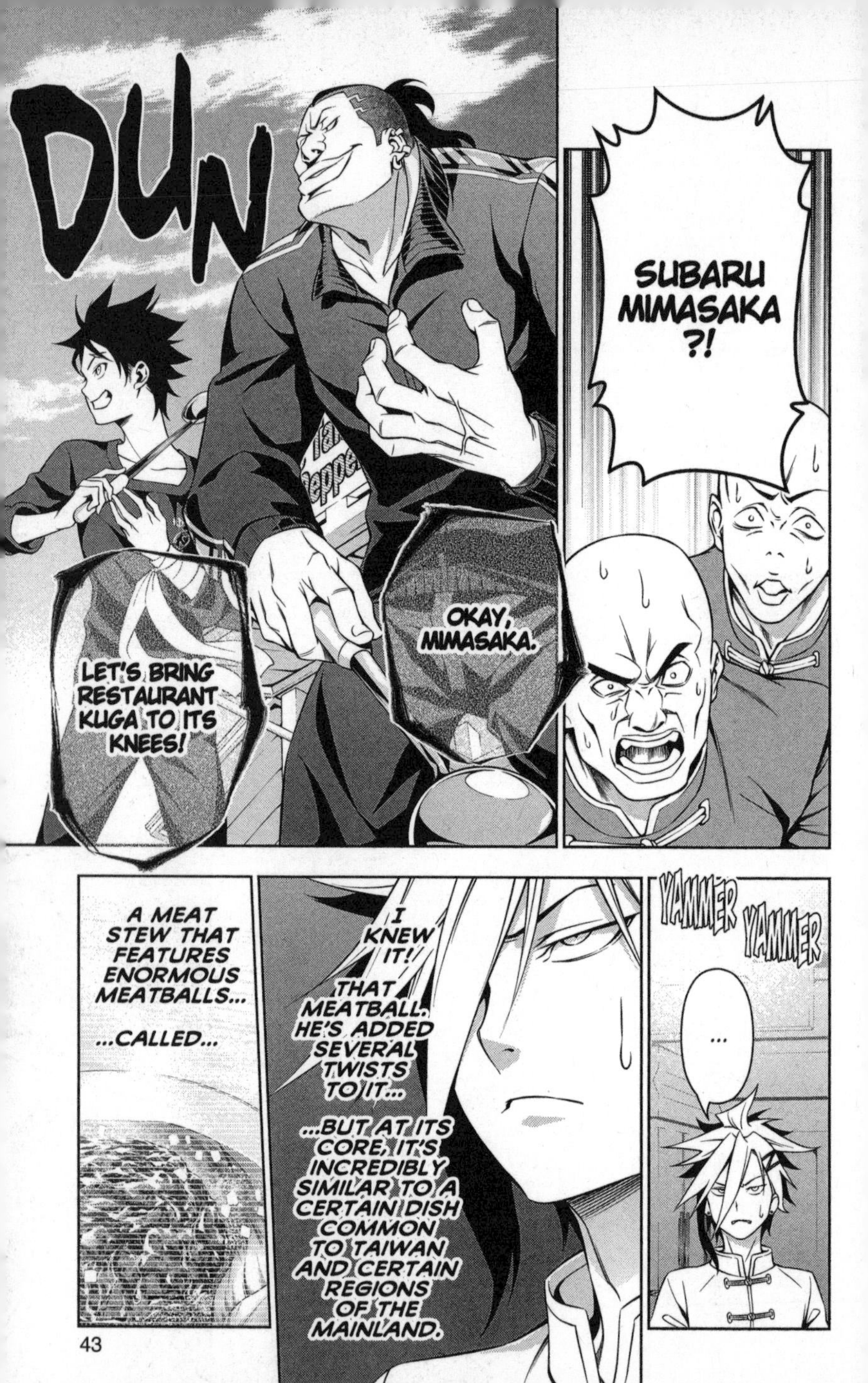
SUBARU MIMASAKA ?!
DUN
OKAY, MIMASAKA.
LET'S BRING RESTAURANT KUGA TO ITS KNEES!
YAMMER YAMMER
...
I KNEW IT!
THAT MEATBALL. HE'S ADDED SEVERAL TWISTS TO IT...
...BUT AT ITS CORE, IT'S INCREDIBLY SIMILAR TO A CERTAIN DISH COMMON TO TAIWAN AND CERTAIN REGIONS OF THE MAINLAND.
A MEAT STEW THAT FEATURES ENORMOUS MEATBALLS...
...CALLED...

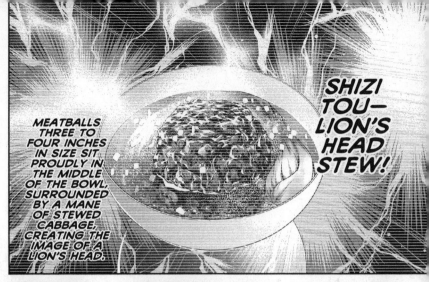

SHIZI TOU— LION'S HEAD STEW!

MEATBALLS THREE TO FOUR INCHES IN SIZE SIT PROUDLY IN THE MIDDLE OF THE BOWL, SURROUNDED BY A MANE OF STEWED CABBAGE, CREATING THE IMAGE OF A LION'S HEAD.

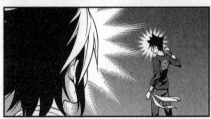

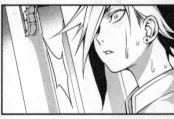

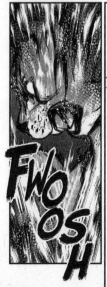

FWOOSH

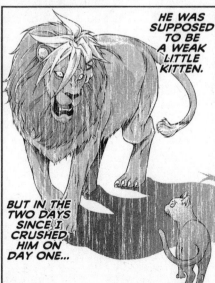

HE WAS SUPPOSED TO BE A WEAK LITTLE KITTEN.

BUT IN THE TWO DAYS SINCE I CRUSHED HIM ON DAY ONE...

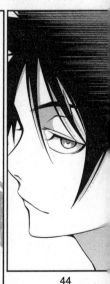

44

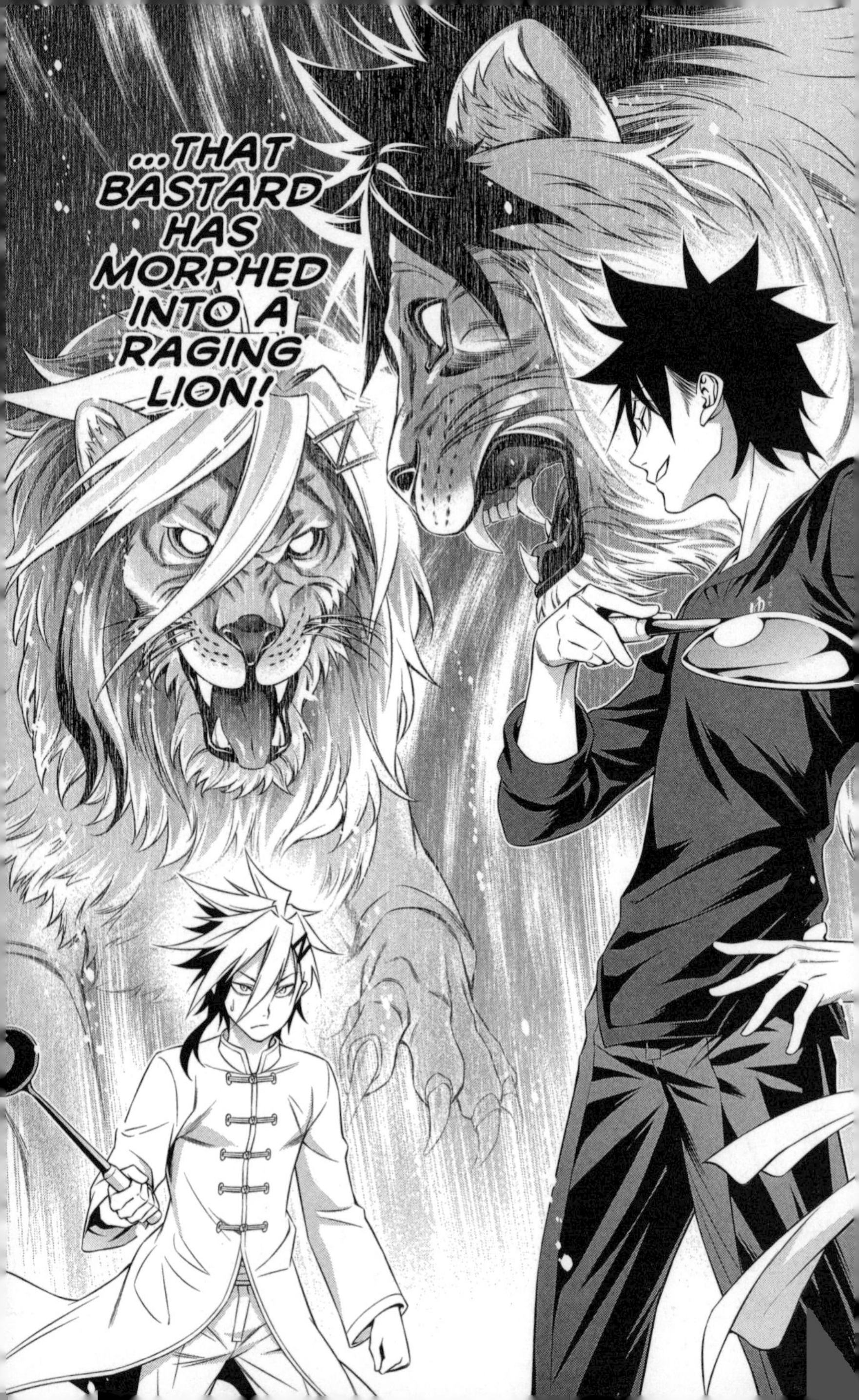
...THAT BASTARD HAS MORPHED INTO A RAGING LION!

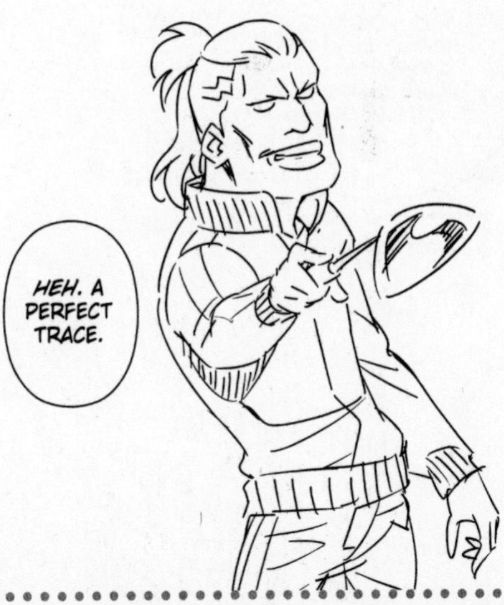
HEH. A PERFECT TRACE.

130 A PRIDE OF YOUNG LIONS

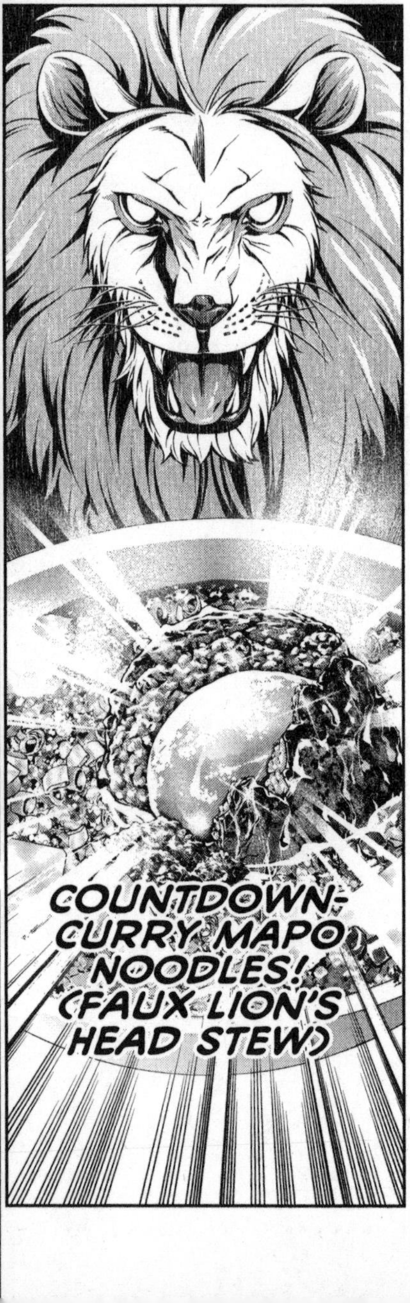
COUNTDOWN-CURRY MAPO NOODLES! (FAUX LION'S HEAD STEW)

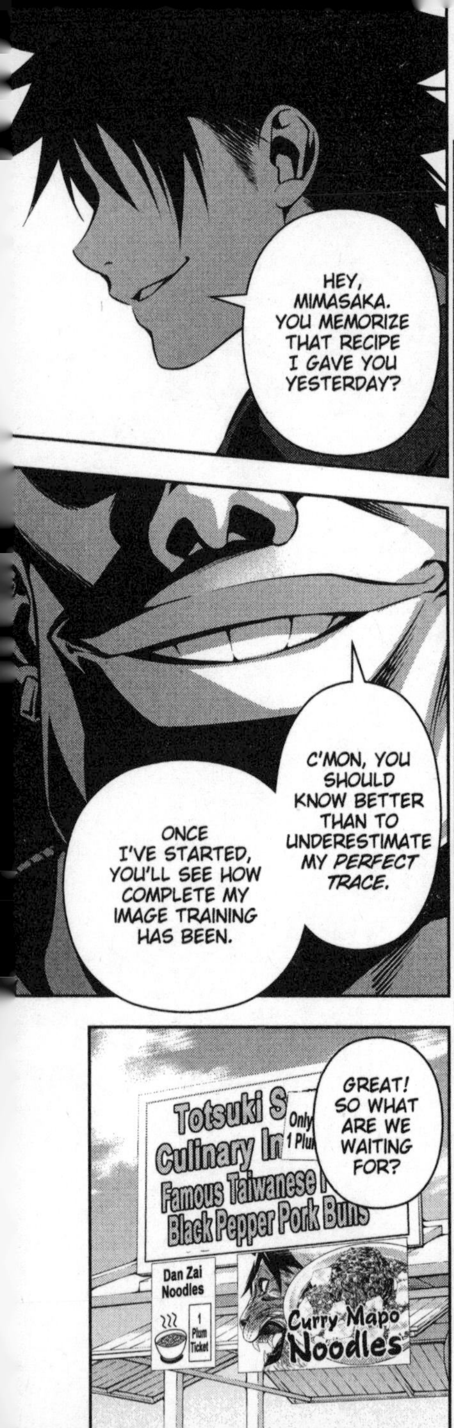
HEY, MIMASAKA. YOU MEMORIZE THAT RECIPE I GAVE YOU YESTERDAY?
C'MON, YOU SHOULD KNOW BETTER THAN TO UNDERESTIMATE MY *PERFECT TRACE.*
ONCE I'VE STARTED, YOU'LL SEE HOW COMPLETE MY IMAGE TRAINING HAS BEEN.
GREAT! SO WHAT ARE WE WAITING FOR?
Famous Taiwanese
Black Pepper Pork Buns
Dan Zai Noodles
1 Plum Ticket
Curry Mapo Noodles

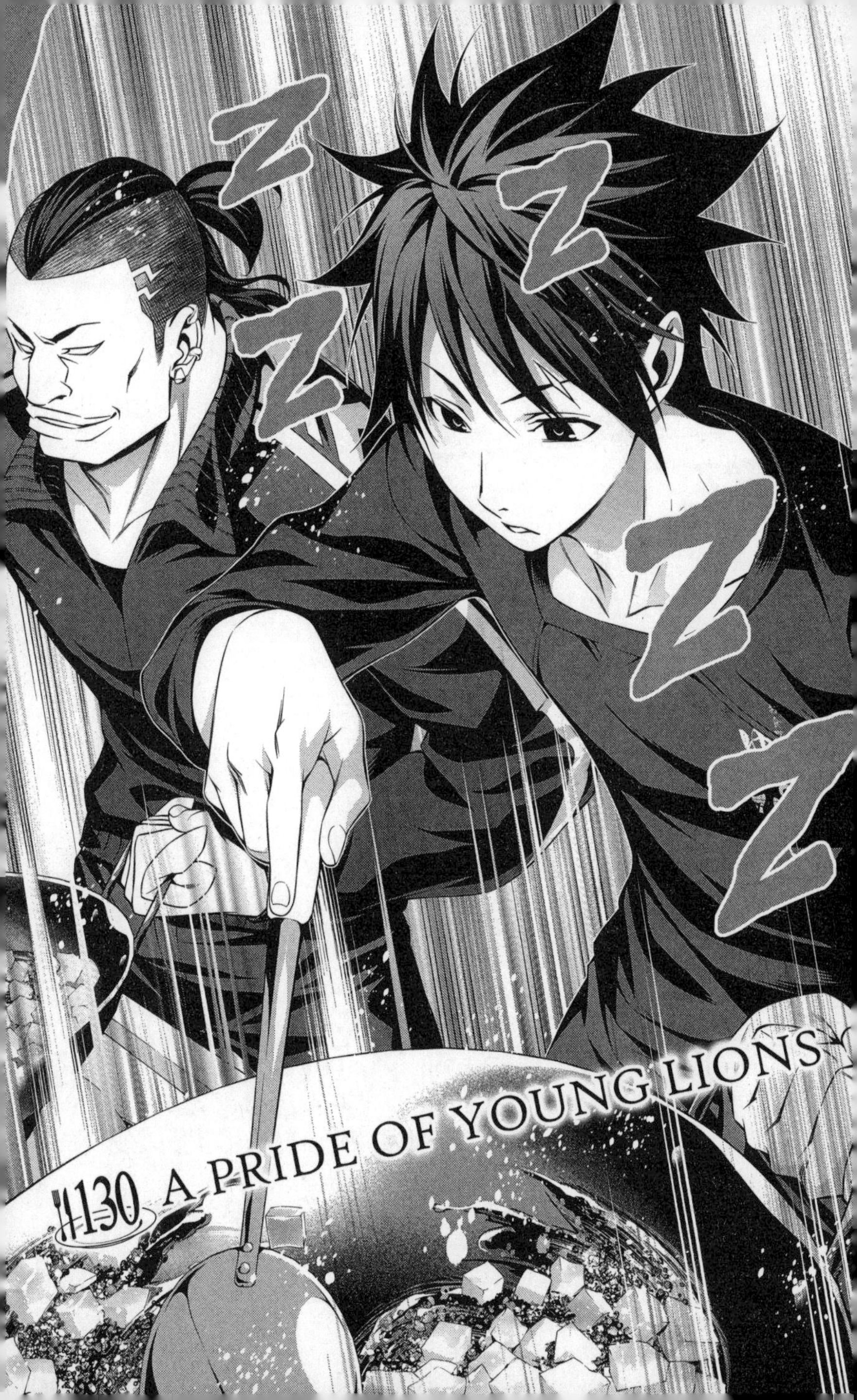

ZZZZZZ
130 A PRIDE OF YOUNG LIONS

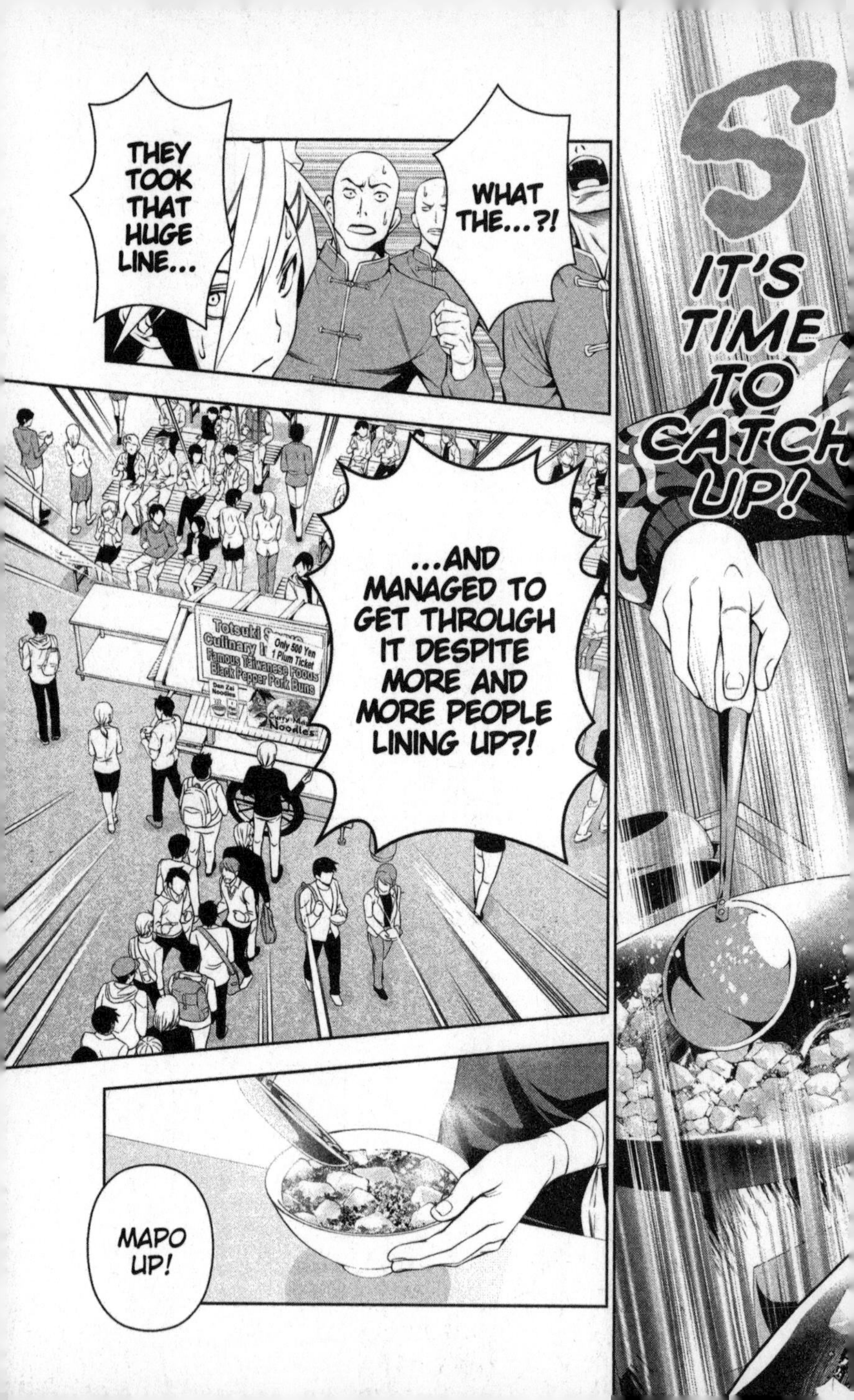
S
IT'S TIME TO CATCH UP!
WHAT THE...?!
THEY TOOK THAT HUGE LINE...
...AND MANAGED TO GET THROUGH IT DESPITE MORE AND MORE PEOPLE LINING UP?!
Totsuki
Culinary
Only 500 Yen
1 Plum Ticket
Famous Taiwanese Foods
Black Pepper Pork Buns
Dan Zai Noodles
Noodles
MAPO UP!

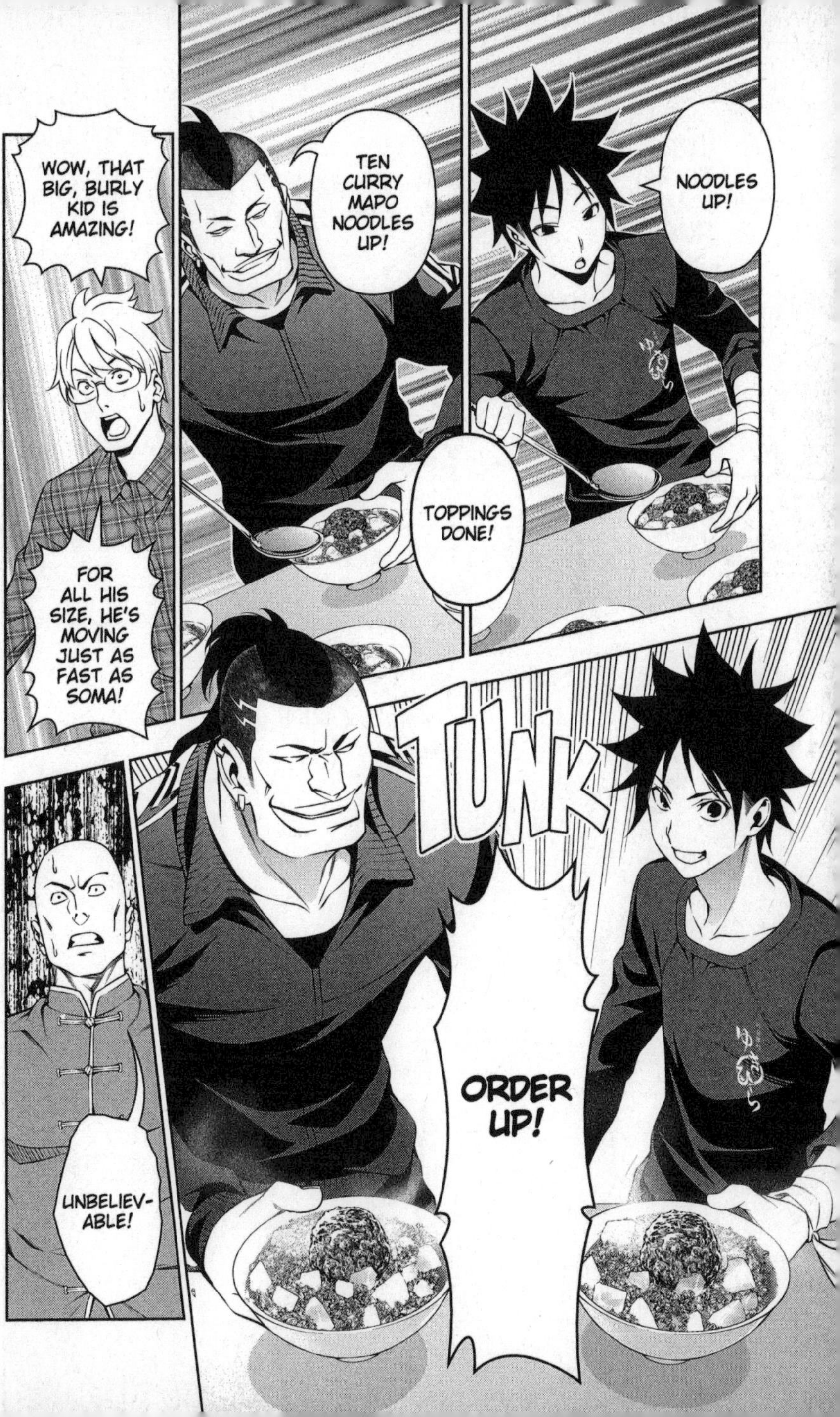
NOODLES UP!
TEN CURRY MAPO NOODLES UP!
TOPPINGS DONE!
WOW, THAT BIG, BURLY KID IS AMAZING!
FOR ALL HIS SIZE, HE'S MOVING JUST AS FAST AS SOMA!
TUNK
ORDER UP!
UNBELIEV-ABLE!

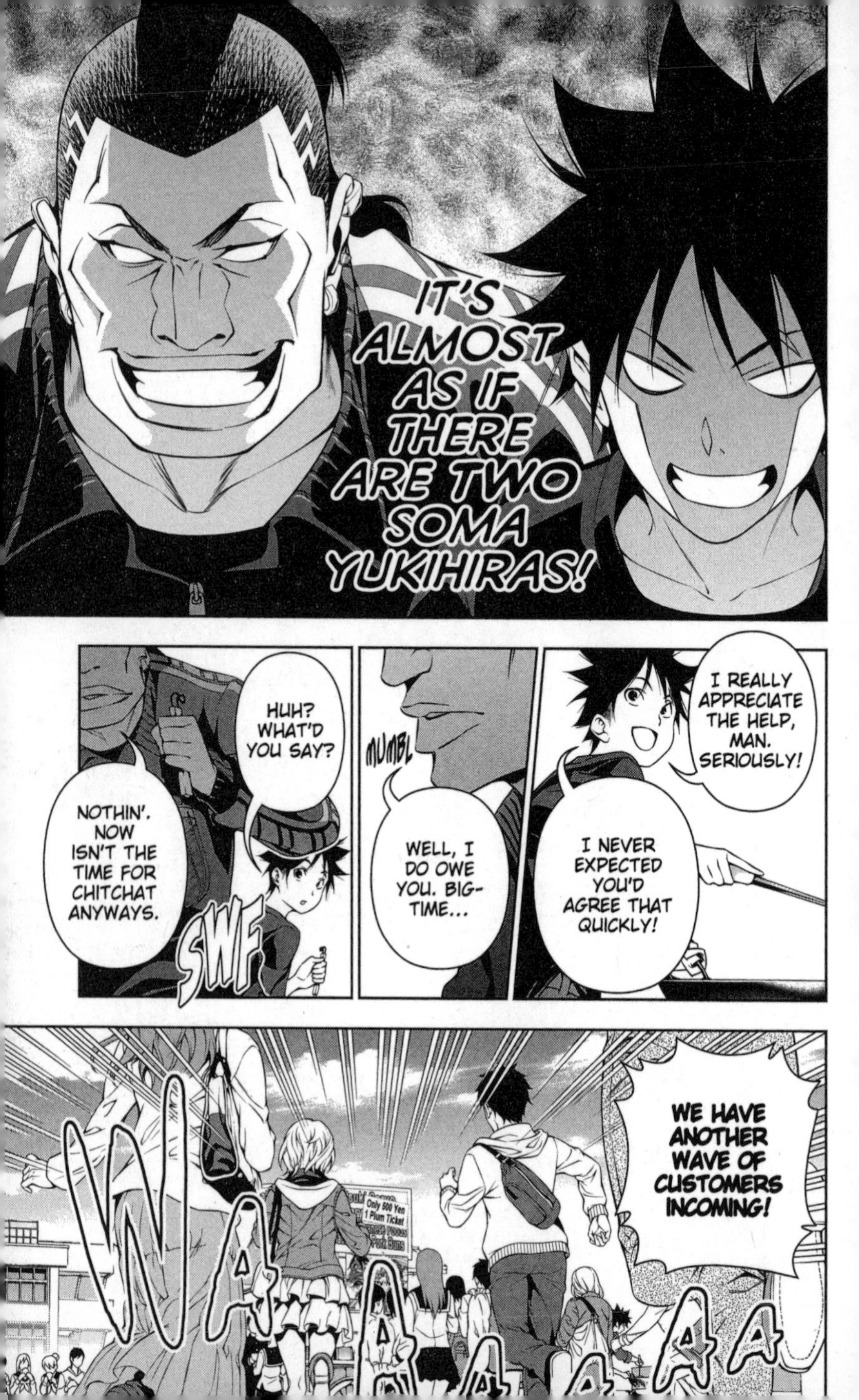

IT'S ALMOST AS IF THERE ARE TWO SOMA YUKIHIRAS!
I REALLY APPRECIATE THE HELP, MAN. SERIOUSLY!
I NEVER EXPECTED YOU'D AGREE THAT QUICKLY!
MUMBL
WELL, I DO OWE YOU. BIG-TIME...
HUH? WHAT'D YOU SAY?
NOTHIN'. NOW ISN'T THE TIME FOR CHITCHAT ANYWAYS.
SWF
WE HAVE ANOTHER WAVE OF CUSTOMERS INCOMING!
Only 500 Yen
1 Plum Ticket
WAAAAAAA

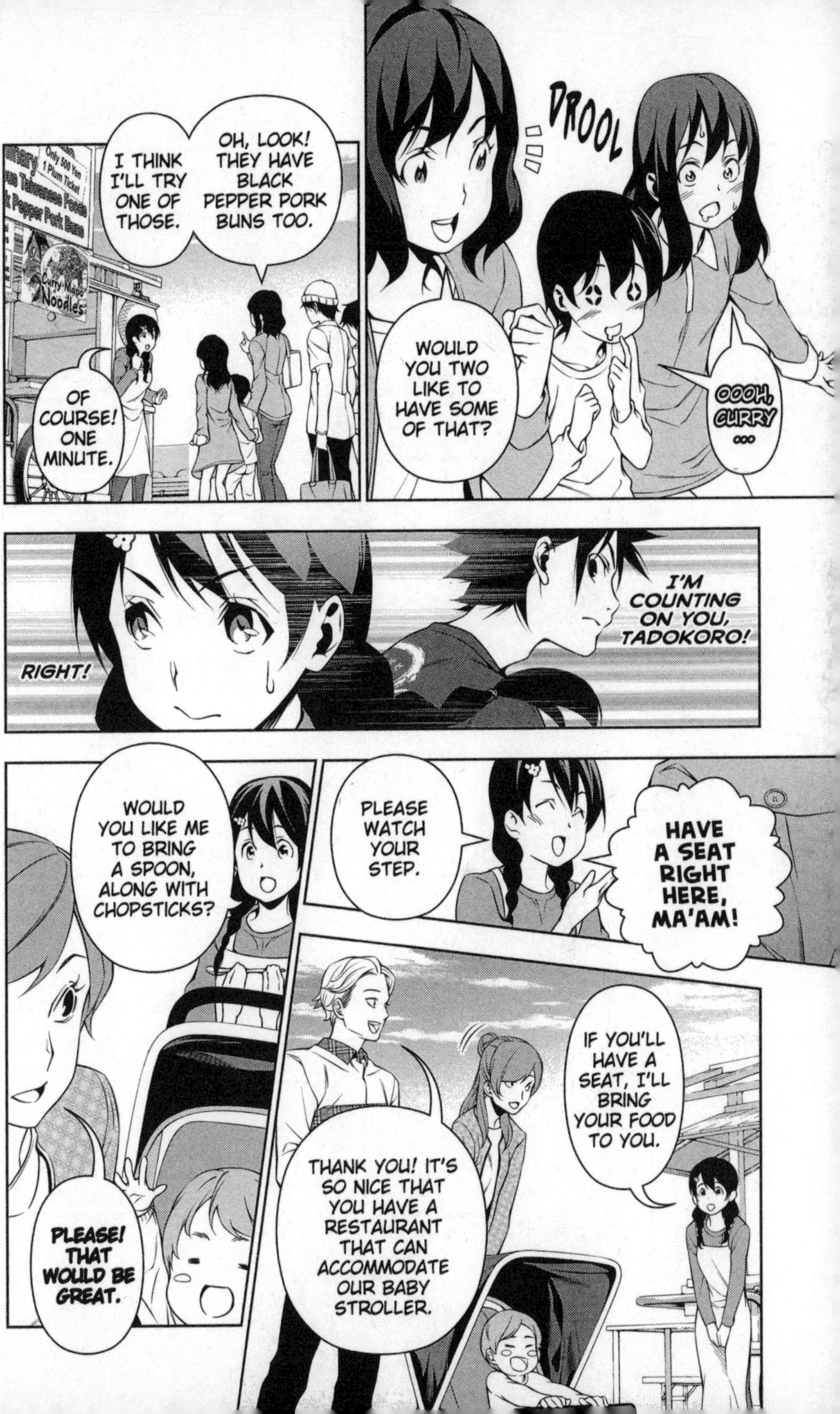
DROOL
OOOH, CURRY...
WOULD YOU TWO LIKE TO HAVE SOME OF THAT?
OH, LOOK! THEY HAVE BLACK PEPPER PORK BUNS TOO.
I THINK I'LL TRY ONE OF THOSE.
Only 500 Yen
1 Plum Ticket
Curry Mapo Noodles
OF COURSE! ONE MINUTE.
I'M COUNTING ON YOU, TADOKORO!
RIGHT!
HAVE A SEAT RIGHT HERE, MA'AM!
PLEASE WATCH YOUR STEP.
IF YOU'LL HAVE A SEAT, I'LL BRING YOUR FOOD TO YOU.
THANK YOU! IT'S SO NICE THAT YOU HAVE A RESTAURANT THAT CAN ACCOMMODATE OUR BABY STROLLER.
WOULD YOU LIKE ME TO BRING A SPOON, ALONG WITH CHOPSTICKS?
PLEASE! THAT WOULD BE GREAT.

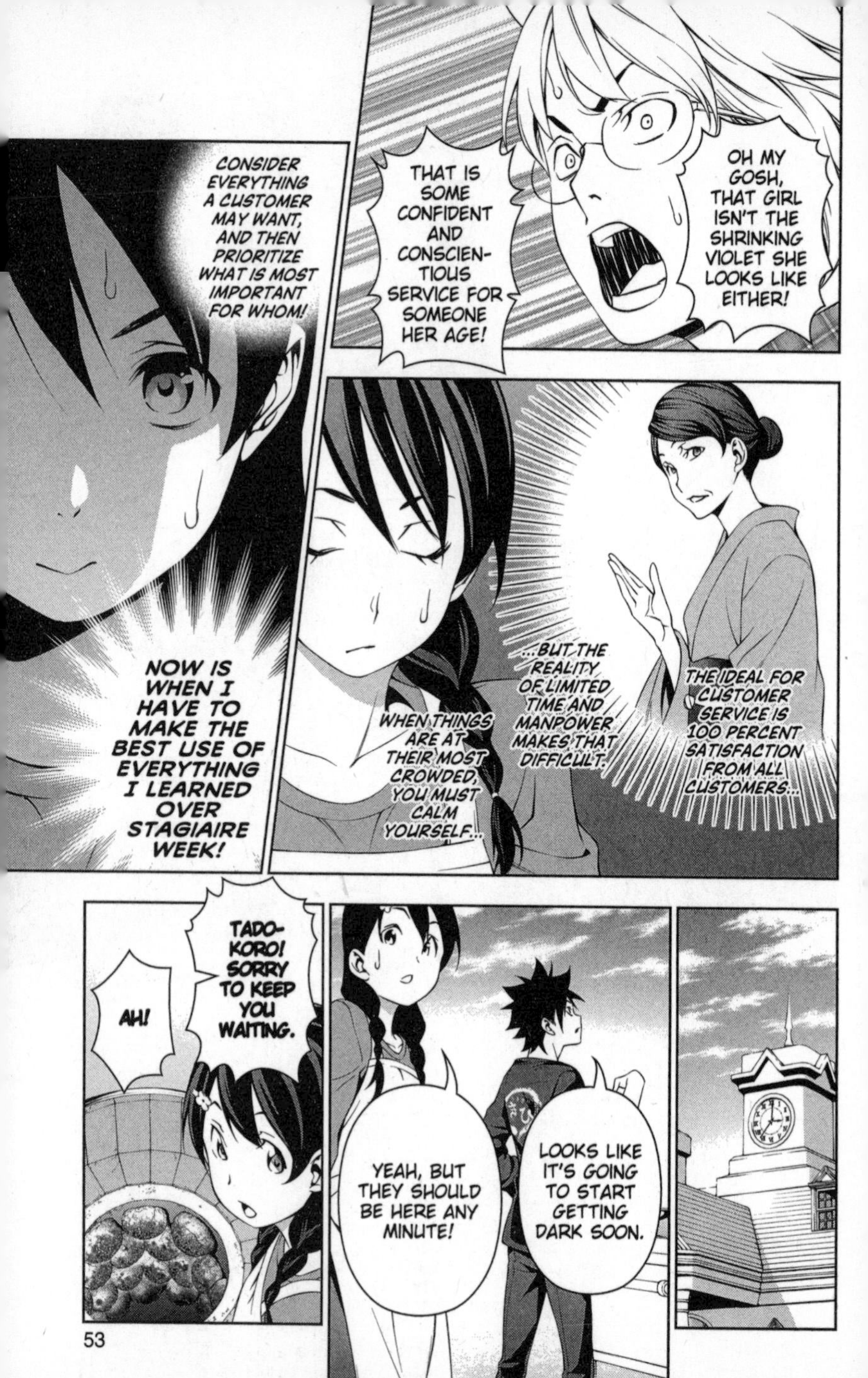
OH MY GOSH, THAT GIRL ISN'T THE SHRINKING VIOLET SHE LOOKS LIKE EITHER!
THAT IS SOME CONFIDENT AND CONSCIEN-TIOUS SERVICE FOR SOMEONE HER AGE!
THE IDEAL FOR CUSTOMER SERVICE IS 100 PERCENT SATISFACTION FROM ALL CUSTOMERS...
...BUT THE REALITY OF LIMITED TIME AND MANPOWER MAKES THAT DIFFICULT.
WHEN THINGS ARE AT THEIR MOST CROWDED, YOU MUST CALM YOURSELF...
CONSIDER EVERYTHING A CUSTOMER MAY WANT, AND THEN PRIORITIZE WHAT IS MOST IMPORTANT FOR WHOM!
NOW IS WHEN I HAVE TO MAKE THE BEST USE OF EVERYTHING I LEARNED OVER STAGIAIRE WEEK!
LOOKS LIKE IT'S GOING TO START GETTING DARK SOON.
YEAH, BUT THEY SHOULD BE HERE ANY MINUTE!
TADO-KORO! SORRY TO KEEP YOU WAITING.
AH!

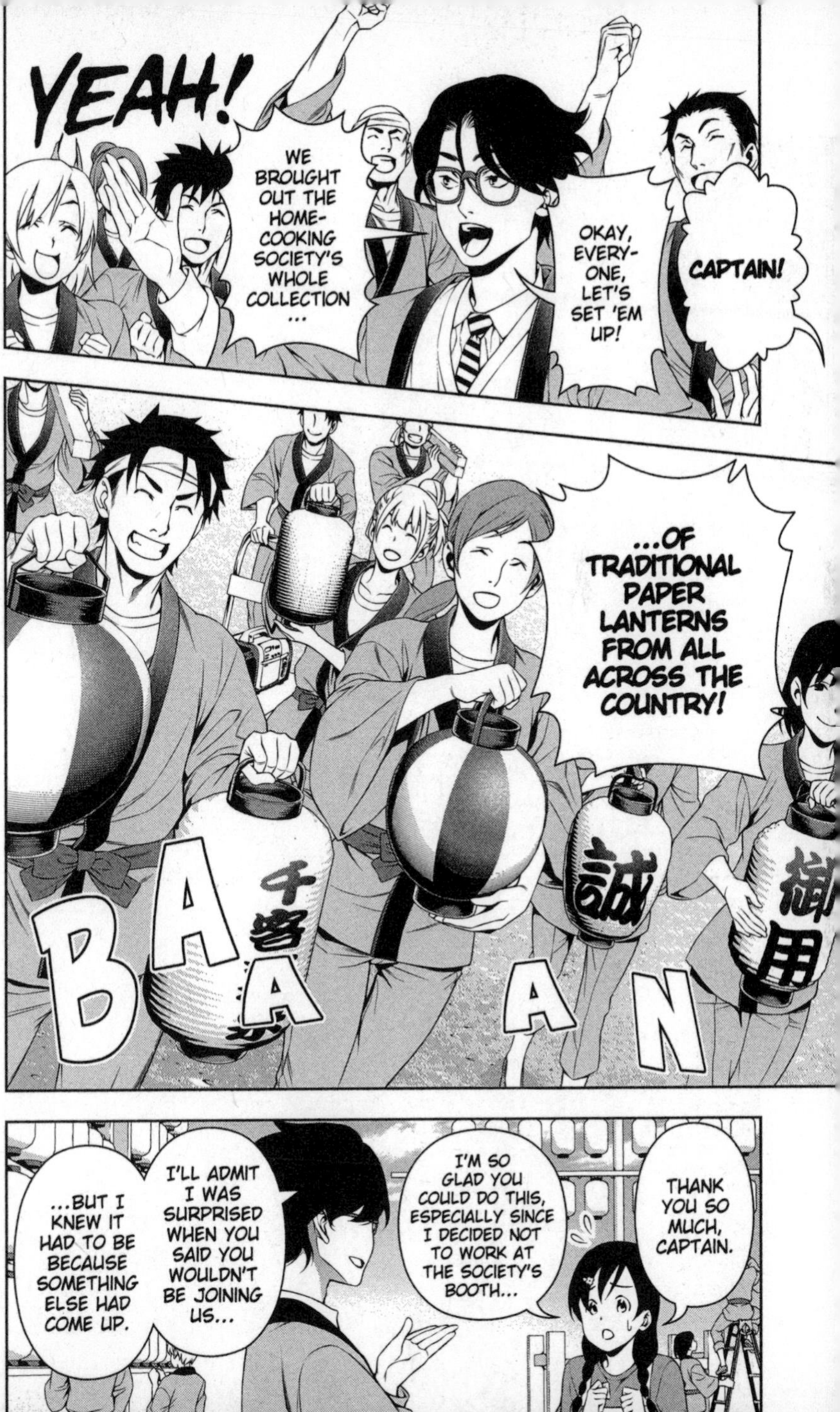
CAPTAIN!
OKAY, EVERYONE, LET'S SET 'EM UP!
YEAH!
WE BROUGHT OUT THE HOME-COOKING SOCIETY'S WHOLE COLLECTION...
...OF TRADITIONAL PAPER LANTERNS FROM ALL ACROSS THE COUNTRY!
BAAAN
THANK YOU SO MUCH, CAPTAIN.
I'M SO GLAD YOU COULD DO THIS, ESPECIALLY SINCE I DECIDED NOT TO WORK AT THE SOCIETY'S BOOTH...
I'LL ADMIT I WAS SURPRISED WHEN YOU SAID YOU WOULDN'T BE JOINING US...
...BUT I KNEW IT HAD TO BE BECAUSE SOMETHING ELSE HAD COME UP.

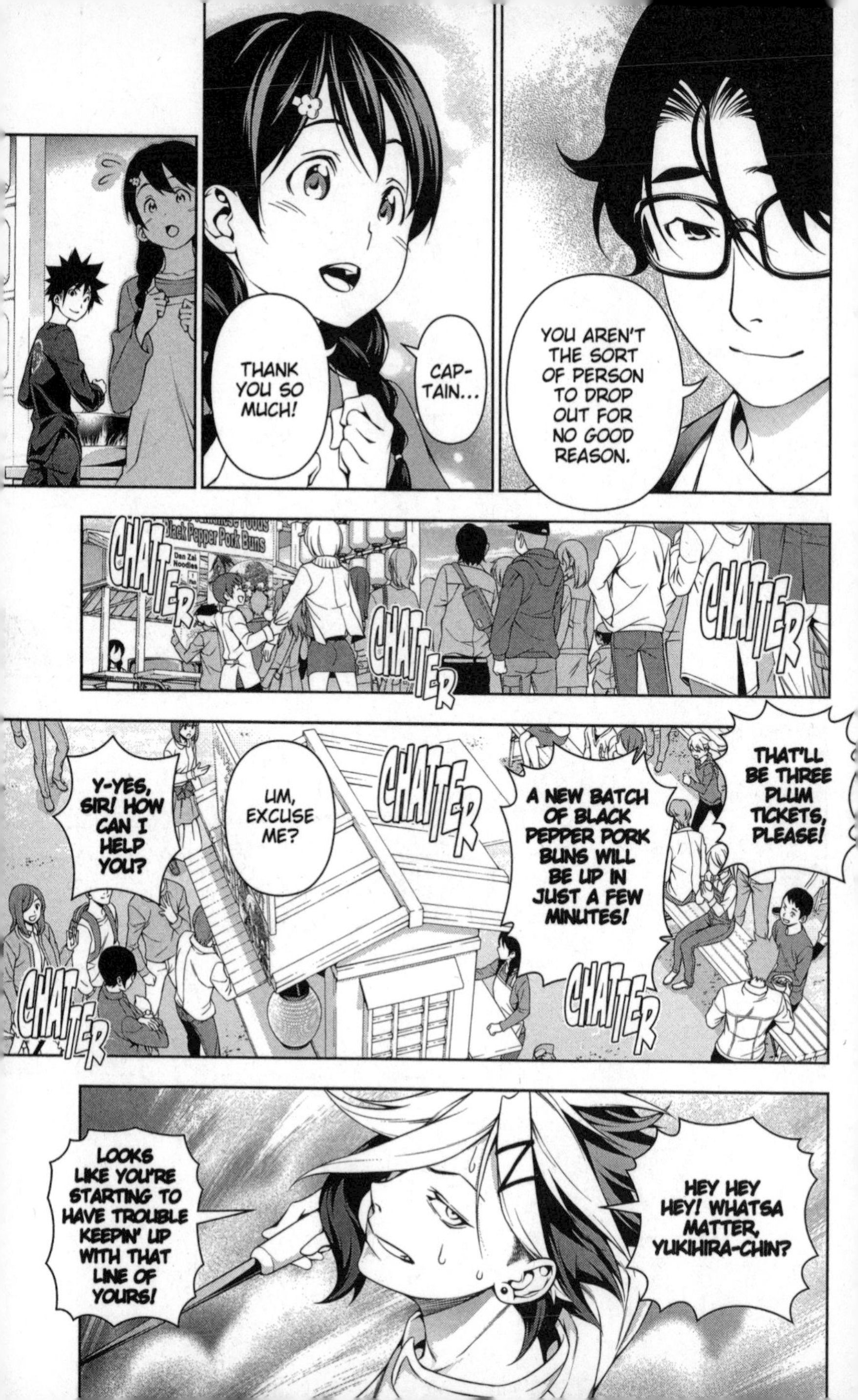
YOU AREN'T THE SORT OF PERSON TO DROP OUT FOR NO GOOD REASON.
CAP-TAIN...
THANK YOU SO MUCH!
Black Pepper Pork Buns
Dan Zai Noodles
CHATTER
CHATTER
CHATTER
THAT'LL BE THREE PLUM TICKETS, PLEASE!
A NEW BATCH OF BLACK PEPPER PORK BUNS WILL BE UP IN JUST A FEW MINUTES!
CHATTER
CHATTER
UM, EXCUSE ME?
Y-YES, SIR! HOW CAN I HELP YOU?
CHATTER
HEY HEY HEY! WHATSA MATTER, YUKIHIRA-CHIN?
LOOKS LIKE YOU'RE STARTING TO HAVE TROUBLE KEEPIN' UP WITH THAT LINE OF YOURS!

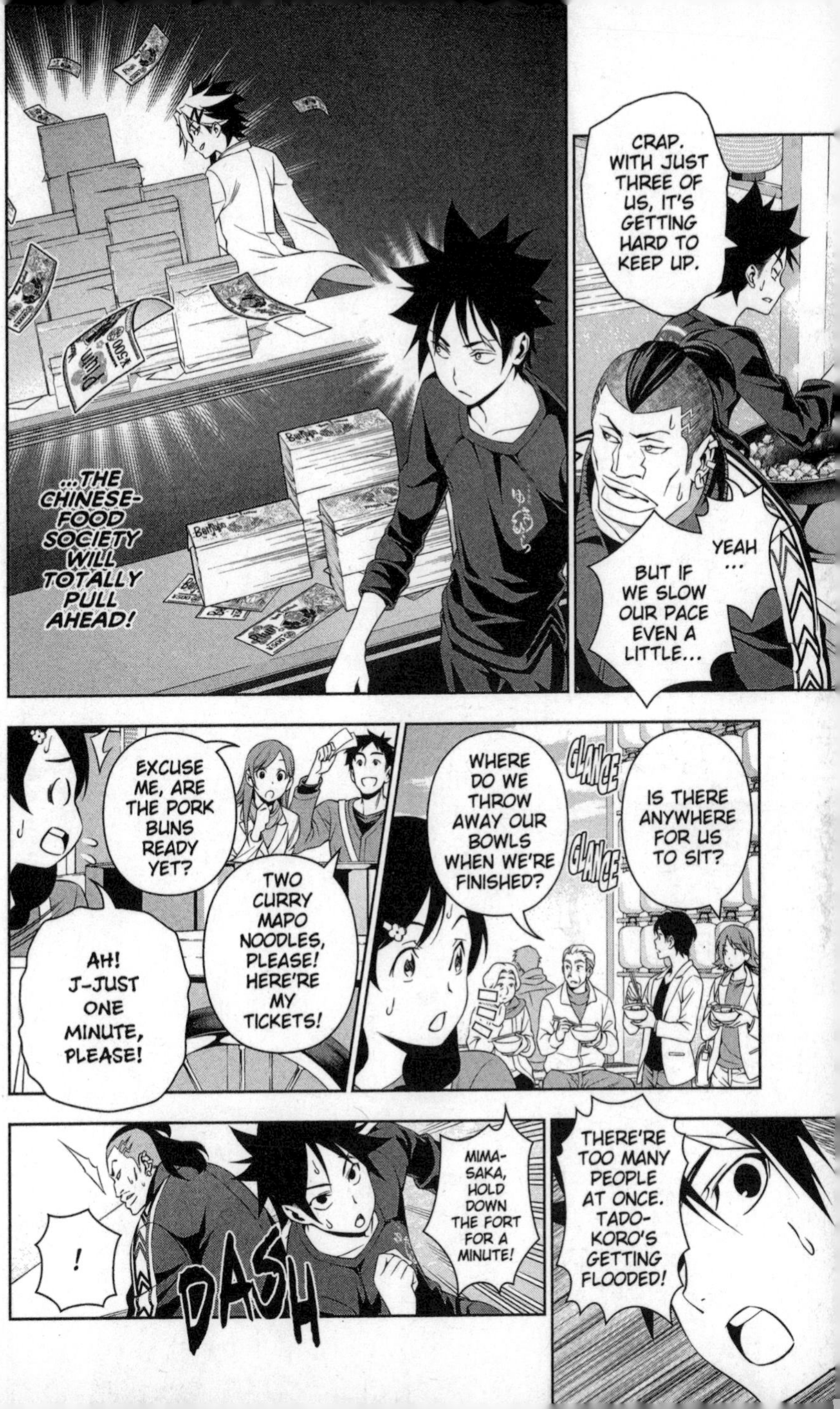
CRAP. WITH JUST THREE OF US, IT'S GETTING HARD TO KEEP UP.
YEAH...
BUT IF WE SLOW OUR PACE EVEN A LITTLE...
...THE CHINESE-FOOD SOCIETY WILL TOTALLY PULL AHEAD!
IS THERE ANYWHERE FOR US TO SIT?
GLANCE
GLANCE
WHERE DO WE THROW AWAY OUR BOWLS WHEN WE'RE FINISHED?
EXCUSE ME, ARE THE PORK BUNS READY YET?
TWO CURRY MAPO NOODLES, PLEASE! HERE'RE MY TICKETS!
AH! J-JUST ONE MINUTE, PLEASE!
THERE'RE TOO MANY PEOPLE AT ONCE. TADO-KORO'S GETTING FLOODED!
MIMA-SAKA, HOLD DOWN THE FORT FOR A MINUTE!
!
DASH

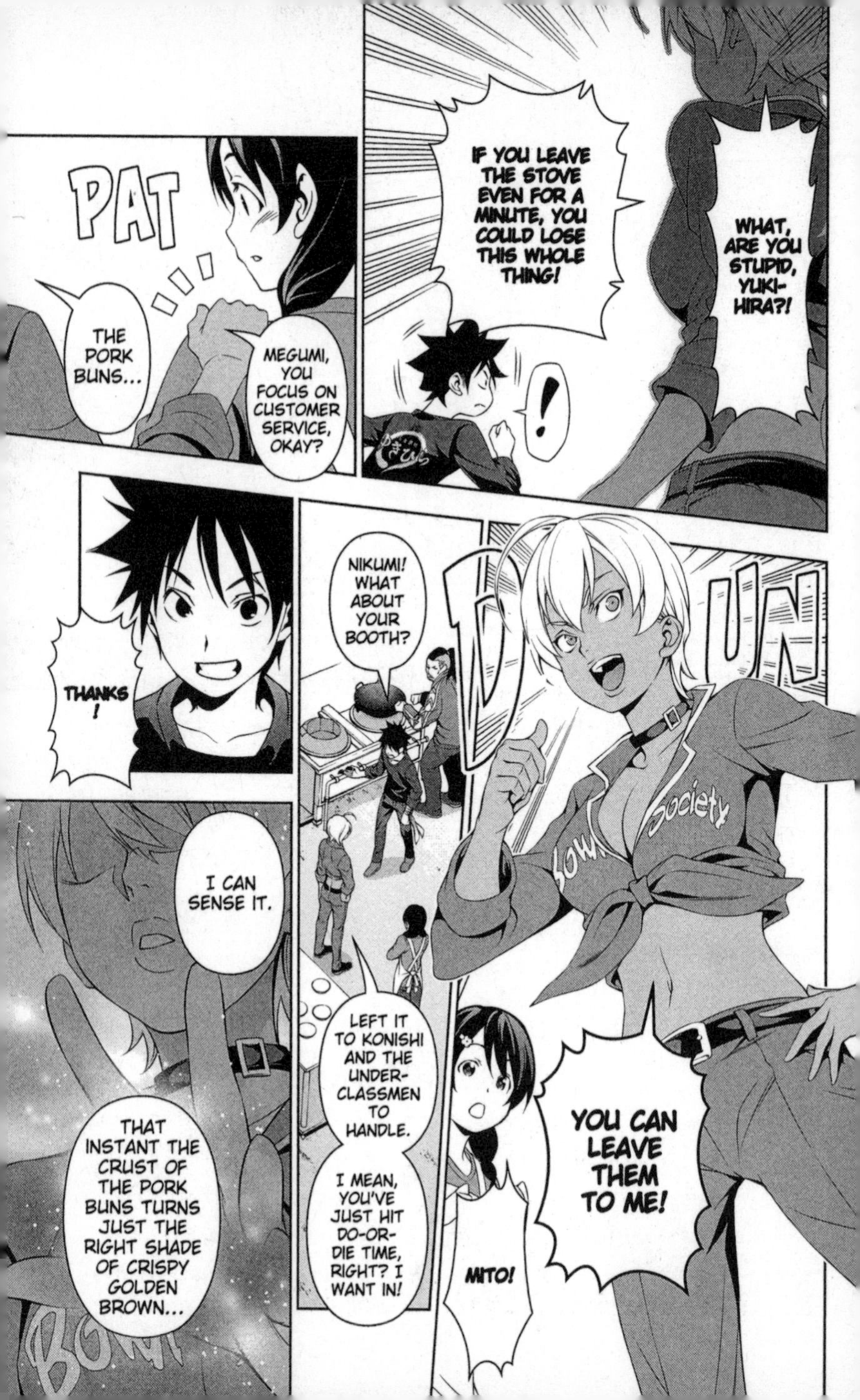
WHAT, ARE YOU STUPID, YUKI-HIRA?!
IF YOU LEAVE THE STOVE EVEN FOR A MINUTE, YOU COULD LOSE THIS WHOLE THING!
!
PAT
MEGUMI, YOU FOCUS ON CUSTOMER SERVICE, OKAY?
...
THE PORK BUNS...
YOU CAN LEAVE THEM TO ME!
MITO!
NIKUMI! WHAT ABOUT YOUR BOOTH?
LEFT IT TO KONISHI AND THE UNDER-CLASSMEN TO HANDLE.
I MEAN, YOU'VE JUST HIT DO-OR-DIE TIME, RIGHT? I WANT IN!
THANKS!
I CAN SENSE IT.
THAT INSTANT THE CRUST OF THE PORK BUNS TURNS JUST THE RIGHT SHADE OF CRISPY GOLDEN BROWN...

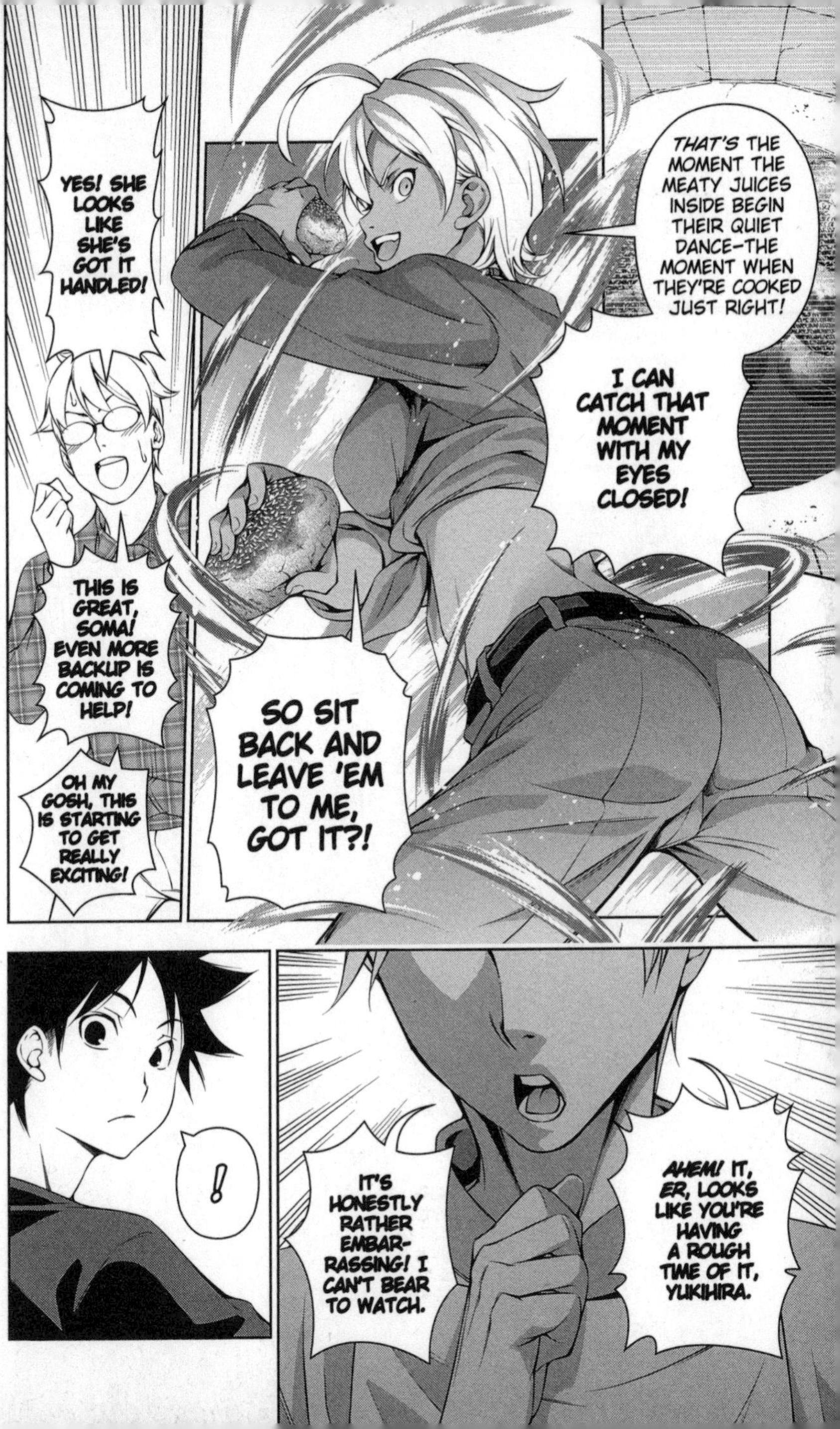

THAT'S THE MOMENT THE MEATY JUICES INSIDE BEGIN THEIR QUIET DANCE—THE MOMENT WHEN THEY'RE COOKED JUST RIGHT!
I CAN CATCH THAT MOMENT WITH MY EYES CLOSED!
SO SIT BACK AND LEAVE 'EM TO ME, GOT IT?!
YES! SHE LOOKS LIKE SHE'S GOT IT HANDLED!
THIS IS GREAT, SOMA! EVEN MORE BACKUP IS COMING TO HELP!
OH MY GOSH, THIS IS STARTING TO GET REALLY EXCITING!
AHEM! IT, *ER,* LOOKS LIKE YOU'RE HAVING A ROUGH TIME OF IT, YUKIHIRA.
IT'S HONESTLY RATHER EMBAR-RASSING! I CAN'T BEAR TO WATCH.
!

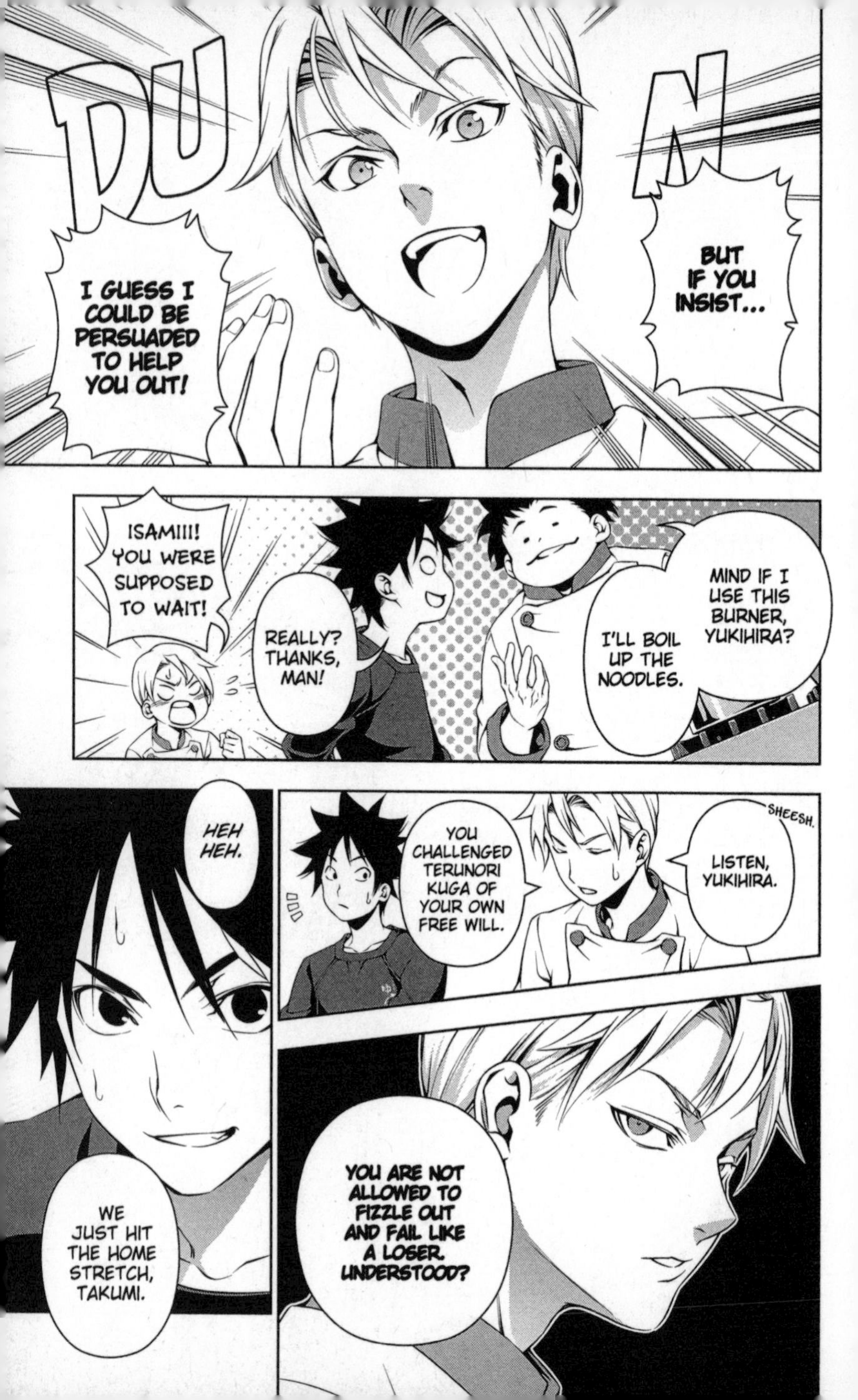
DU
N
BUT IF YOU INSIST...
I GUESS I COULD BE PERSUADED TO HELP YOU OUT!
MIND IF I USE THIS BURNER, YUKIHIRA?
I'LL BOIL UP THE NOODLES.
REALLY? THANKS, MAN!
ISAMIII! YOU WERE SUPPOSED TO WAIT!
SHEESH.
LISTEN, YUKIHIRA.
YOU CHALLENGED TERUNORI KUGA OF YOUR OWN FREE WILL.
YOU ARE NOT ALLOWED TO FIZZLE OUT AND FAIL LIKE A LOSER. UNDERSTOOD?
HEH HEH.
WE JUST HIT THE HOME STRETCH, TAKUMI.

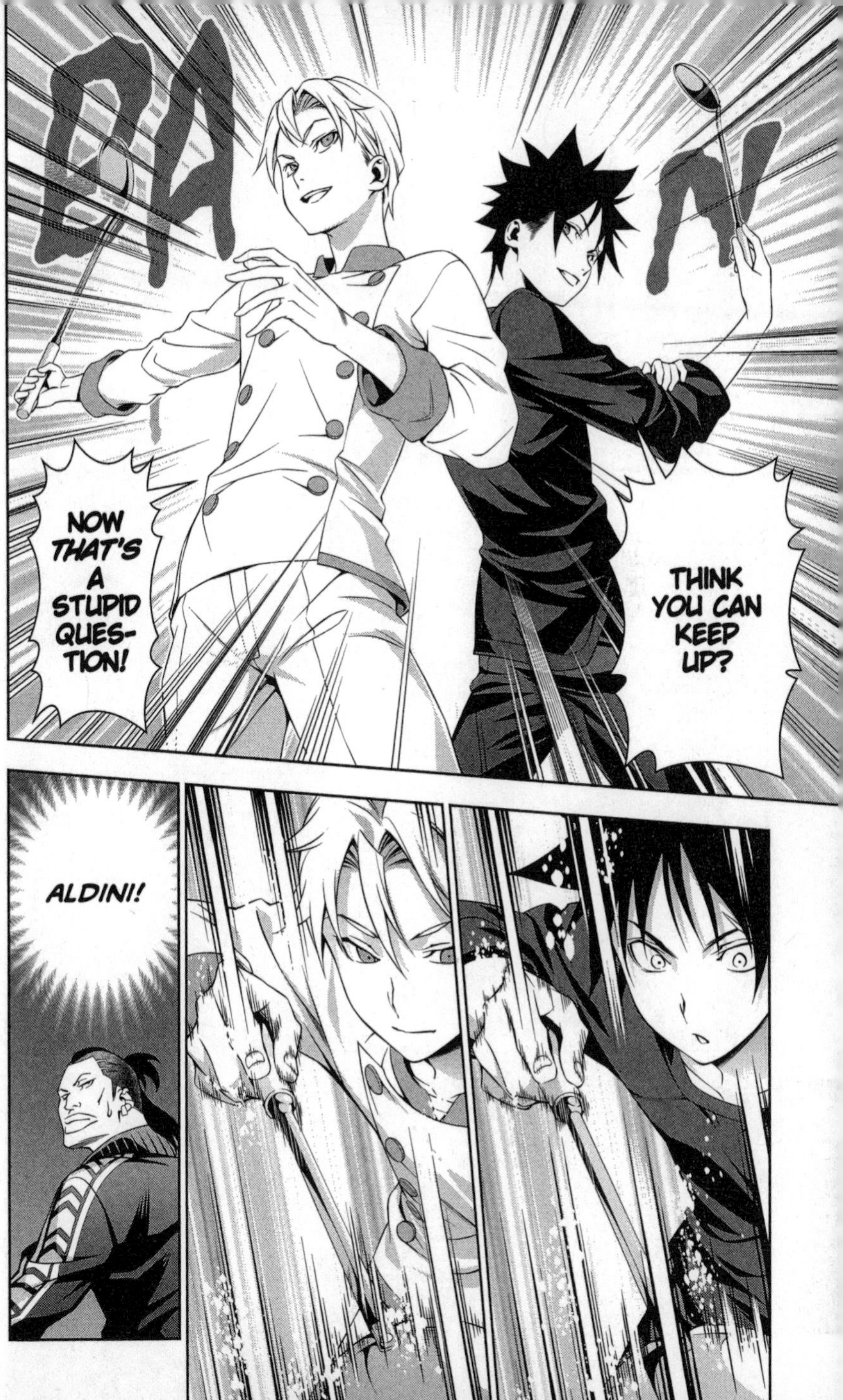
DAN
THINK YOU CAN KEEP UP?
NOW THAT'S A STUPID QUESTION!
ALDINI!

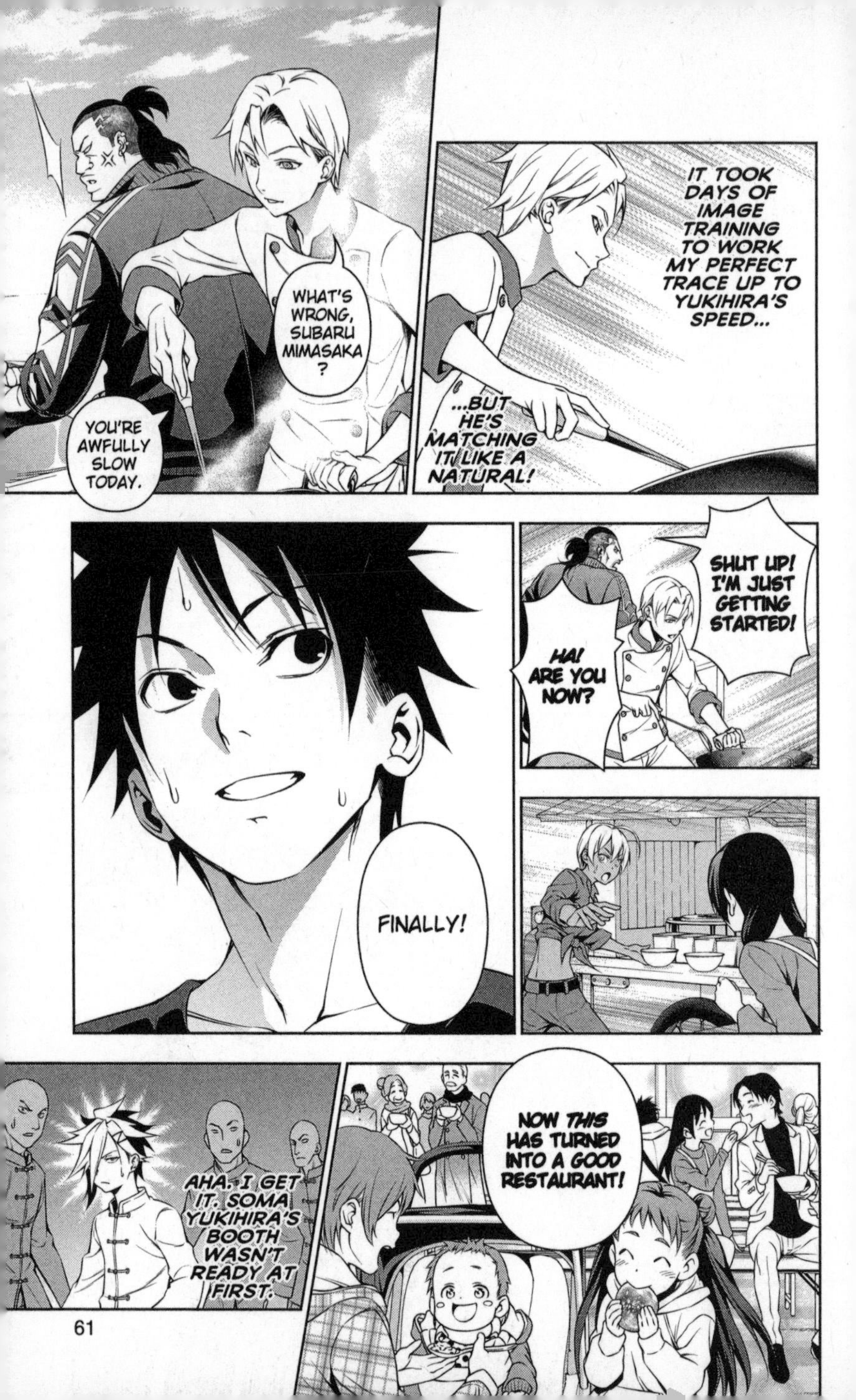
IT TOOK DAYS OF IMAGE TRAINING TO WORK MY PERFECT TRACE UP TO YUKIHIRA'S SPEED...
...BUT HE'S MATCHING IT LIKE A NATURAL!
WHAT'S WRONG, SUBARU MIMASAKA?
YOU'RE AWFULLY SLOW TODAY.
SHUT UP! I'M JUST GETTING STARTED!
HA! ARE YOU NOW?
FINALLY!
NOW THIS HAS TURNED INTO A GOOD RESTAURANT!
AHA. I GET IT. SOMA YUKIHIRA'S BOOTH WASN'T READY AT FIRST.

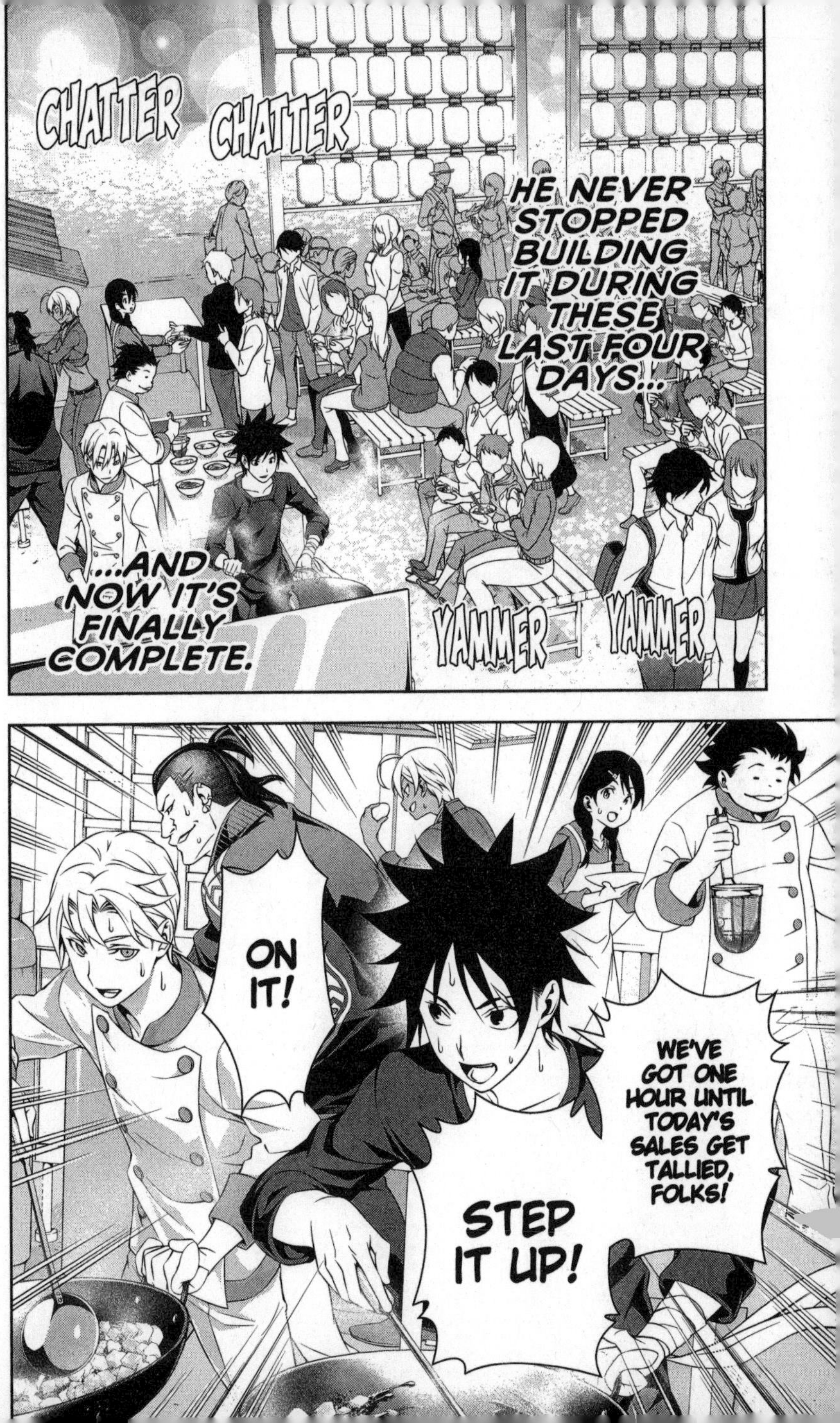
HE NEVER STOPPED BUILDING IT DURING THESE LAST FOUR DAYS...
CHATTER CHATTER
YAMMER YAMMER
...AND NOW IT'S FINALLY COMPLETE.
WE'VE GOT ONE HOUR UNTIL TODAY'S SALES GET TALLIED, FOLKS!
STEP IT UP!
ON IT!

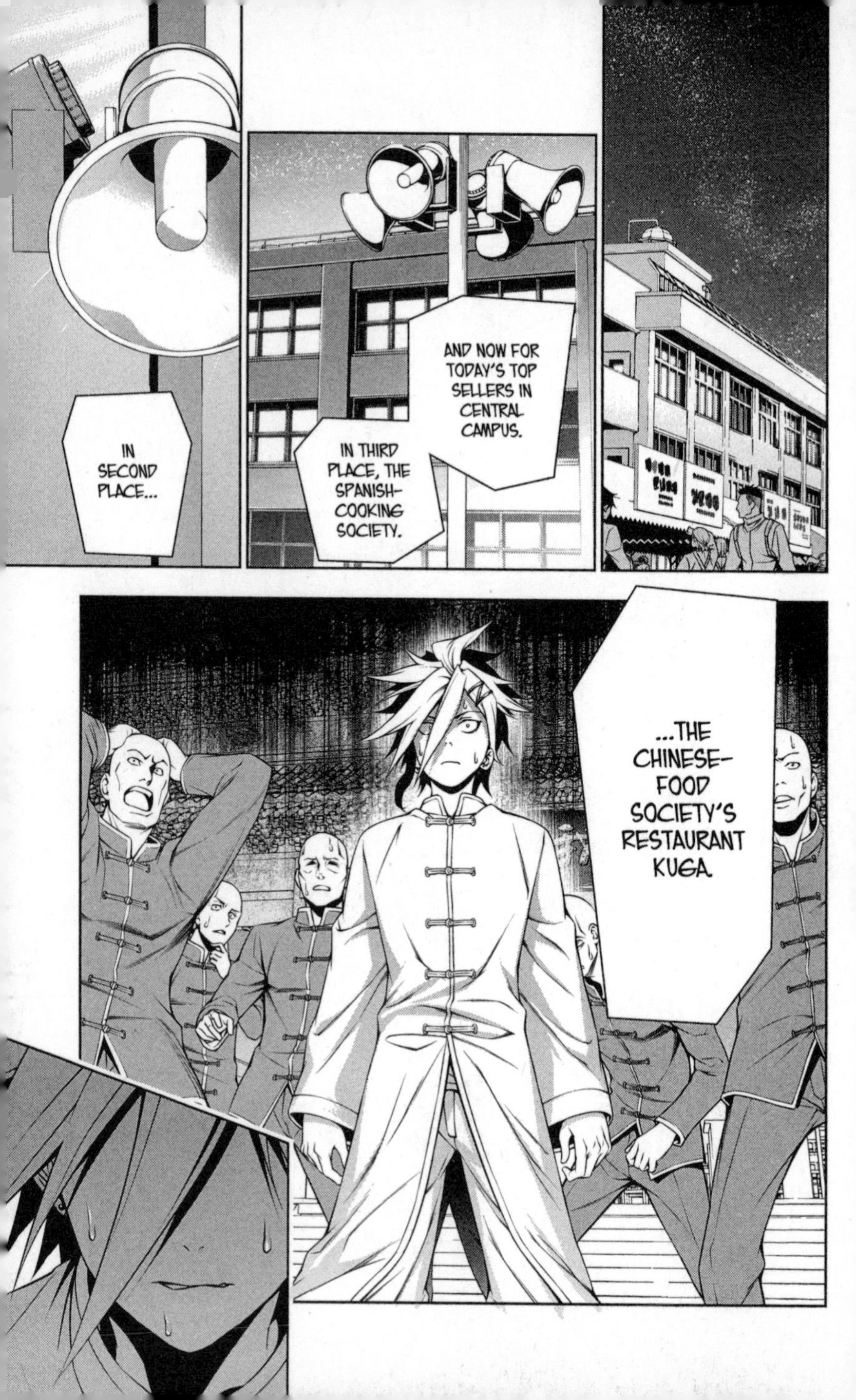
AND NOW FOR TODAY'S TOP SELLERS IN CENTRAL CAMPUS.
IN THIRD PLACE, THE SPANISH-COOKING SOCIETY.
IN SECOND PLACE...
...THE CHINESE-FOOD SOCIETY'S RESTAURANT KUGA.

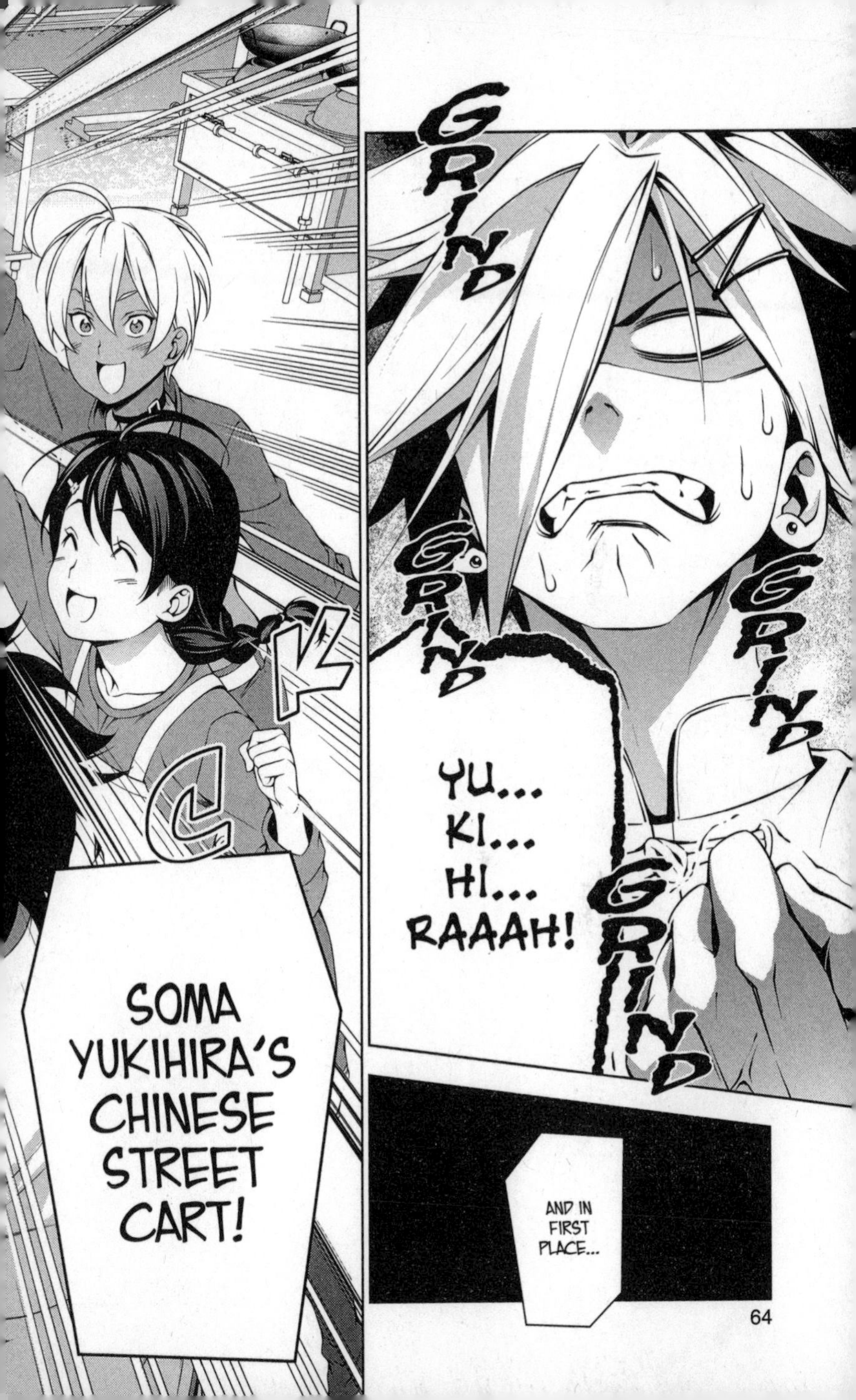
GRIND
GRIND
GRIND
GRIND
YU... KI... HI... RAAAH!
AND IN FIRST PLACE...
SOMA YUKIHIRA'S CHINESE STREET CART!

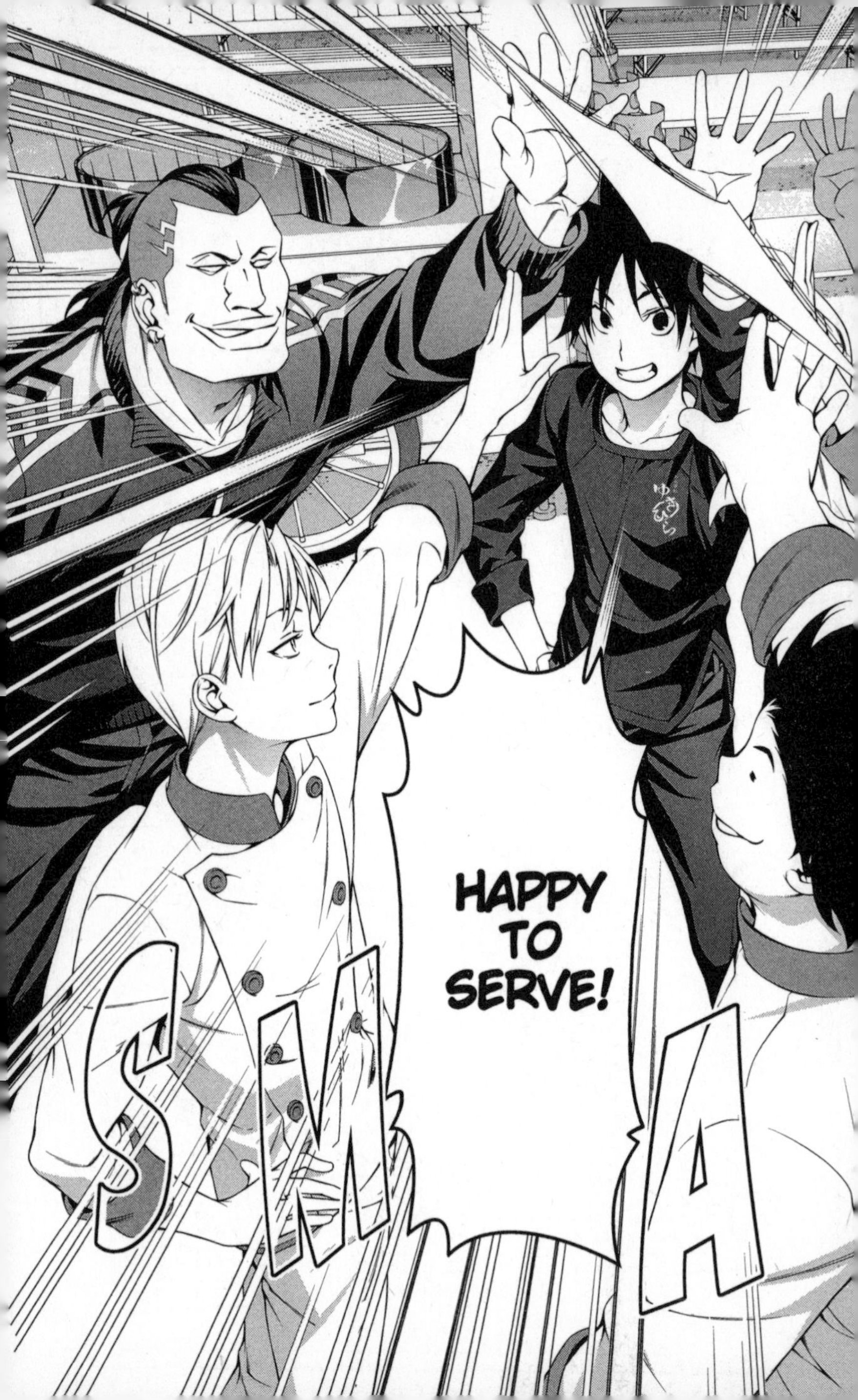
HAPPY TO SERVE!
SMA

VOLUME 16
SPECIAL SUPPLEMENT!

HOMEMADE BLACK PEPPER PORK BUNS

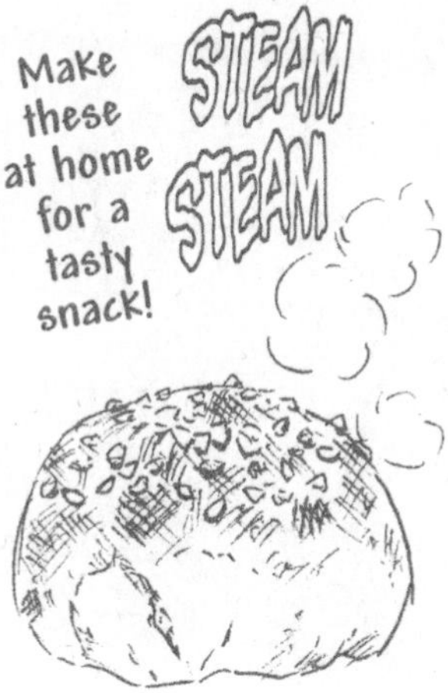

Make these at home for a tasty snack!

INGREDIENTS
(MAKES 8)

★ DOUGH	★ FILLING
100 GRAMS EACH BREAD FLOUR, ALL-PURPOSE FLOUR	250 GRAMS THIN-SLICED PORK
1½ TEASPOONS DRY YEAST	A 2 TEASPOONS BLACK PEPPER
1 TABLESPOON SUGAR	1 TABLESPOON EACH SAKE, SOY SAUCE, SESAME SEED OIL
¼ TEASPOON SALT	½ TABLESPOON OYSTER SAUCE
130 CC WARM WATER	⅛ TEASPOON FIVE-SPICE POWDER
1 TABLESPOON SESAME SEED OIL	CHOPPED SPRING ONION, EGG YOLK, WHITE SESAME SEEDS

1) IN A SMALL BOWL, POUR THE DRY YEAST INTO THE WARM WATER AND STIR TOGETHER.

2) WHISK THE BREAD FLOUR, ALL-PURPOSE FLOUR, SUGAR, SALT AND SESAME SEED OIL TOGETHER IN A LARGE BOWL. POUR IN (1) AND MIX THOROUGHLY.

3) TURN THE DOUGH OUT OF THE BOWL ONTO A LIGHTLY FLOURED SURFACE. KNEAD AND FOLD IT TOGETHER FIRMLY, USING THE HEELS OF YOUR HANDS, UNTIL THE DOUGH IS SMOOTH AND ELASTIC. MOLD THE DOUGH INTO A ROUND, PLACE IT BACK IN THE BOWL, COVER WITH PLASTIC WRAP AND SET IT IN AN OVEN PREHEATED TO 113°F. LET IT RISE FOR 30 MINUTES.

4) CHOP THE THIN-SLICED PORK INTO STRIPS ABOUT 5 MM WIDE. PUT IN A BOWL, ADD (A) AND MIX THOROUGHLY.

5) ONCE (3) HAS FINISHED RISING, TAKE THE DOUGH OUT OF THE BOWL AND SPLIT IT INTO 8 EQUAL PORTIONS. ROLL EACH PORTION INTO A BALL, AND THEN USE THE PALM OF YOUR HAND TO FLATTEN EACH ONE INTO A CIRCLE THAT'S APPROXIMATELY 10 CM ACROSS.

6) HOLDING ONE DISK OF DOUGH IN YOUR LEFT HAND, PUT A HEAPING HELPING OF THE MEAT FROM (4) IN THE MIDDLE OF IT AND SPRINKLE WITH CHOPPED SPRING ONION. USING YOUR RIGHT THUMB AND FOREFINGER, PINCH THE EDGES OF THE DOUGH TOGETHER TO SEAL THE BUN CLOSED. REPEAT FOR ALL 8 PORTIONS.

7) ARRANGE ALL 8 BUNS ON A BAKING SHEET LINED WITH PARCHMENT PAPER, AND COVER WITH A CLEAN KITCHEN TOWEL. PUT THE BAKING SHEET BACK IN THE OVEN AT 113°F, AND LET THE DOUGH RISE A SECOND TIME FOR 20 MINUTES.

8) BRUSH THE TOP OF EACH BUN WITH EGG YOLK. POUR WHITE SESAME SEEDS INTO A BOWL. TAKING EACH BUN BY THE BOTTOM, FLIP IT OVER AND PRESS THE TOP INTO THE SESAME SEEDS TO LIGHTLY COAT. THEN BAKE THE BUNS IN AN OVEN HEATED TO 355°F FOR 25 MINUTES. AND DONE!

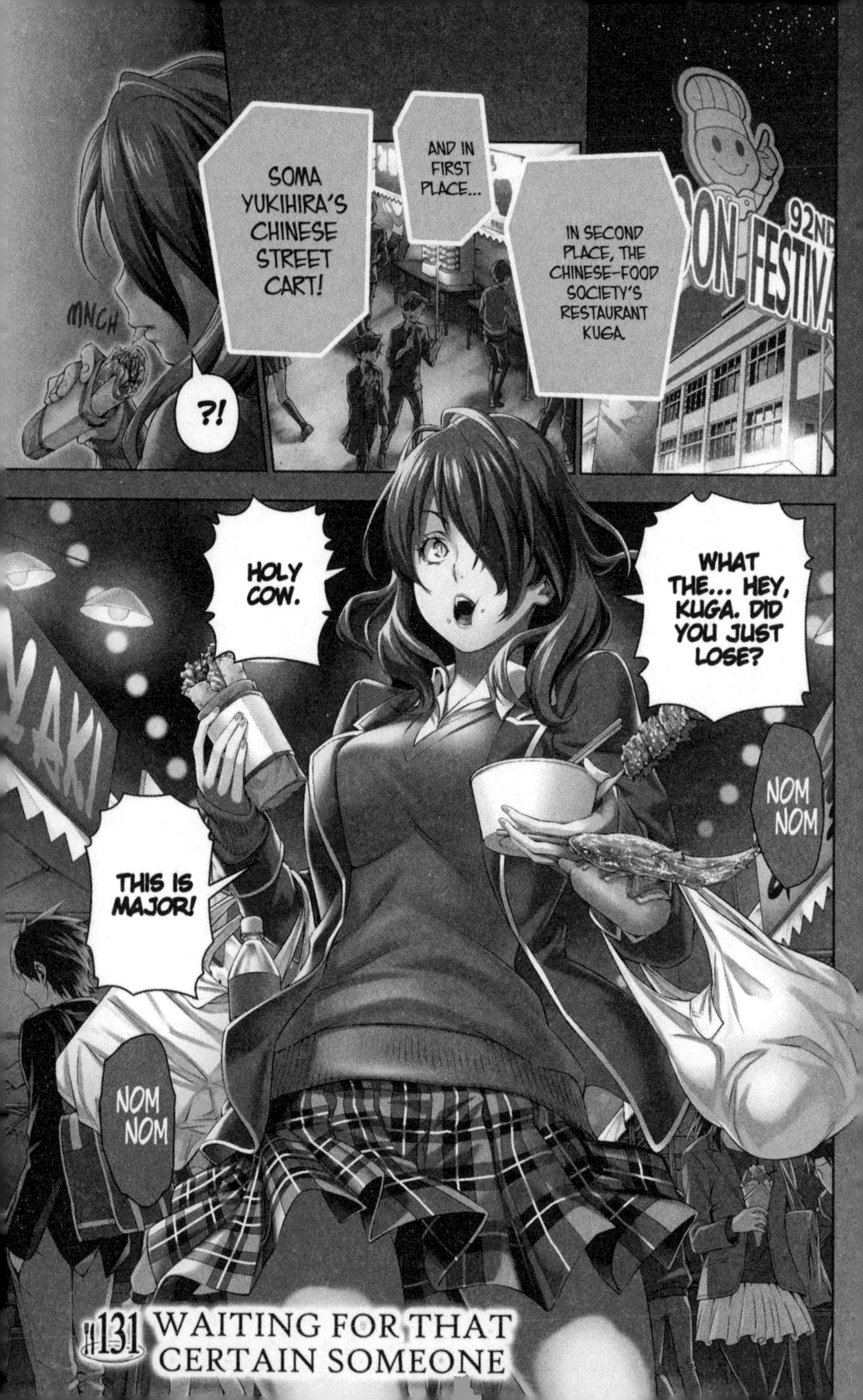
92ND
IN SECOND PLACE, THE CHINESE-FOOD SOCIETY'S RESTAURANT KUGA.
AND IN FIRST PLACE...
SOMA YUKIHIRA'S CHINESE STREET CART!
MNCH
?!
WHAT THE... HEY, KUGA. DID YOU JUST LOSE?
NOM NOM
HOLY COW.
THIS IS MAJOR!
NOM NOM

131 WAITING FOR THAT CERTAIN SOMEONE

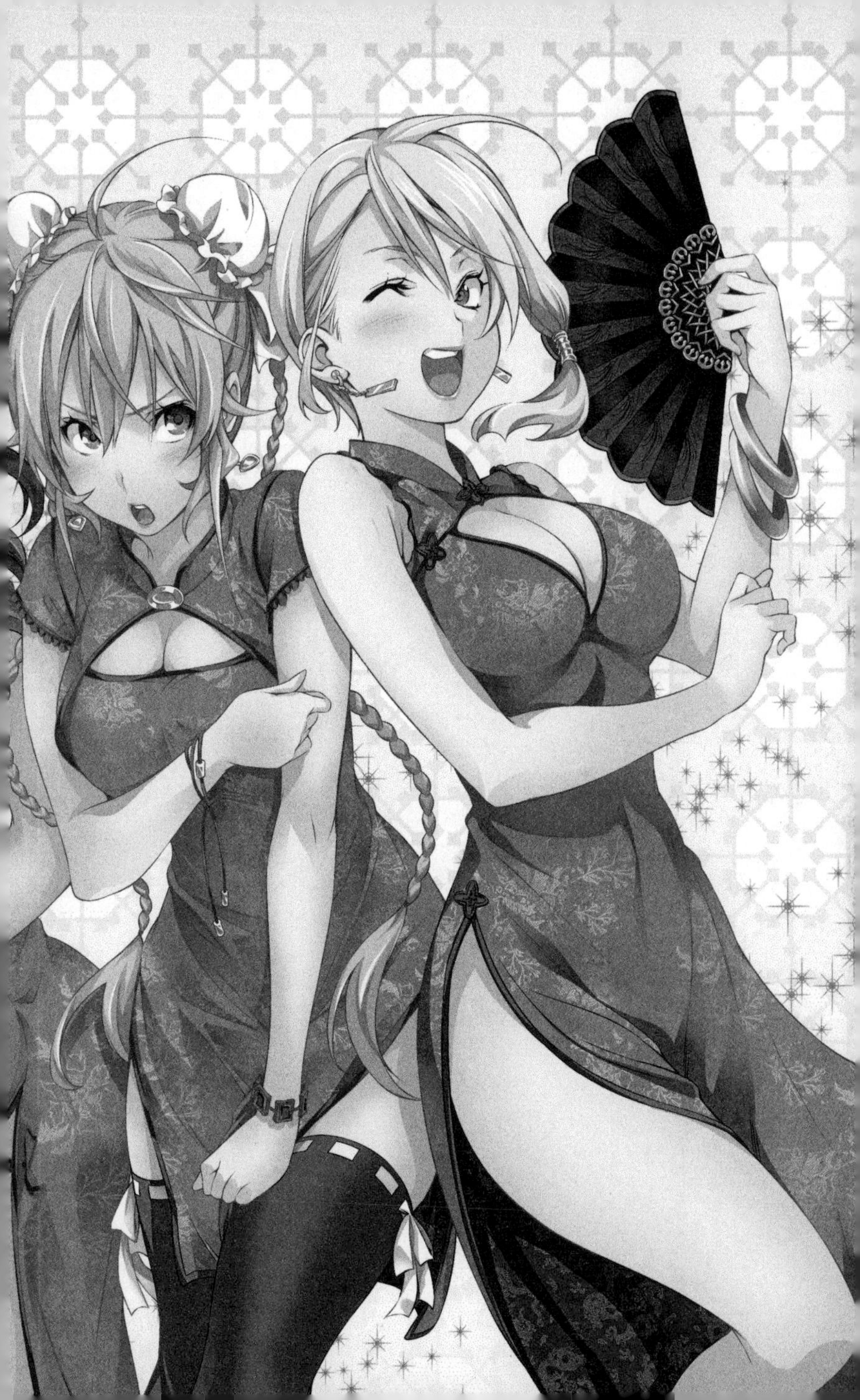

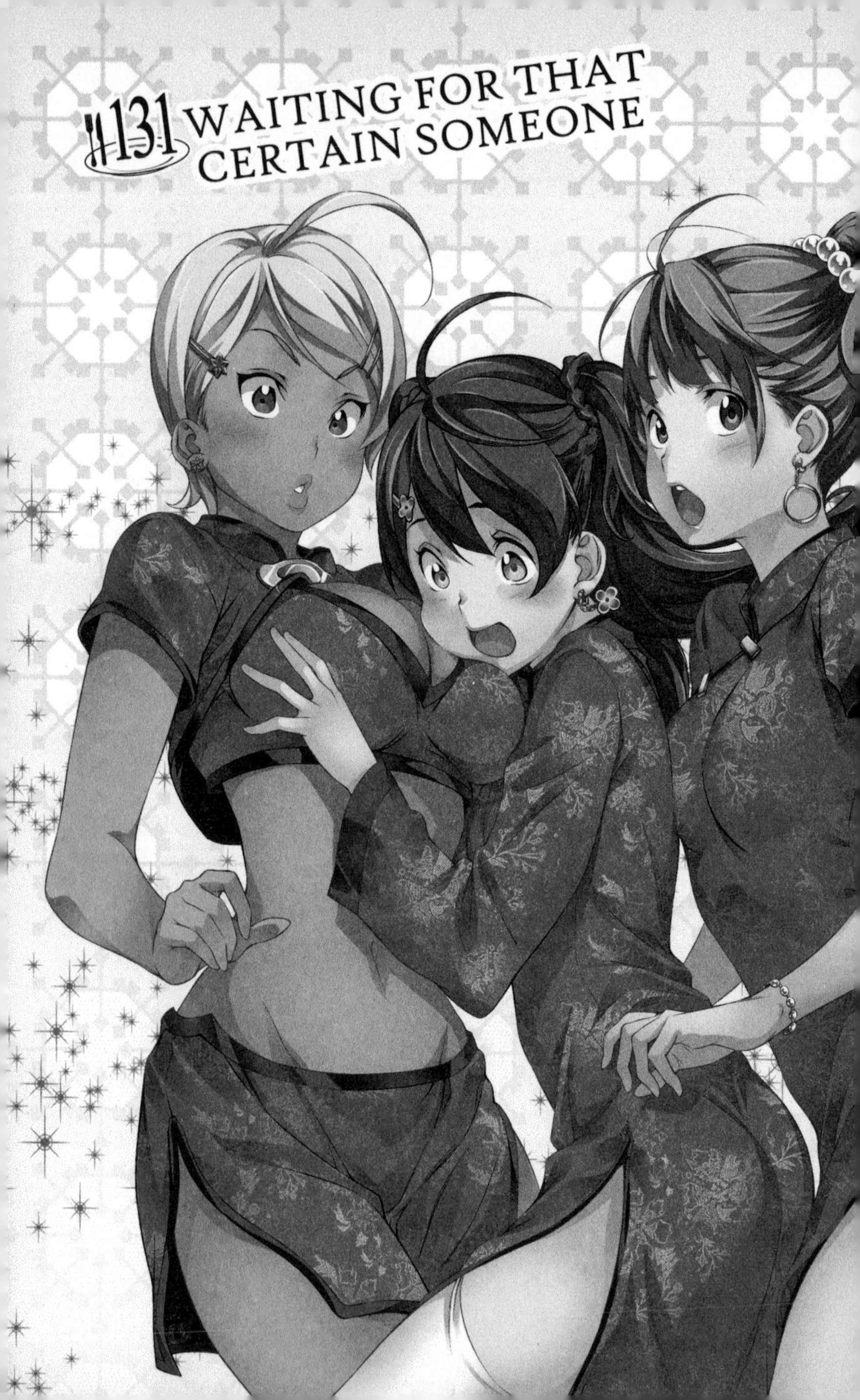

#131
WAITING FOR THAT
CERTAIN SOMEONE

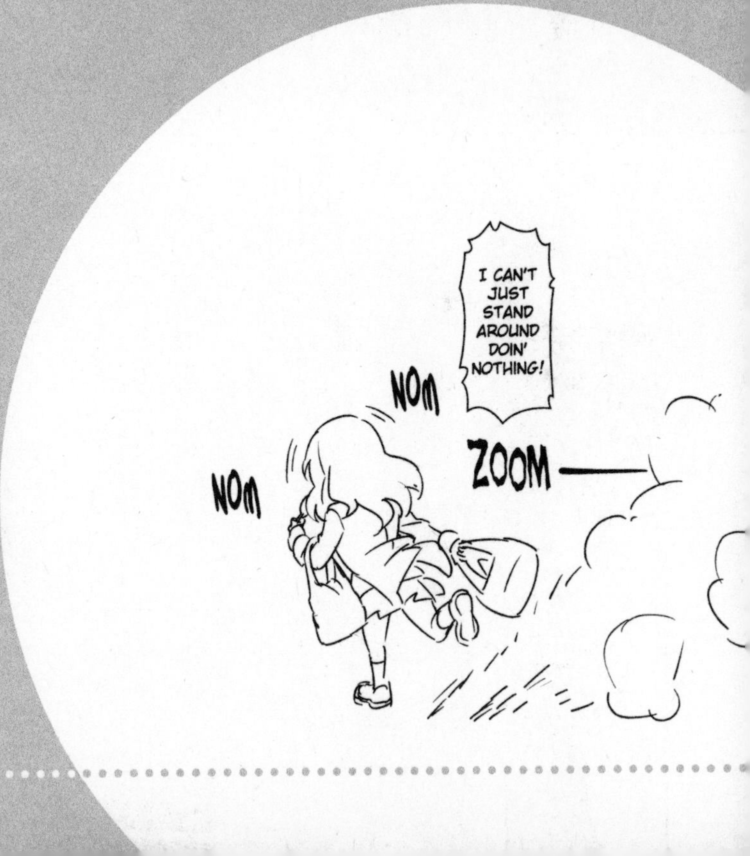
I CAN'T JUST STAND AROUND DOIN' NOTHING!
NOM
ZOOM
NOM

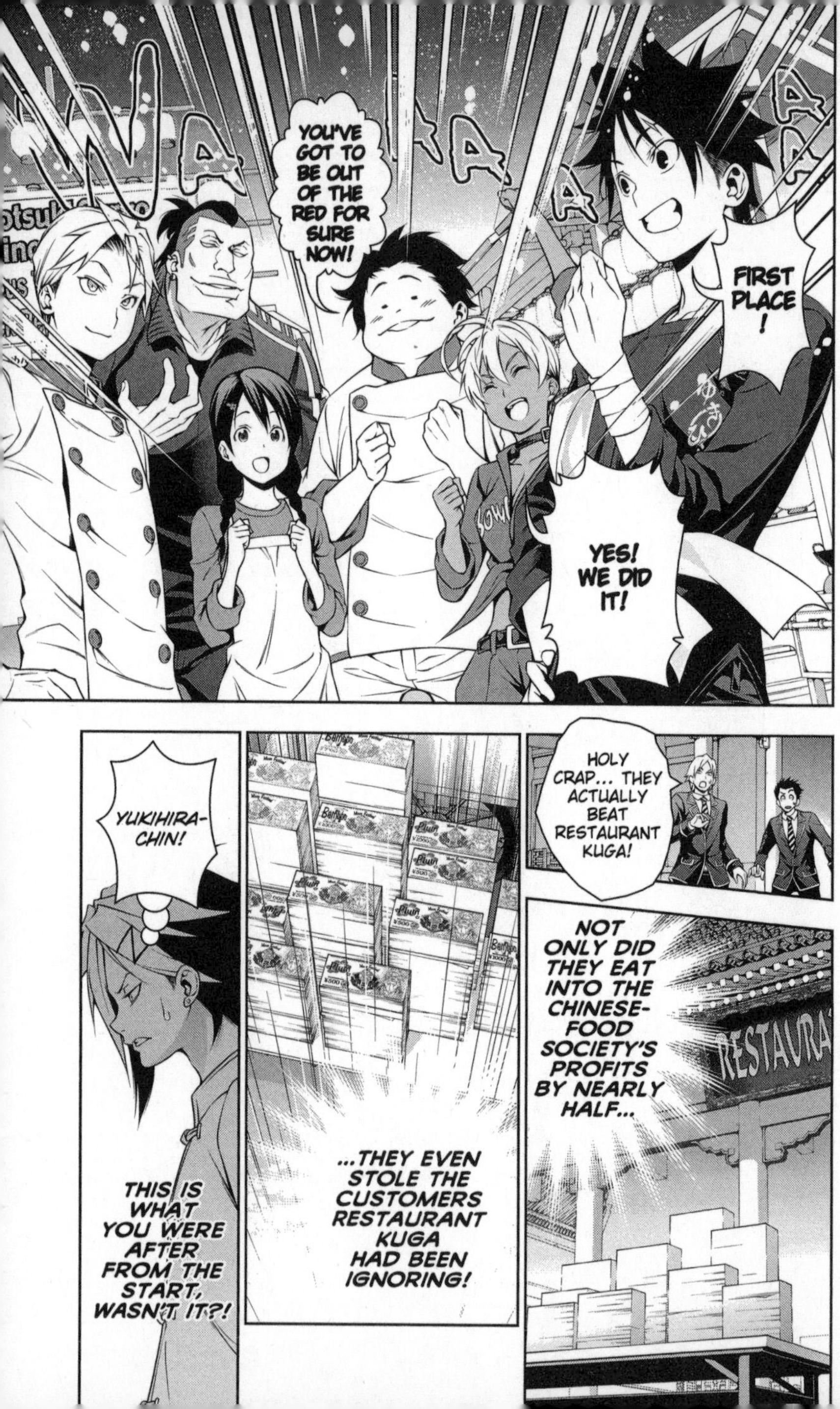
FIRST PLACE!
YES! WE DID IT!
YOU'VE GOT TO BE OUT OF THE RED FOR SURE NOW!
HOLY CRAP... THEY ACTUALLY BEAT RESTAURANT KUGA!
NOT ONLY DID THEY EAT INTO THE CHINESE-FOOD SOCIETY'S PROFITS BY NEARLY HALF...
...THEY EVEN STOLE THE CUSTOMERS RESTAURANT KUGA HAD BEEN IGNORING!
YUKIHIRA-CHIN!
THIS IS WHAT YOU WERE AFTER FROM THE START, WASN'T IT?!

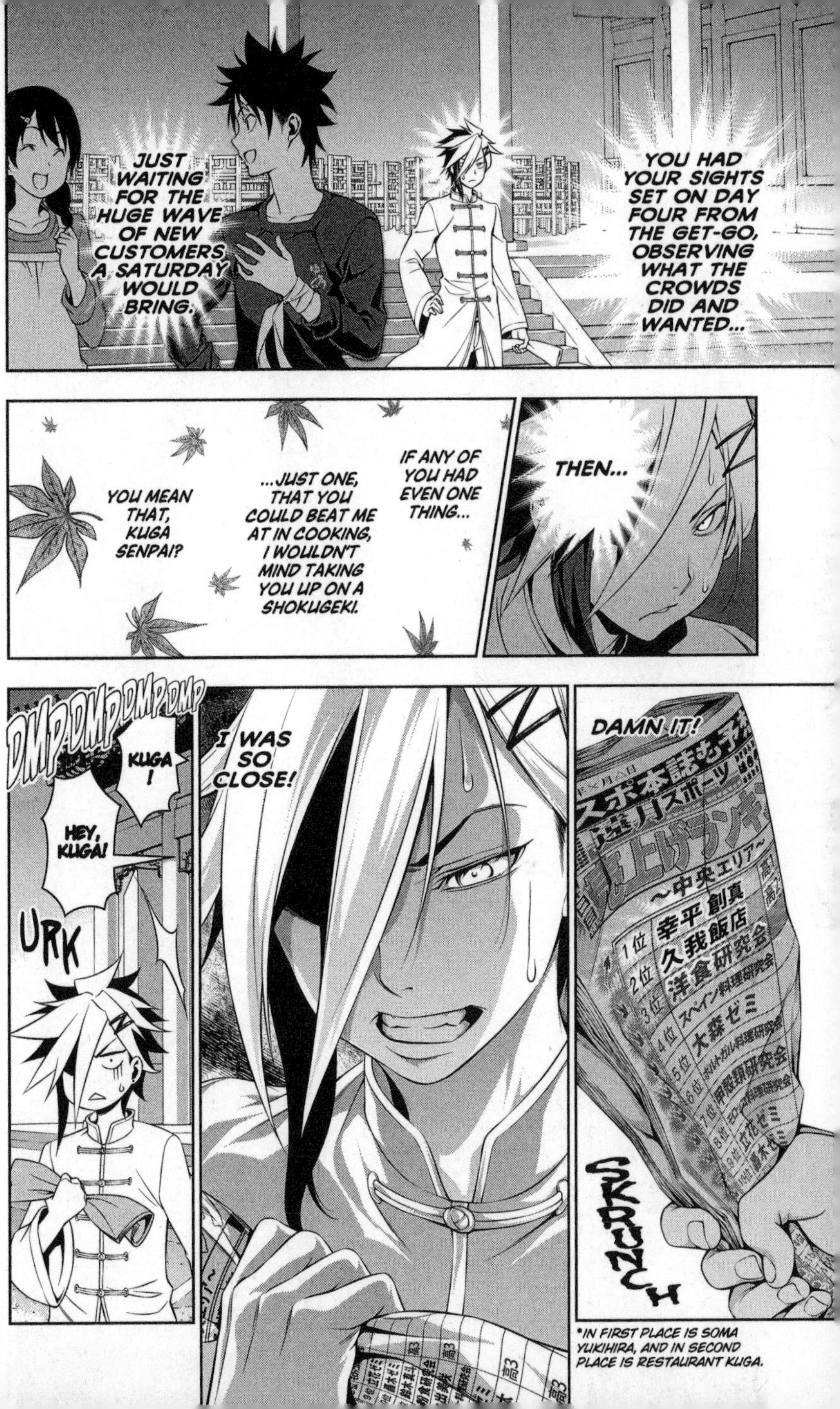
YOU HAD YOUR SIGHTS SET ON DAY FOUR FROM THE GET-GO, OBSERVING WHAT THE CROWDS DID AND WANTED...
JUST WAITING FOR THE HUGE WAVE OF NEW CUSTOMERS A SATURDAY WOULD BRING.
THEN...
IF ANY OF YOU HAD EVEN ONE THING...
...JUST ONE, THAT YOU COULD BEAT ME AT IN COOKING, I WOULDN'T MIND TAKING YOU UP ON A SHOKUGEKI.
YOU MEAN THAT, KUGA SENPAI?
DAMN IT!
～中央エリア～
幸平創真
1位 久我飯店
2位 洋食研究会
3位 スペイン料理研究会
4位 大森ゼミ
SKRUNCH
I WAS SO CLOSE!
DMP DMP DMP DMP
KUGA!
HEY, KUGA!
URK
*IN FIRST PLACE IS SOMA YUKIHIRA, AND IN SECOND PLACE IS RESTAURANT KUGA.

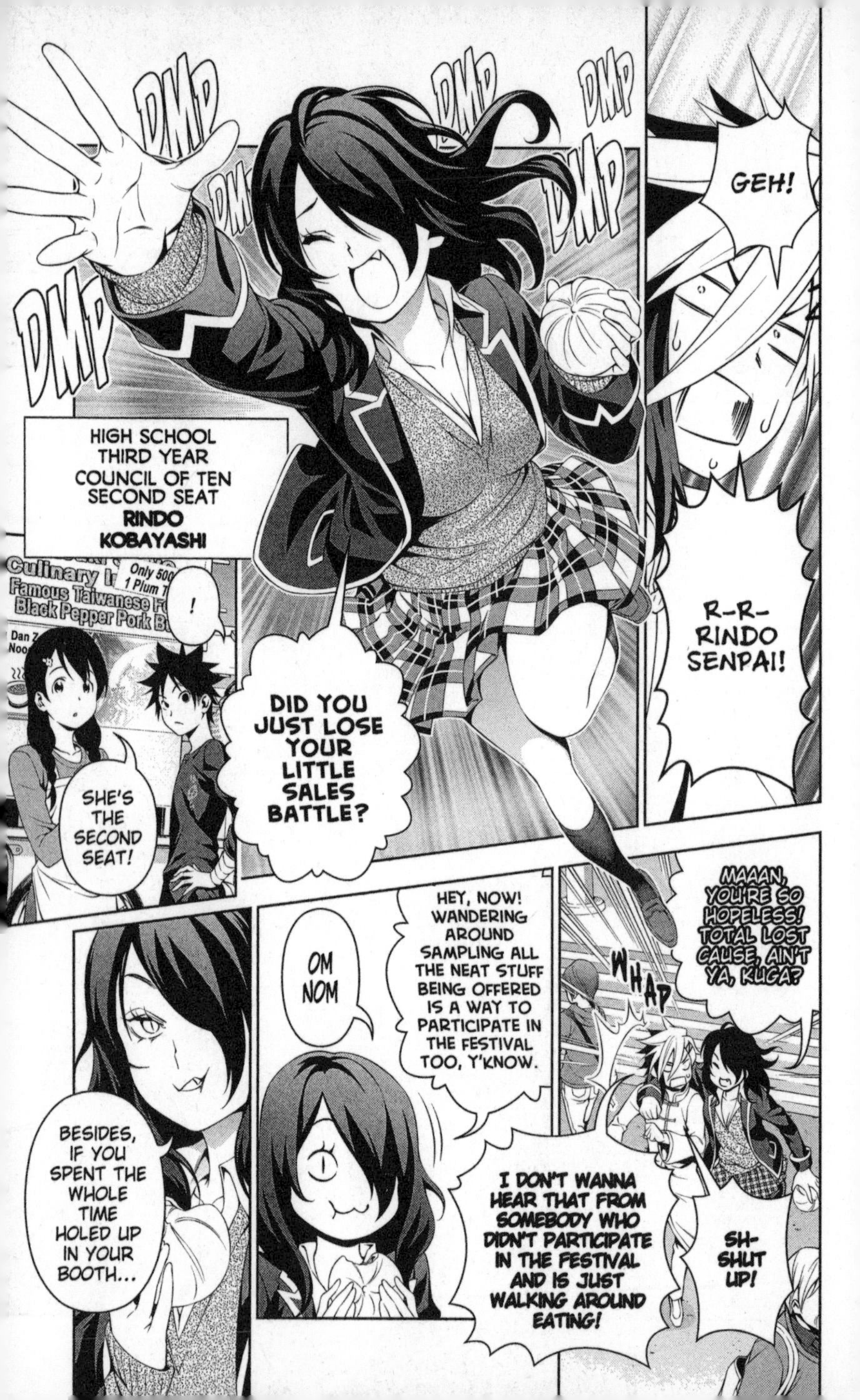
GEH!
R-R-RINDO SENPAI!
DMP DMP DMP DMP DMP DMP
HIGH SCHOOL THIRD YEAR COUNCIL OF TEN SECOND SEAT RINDO KOBAYASHI
DID YOU JUST LOSE YOUR LITTLE SALES BATTLE?
Famous Taiwanese
Black Pepper Pork
!
SHE'S THE SECOND SEAT!
MAAAN, YOU'RE SO HOPELESS! TOTAL LOST CAUSE, AIN'T YA, KUGA?
WHAP
SH-SHUT UP!
I DON'T WANNA HEAR THAT FROM SOMEBODY WHO DIDN'T PARTICIPATE IN THE FESTIVAL AND IS JUST WALKING AROUND EATING!
HEY, NOW! WANDERING AROUND SAMPLING ALL THE NEAT STUFF BEING OFFERED IS A WAY TO PARTICIPATE IN THE FESTIVAL TOO, Y'KNOW.
OM NOM
BESIDES, IF YOU SPENT THE WHOLE TIME HOLED UP IN YOUR BOOTH...

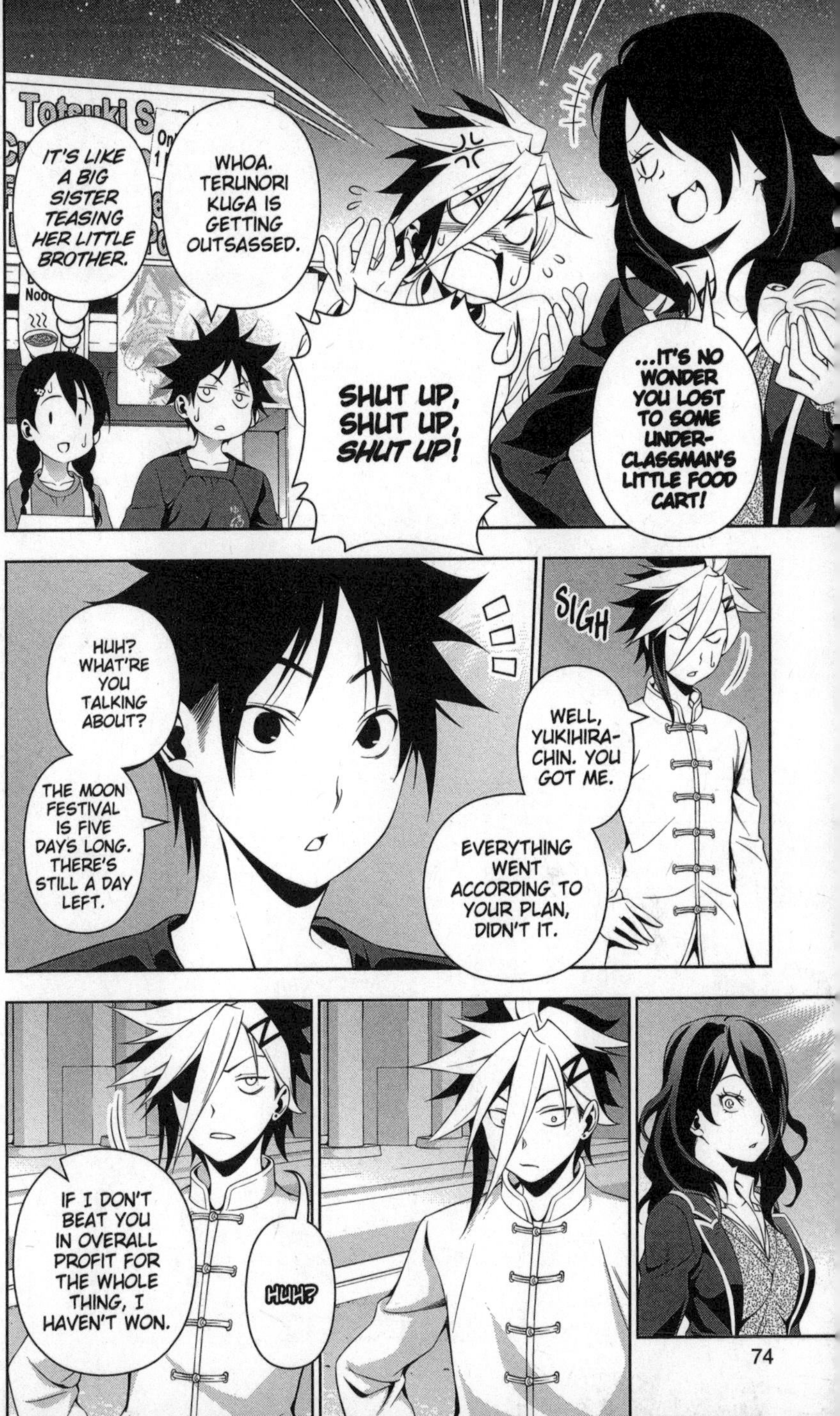

...IT'S NO WONDER YOU LOST TO SOME UNDER-CLASSMAN'S LITTLE FOOD CART!
SHUT UP, SHUT UP, SHUT UP!
WHOA. TERUNORI KUGA IS GETTING OUTSASSED.
IT'S LIKE A BIG SISTER TEASING HER LITTLE BROTHER.
SIGH
WELL, YUKIHIRA-CHIN. YOU GOT ME.
EVERYTHING WENT ACCORDING TO YOUR PLAN, DIDN'T IT.
HUH? WHAT'RE YOU TALKING ABOUT?
THE MOON FESTIVAL IS FIVE DAYS LONG. THERE'S STILL A DAY LEFT.
IF I DON'T BEAT YOU IN OVERALL PROFIT FOR THE WHOLE THING, I HAVEN'T WON.
HUH?

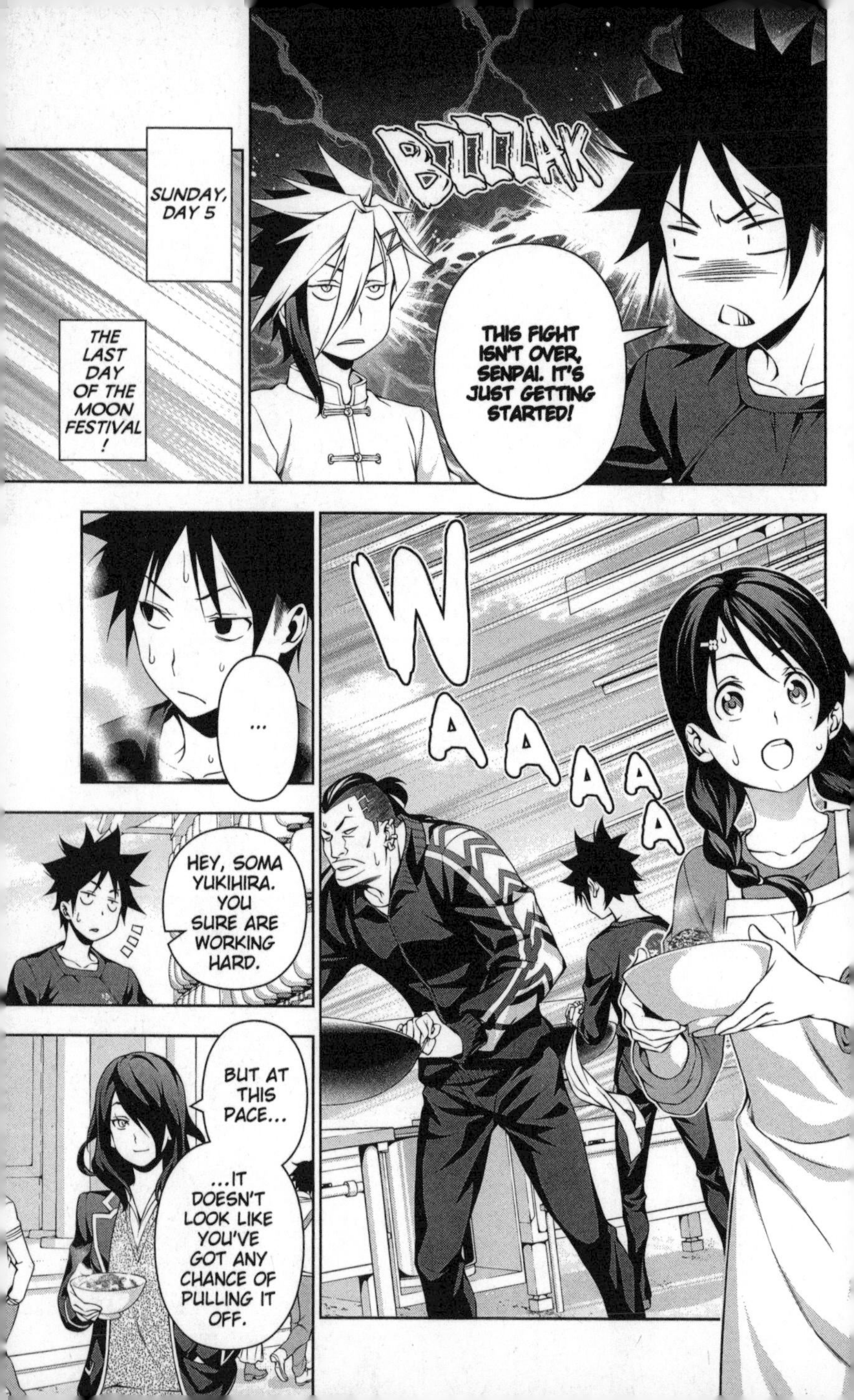
BZZZAK
THIS FIGHT ISN'T OVER, SENPAI. IT'S JUST GETTING STARTED!
SUNDAY, DAY 5
THE LAST DAY OF THE MOON FESTIVAL!
WAAAAAA
...
HEY, SOMA YUKIHIRA. YOU SURE ARE WORKING HARD.
BUT AT THIS PACE...
...IT DOESN'T LOOK LIKE YOU'VE GOT ANY CHANCE OF PULLING IT OFF.

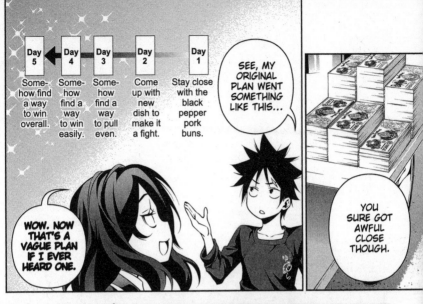

Day 5	Day 4	Day 3	Day 2	Day 1
Somehow find a way to win overall.	Somehow find a way to win easily.	Somehow find a way to pull even.	Come up with new dish to make it a fight.	Stay close with the black pepper pork buns.

SEE, MY ORIGINAL PLAN WENT SOMETHING LIKE THIS...

WOW. NOW THAT'S A VAGUE PLAN IF I EVER HEARD ONE.

YOU SURE GOT AWFUL CLOSE THOUGH.

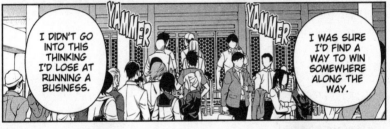

I DIDN'T GO INTO THIS THINKING I'D LOSE AT RUNNING A BUSINESS.

YAMMER

YAMMER

I WAS SURE I'D FIND A WAY TO WIN SOMEWHERE ALONG THE WAY.

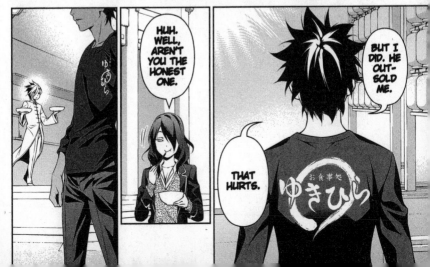

HUH. WELL, AREN'T YOU THE HONEST ONE.

BUT I DID. HE OUT-SOLD ME.

THAT HURTS.

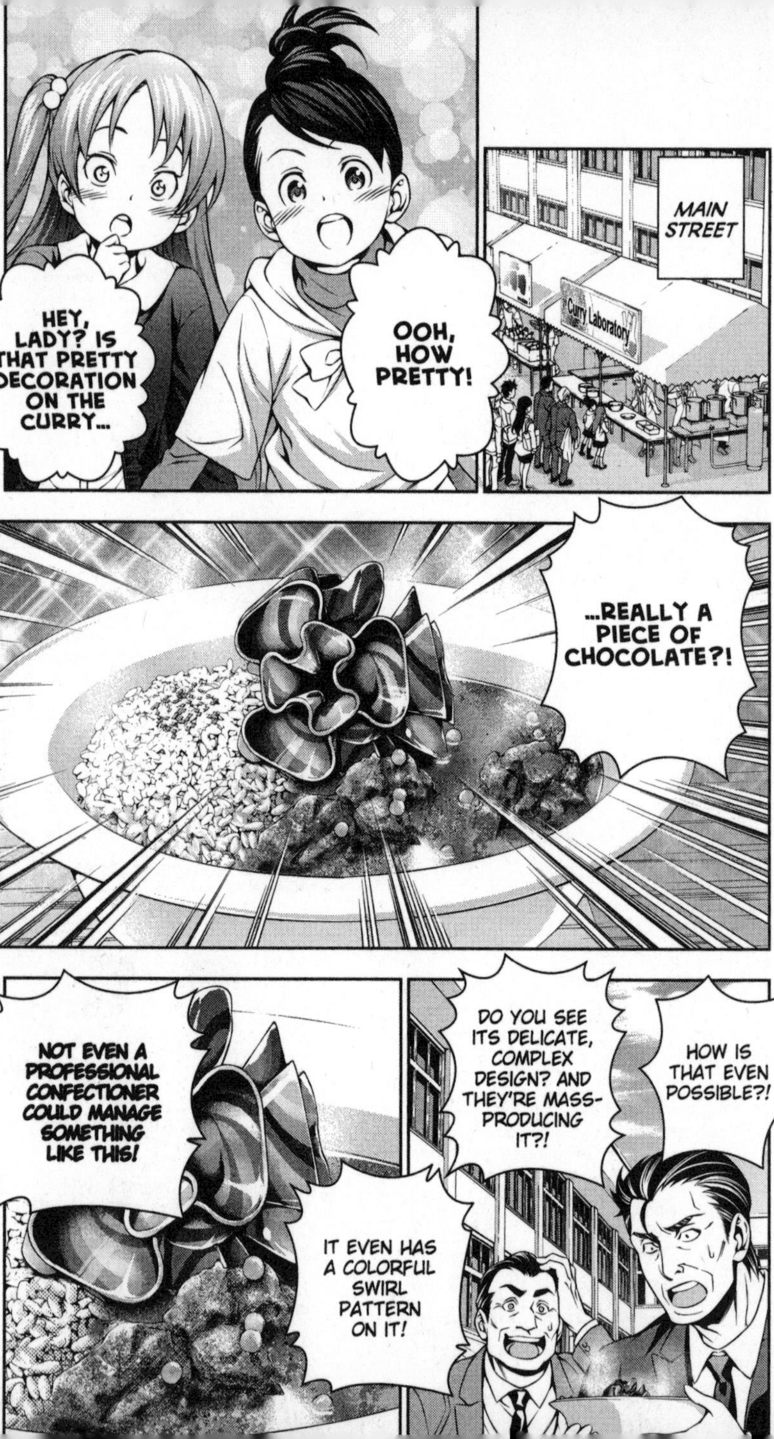
MAIN STREET
Curry Laboratory
OOH, HOW PRETTY!
HEY, LADY? IS THAT PRETTY DECORATION ON THE CURRY...
...REALLY A PIECE OF CHOCOLATE?!
HOW IS THAT EVEN POSSIBLE?!
DO YOU SEE ITS DELICATE, COMPLEX DESIGN? AND THEY'RE MASS-PRODUCING IT?!
IT EVEN HAS A COLORFUL SWIRL PATTERN ON IT!
NOT EVEN A PROFESSIONAL CONFECTIONER COULD MANAGE SOMETHING LIKE THIS!

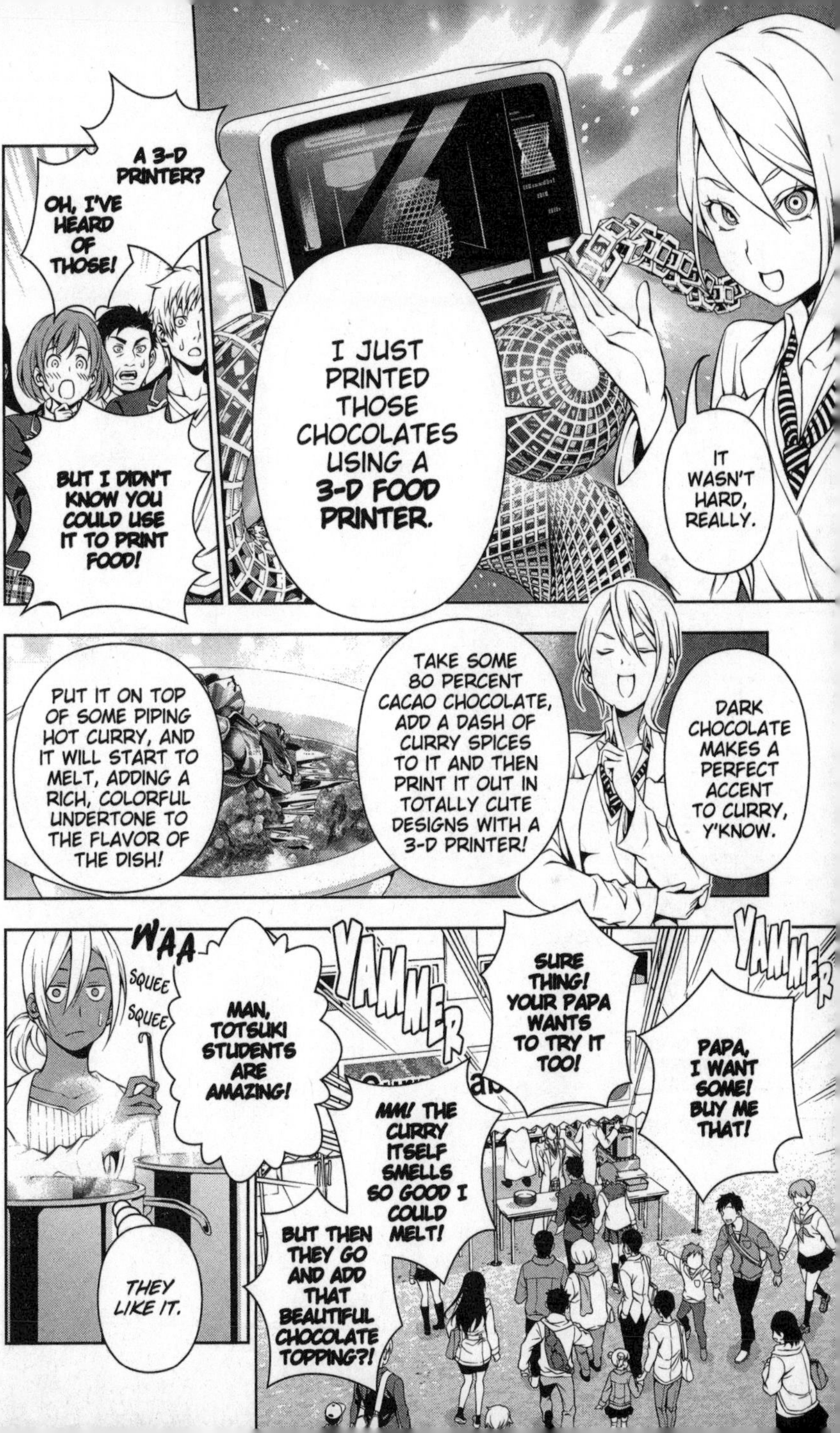
IT WASN'T HARD, REALLY.
I JUST PRINTED THOSE CHOCOLATES USING A 3-D FOOD PRINTER.
A 3-D PRINTER?
OH, I'VE HEARD OF THOSE!
BUT I DIDN'T KNOW YOU COULD USE IT TO PRINT FOOD!
DARK CHOCOLATE MAKES A PERFECT ACCENT TO CURRY, Y'KNOW.
TAKE SOME 80 PERCENT CACAO CHOCOLATE, ADD A DASH OF CURRY SPICES TO IT AND THEN PRINT IT OUT IN TOTALLY CUTE DESIGNS WITH A 3-D PRINTER!
PUT IT ON TOP OF SOME PIPING HOT CURRY, AND IT WILL START TO MELT, ADDING A RICH, COLORFUL UNDERTONE TO THE FLAVOR OF THE DISH!
YAMMER
PAPA, I WANT SOME! BUY ME THAT!
SURE THING! YOUR PAPA WANTS TO TRY IT TOO!
YAMMER
MM! THE CURRY ITSELF SMELLS SO GOOD I COULD MELT!
BUT THEN THEY GO AND ADD THAT BEAUTIFUL CHOCOLATE TOPPING?!
MAN, TOTSUKI STUDENTS ARE AMAZING!
WAA
SQUEE
SQUEE
THEY LIKE IT.

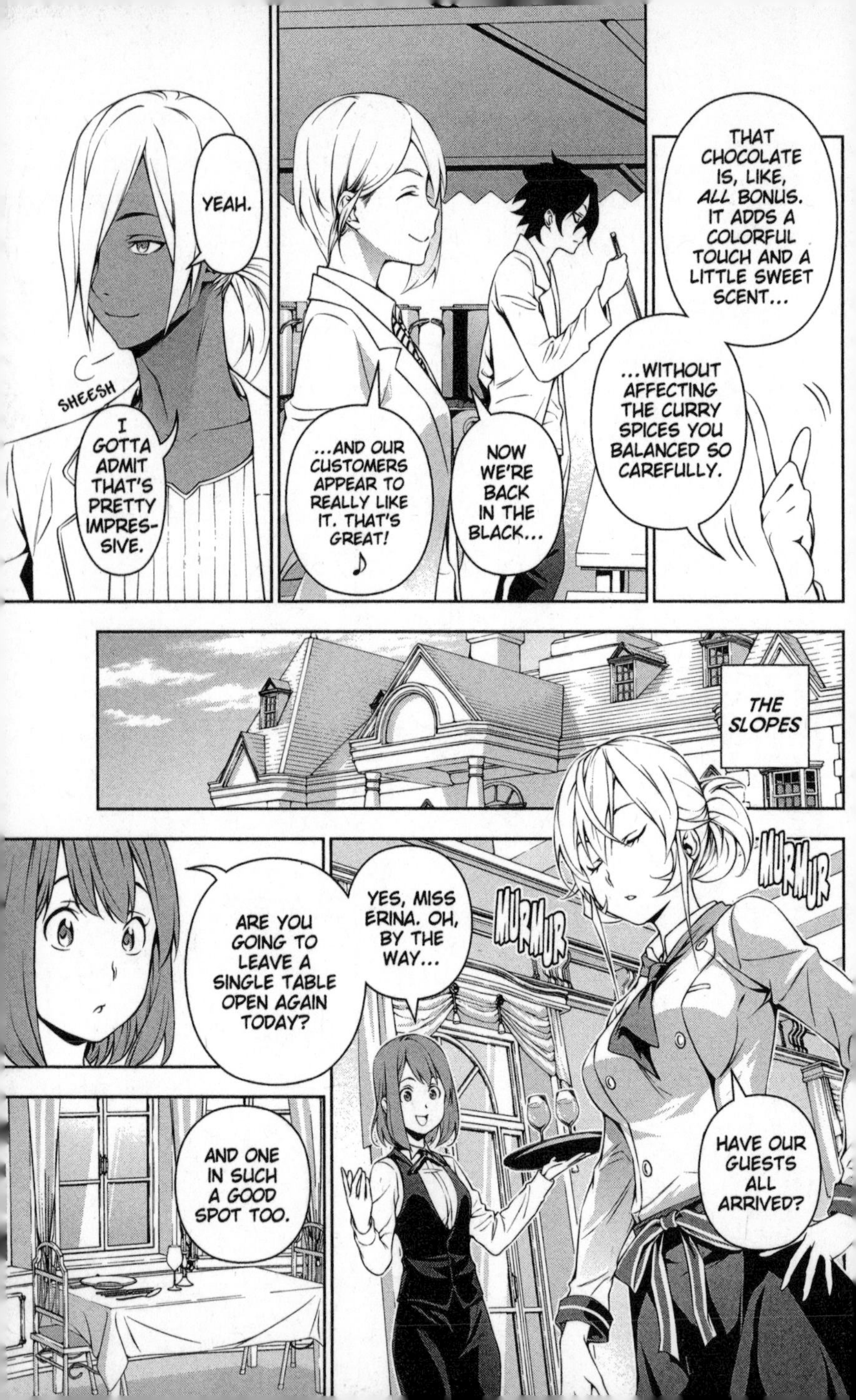
THAT CHOCOLATE IS, LIKE, *ALL* BONUS. IT ADDS A COLORFUL TOUCH AND A LITTLE SWEET SCENT...
...WITHOUT AFFECTING THE CURRY SPICES YOU BALANCED SO CAREFULLY.
NOW WE'RE BACK IN THE BLACK...
...AND OUR CUSTOMERS APPEAR TO REALLY LIKE IT. THAT'S GREAT! ♪
YEAH.
SHEESH
I GOTTA ADMIT THAT'S PRETTY IMPRES-SIVE.
THE SLOPES
MURMUR
MURMUR
HAVE OUR GUESTS ALL ARRIVED?
YES, MISS ERINA. OH, BY THE WAY...
ARE YOU GOING TO LEAVE A SINGLE TABLE OPEN AGAIN TODAY?
AND ONE IN SUCH A GOOD SPOT TOO.

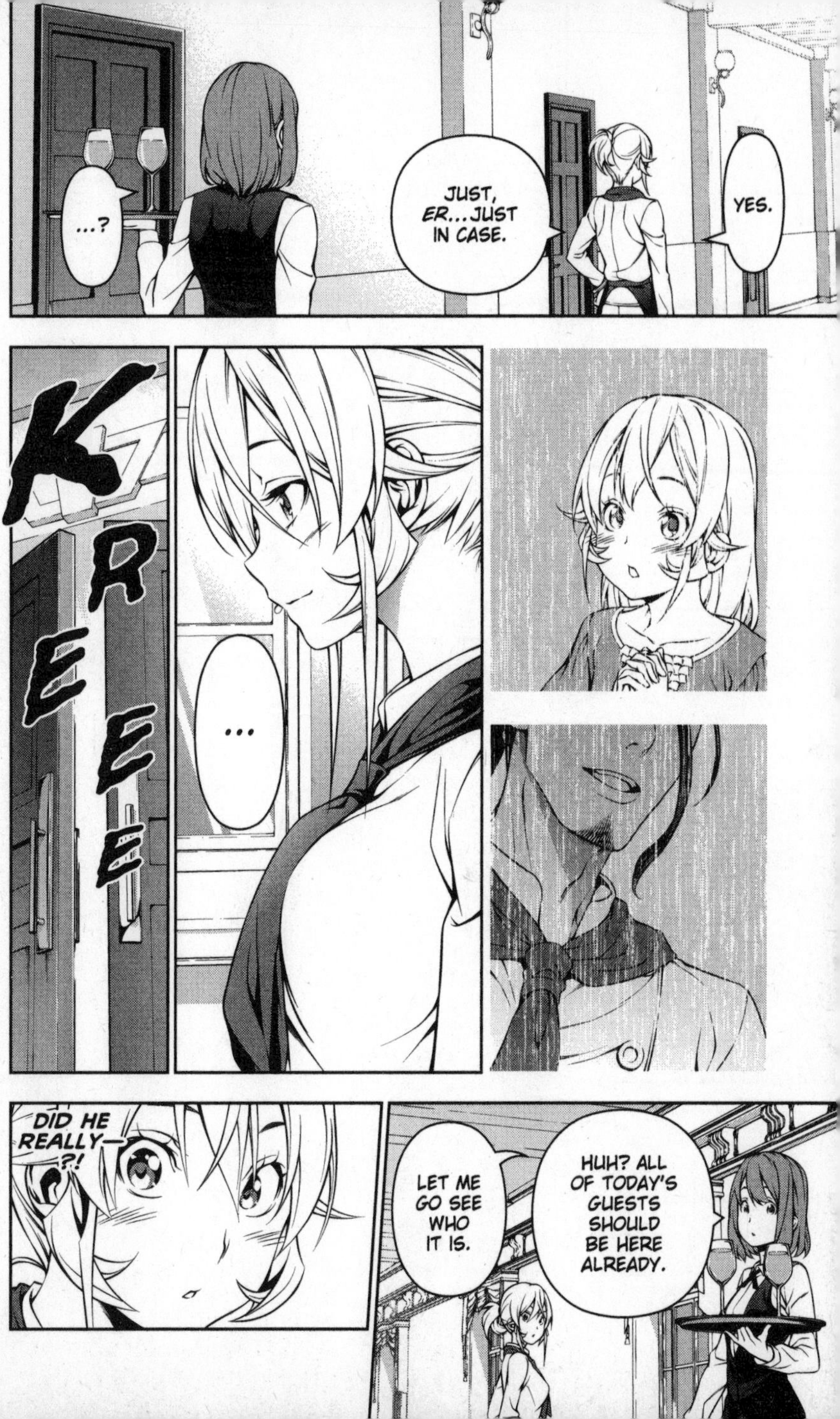
YES.
JUST, ER... JUST IN CASE.
...?
...
KREEEE
HUH? ALL OF TODAY'S GUESTS SHOULD BE HERE ALREADY.
LET ME GO SEE WHO IT IS.
DID HE REALLY—?!

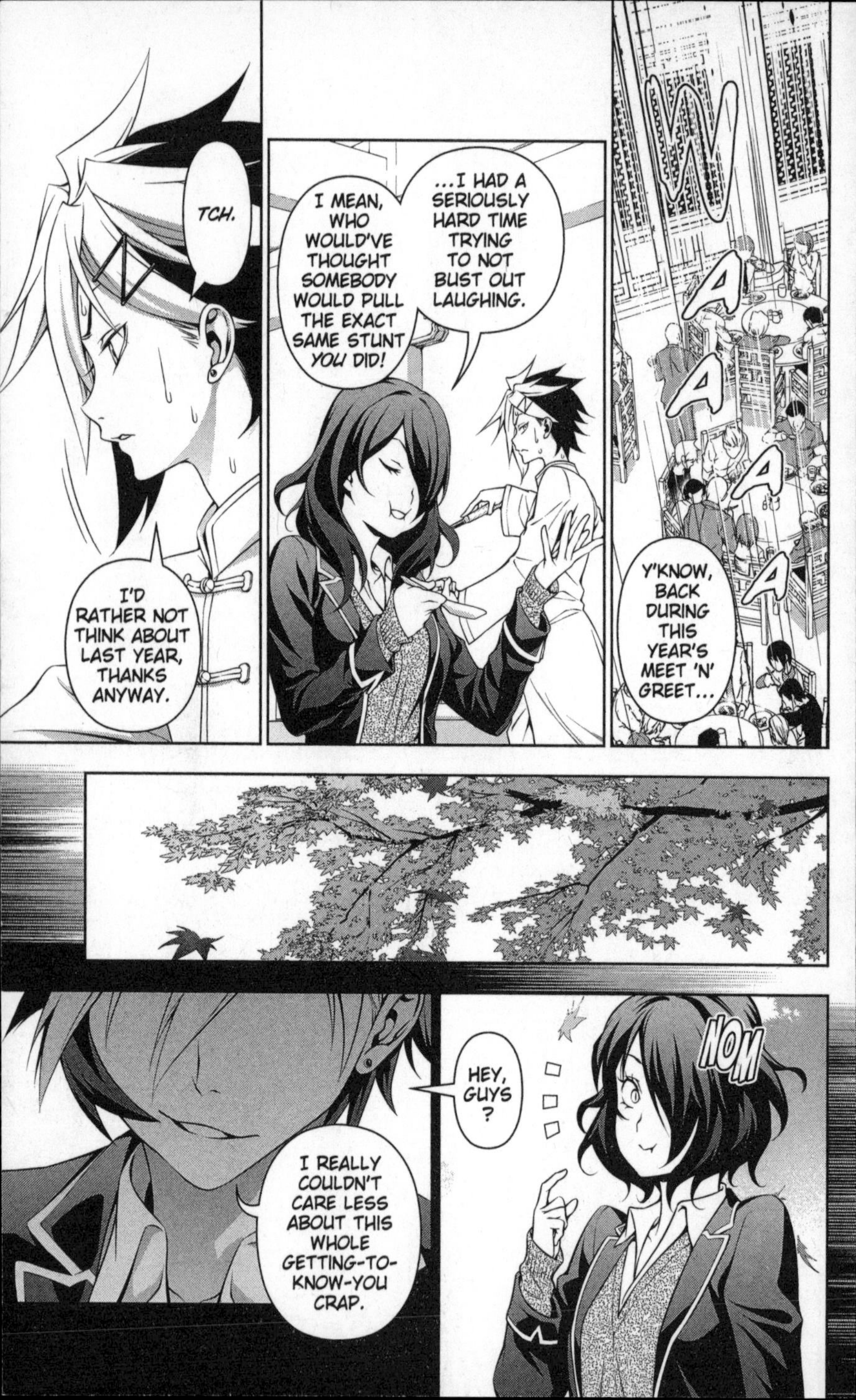
WAAAA
Y'KNOW, BACK DURING THIS YEAR'S MEET 'N' GREET...
...I HAD A SERIOUSLY HARD TIME TRYING TO NOT BUST OUT LAUGHING.
I MEAN, WHO WOULD'VE THOUGHT SOMEBODY WOULD PULL THE EXACT SAME STUNT *YOU* DID!
TCH.
I'D RATHER NOT THINK ABOUT LAST YEAR, THANKS ANYWAY.
NOM
HEY, GUYS?
I REALLY COULDN'T CARE LESS ABOUT THIS WHOLE GETTING-TO-KNOW-YOU CRAP.

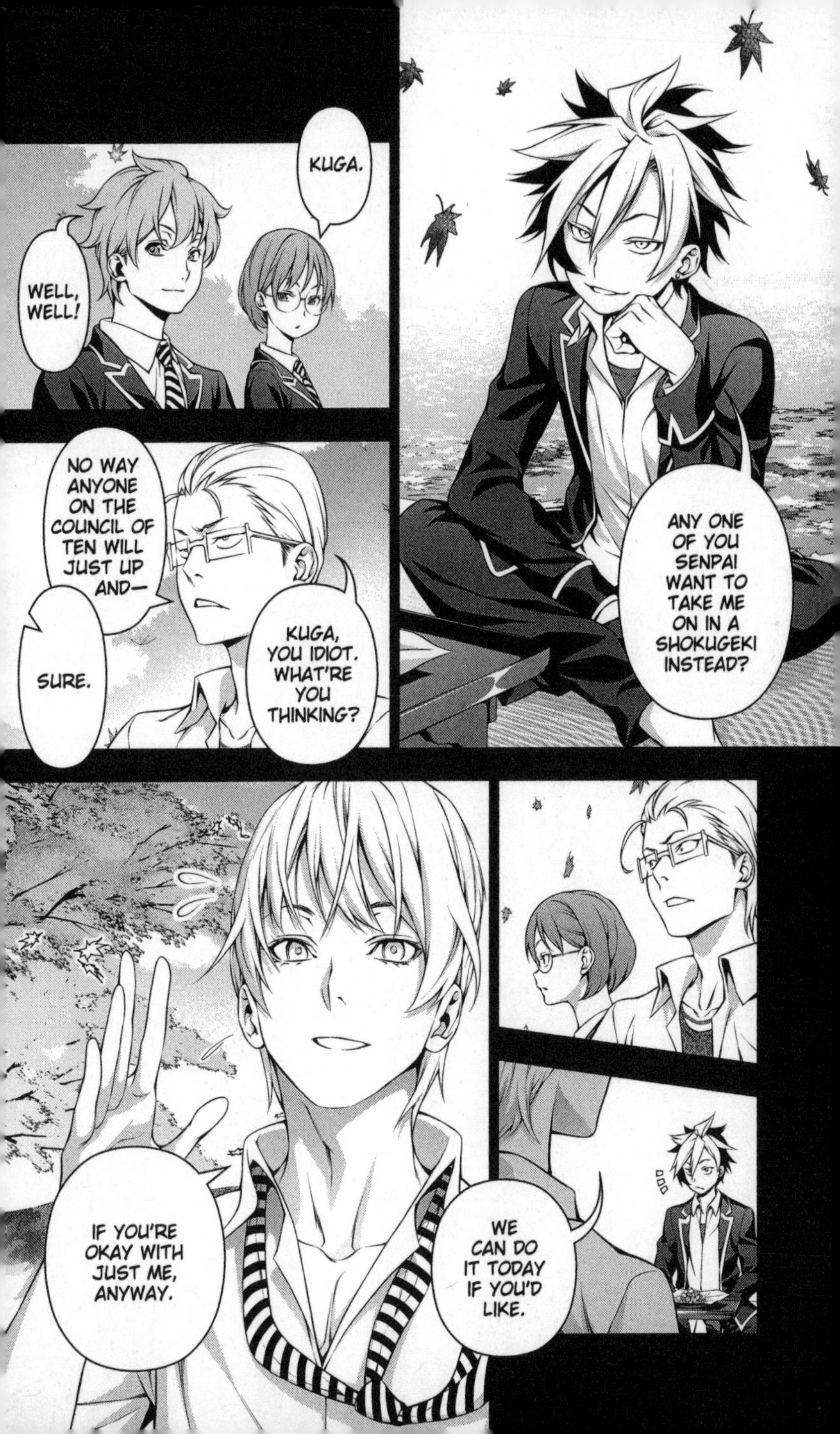
ANY ONE OF YOU SENPAI WANT TO TAKE ME ON IN A SHOKUGEKI INSTEAD?
KUGA.
WELL, WELL!
KUGA, YOU IDIOT. WHAT'RE YOU THINKING?
NO WAY ANYONE ON THE COUNCIL OF TEN WILL JUST UP AND—
SURE.
WE CAN DO IT TODAY IF YOU'D LIKE.
IF YOU'RE OKAY WITH JUST ME, ANYWAY.

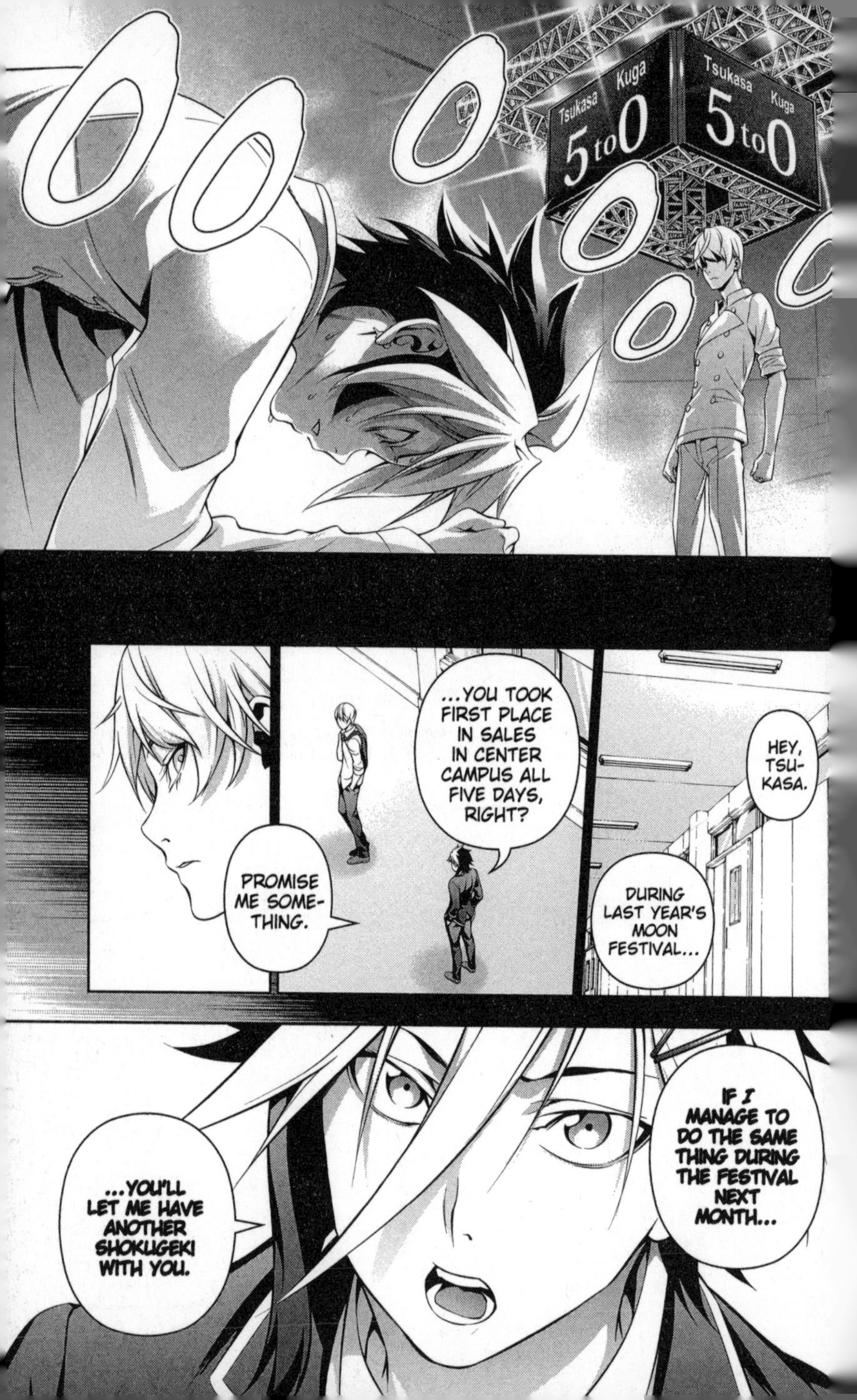
Tsukasa Kuga
5 to 0
Tsukasa Kuga
5 to 0
HEY, TSU-KASA.
DURING LAST YEAR'S MOON FESTIVAL...
...YOU TOOK FIRST PLACE IN SALES IN CENTER CAMPUS ALL FIVE DAYS, RIGHT?
PROMISE ME SOME-THING.
IF I MANAGE TO DO THE SAME THING DURING THE FESTIVAL NEXT MONTH...
...YOU'LL LET ME HAVE ANOTHER SHOKUGEKI WITH YOU.

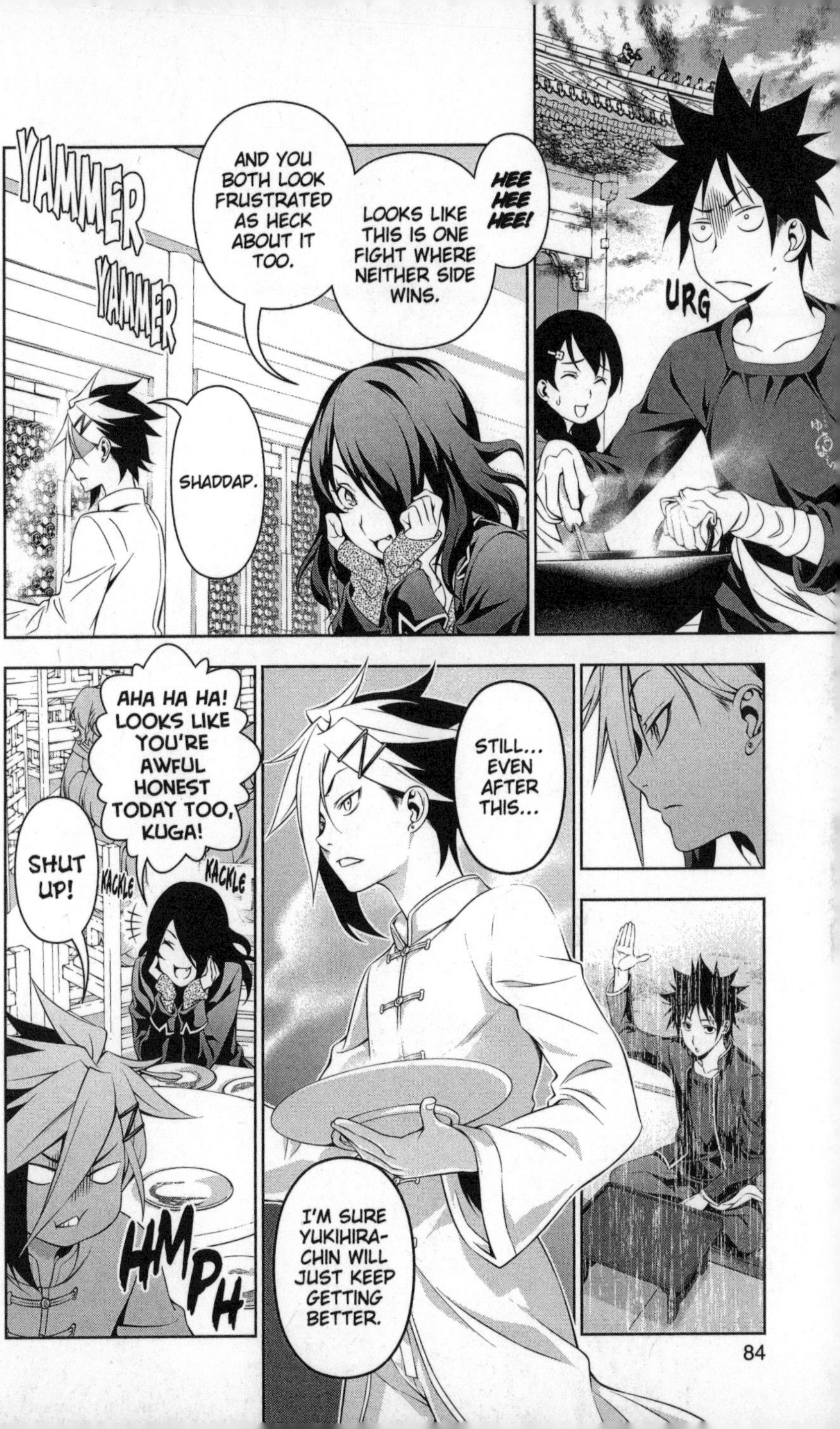
URG
HEE HEE HEE!
LOOKS LIKE THIS IS ONE FIGHT WHERE NEITHER SIDE WINS.
AND YOU BOTH LOOK FRUSTRATED AS HECK ABOUT IT TOO.
SHADDAP.
YAMMER
YAMMER
STILL... EVEN AFTER THIS...
I'M SURE YUKIHIRA-CHIN WILL JUST KEEP GETTING BETTER.
AHA HA HA! LOOKS LIKE YOU'RE AWFUL HONEST TODAY TOO, KUGA!
KACKLE
KACKLE
SHUT UP!
HMPH

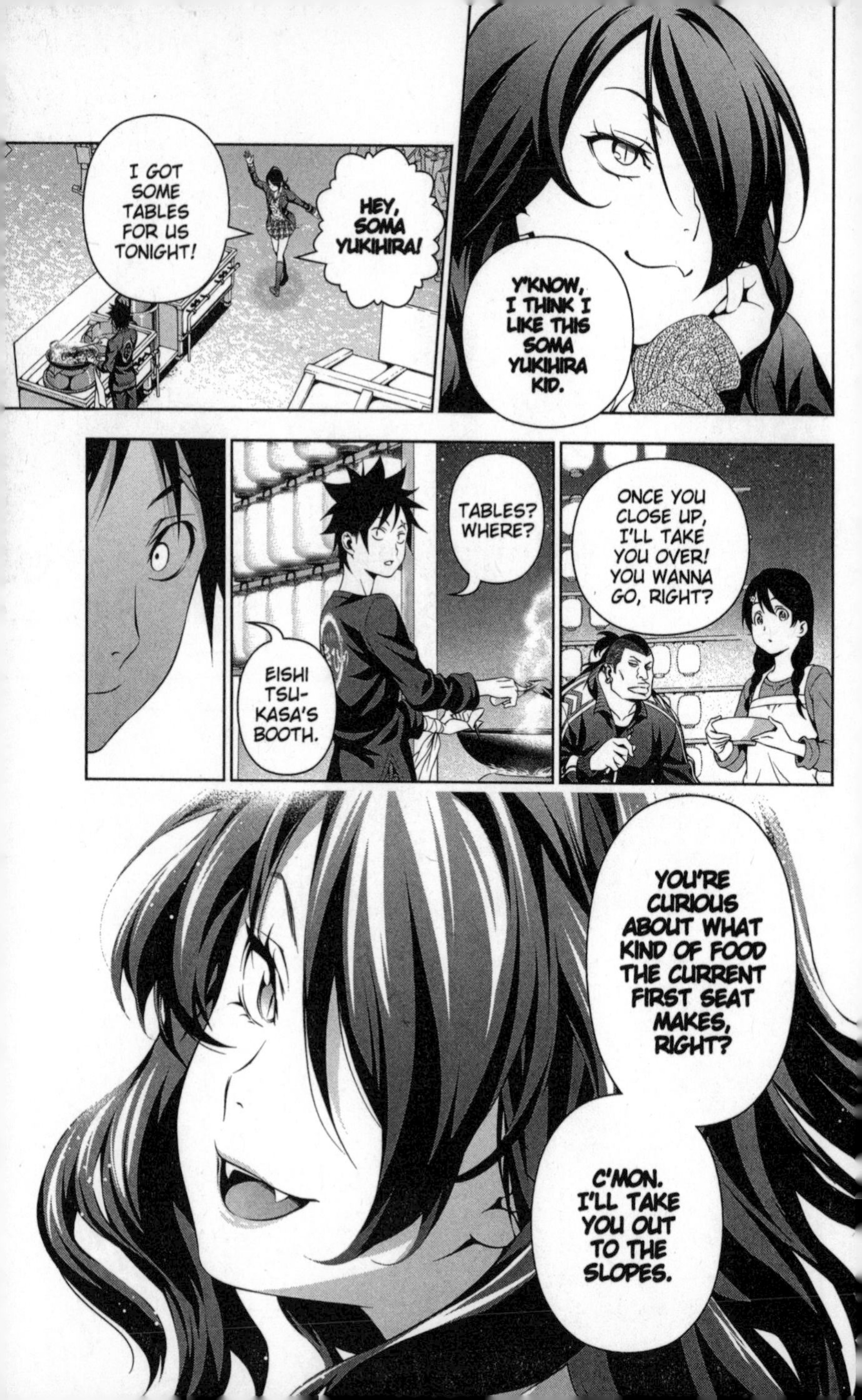
Y'KNOW, I THINK I LIKE THIS SOMA YUKIHIRA KID.
HEY, SOMA YUKIHIRA!
I GOT SOME TABLES FOR US TONIGHT!
ONCE YOU CLOSE UP, I'LL TAKE YOU OVER! YOU WANNA GO, RIGHT?
TABLES? WHERE?
EISHI TSU-KASA'S BOOTH.
YOU'RE CURIOUS ABOUT WHAT KIND OF FOOD THE CURRENT FIRST SEAT MAKES, RIGHT?
C'MON. I'LL TAKE YOU OUT TO THE SLOPES.

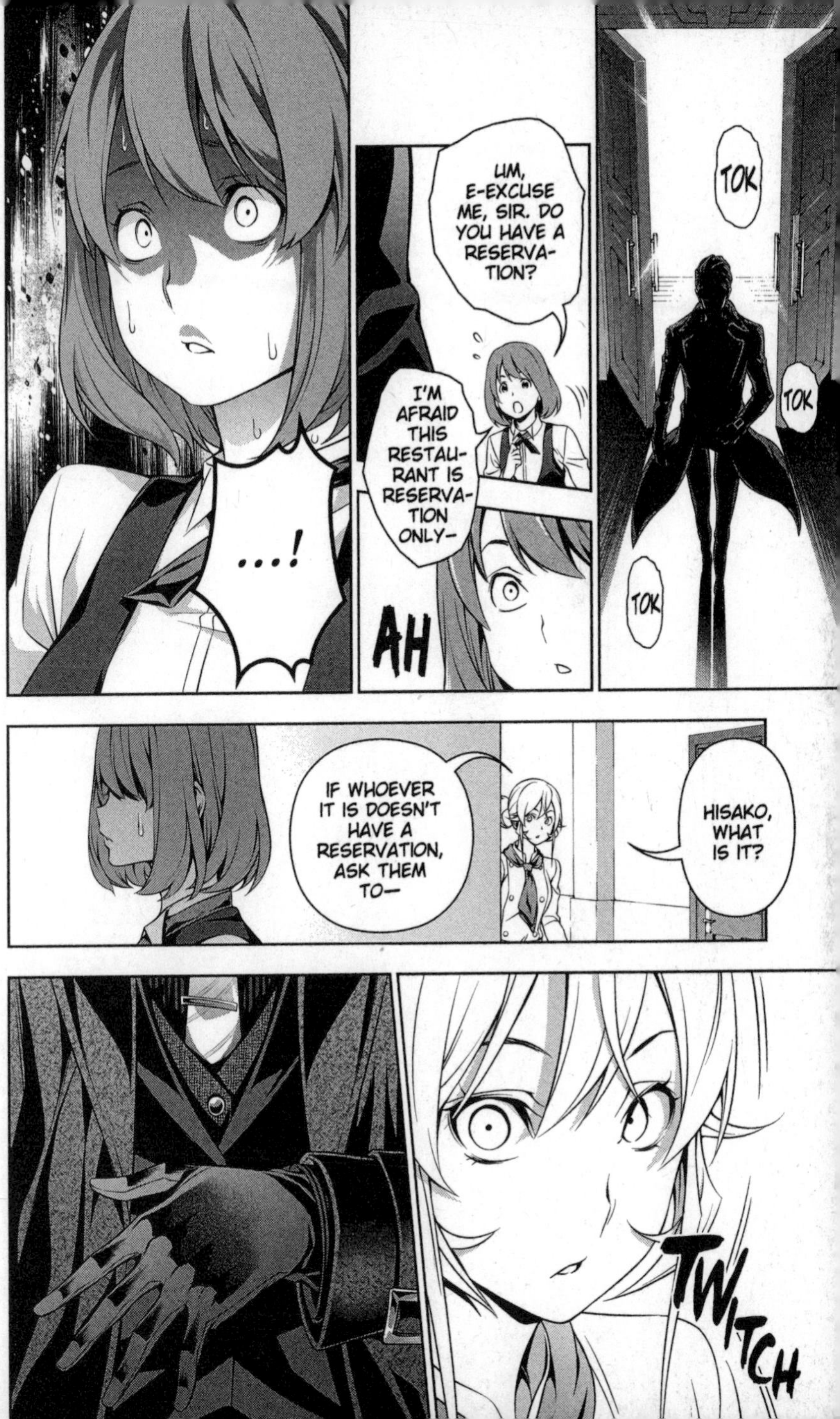
TOK
TOK
TOK
UM, E-EXCUSE ME, SIR. DO YOU HAVE A RESERVATION?
I'M AFRAID THIS RESTAURANT IS RESERVATION ONLY—
AH
...!
HISAKO, WHAT IS IT?
IF WHOEVER IT IS DOESN'T HAVE A RESERVATION, ASK THEM TO—
TWITCH

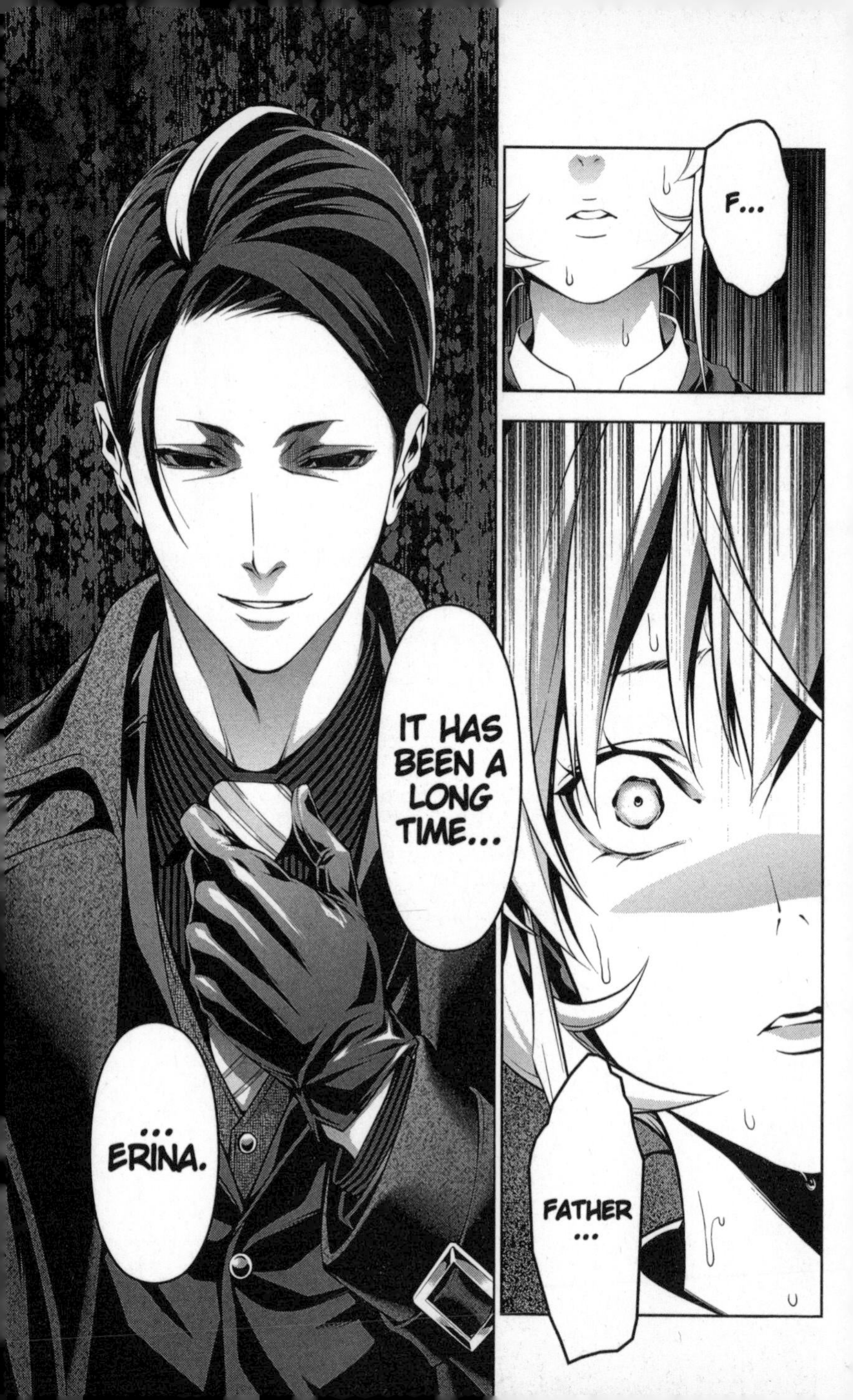
F...
FATHER ...
IT HAS BEEN A LONG TIME...
... ERINA.

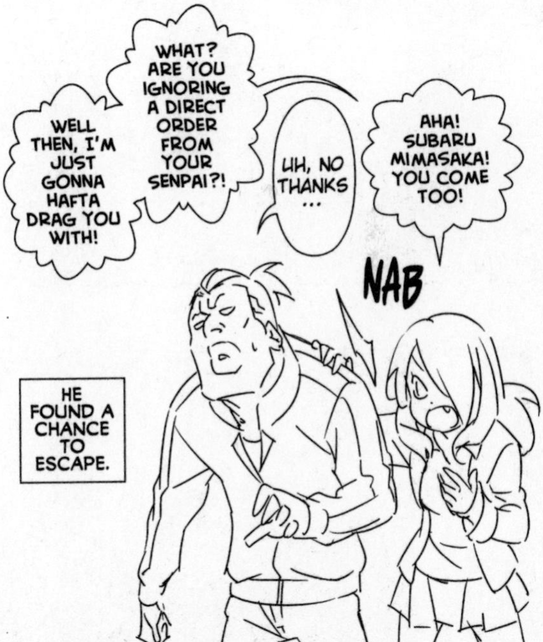
AHA! SUBARU MIMASAKA! YOU COME TOO!
UH, NO THANKS...
WHAT? ARE YOU IGNORING A DIRECT ORDER FROM YOUR SENPAI?!
WELL THEN, I'M JUST GONNA HAFTA DRAG YOU WITH!
NAB
HE FOUND A CHANCE TO ESCAPE.

#132 THE POWER OF THE FIRST SEAT

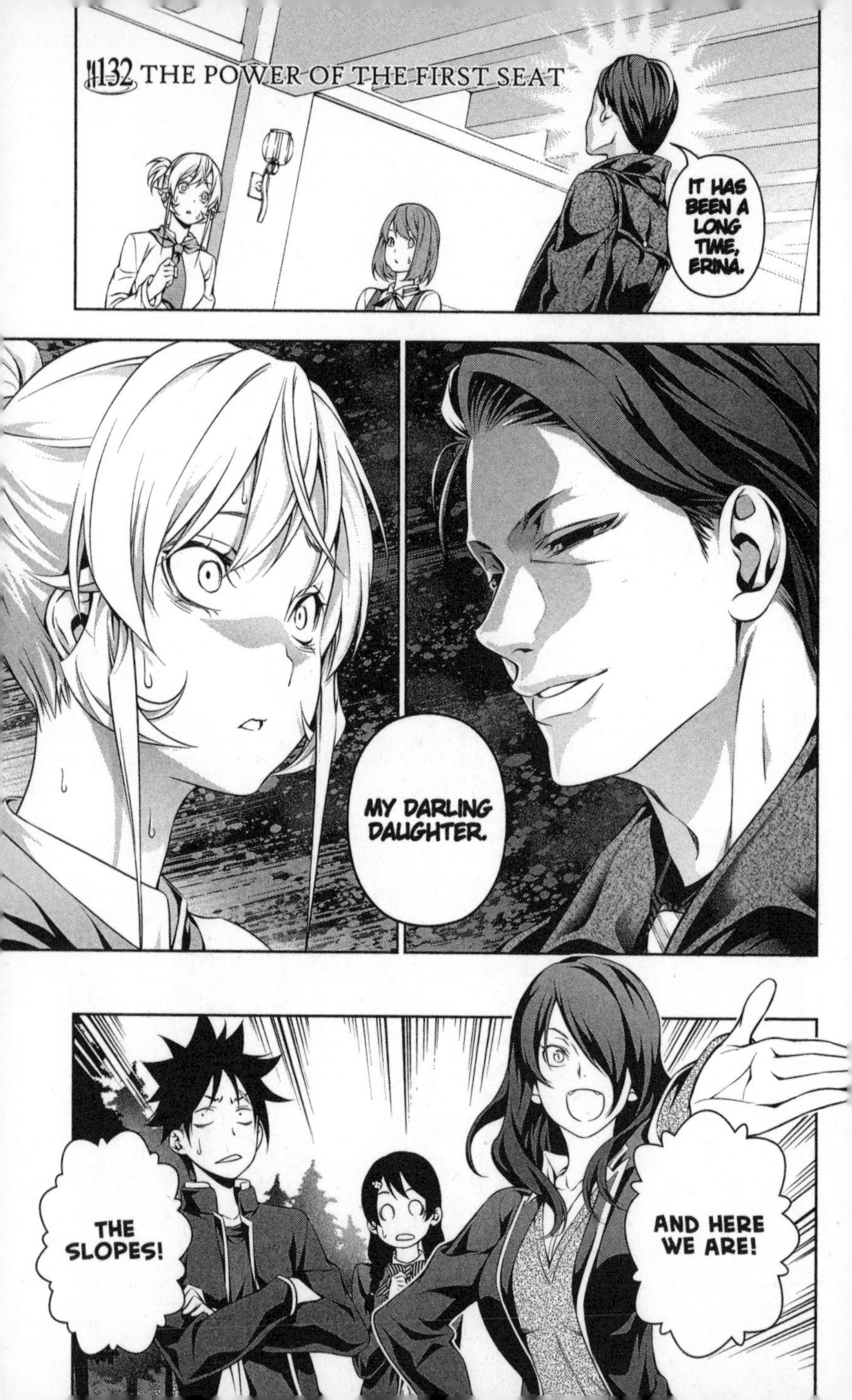
IT HAS BEEN A LONG TIME, ERINA.
MY DARLING DAUGHTER.
AND HERE WE ARE!
THE SLOPES!

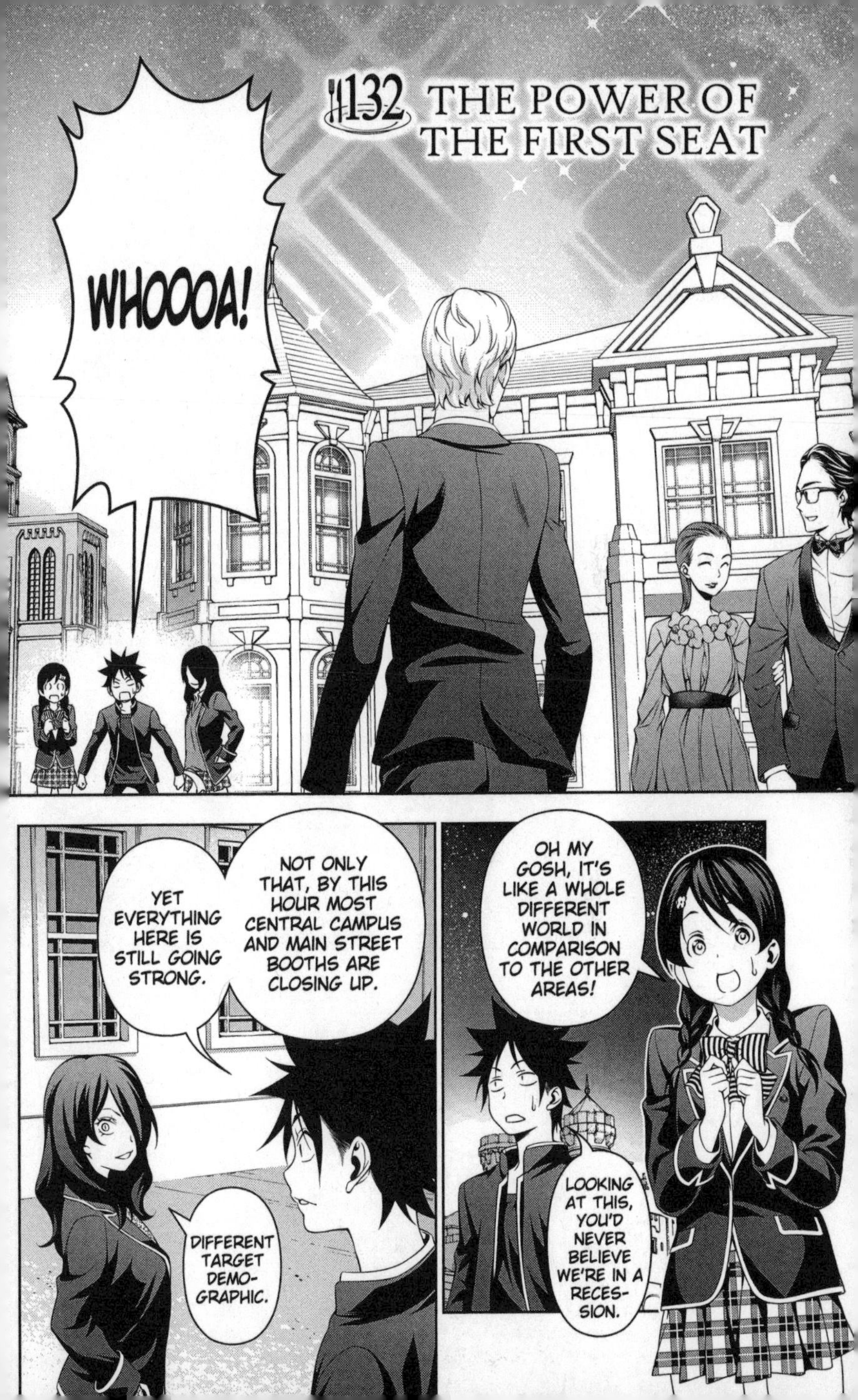
132 THE POWER OF THE FIRST SEAT
WHOOOA!
OH MY GOSH, IT'S LIKE A WHOLE DIFFERENT WORLD IN COMPARISON TO THE OTHER AREAS!
LOOKING AT THIS, YOU'D NEVER BELIEVE WE'RE IN A RECES-SION.
NOT ONLY THAT, BY THIS HOUR MOST CENTRAL CAMPUS AND MAIN STREET BOOTHS ARE CLOSING UP.
YET EVERYTHING HERE IS STILL GOING STRONG.
DIFFERENT TARGET DEMO-GRAPHIC.

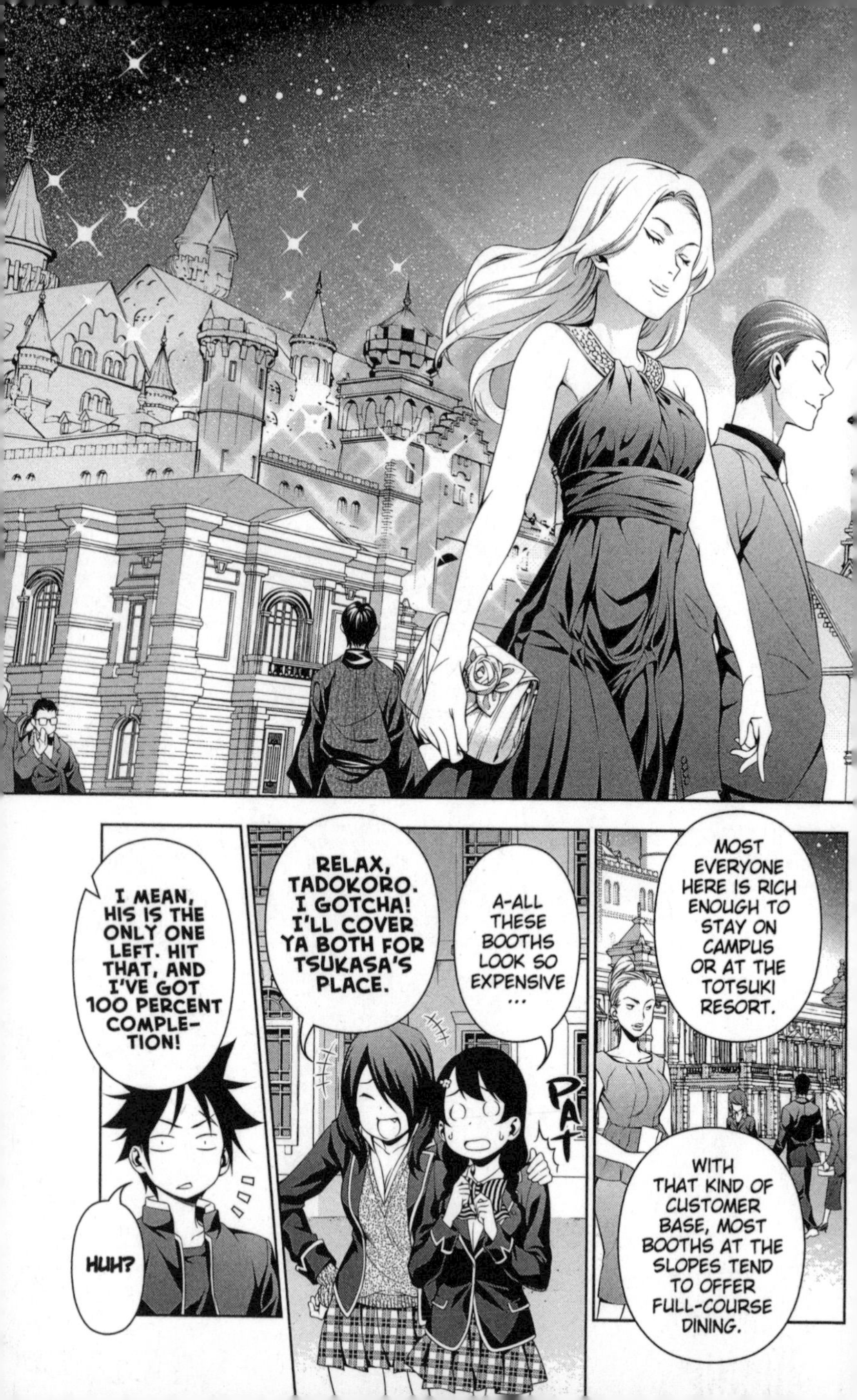
MOST EVERYONE HERE IS RICH ENOUGH TO STAY ON CAMPUS OR AT THE TOTSUKI RESORT.
WITH THAT KIND OF CUSTOMER BASE, MOST BOOTHS AT THE SLOPES TEND TO OFFER FULL-COURSE DINING.
A-ALL THESE BOOTHS LOOK SO EXPENSIVE...
RELAX, TADOKORO. I GOTCHA! I'LL COVER YA BOTH FOR TSUKASA'S PLACE.
PAT
I MEAN, HIS IS THE ONLY ONE LEFT. HIT THAT, AND I'VE GOT 100 PERCENT COMPLETION!
HUH?

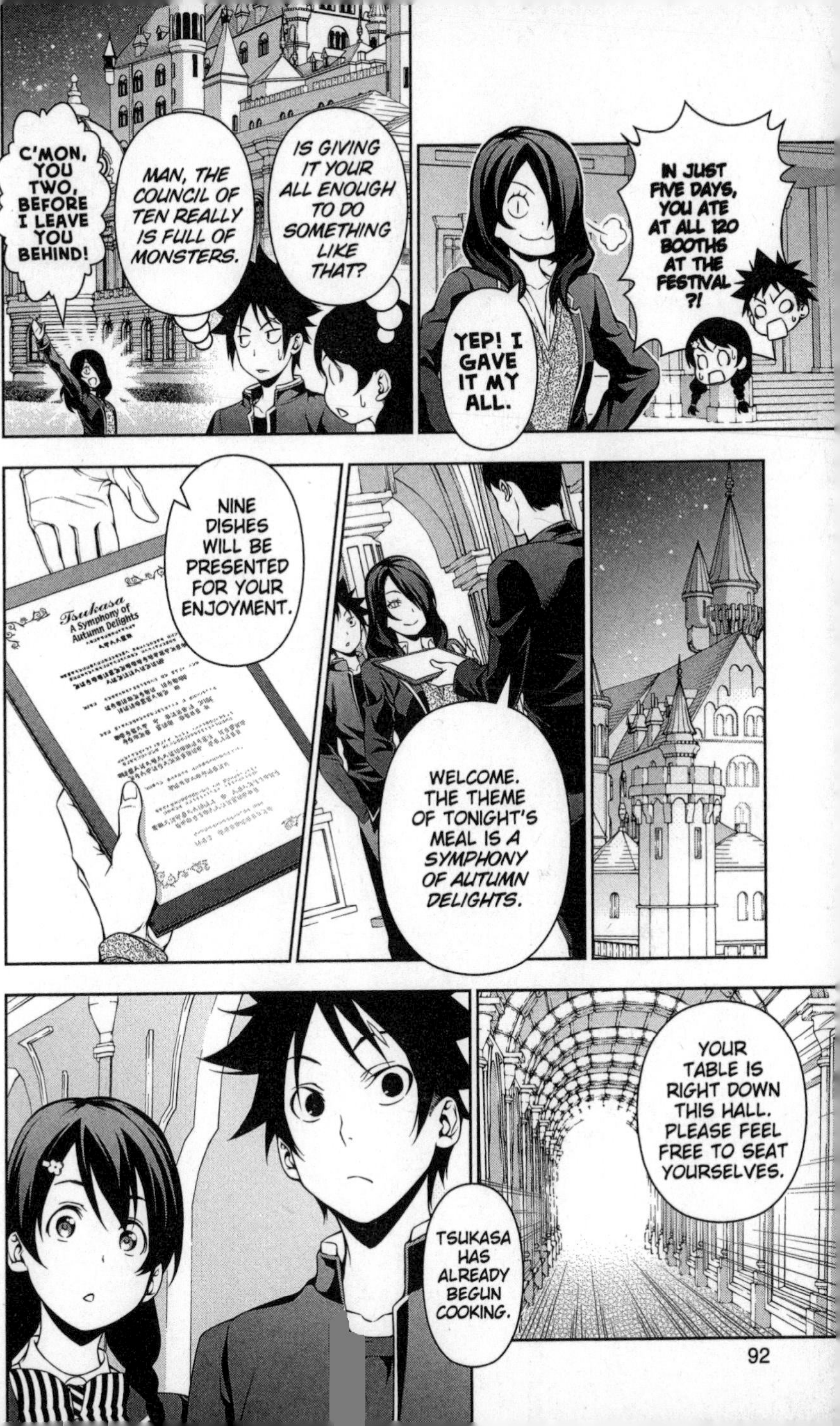
IN JUST FIVE DAYS, YOU ATE AT ALL 120 BOOTHS AT THE FESTIVAL ?!
YEP! I GAVE IT MY ALL.
IS GIVING IT YOUR ALL ENOUGH TO DO SOMETHING LIKE THAT?
MAN, THE COUNCIL OF TEN REALLY IS FULL OF MONSTERS.
C'MON, YOU TWO, BEFORE I LEAVE YOU BEHIND!
WELCOME. THE THEME OF TONIGHT'S MEAL IS A SYMPHONY OF AUTUMN DELIGHTS.
NINE DISHES WILL BE PRESENTED FOR YOUR ENJOYMENT.
Tsukasa
A Symphony of Autumn Delights
YOUR TABLE IS RIGHT DOWN THIS HALL. PLEASE FEEL FREE TO SEAT YOURSELVES.
TSUKASA HAS ALREADY BEGUN COOKING.

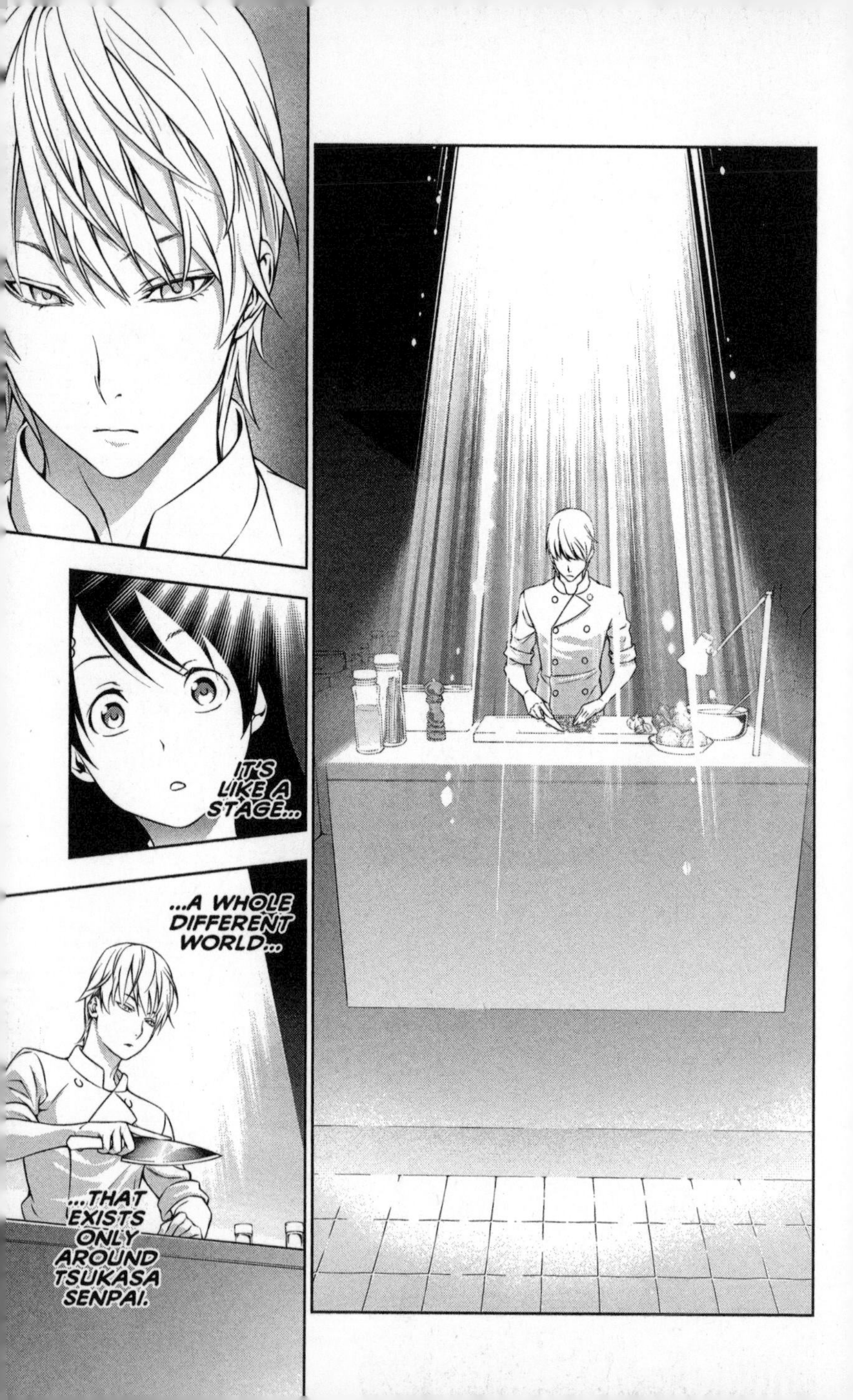
IT'S LIKE A STAGE...
...A WHOLE DIFFERENT WORLD...
...THAT EXISTS ONLY AROUND TSUKASA SENPAI.

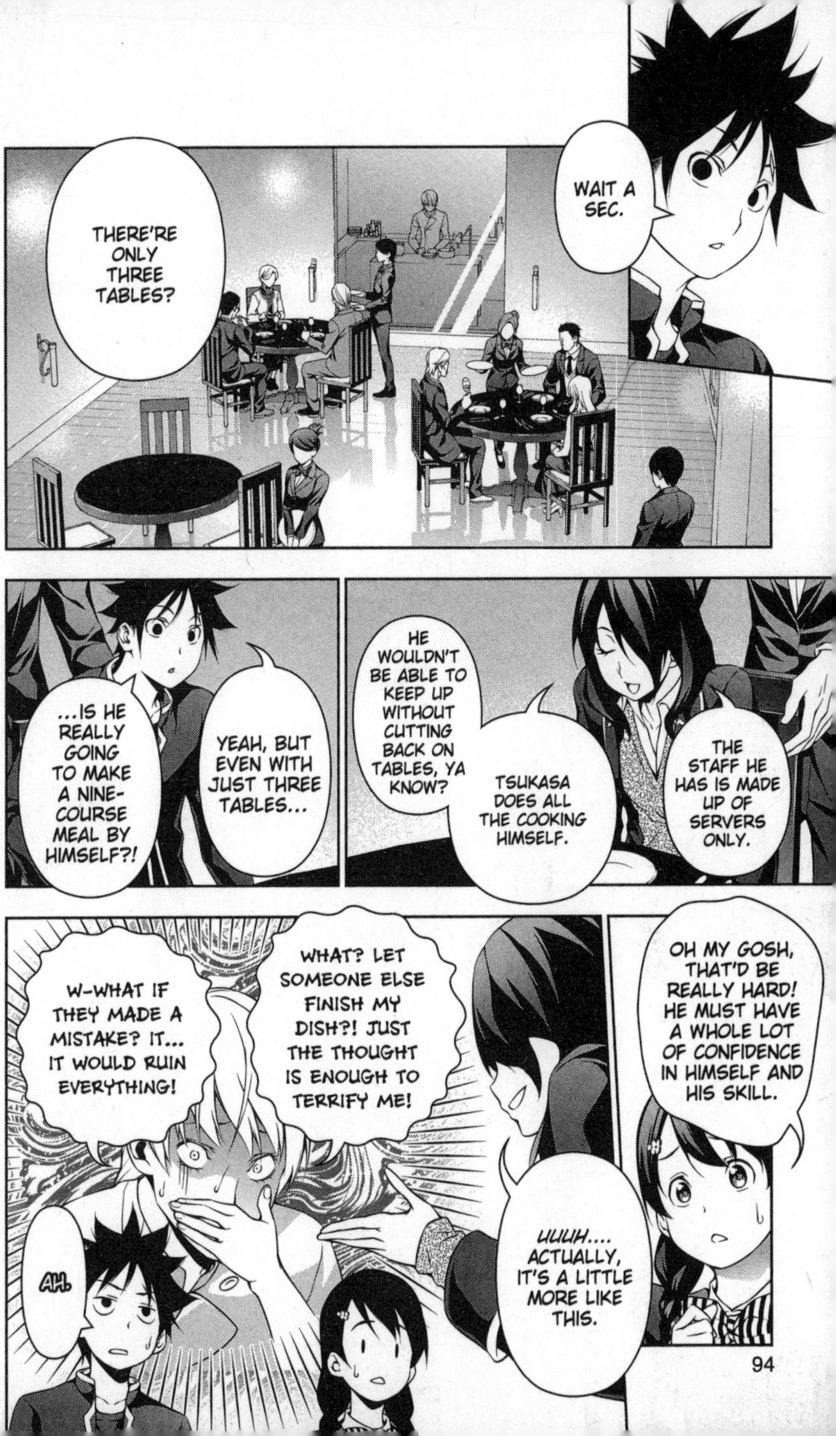
WAIT A SEC.
THERE'RE ONLY THREE TABLES?
THE STAFF HE HAS IS MADE UP OF SERVERS ONLY.
TSUKASA DOES ALL THE COOKING HIMSELF.
HE WOULDN'T BE ABLE TO KEEP UP WITHOUT CUTTING BACK ON TABLES, YA KNOW?
YEAH, BUT EVEN WITH JUST THREE TABLES...
...IS HE REALLY GOING TO MAKE A NINE-COURSE MEAL BY HIMSELF?!
OH MY GOSH, THAT'D BE REALLY HARD! HE MUST HAVE A WHOLE LOT OF CONFIDENCE IN HIMSELF AND HIS SKILL.
UUUH.... ACTUALLY, IT'S A LITTLE MORE LIKE THIS.
WHAT? LET SOMEONE ELSE FINISH MY DISH?! JUST THE THOUGHT IS ENOUGH TO TERRIFY ME!
W-WHAT IF THEY MADE A MISTAKE? IT... IT WOULD RUIN EVERYTHING!
AH.

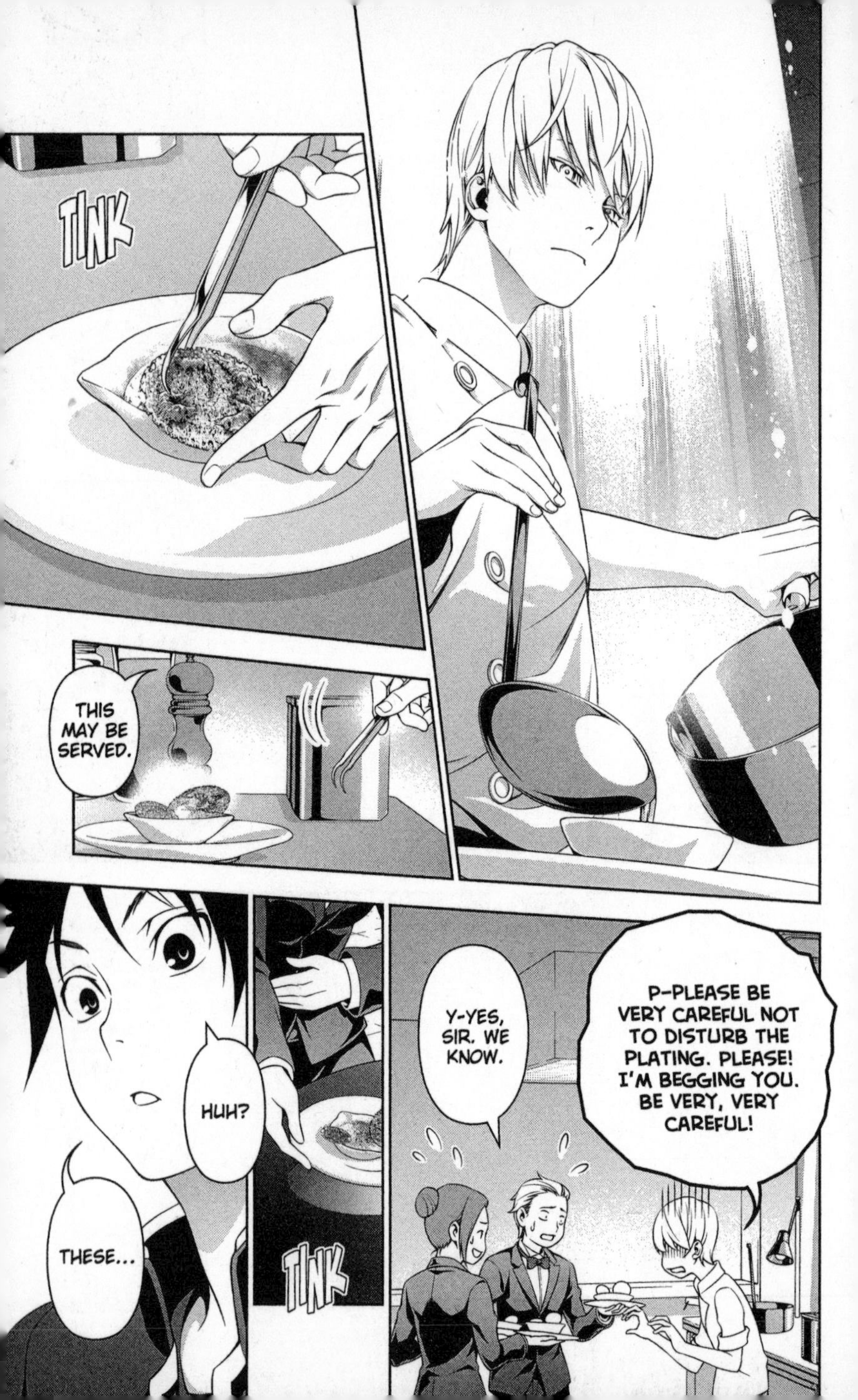
TINK
THIS MAY BE SERVED.
P-PLEASE BE VERY CAREFUL NOT TO DISTURB THE PLATING. PLEASE! I'M BEGGING YOU. BE VERY, VERY CAREFUL!
Y-YES, SIR. WE KNOW.
TINK
HUH?
THESE...

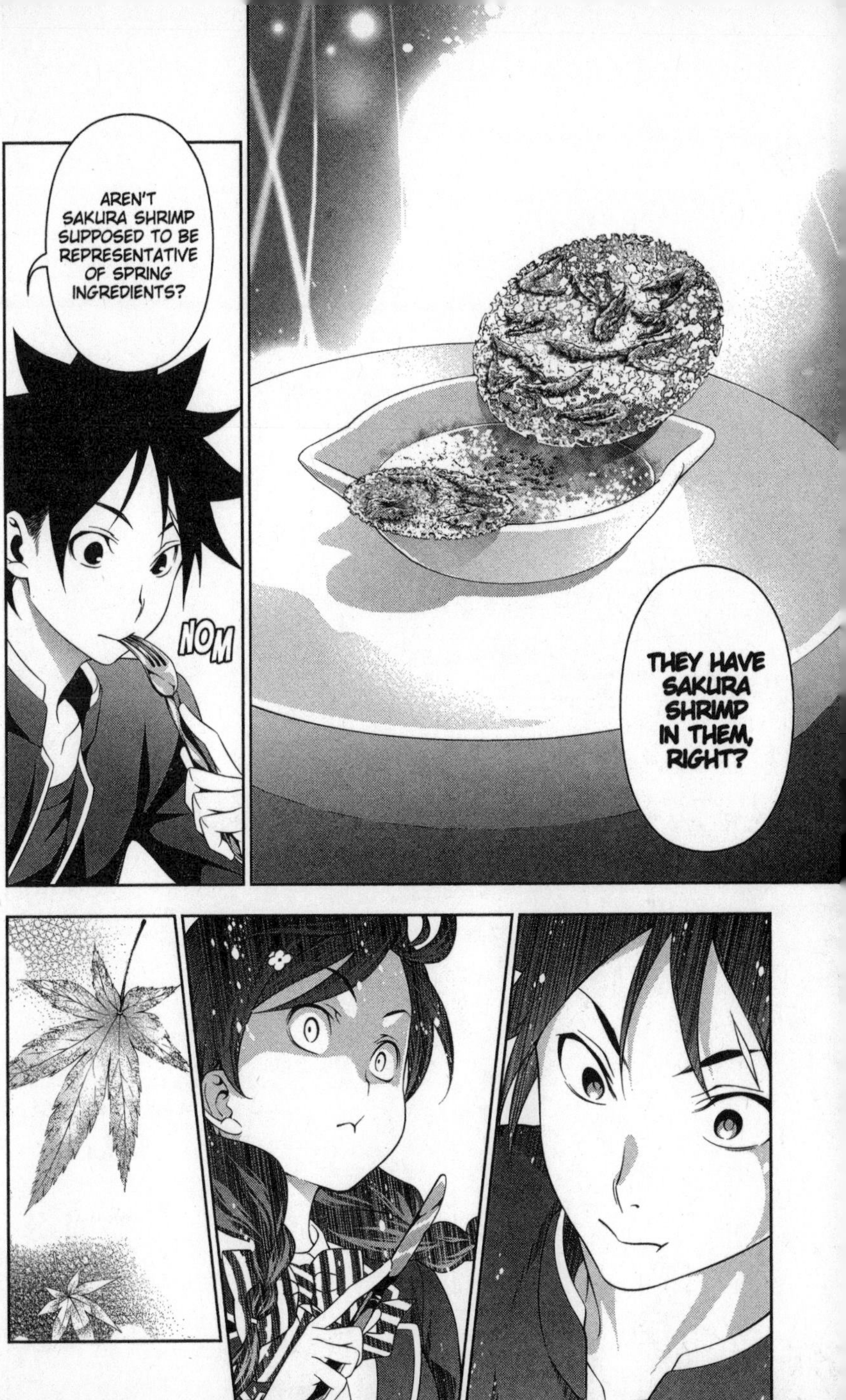
THEY HAVE SAKURA SHRIMP IN THEM, RIGHT?
AREN'T SAKURA SHRIMP SUPPOSED TO BE REPRESENTATIVE OF SPRING INGREDIENTS?
NOM

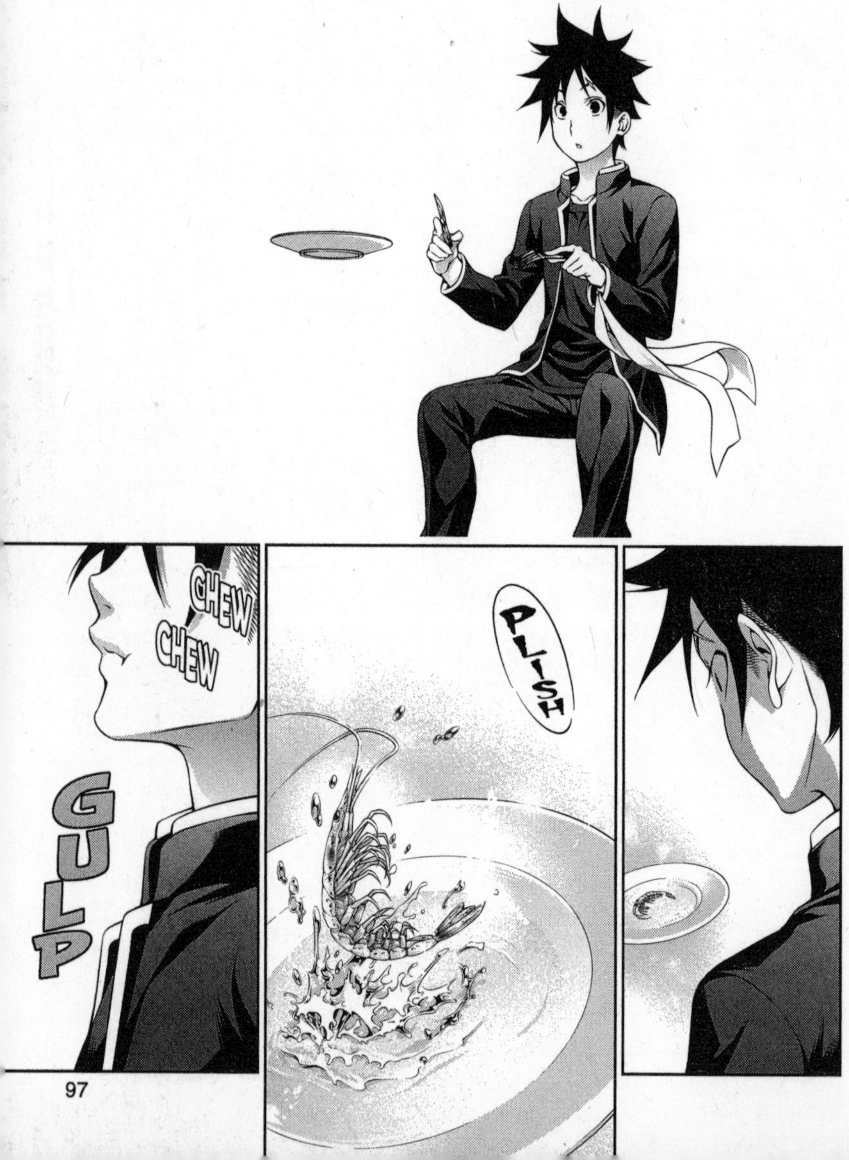
PLISH
CHEW
CHEW
GULP

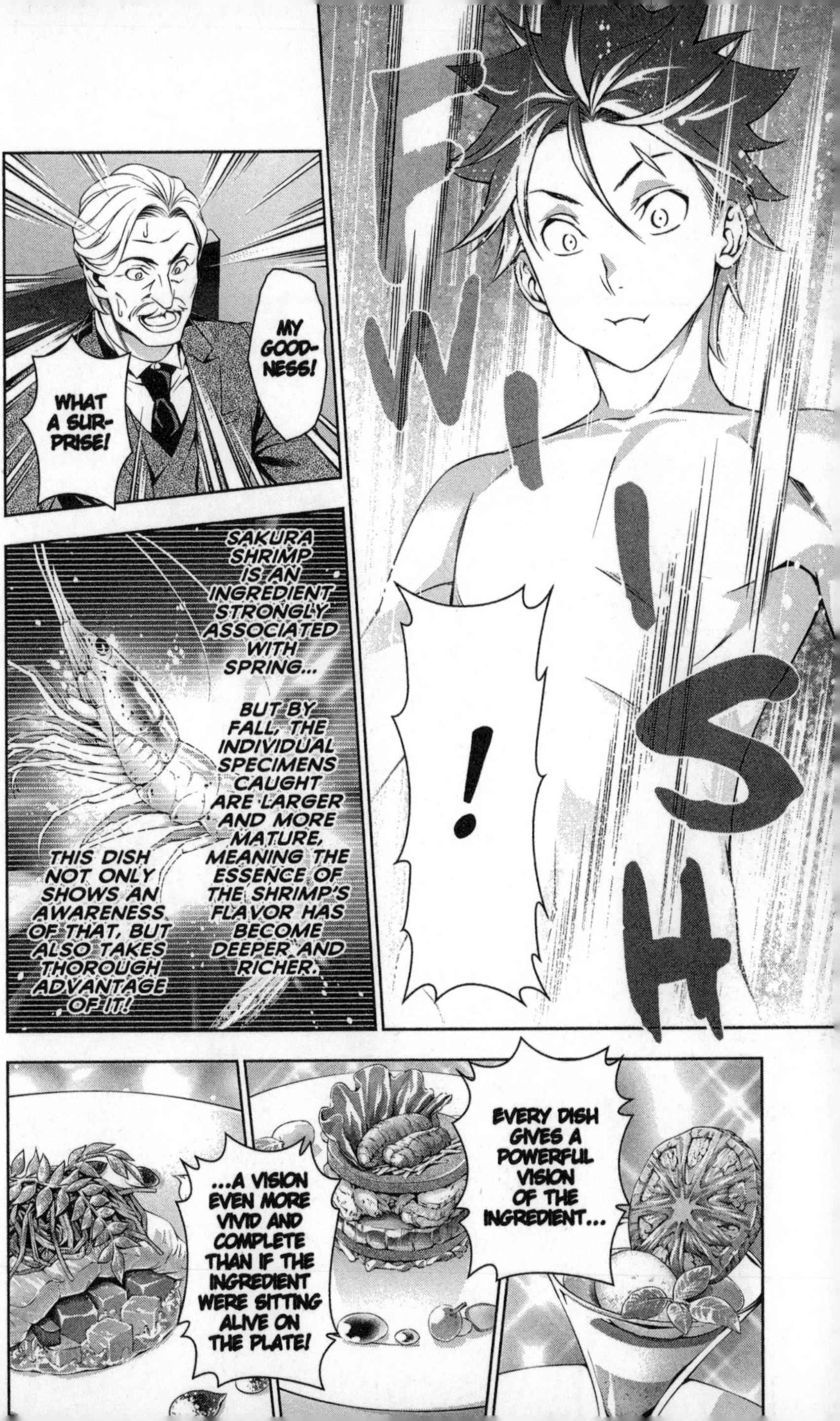
WHISH
!
MY GOODNESS!
WHAT A SURPRISE!
SAKURA SHRIMP IS AN INGREDIENT STRONGLY ASSOCIATED WITH SPRING...
BUT BY FALL, THE INDIVIDUAL SPECIMENS CAUGHT ARE LARGER AND MORE MATURE, MEANING THE ESSENCE OF THE SHRIMP'S FLAVOR HAS BECOME DEEPER AND RICHER.
THIS DISH NOT ONLY SHOWS AN AWARENESS OF THAT, BUT ALSO TAKES THOROUGH ADVANTAGE OF IT!
EVERY DISH GIVES A POWERFUL VISION OF THE INGREDIENT...
...A VISION EVEN MORE VIVID AND COMPLETE THAN IF THE INGREDIENT WERE SITTING ALIVE ON THE PLATE!

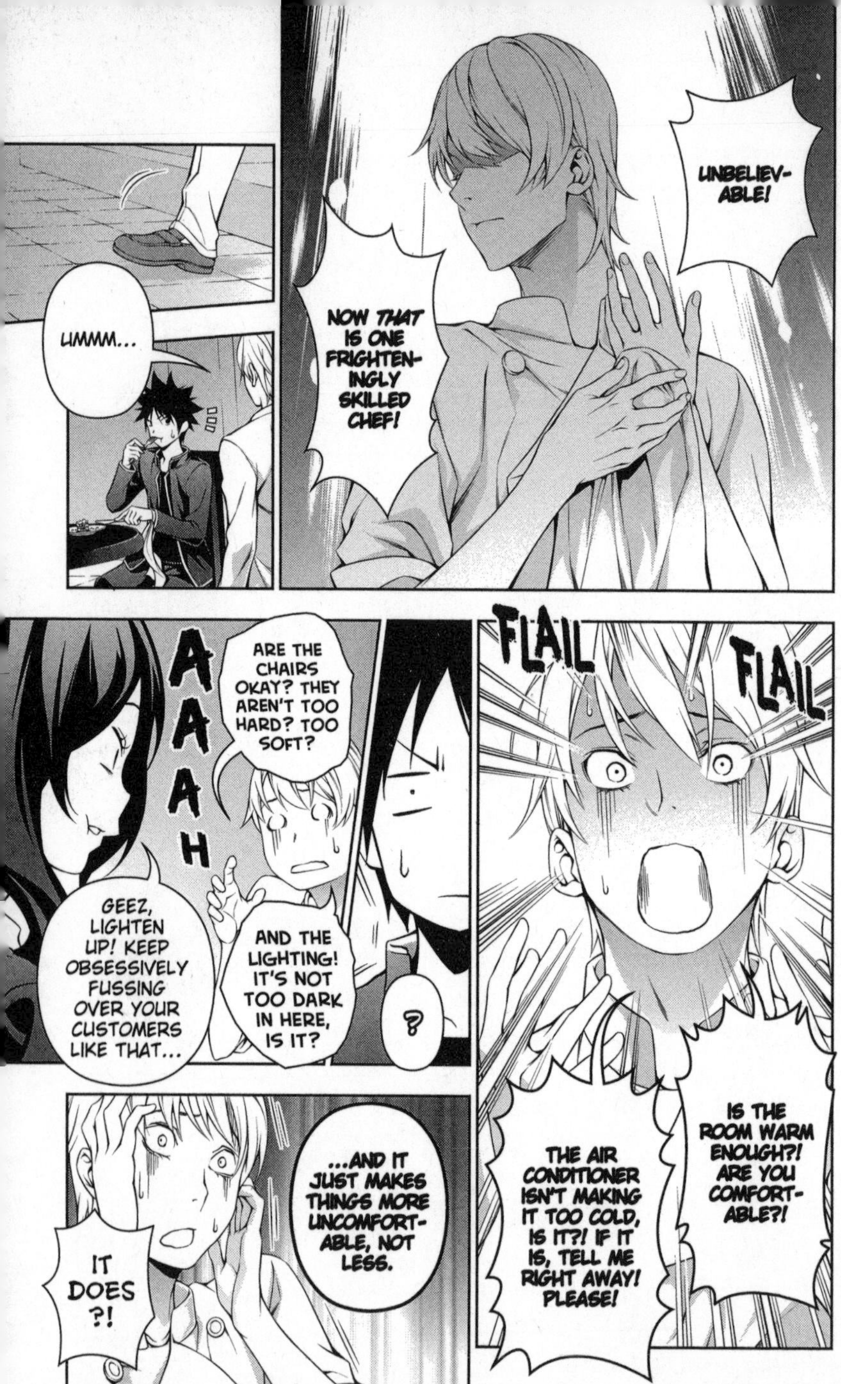
UNBELIEV-ABLE!
NOW THAT IS ONE FRIGHTEN-INGLY SKILLED CHEF!
UMMM...
FLAIL
FLAIL
IS THE ROOM WARM ENOUGH?! ARE YOU COMFORT-ABLE?!
THE AIR CONDITIONER ISN'T MAKING IT TOO COLD, IS IT?! IF IT IS, TELL ME RIGHT AWAY! PLEASE!
ARE THE CHAIRS OKAY? THEY AREN'T TOO HARD? TOO SOFT?
AAAH
AND THE LIGHTING! IT'S NOT TOO DARK IN HERE, IS IT?
?
GEEZ, LIGHTEN UP! KEEP OBSESSIVELY FUSSING OVER YOUR CUSTOMERS LIKE THAT...
...AND IT JUST MAKES THINGS MORE UNCOMFORT-ABLE, NOT LESS.
IT DOES ?!

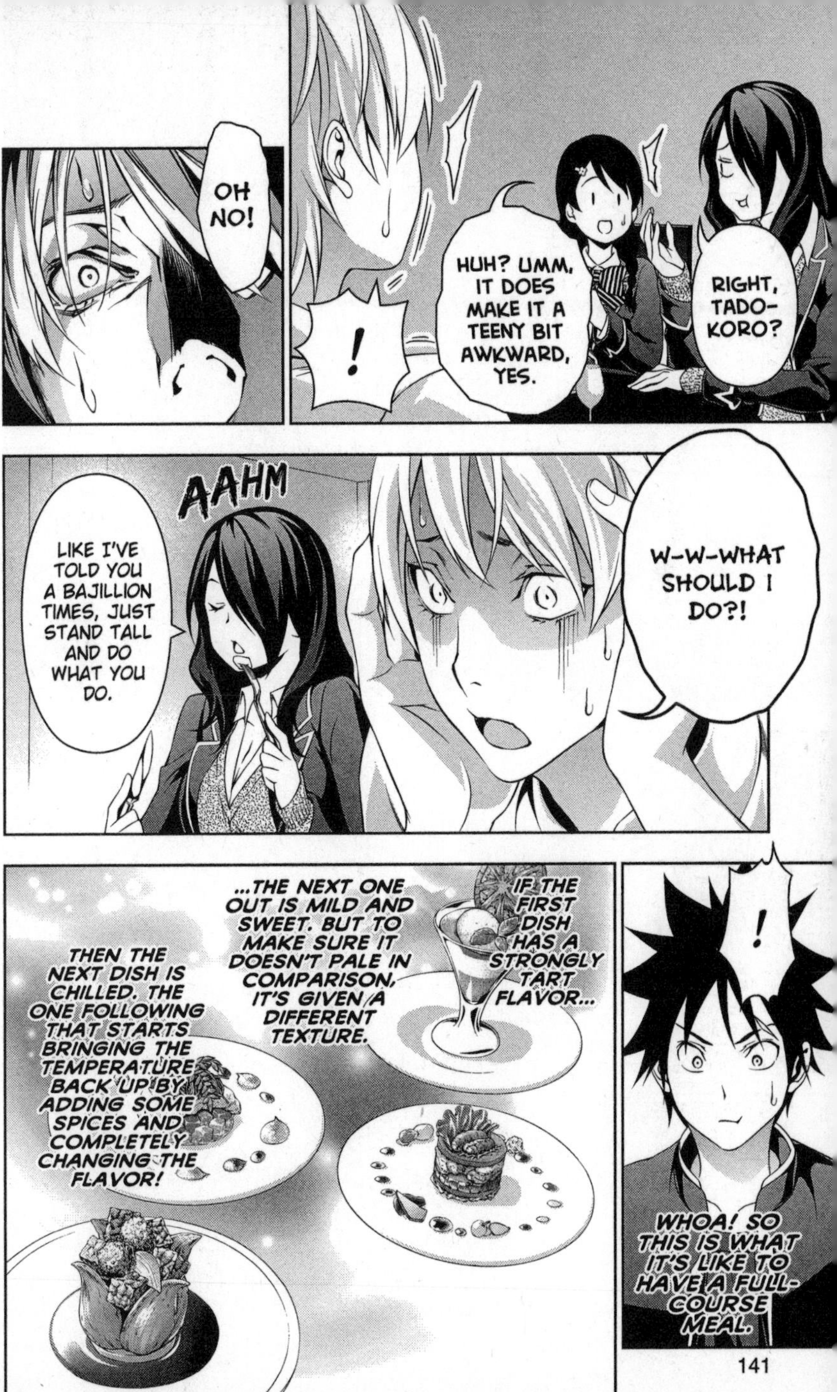
RIGHT, TADO-KORO?
HUH? UMM, IT DOES MAKE IT A TEENY BIT AWKWARD, YES.
!
OH NO!
W-W-WHAT SHOULD I DO?!
AAHM
LIKE I'VE TOLD YOU A BAJILLION TIMES, JUST STAND TALL AND DO WHAT YOU DO.
!
WHOA! SO THIS IS WHAT IT'S LIKE TO HAVE A FULL-COURSE MEAL.
IF THE FIRST DISH HAS A STRONGLY TART FLAVOR...
...THE NEXT ONE OUT IS MILD AND SWEET. BUT TO MAKE SURE IT DOESN'T PALE IN COMPARISON, IT'S GIVEN A DIFFERENT TEXTURE.
THEN THE NEXT DISH IS CHILLED. THE ONE FOLLOWING THAT STARTS BRINGING THE TEMPERATURE BACK UP BY ADDING SOME SPICES AND COMPLETELY CHANGING THE FLAVOR!

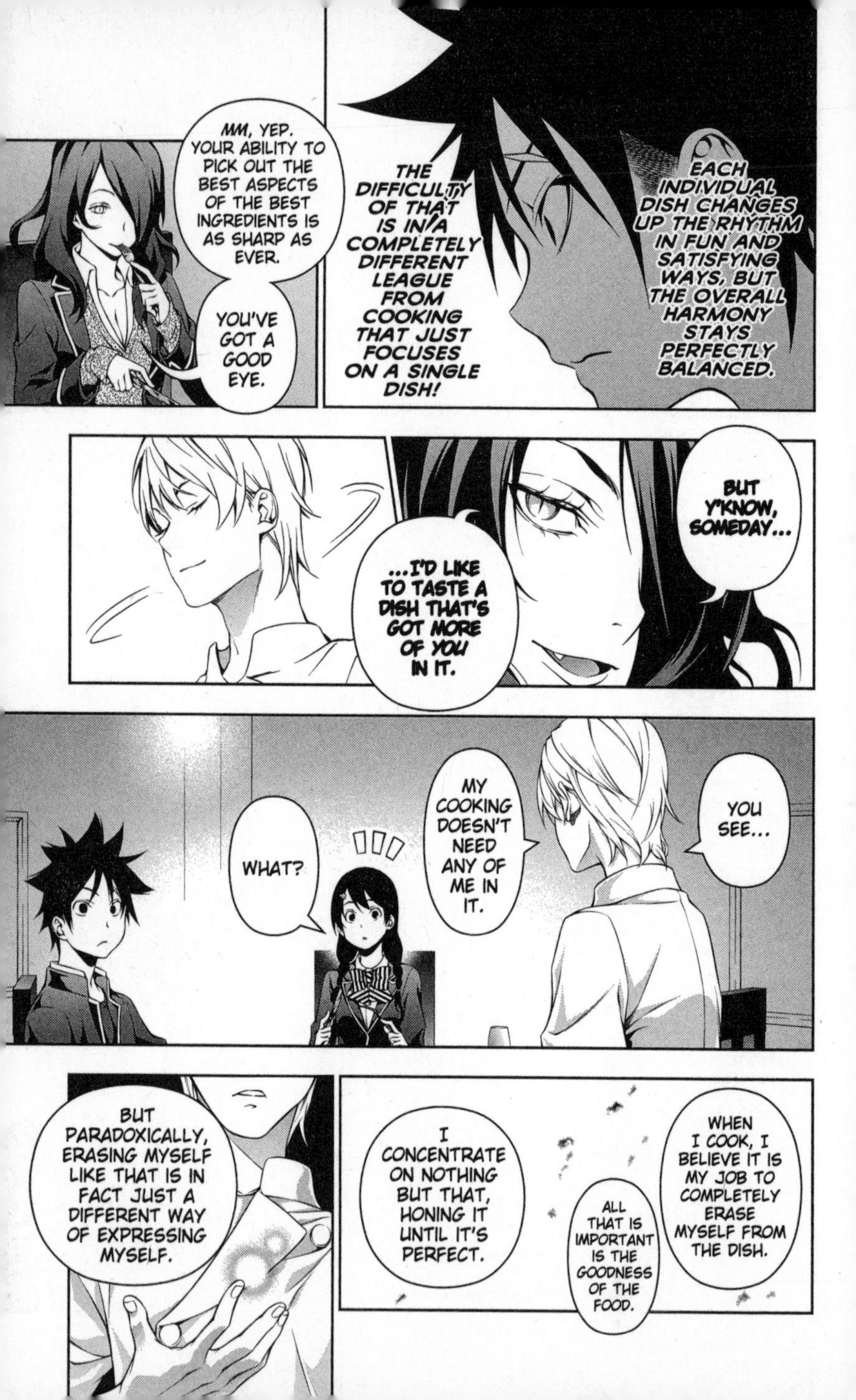
EACH INDIVIDUAL DISH CHANGES UP THE RHYTHM IN FUN AND SATISFYING WAYS, BUT THE OVERALL HARMONY STAYS PERFECTLY BALANCED.
THE DIFFICULTY OF THAT IS IN A COMPLETELY DIFFERENT LEAGUE FROM COOKING THAT JUST FOCUSES ON A SINGLE DISH!
MM, YEP. YOUR ABILITY TO PICK OUT THE BEST ASPECTS OF THE BEST INGREDIENTS IS AS SHARP AS EVER.
YOU'VE GOT A GOOD EYE.
BUT Y'KNOW, SOMEDAY...
...I'D LIKE TO TASTE A DISH THAT'S GOT MORE OF YOU IN IT.
YOU SEE...
MY COOKING DOESN'T NEED ANY OF ME IN IT.
WHAT?
WHEN I COOK, I BELIEVE IT IS MY JOB TO COMPLETELY ERASE MYSELF FROM THE DISH.
ALL THAT IS IMPORTANT IS THE GOODNESS OF THE FOOD.
I CONCENTRATE ON NOTHING BUT THAT, HONING IT UNTIL IT'S PERFECT.
BUT PARADOXICALLY, ERASING MYSELF LIKE THAT IS IN FACT JUST A DIFFERENT WAY OF EXPRESSING MYSELF.

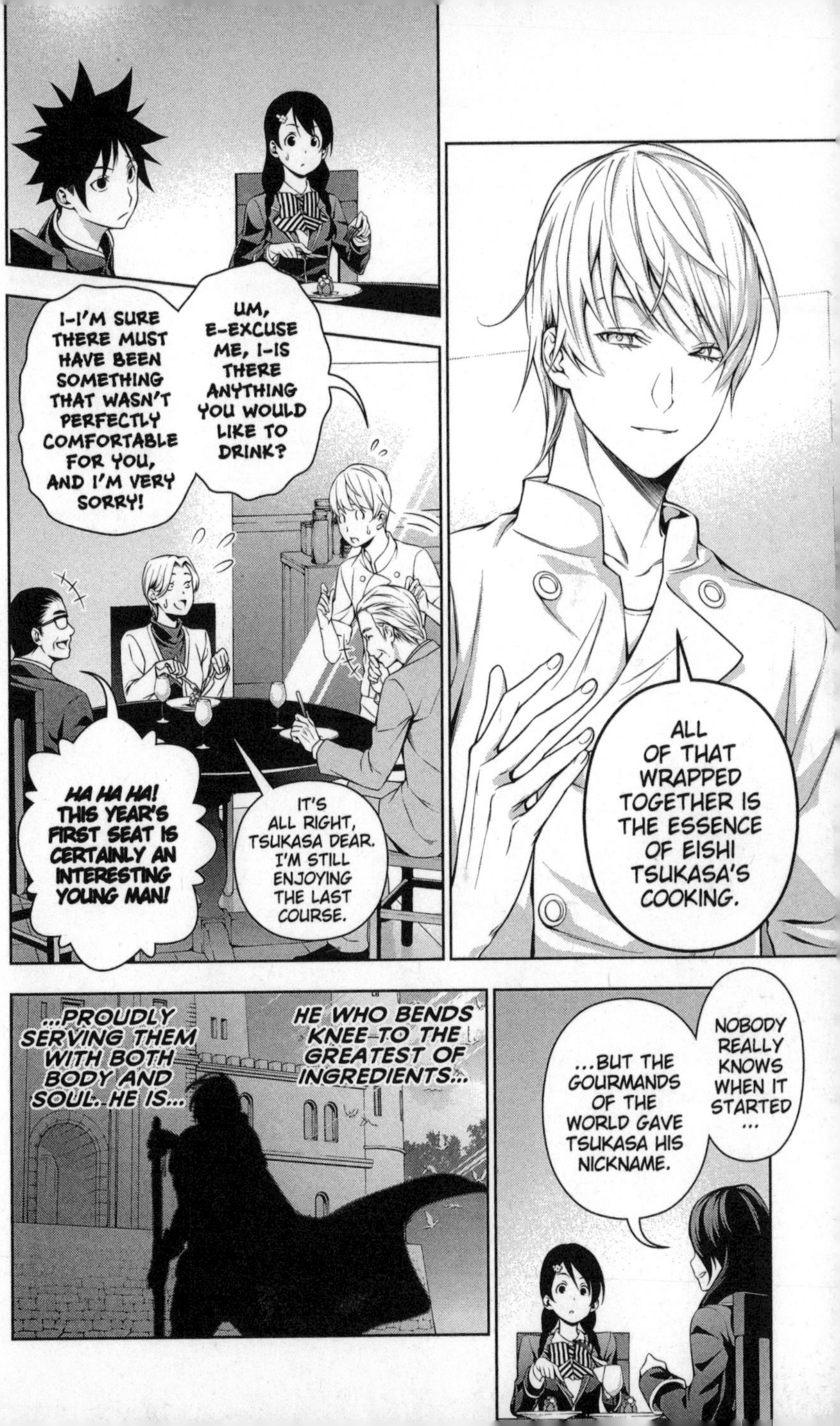
ALL OF THAT WRAPPED TOGETHER IS THE ESSENCE OF EISHI TSUKASA'S COOKING.
UM, E-EXCUSE ME, I-IS THERE ANYTHING YOU WOULD LIKE TO DRINK?
I-I'M SURE THERE MUST HAVE BEEN SOMETHING THAT WASN'T PERFECTLY COMFORTABLE FOR YOU, AND I'M VERY SORRY!
IT'S ALL RIGHT, TSUKASA DEAR. I'M STILL ENJOYING THE LAST COURSE.
HA HA HA! THIS YEAR'S FIRST SEAT IS CERTAINLY AN INTERESTING YOUNG MAN!
NOBODY REALLY KNOWS WHEN IT STARTED ...
...BUT THE GOURMANDS OF THE WORLD GAVE TSUKASA HIS NICKNAME.
HE WHO BENDS KNEE TO THE GREATEST OF INGREDIENTS...
...PROUDLY SERVING THEM WITH BOTH BODY AND SOUL. HE IS...

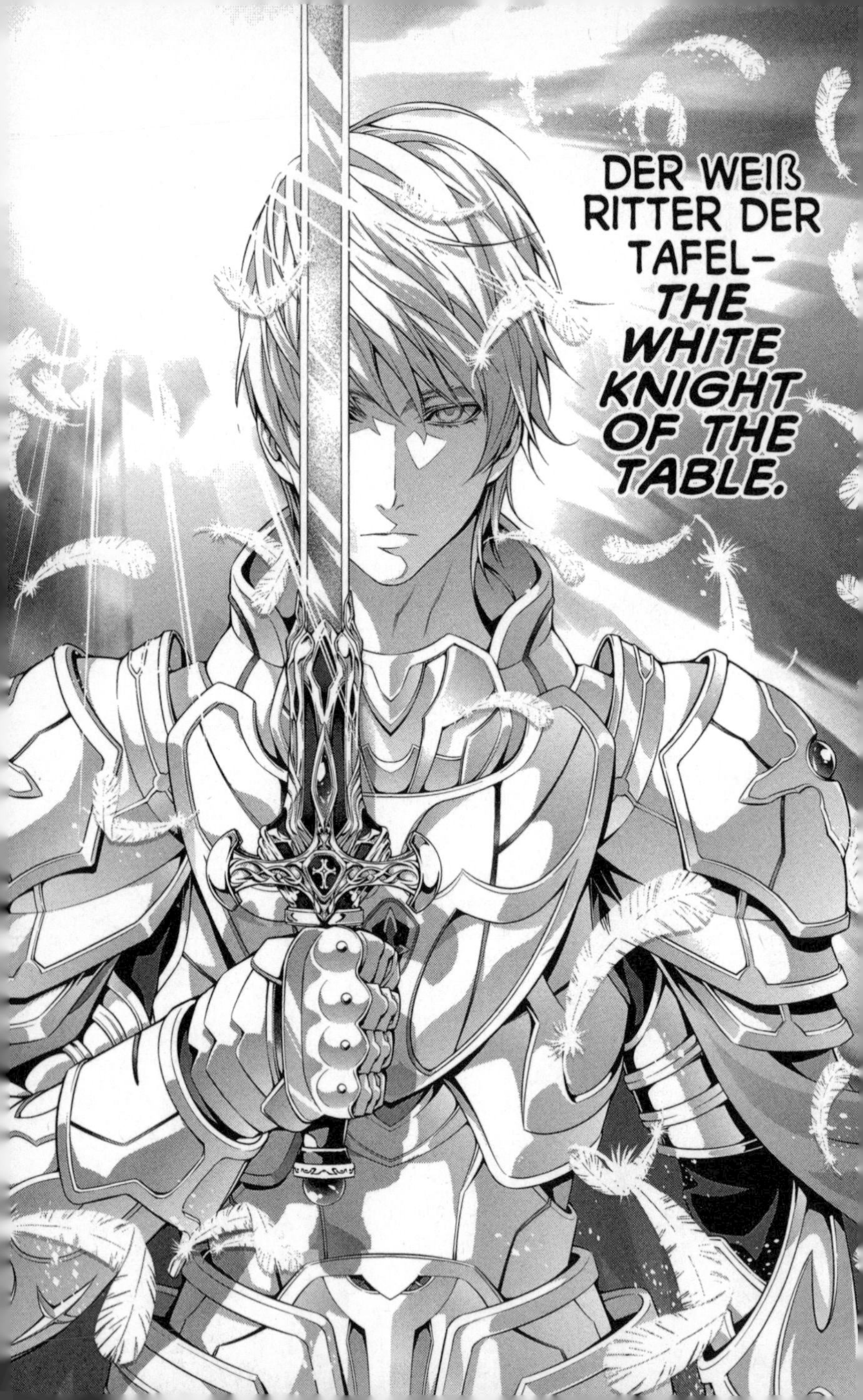
DER WEIß RITTER DER TAFEL—*THE WHITE KNIGHT OF THE TABLE.*

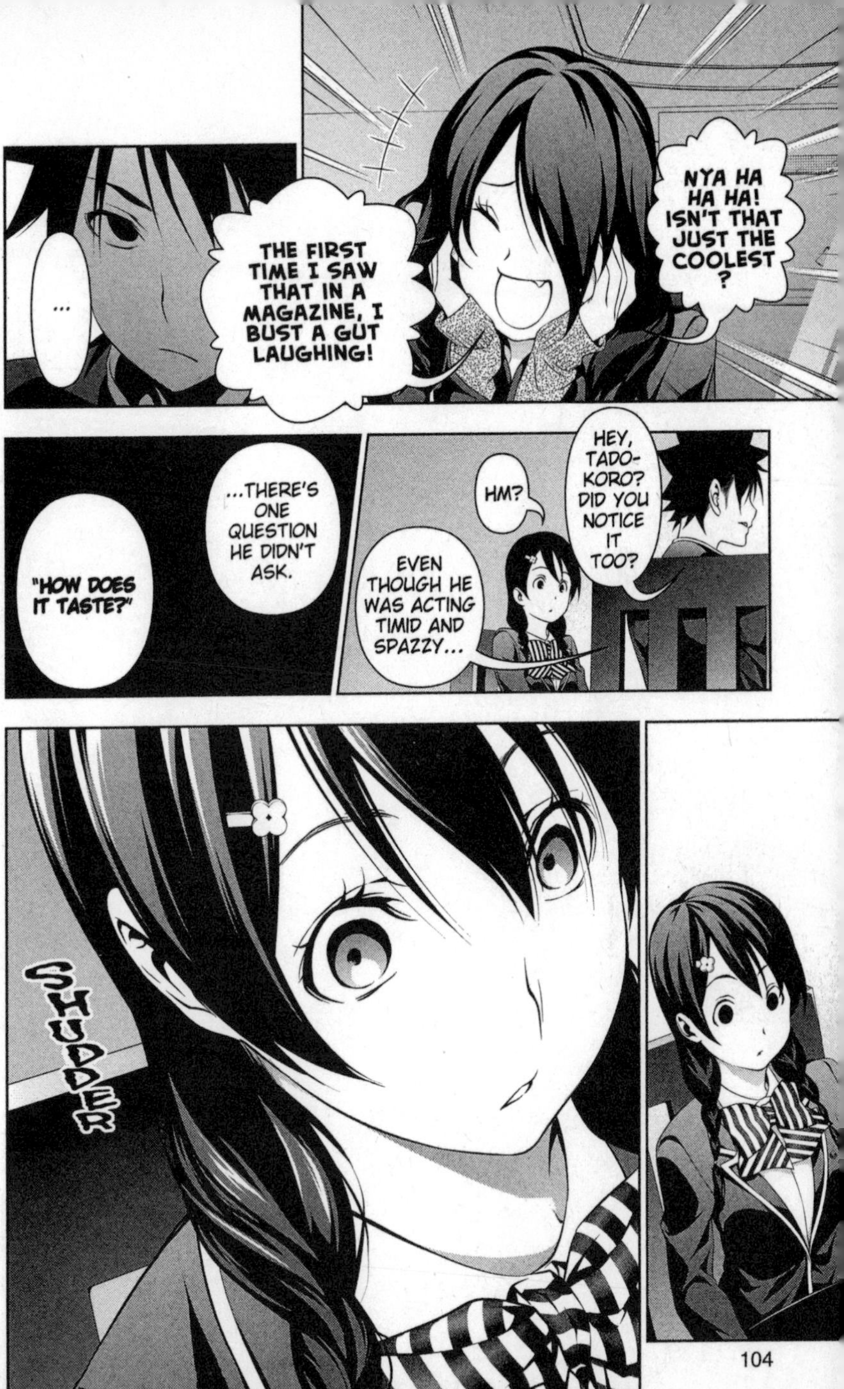
NYA HA HA HA! ISN'T THAT JUST THE COOLEST?
THE FIRST TIME I SAW THAT IN A MAGAZINE, I BUST A GUT LAUGHING!
...
HEY, TADOKORO? DID YOU NOTICE IT TOO?
HM?
EVEN THOUGH HE WAS ACTING TIMID AND SPAZZY...
...THERE'S ONE QUESTION HE DIDN'T ASK.
"HOW DOES IT TASTE?"
SHUDDER

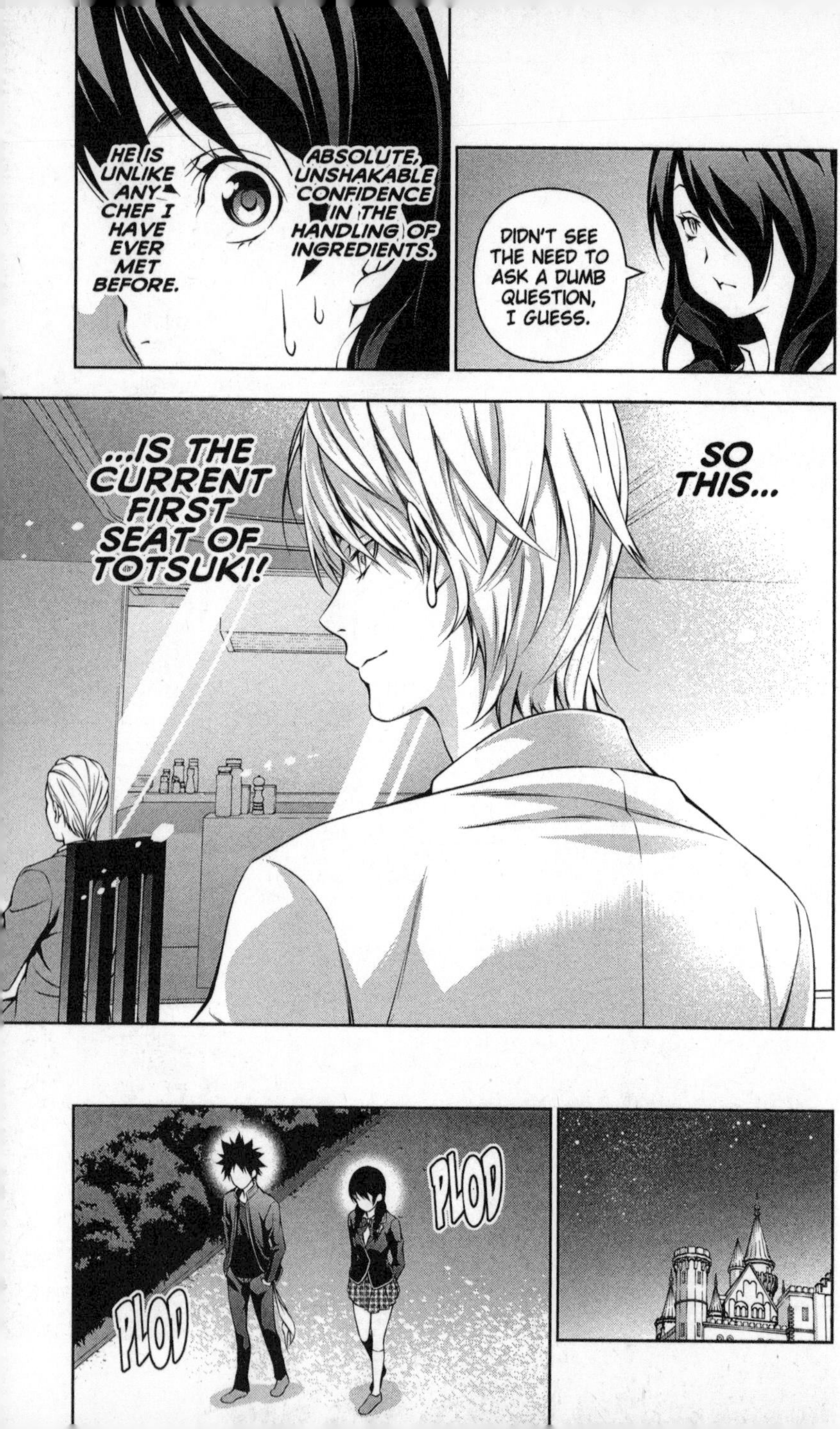
DIDN'T SEE THE NEED TO ASK A DUMB QUESTION, I GUESS.
ABSOLUTE, UNSHAKABLE CONFIDENCE IN THE HANDLING OF INGREDIENTS.
HE IS UNLIKE ANY CHEF I HAVE EVER MET BEFORE.
SO THIS...
...IS THE CURRENT FIRST SEAT OF TOTSUKI!
PLOD
PLOD

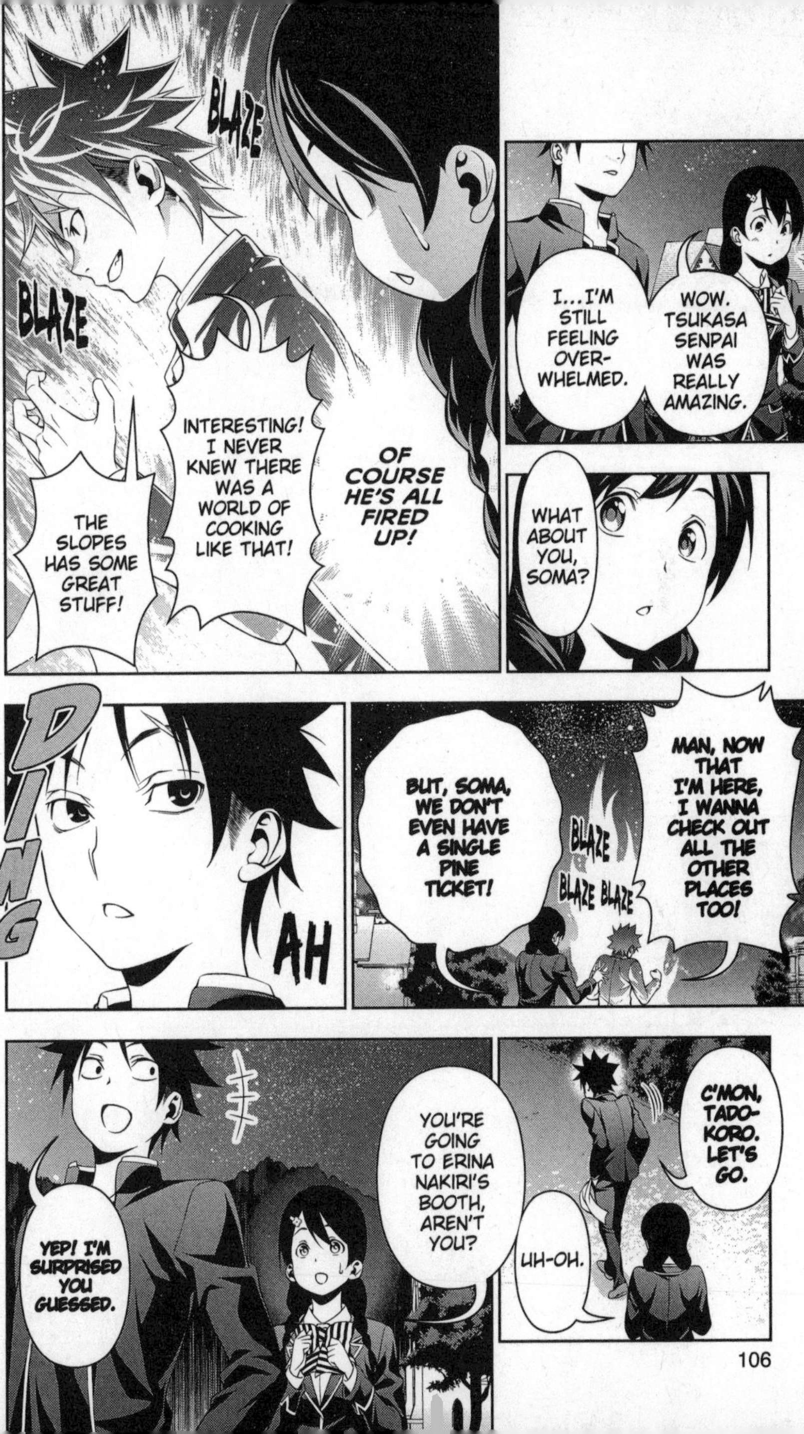
WOW. TSUKASA SENPAI WAS REALLY AMAZING.
I...I'M STILL FEELING OVER-WHELMED.
WHAT ABOUT YOU, SOMA?
BLAZE
OF COURSE HE'S ALL FIRED UP!
INTERESTING! I NEVER KNEW THERE WAS A WORLD OF COOKING LIKE THAT!
BLAZE
THE SLOPES HAS SOME GREAT STUFF!
MAN, NOW THAT I'M HERE, I WANNA CHECK OUT ALL THE OTHER PLACES TOO!
BLAZE BLAZE BLAZE
BUT, SOMA, WE DON'T EVEN HAVE A SINGLE PINE TICKET!
AH
DING
C'MON, TADOKORO. LET'S GO.
UH-OH.
YOU'RE GOING TO ERINA NAKIRI'S BOOTH, AREN'T YOU?
YEP! I'M SURPRISED YOU GUESSED.

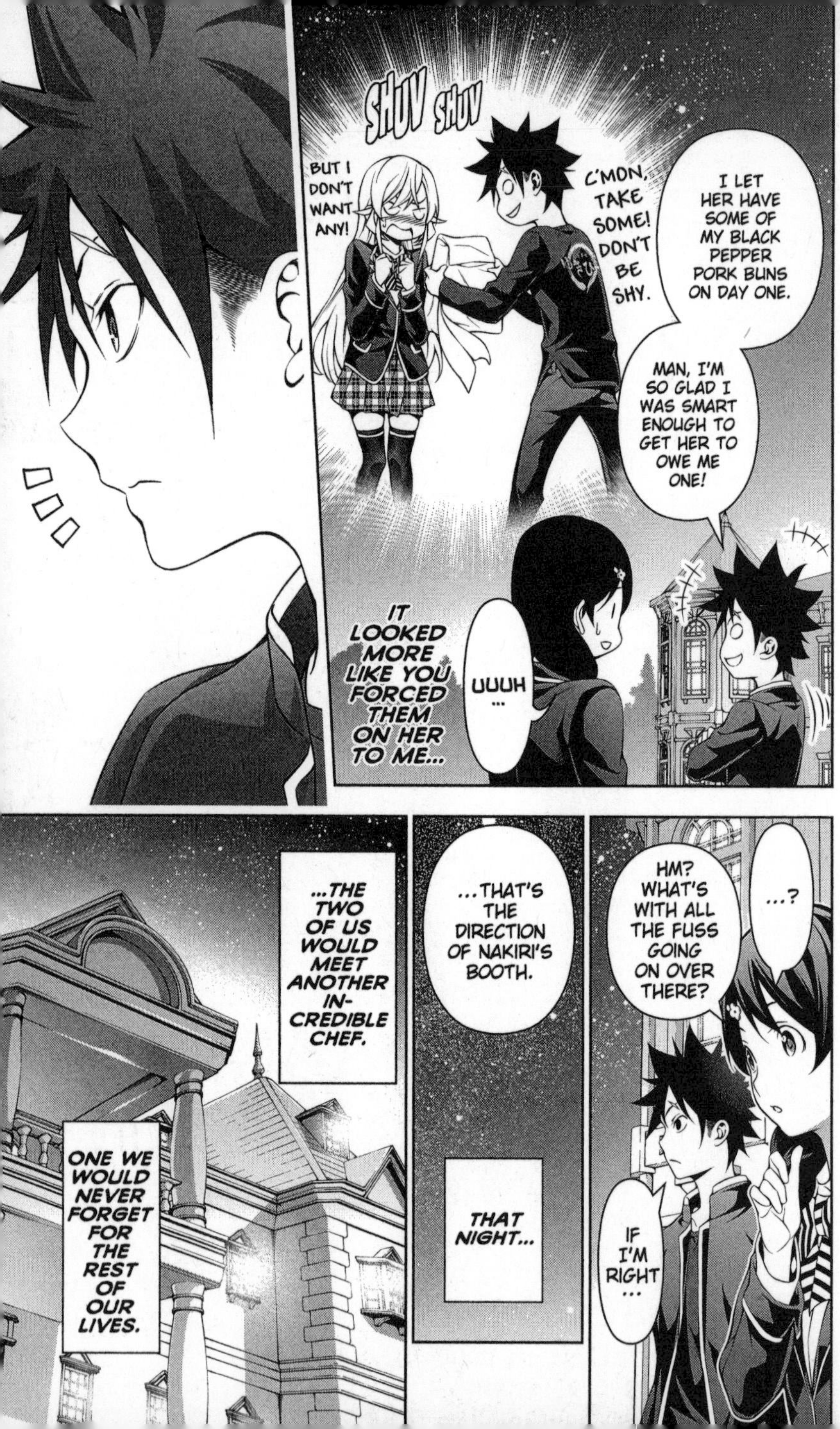
I LET HER HAVE SOME OF MY BLACK PEPPER PORK BUNS ON DAY ONE.
SHUV SHUV
C'MON, TAKE SOME! DON'T BE SHY.
BUT I DON'T WANT ANY!
MAN, I'M SO GLAD I WAS SMART ENOUGH TO GET HER TO OWE ME ONE!
UUUH...
IT LOOKED MORE LIKE YOU FORCED THEM ON HER TO ME...
...?
HM? WHAT'S WITH ALL THE FUSS GOING ON OVER THERE?
IF I'M RIGHT...
...THAT'S THE DIRECTION OF NAKIRI'S BOOTH.
THAT NIGHT...
...THE TWO OF US WOULD MEET ANOTHER IN-CREDIBLE CHEF.
ONE WE WOULD NEVER FORGET FOR THE REST OF OUR LIVES.

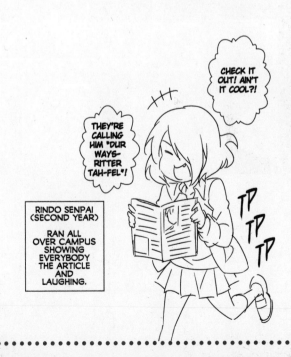

CHECK IT OUT! AIN'T IT COOL?!

THEY'RE CALLING HIM "DUR WAYS-RITTER TAH-FEL"!

RINDO SENPAI (SECOND YEAR)

RAN ALL OVER CAMPUS SHOWING EVERYBODY THE ARTICLE AND LAUGHING.

TP TP TP

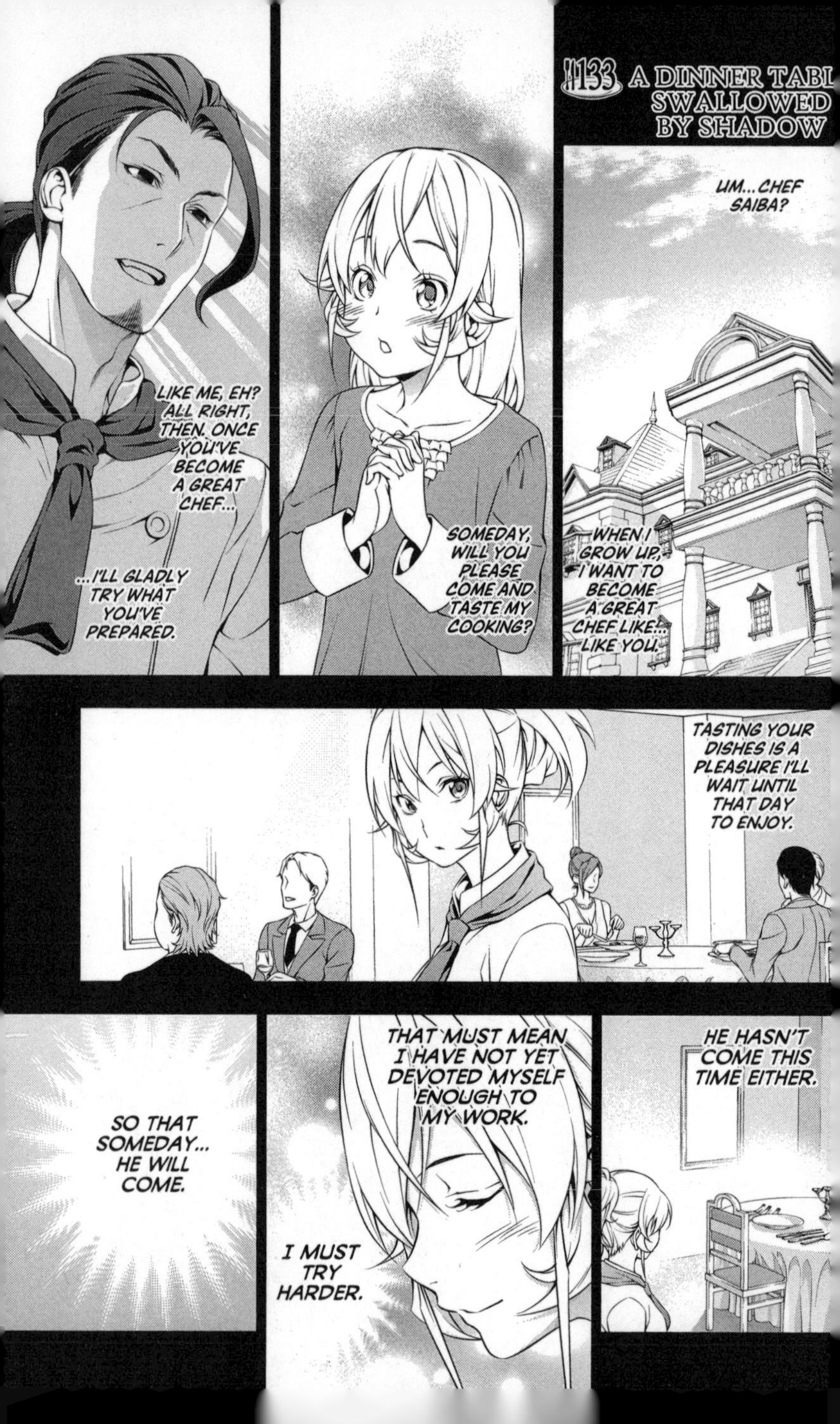
#133 A DINNER TABL SWALLOWED BY SHADOW
UM... CHEF SAIBA?
WHEN I GROW UP, I WANT TO BECOME A GREAT CHEF LIKE... LIKE YOU.
SOMEDAY, WILL YOU PLEASE COME AND TASTE MY COOKING?
LIKE ME, EH? ALL RIGHT, THEN. ONCE YOU'VE BECOME A GREAT CHEF...
...I'LL GLADLY TRY WHAT YOU'VE PREPARED.
TASTING YOUR DISHES IS A PLEASURE I'LL WAIT UNTIL THAT DAY TO ENJOY.
HE HASN'T COME THIS TIME EITHER.
THAT MUST MEAN I HAVE NOT YET DEVOTED MYSELF ENOUGH TO MY WORK.
I MUST TRY HARDER.
SO THAT SOMEDAY... HE WILL COME.

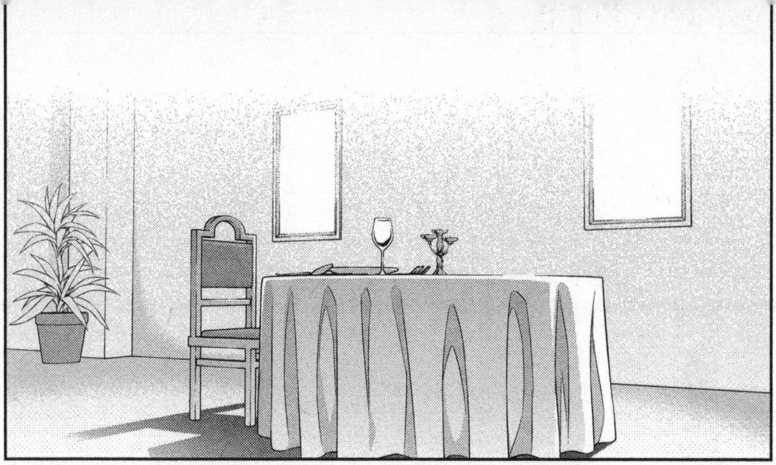
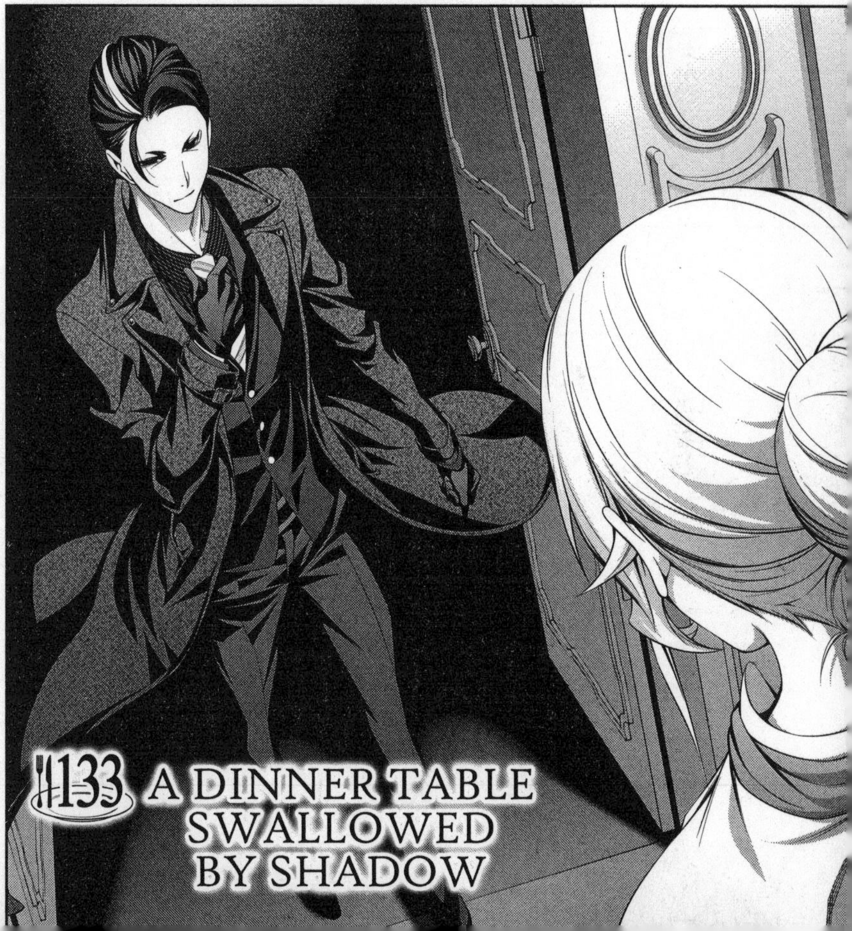
133 A DINNER TABLE SWALLOWED BY SHADOW

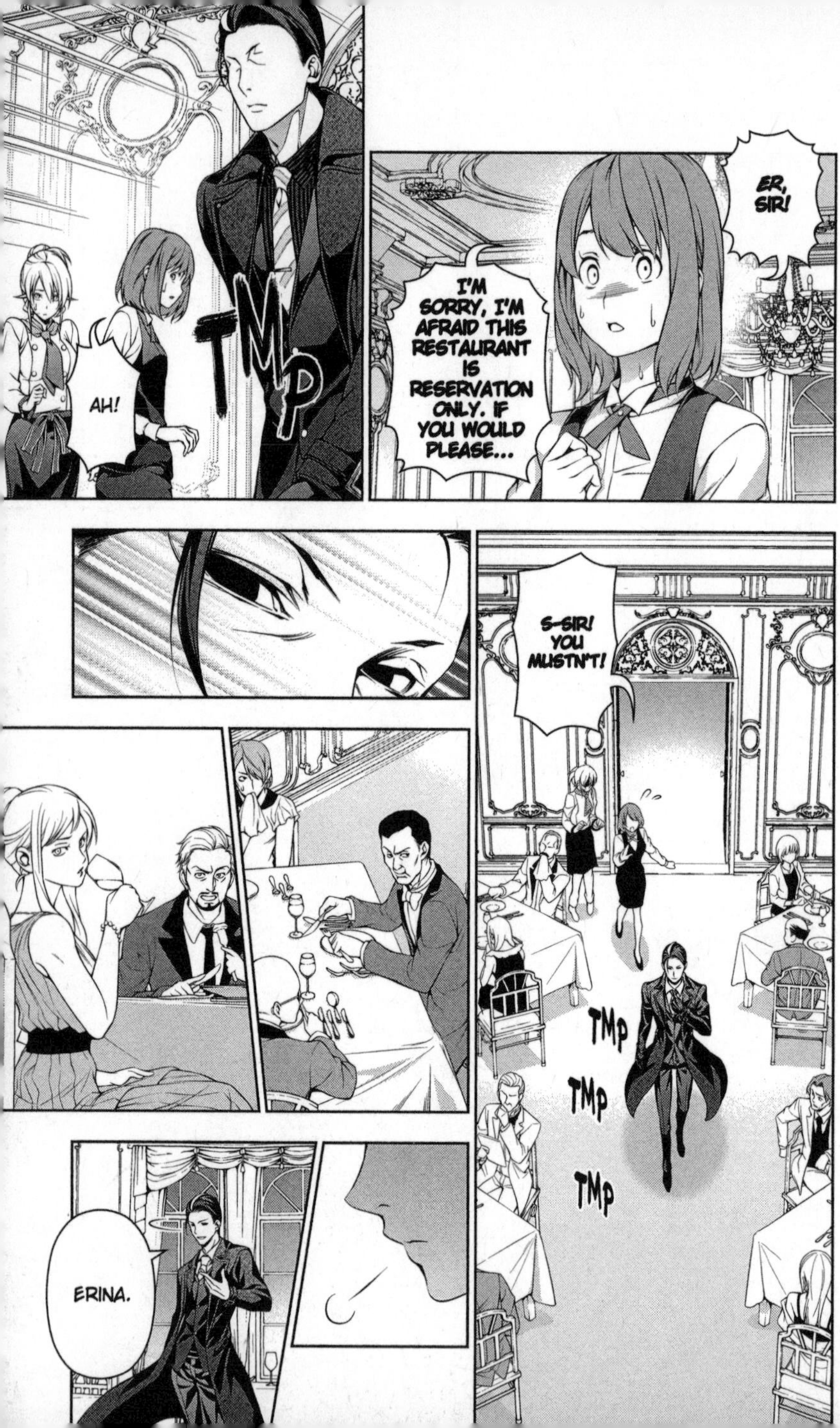
ER, SIR!
I'M SORRY, I'M AFRAID THIS RESTAURANT IS RESERVATION ONLY. IF YOU WOULD PLEASE...
TMP
AH!
S-SIR! YOU MUSTN'T!
TMP
TMP
TMP
ERINA.

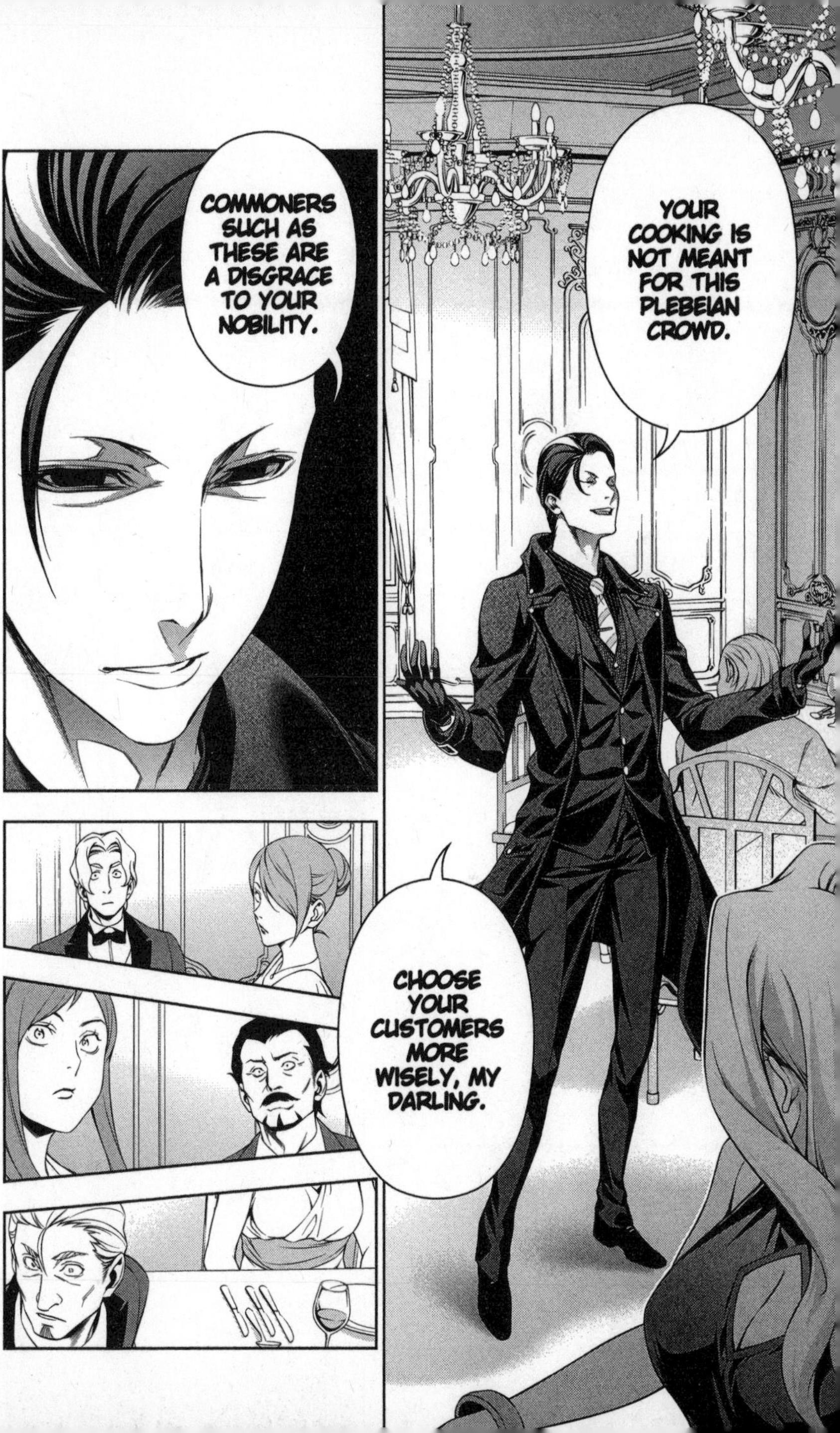
YOUR COOKING IS NOT MEANT FOR THIS PLEBEIAN CROWD.
CHOOSE YOUR CUSTOMERS MORE WISELY, MY DARLING.
COMMONERS SUCH AS THESE ARE A DISGRACE TO YOUR NOBILITY.

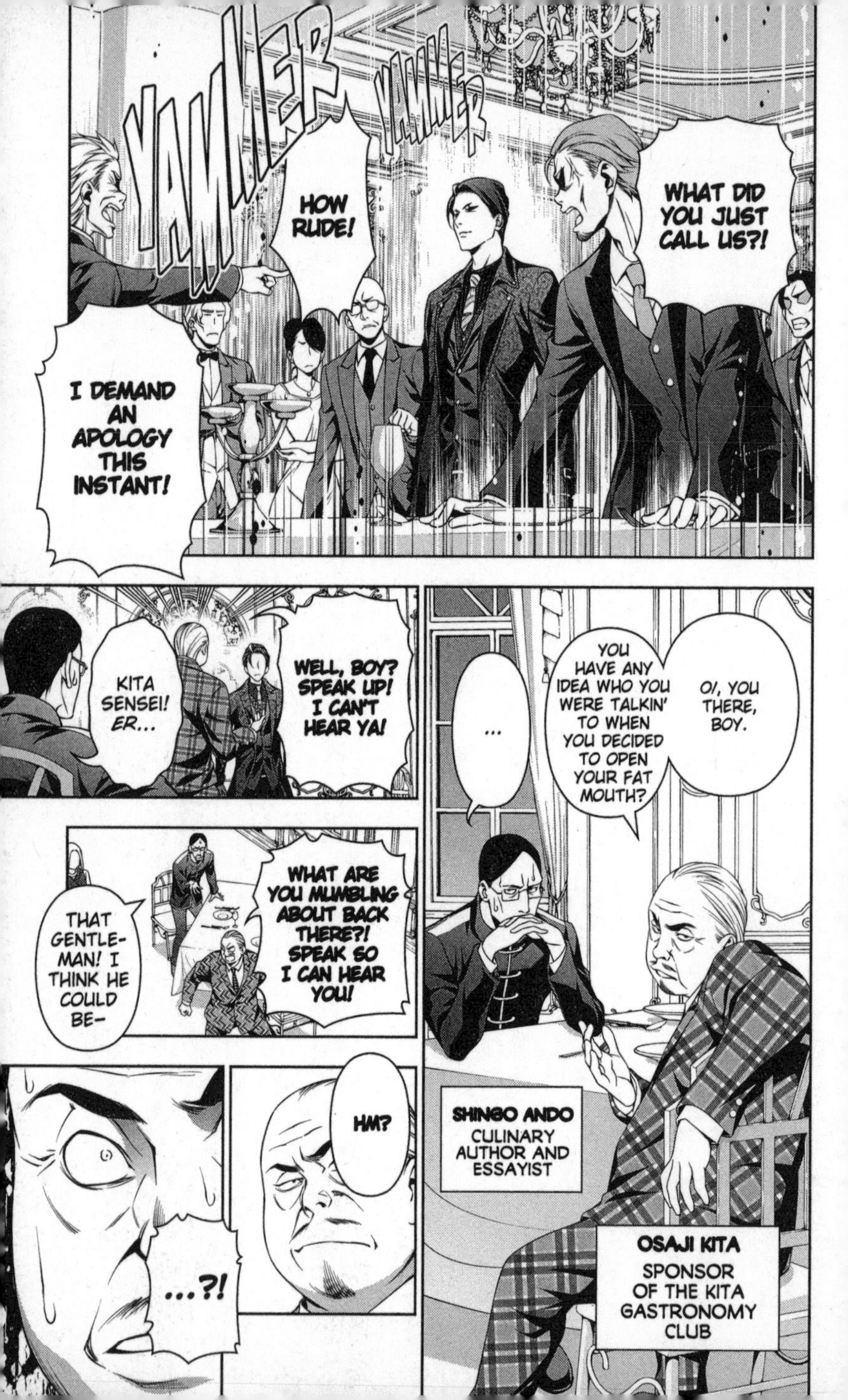
WHAT DID YOU JUST CALL US?!
YAMMER
YAMMER
HOW RUDE!
I DEMAND AN APOLOGY THIS INSTANT!
OI, YOU THERE, BOY.
YOU HAVE ANY IDEA WHO YOU WERE TALKIN' TO WHEN YOU DECIDED TO OPEN YOUR FAT MOUTH?
...
SHINGO ANDO
CULINARY AUTHOR AND ESSAYIST
OSAJI KITA
SPONSOR OF THE KITA GASTRONOMY CLUB
WELL, BOY? SPEAK UP! I CAN'T HEAR YA!
KITA SENSEI! ER...
WHAT ARE YOU MUMBLING ABOUT BACK THERE?! SPEAK SO I CAN HEAR YOU!
THAT GENTLEMAN! I THINK HE COULD BE-
HM?
...?!

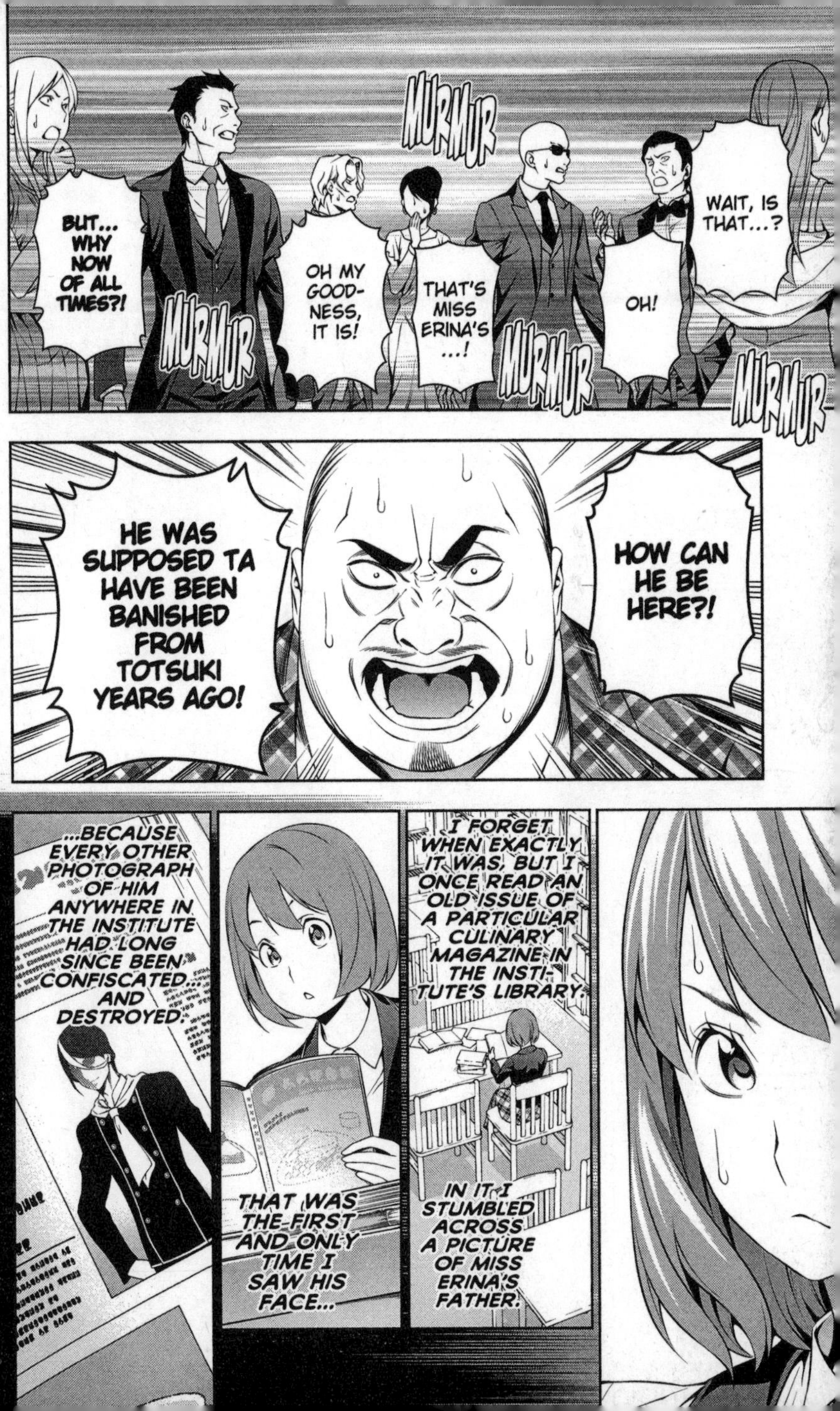
WAIT, IS THAT...?
MURMUR
OH!
MURMUR
THAT'S MISS ERINA'S ...!
MURMUR
OH MY GOODNESS, IT IS!
MURMUR
BUT... WHY NOW OF ALL TIMES?!
HOW CAN HE BE HERE?!
HE WAS SUPPOSED TA HAVE BEEN BANISHED FROM TOTSUKI YEARS AGO!
I FORGET WHEN EXACTLY IT WAS, BUT I ONCE READ AN OLD ISSUE OF A PARTICULAR CULINARY MAGAZINE IN THE INSTITUTE'S LIBRARY.
IN IT I STUMBLED ACROSS A PICTURE OF MISS ERINA'S FATHER.
THAT WAS THE FIRST AND ONLY TIME I SAW HIS FACE...
...BECAUSE EVERY OTHER PHOTOGRAPH OF HIM ANYWHERE IN THE INSTITUTE HAD LONG SINCE BEEN CONFISCATED... AND DESTROYED.

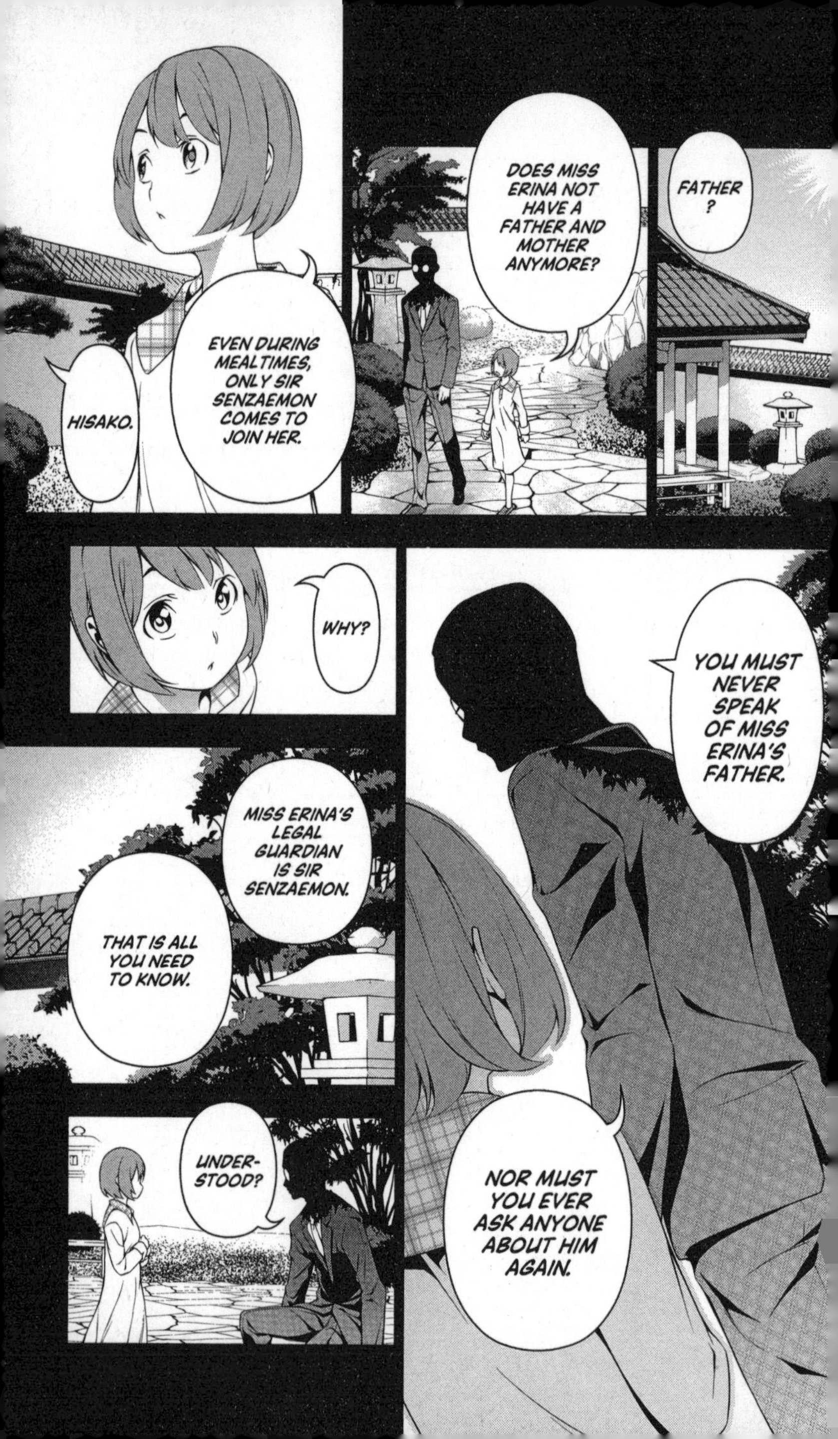
FATHER?
DOES MISS ERINA NOT HAVE A FATHER AND MOTHER ANYMORE?
EVEN DURING MEALTIMES, ONLY SIR SENZAEMON COMES TO JOIN HER.
HISAKO.
YOU MUST NEVER SPEAK OF MISS ERINA'S FATHER.
NOR MUST YOU EVER ASK ANYONE ABOUT HIM AGAIN.
WHY?
MISS ERINA'S LEGAL GUARDIAN IS SIR SENZAEMON.
THAT IS ALL YOU NEED TO KNOW.
UNDER-STOOD?

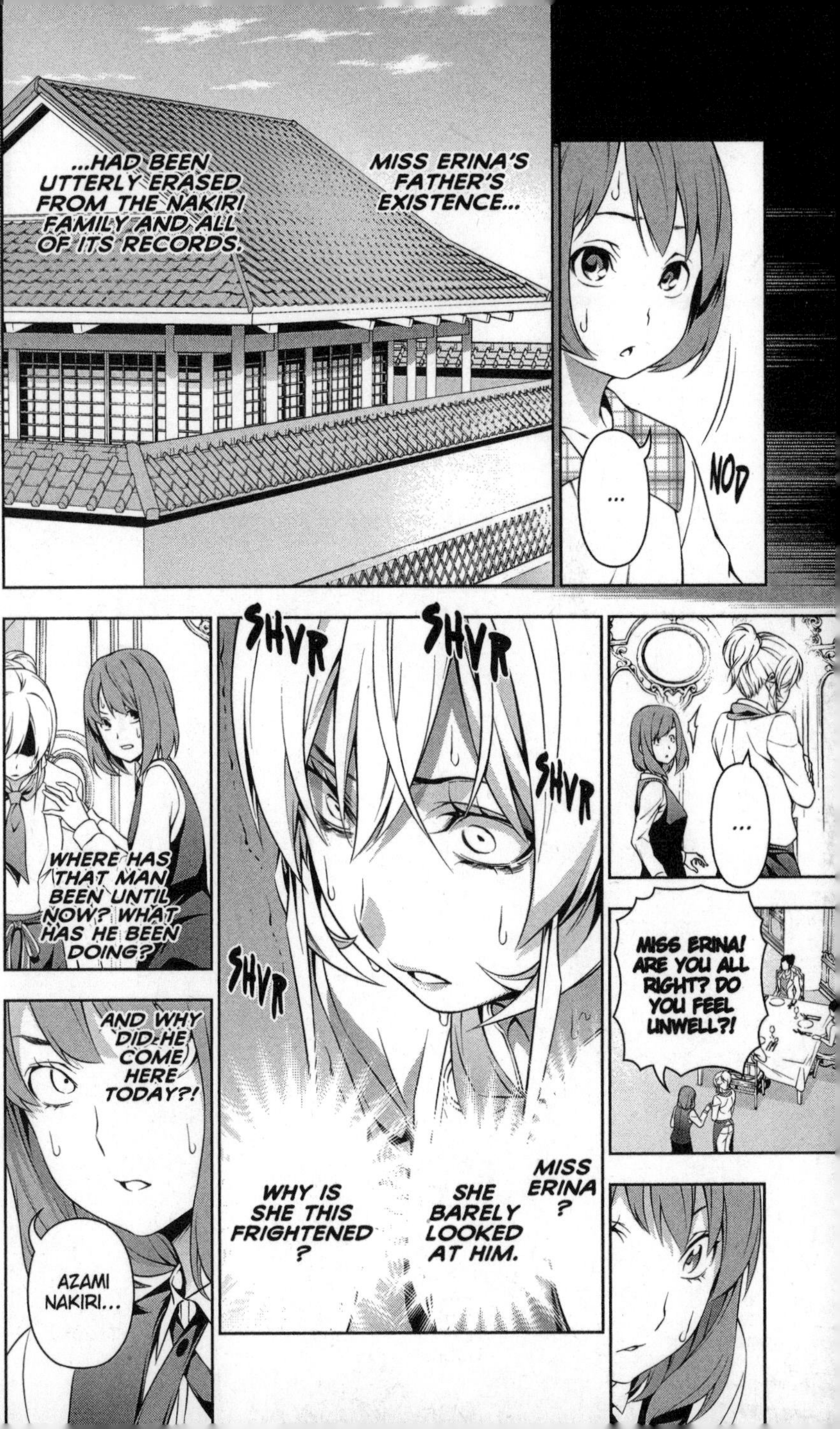
...
NOD
MISS ERINA'S FATHER'S EXISTENCE...
...HAD BEEN UTTERLY ERASED FROM THE NAKIRI FAMILY AND ALL OF ITS RECORDS.
...
MISS ERINA! ARE YOU ALL RIGHT? DO YOU FEEL UNWELL?!
SHVR
SHVR
SHVR
SHVR
MISS ERINA?
SHE BARELY LOOKED AT HIM.
WHY IS SHE THIS FRIGHTENED?
WHERE HAS THAT MAN BEEN UNTIL NOW? WHAT HAS HE BEEN DOING?
AND WHY DID HE COME HERE TODAY?!
AZAMI NAKIRI...

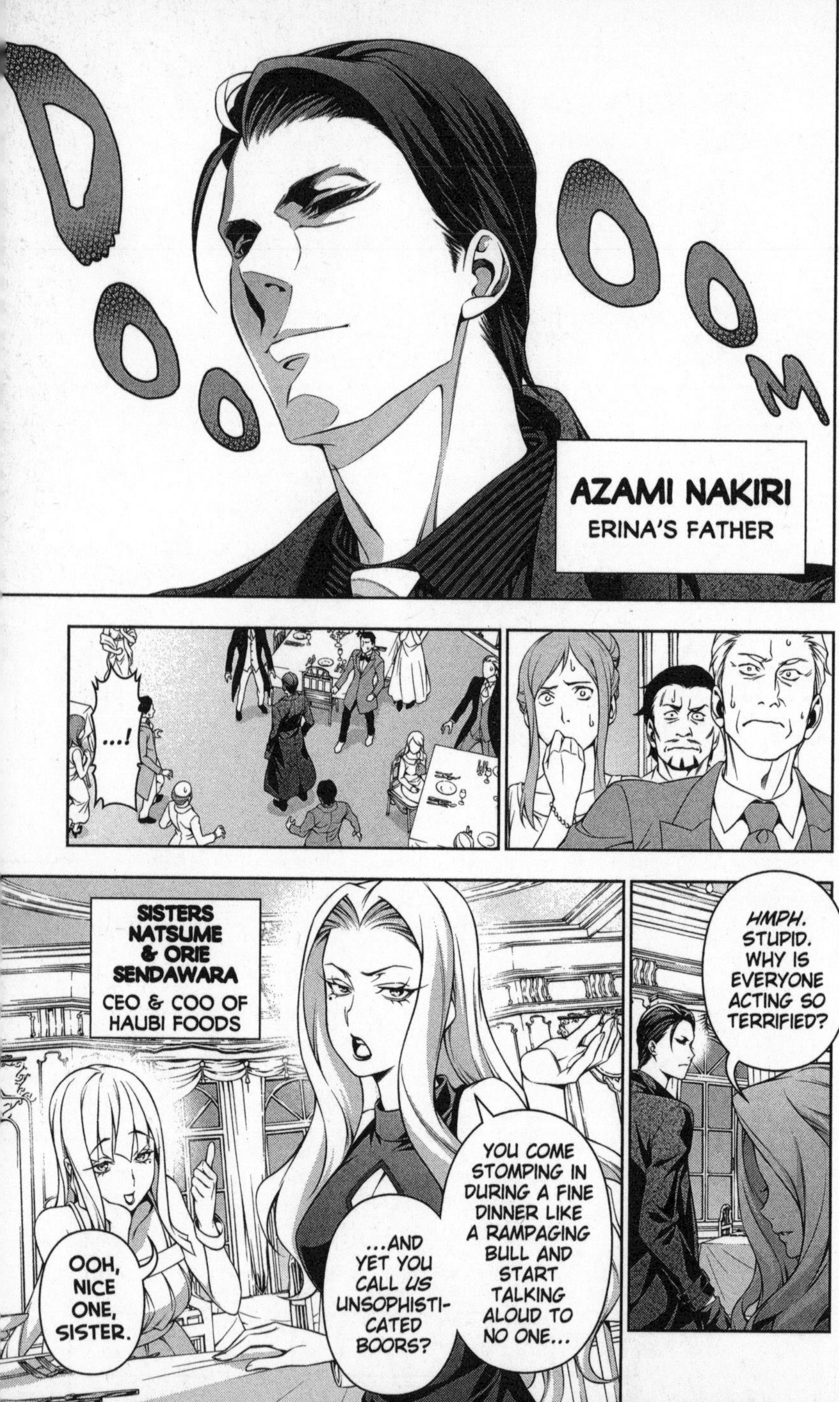
DOOOOOOM
AZAMI NAKIRI
ERINA'S FATHER
...!
HMPH. STUPID. WHY IS EVERYONE ACTING SO TERRIFIED?
SISTERS NATSUME & ORIE SENDAWARA
CEO & COO OF HAUBI FOODS
YOU COME STOMPING IN DURING A FINE DINNER LIKE A RAMPAGING BULL AND START TALKING ALOUD TO NO ONE...
...AND YET YOU CALL *US* UNSOPHISTI-CATED BOORS?
OOH, NICE ONE, SISTER.

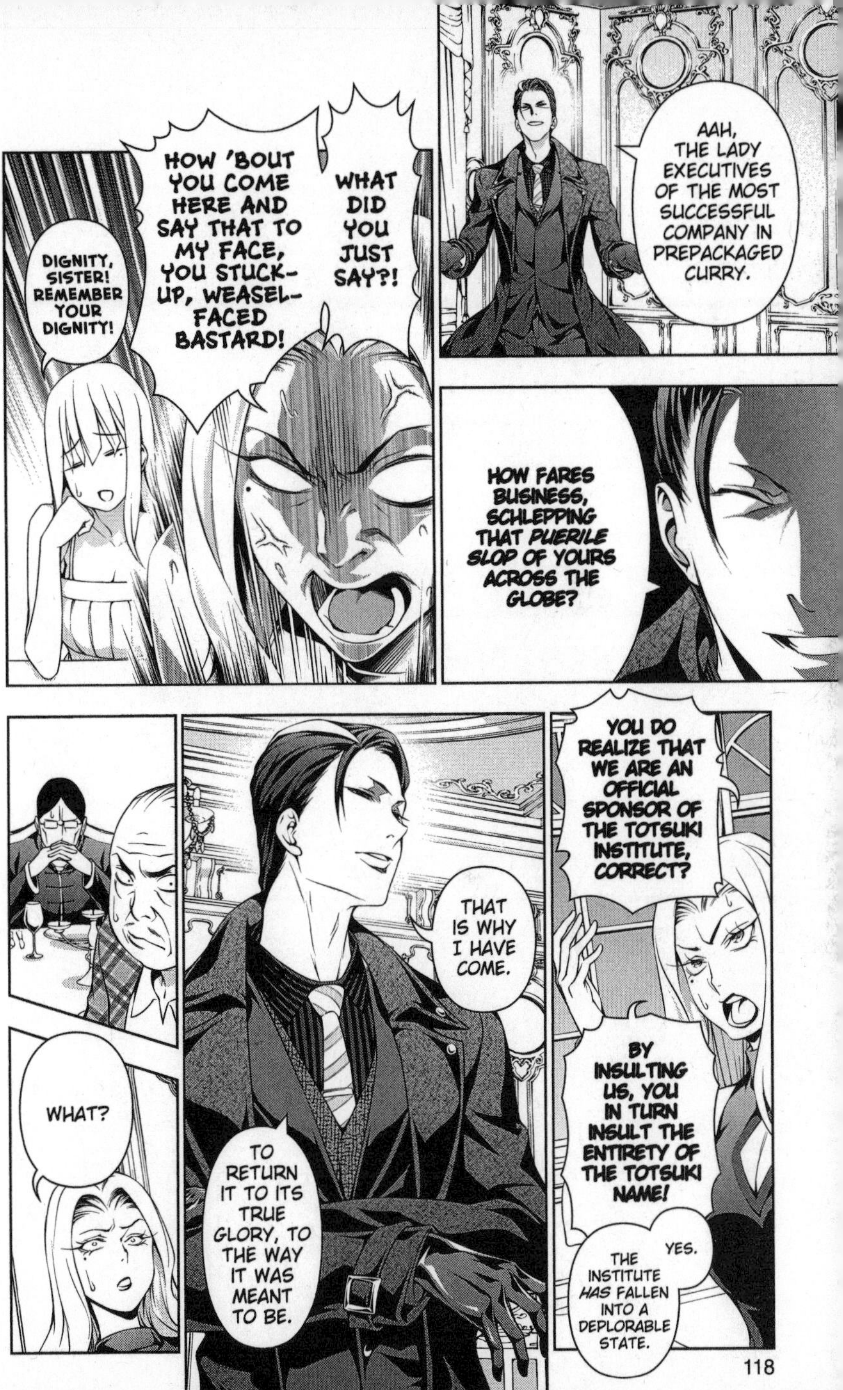
AAH, THE LADY EXECUTIVES OF THE MOST SUCCESSFUL COMPANY IN PREPACKAGED CURRY.
HOW FARES BUSINESS, SCHLEPPING THAT *PUERILE* SLOP OF YOURS ACROSS THE GLOBE?
WHAT DID YOU JUST SAY?!
HOW 'BOUT YOU COME HERE AND SAY THAT TO MY FACE, YOU STUCK-UP, WEASEL-FACED BASTARD!
DIGNITY, SISTER! REMEMBER YOUR DIGNITY!
YOU DO REALIZE THAT WE ARE AN OFFICIAL SPONSOR OF THE TOTSUKI INSTITUTE, CORRECT?
BY INSULTING US, YOU IN TURN INSULT THE ENTIRETY OF THE TOTSUKI NAME!
YES.
THE INSTITUTE *HAS* FALLEN INTO A DEPLORABLE STATE.
THAT IS WHY I HAVE COME.
TO RETURN IT TO ITS TRUE GLORY, TO THE WAY IT WAS MEANT TO BE.
WHAT?

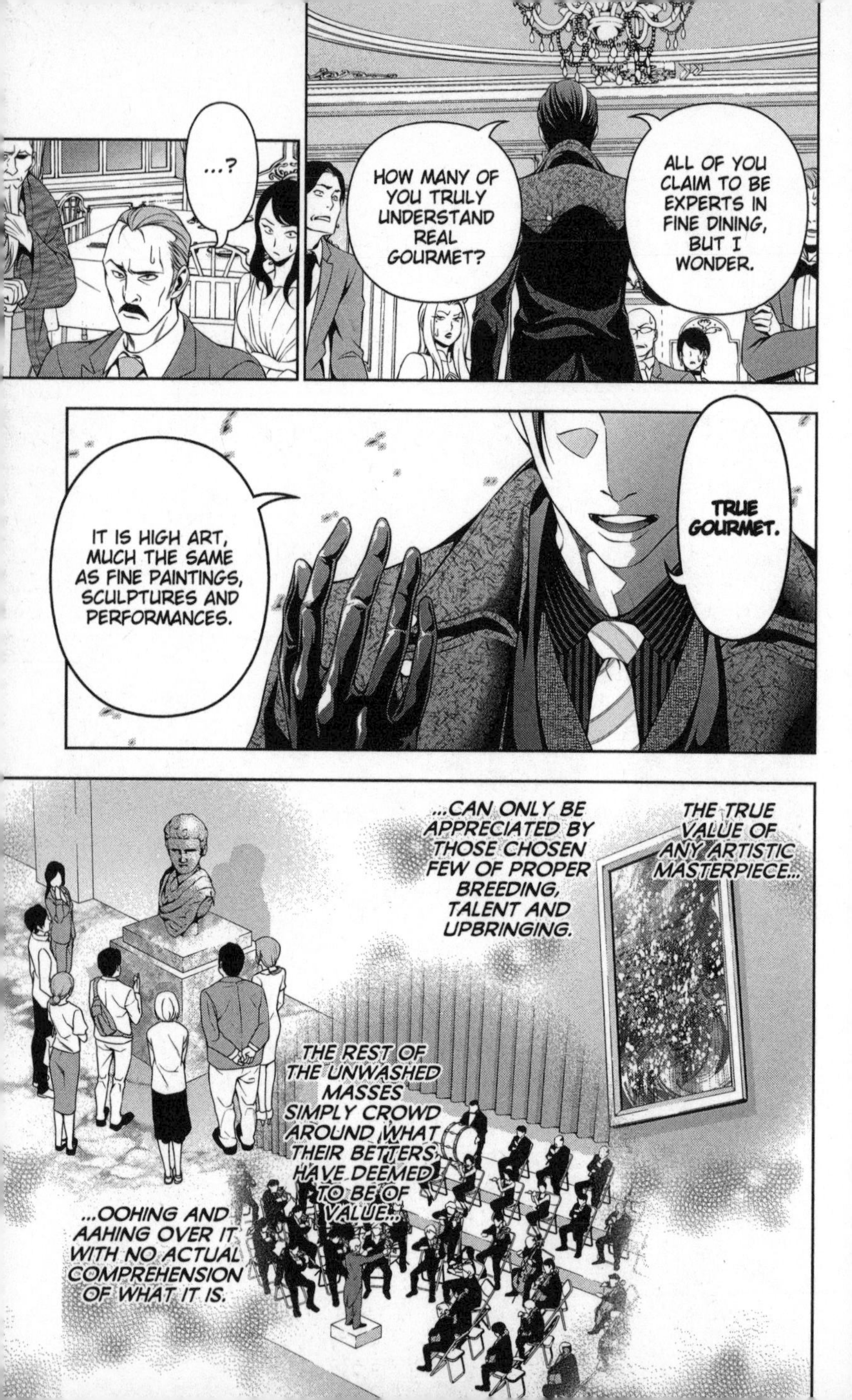
ALL OF YOU CLAIM TO BE EXPERTS IN FINE DINING, BUT I WONDER.
HOW MANY OF YOU TRULY UNDERSTAND REAL GOURMET?
...?
TRUE GOURMET.
IT IS HIGH ART, MUCH THE SAME AS FINE PAINTINGS, SCULPTURES AND PERFORMANCES.
THE TRUE VALUE OF ANY ARTISTIC MASTERPIECE...
...CAN ONLY BE APPRECIATED BY THOSE CHOSEN FEW OF PROPER BREEDING, TALENT AND UPBRINGING.
THE REST OF THE UNWASHED MASSES SIMPLY CROWD AROUND WHAT THEIR BETTERS HAVE DEEMED TO BE OF VALUE...
...OOHING AND AAHING OVER IT WITH NO ACTUAL COMPREHENSION OF WHAT IT IS.

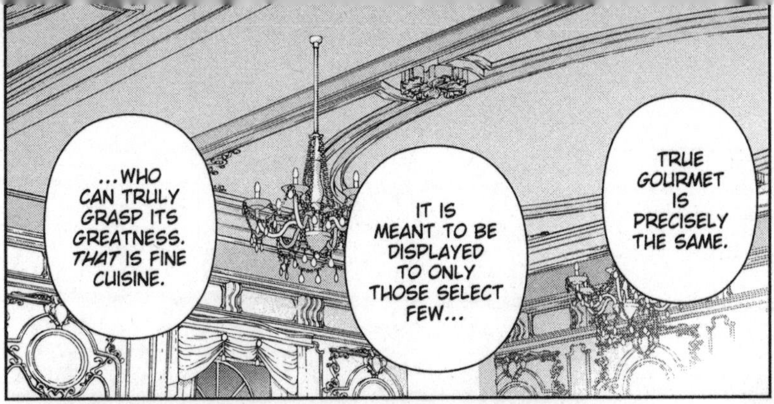
TRUE GOURMET IS PRECISELY THE SAME.
IT IS MEANT TO BE DISPLAYED TO ONLY THOSE SELECT FEW...
...WHO CAN TRULY GRASP ITS GREATNESS. *THAT* IS FINE CUISINE.

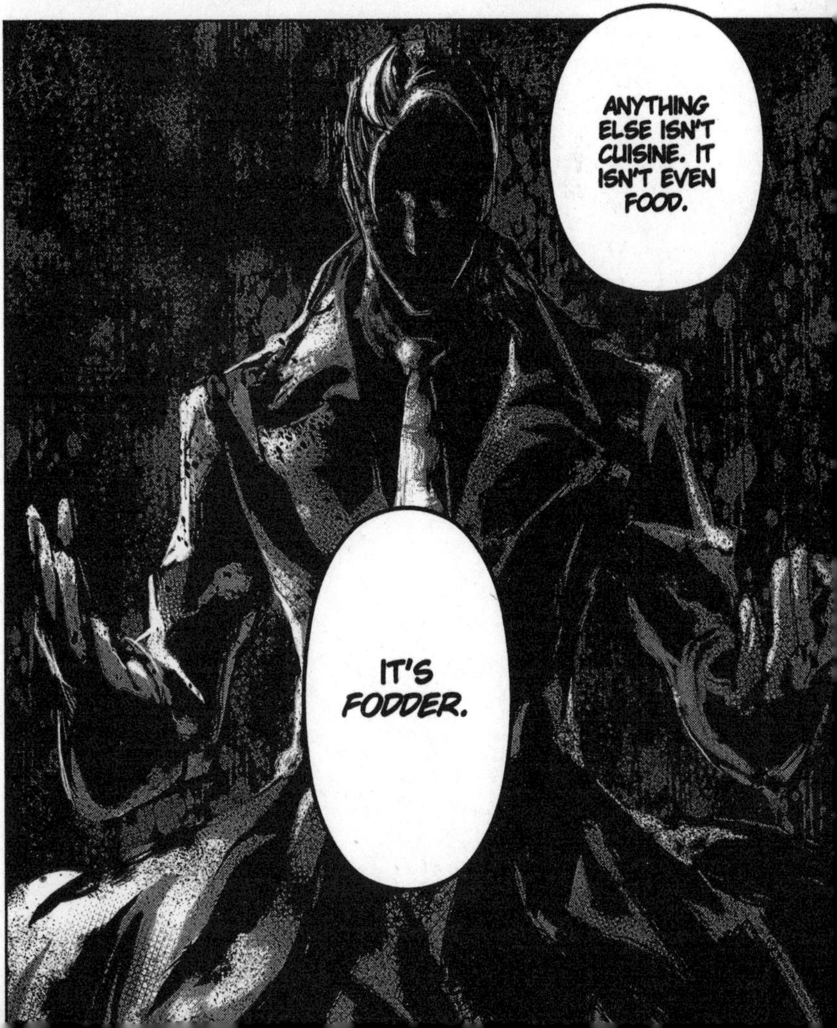
ANYTHING ELSE ISN'T CUISINE. IT ISN'T EVEN FOOD.
IT'S FODDER.

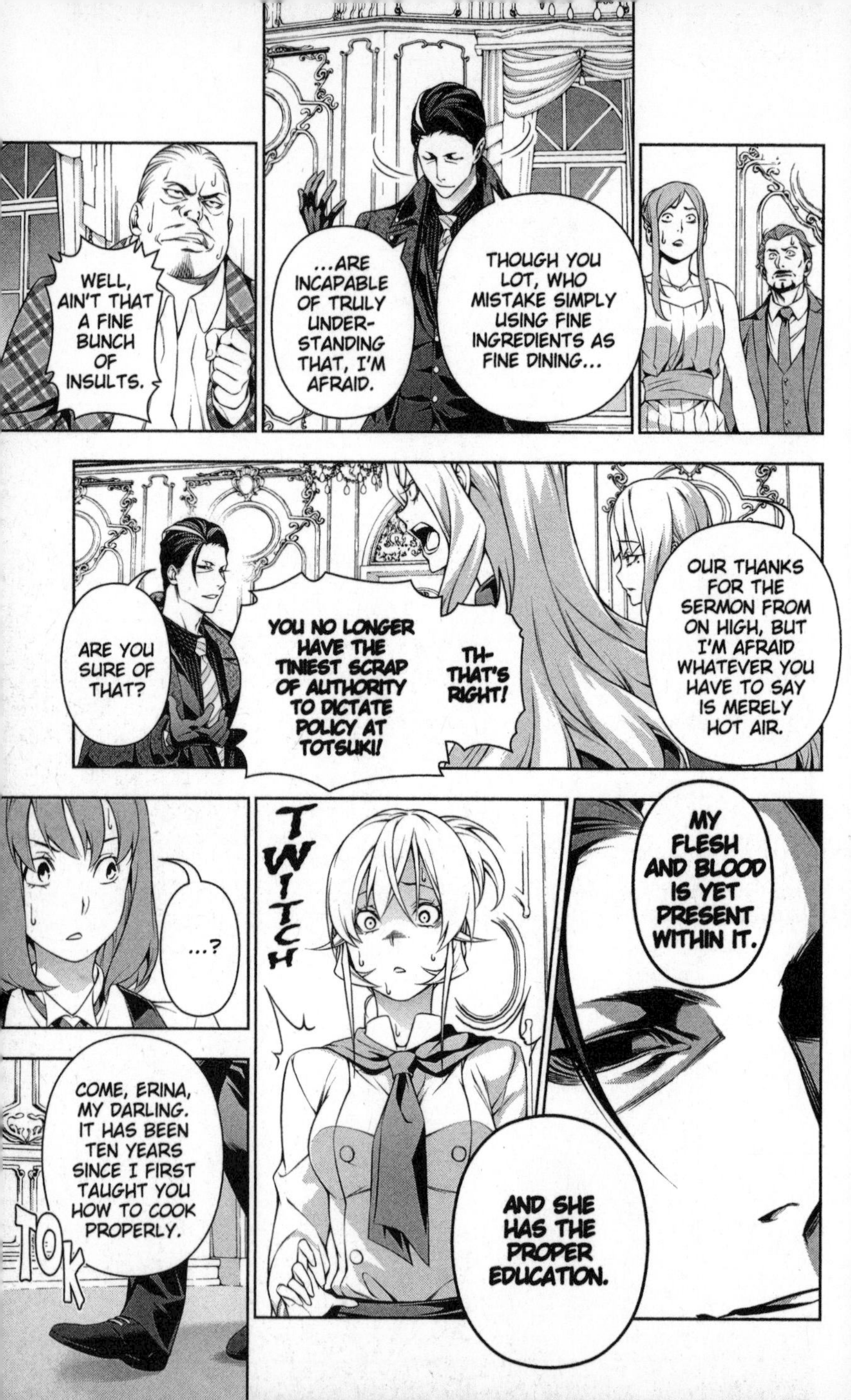
THOUGH YOU LOT, WHO MISTAKE SIMPLY USING FINE INGREDIENTS AS FINE DINING...
...ARE INCAPABLE OF TRULY UNDER-STANDING THAT, I'M AFRAID.
WELL, AIN'T THAT A FINE BUNCH OF INSULTS.
OUR THANKS FOR THE SERMON FROM ON HIGH, BUT I'M AFRAID WHATEVER YOU HAVE TO SAY IS MERELY HOT AIR.
TH-THAT'S RIGHT!
YOU NO LONGER HAVE THE TINIEST SCRAP OF AUTHORITY TO DICTATE POLICY AT TOTSUKI!
ARE YOU SURE OF THAT?
MY FLESH AND BLOOD IS YET PRESENT WITHIN IT.
AND SHE HAS THE PROPER EDUCATION.
TWITCH
...?
COME, ERINA, MY DARLING. IT HAS BEEN TEN YEARS SINCE I FIRST TAUGHT YOU HOW TO COOK PROPERLY.
TOK

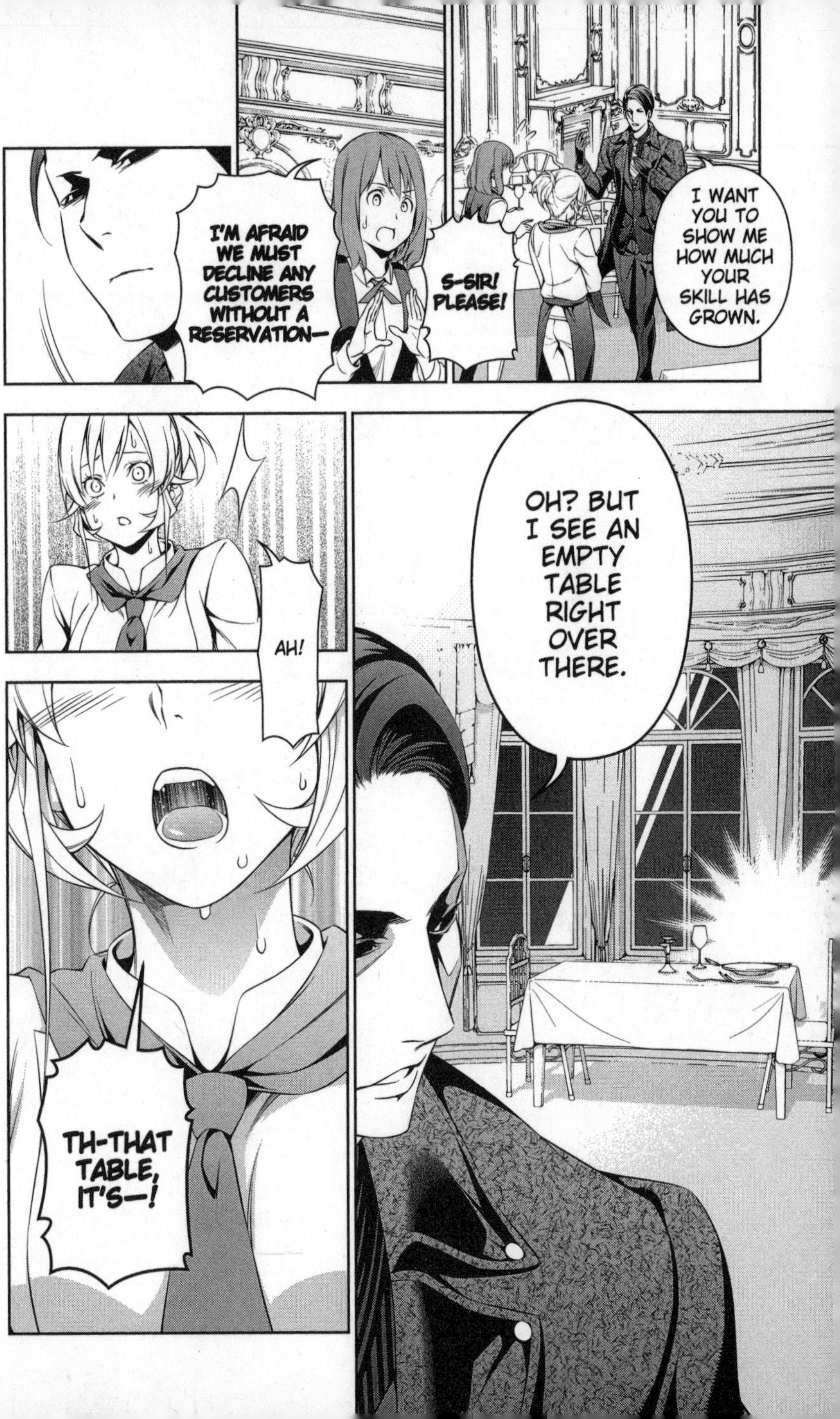
I WANT YOU TO SHOW ME HOW MUCH YOUR SKILL HAS GROWN.
S-SIR! PLEASE!
I'M AFRAID WE MUST DECLINE ANY CUSTOMERS WITHOUT A RESERVATION—
OH? BUT I SEE AN EMPTY TABLE RIGHT OVER THERE.
AH!
TH-THAT TABLE, IT'S—!

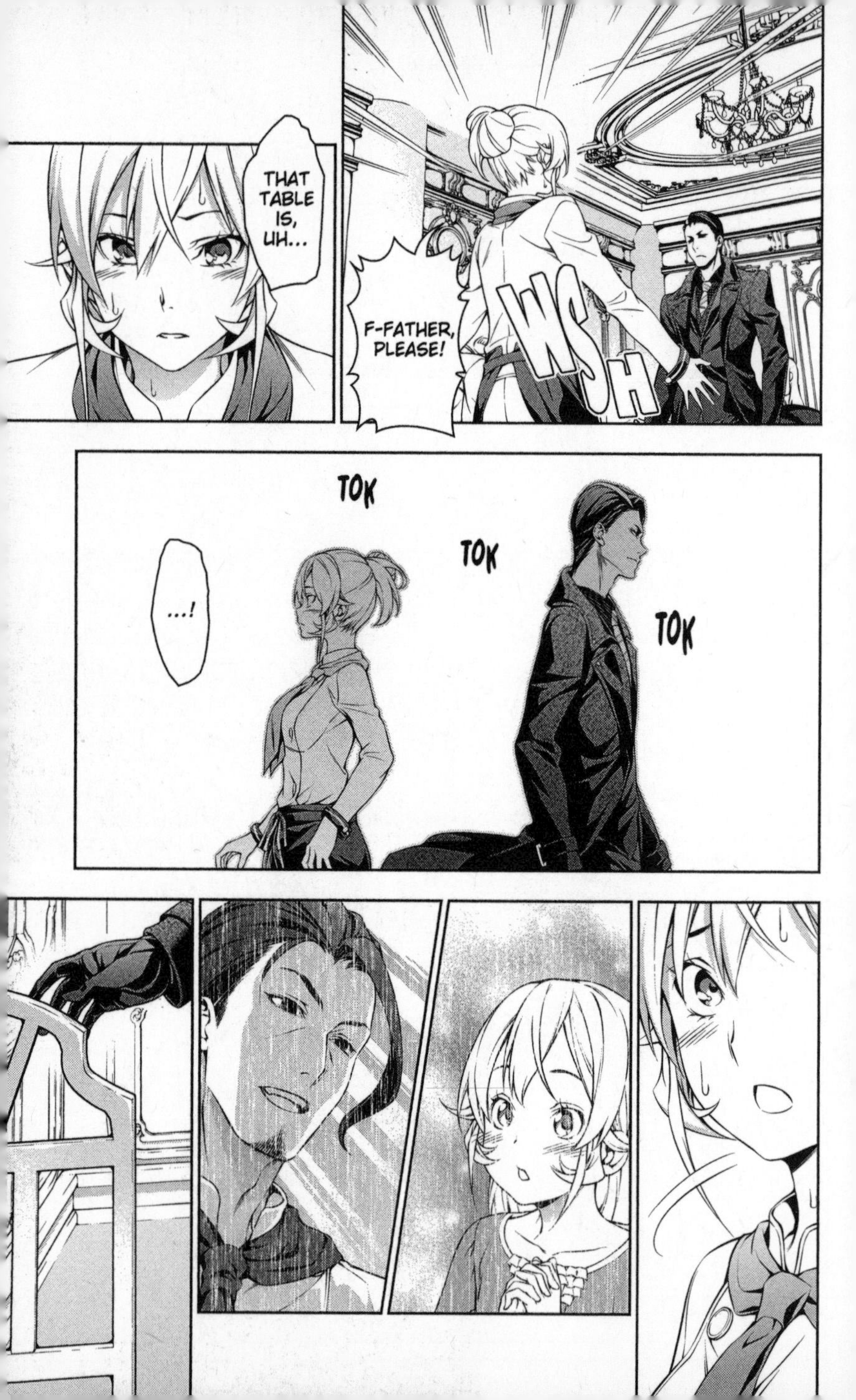
F-FATHER, PLEASE!
WSH
THAT TABLE IS, UH...
TOK
TOK
TOK
...!

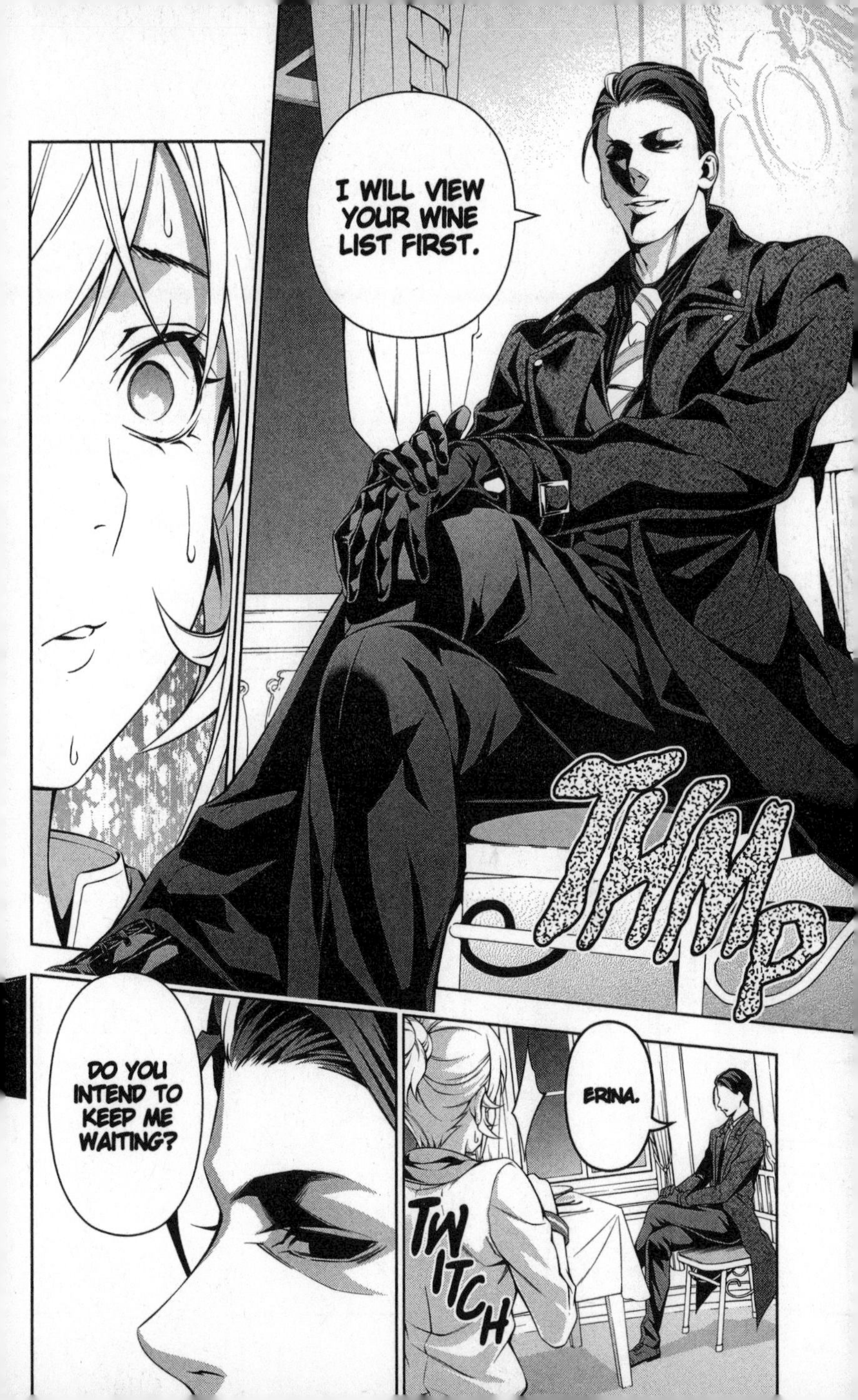
I WILL VIEW YOUR WINE LIST FIRST.
THMP
ERINA.
TWITCH
DO YOU INTEND TO KEEP ME WAITING?

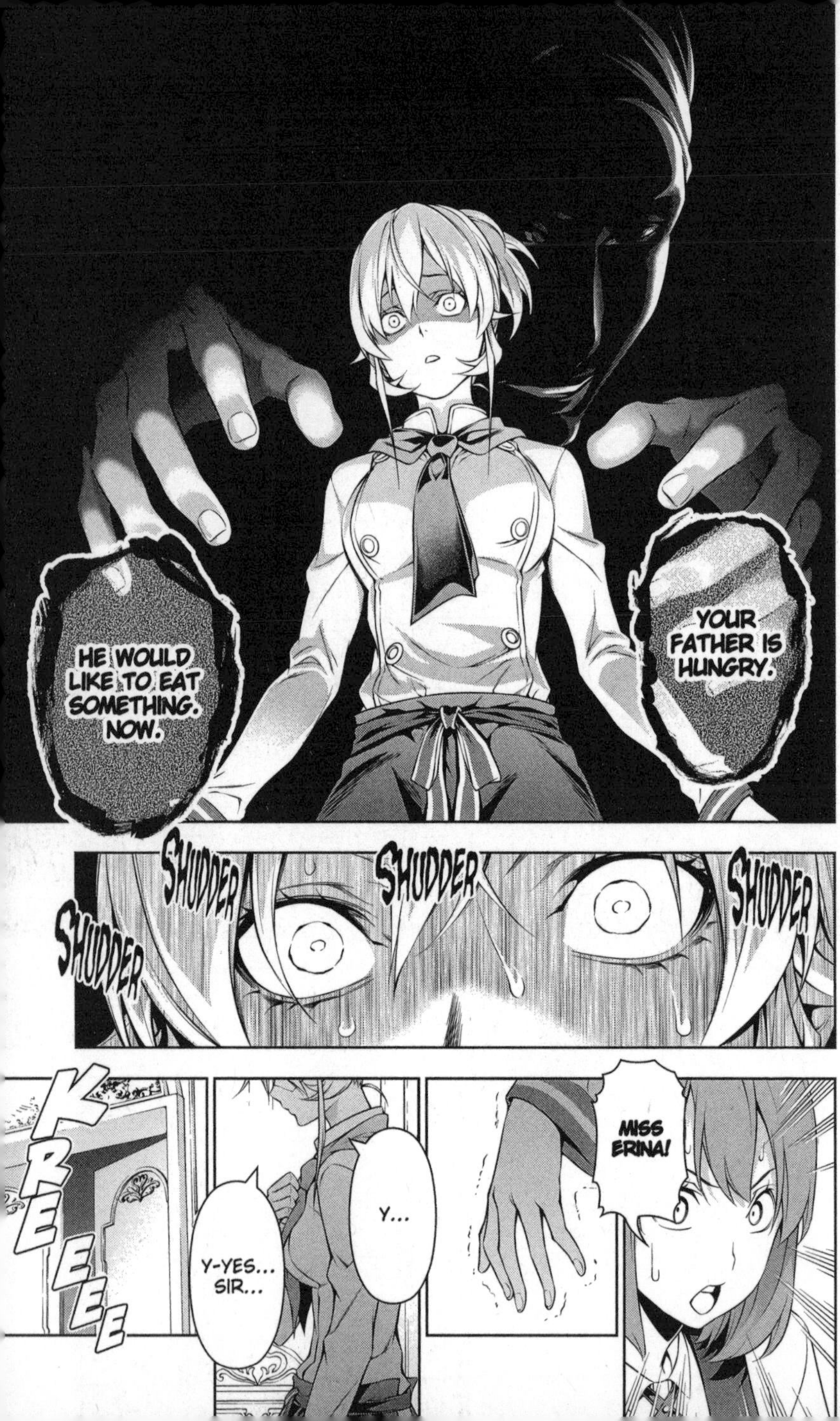
YOUR FATHER IS HUNGRY.
HE WOULD LIKE TO EAT SOMETHING. NOW.
SHUDDER
SHUDDER
SHUDDER
SHUDDER
MISS ERINA!
Y...
Y-YES... SIR...
KREEEE

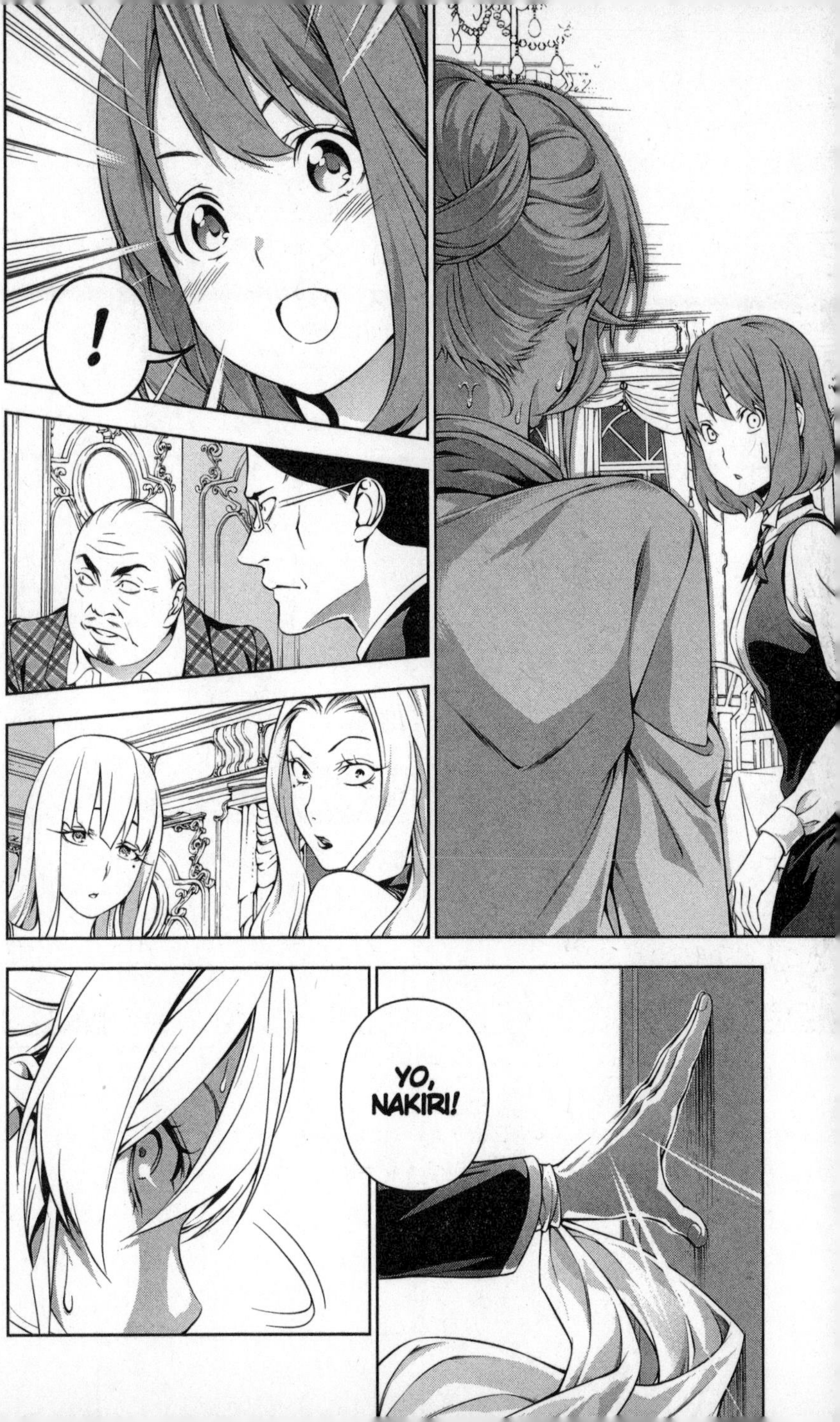
!
YO, NAKIRI!

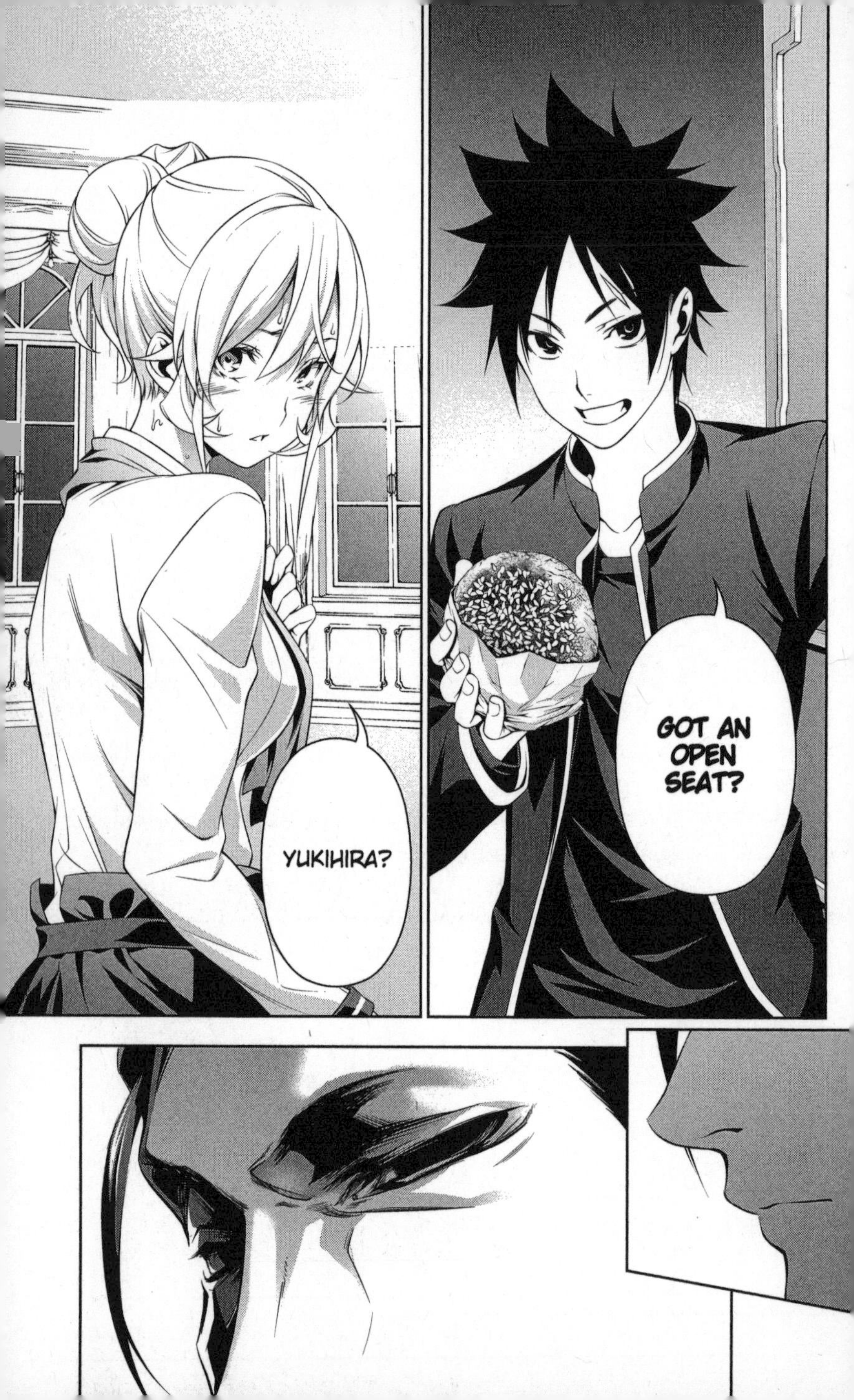
GOT AN OPEN SEAT?
YUKIHIRA?

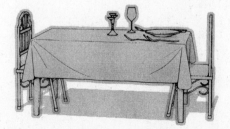

134 BLACK CLOUDS HIDE THE MOON

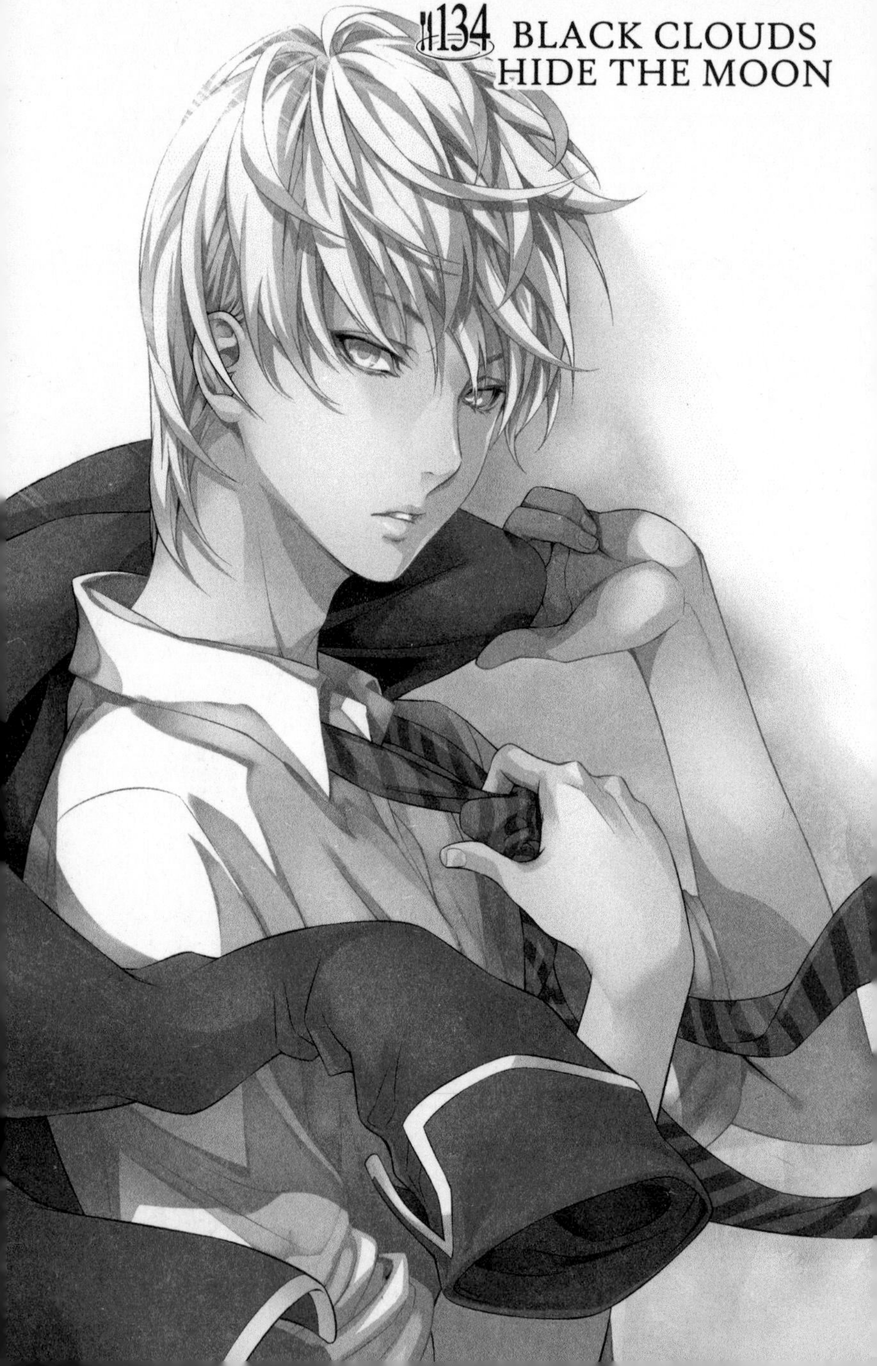

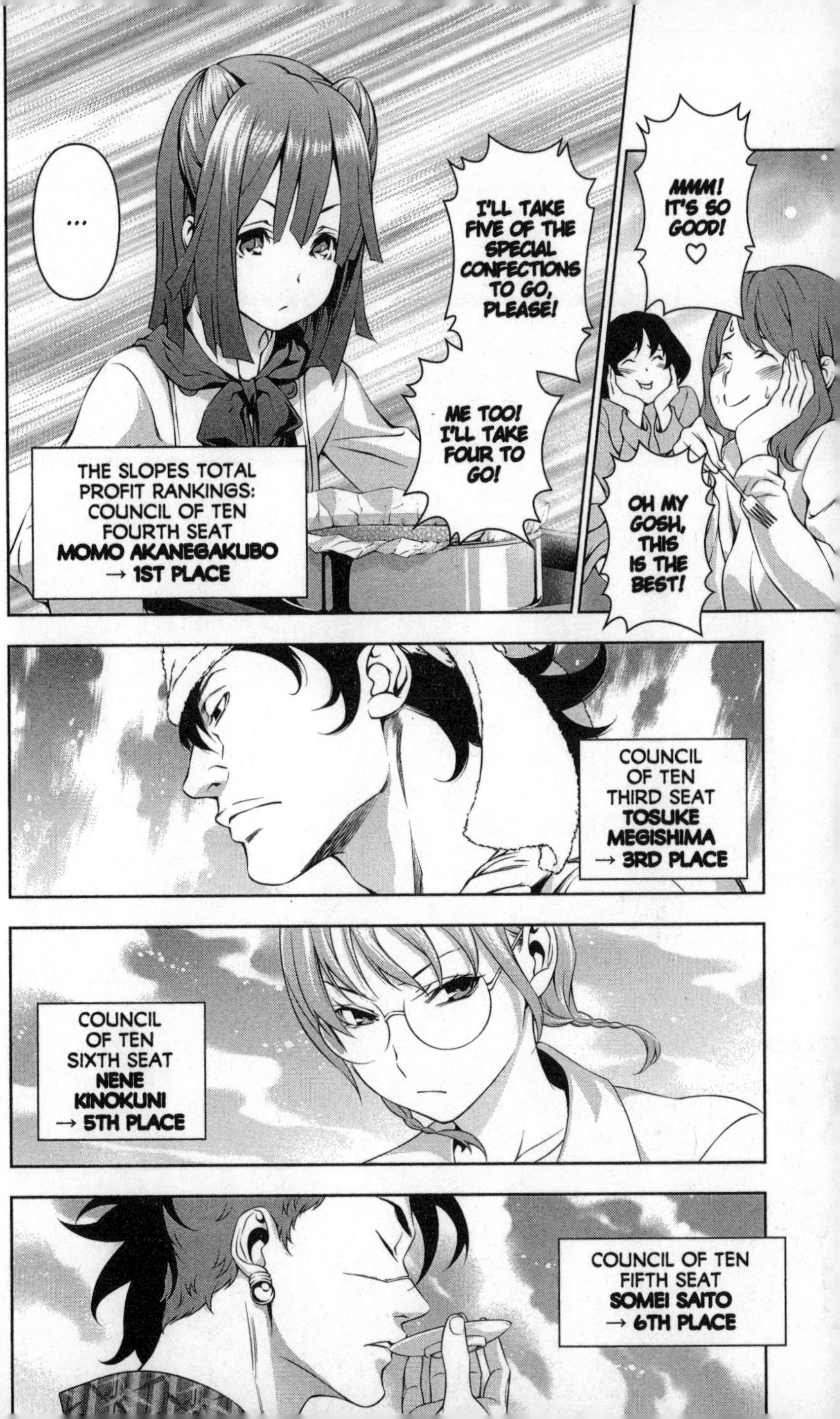
MMM! IT'S SO GOOD! ♡
OH MY GOSH, THIS IS THE BEST!
I'LL TAKE FIVE OF THE SPECIAL CONFECTIONS TO GO, PLEASE!
ME TOO! I'LL TAKE FOUR TO GO!
...
THE SLOPES TOTAL PROFIT RANKINGS: COUNCIL OF TEN FOURTH SEAT MOMO AKANEGAKUBO → 1ST PLACE
COUNCIL OF TEN THIRD SEAT TOSUKE MEGISHIMA → 3RD PLACE
COUNCIL OF TEN SIXTH SEAT NENE KINOKUNI → 5TH PLACE
COUNCIL OF TEN FIFTH SEAT SOMEI SAITO → 6TH PLACE

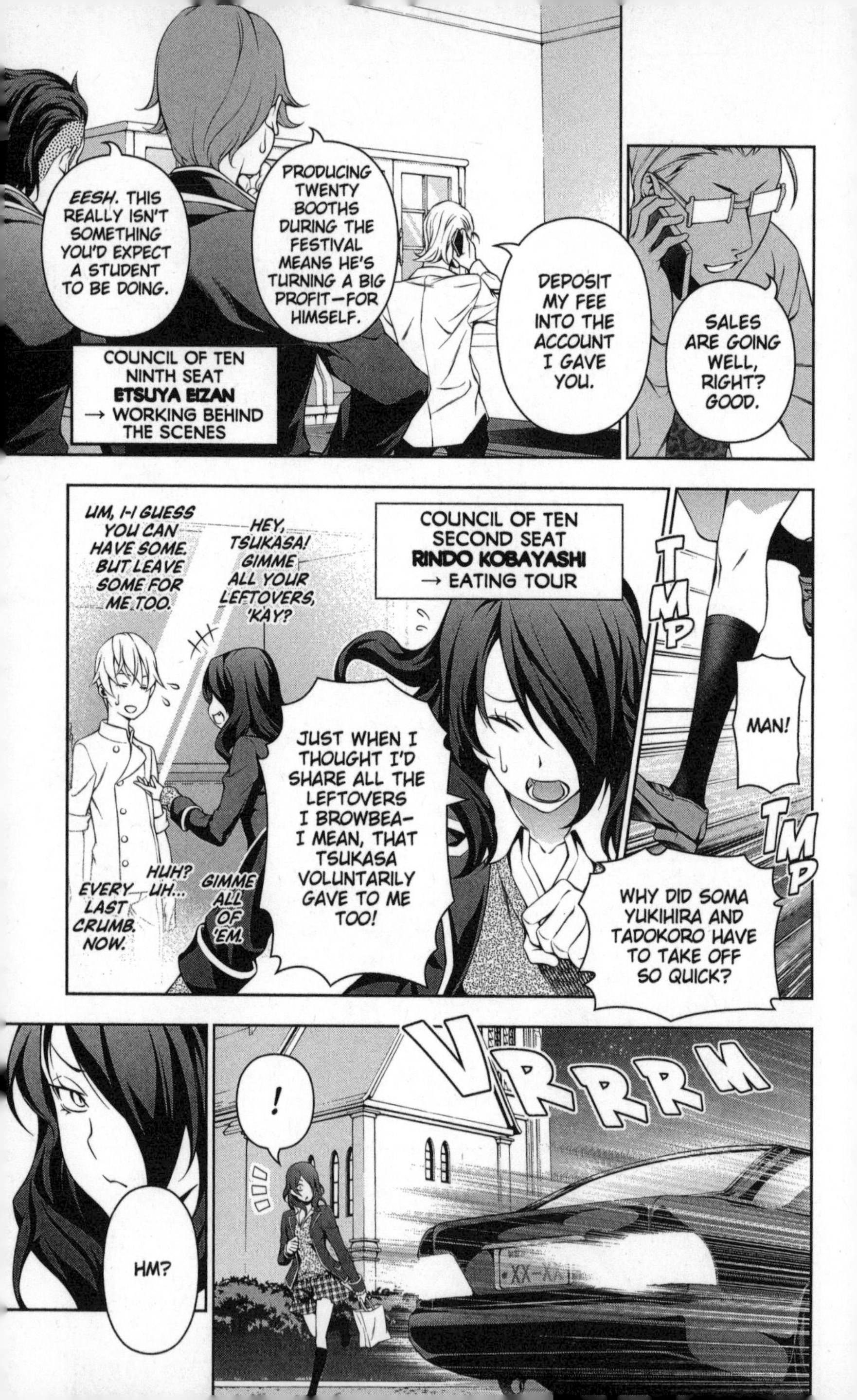
SALES ARE GOING WELL, RIGHT? GOOD.
DEPOSIT MY FEE INTO THE ACCOUNT I GAVE YOU.
PRODUCING TWENTY BOOTHS DURING THE FESTIVAL MEANS HE'S TURNING A BIG PROFIT—FOR HIMSELF.
EESH. THIS REALLY ISN'T SOMETHING YOU'D EXPECT A STUDENT TO BE DOING.
COUNCIL OF TEN NINTH SEAT **ETSUYA EIZAN** → WORKING BEHIND THE SCENES
TMP
MAN!
TMP
WHY DID SOMA YUKIHIRA AND TADOKORO HAVE TO TAKE OFF SO QUICK?
COUNCIL OF TEN SECOND SEAT **RINDO KOBAYASHI** → EATING TOUR
JUST WHEN I THOUGHT I'D SHARE ALL THE LEFTOVERS I BROWBEA- I MEAN, THAT TSUKASA VOLUNTARILY GAVE TO ME TOO!
HEY, TSUKASA! GIMME ALL YOUR LEFTOVERS, 'KAY?
UM, I-I GUESS YOU CAN HAVE SOME. BUT LEAVE SOME FOR ME TOO.
GIMME ALL OF 'EM.
HUH? UH...
EVERY LAST CRUMB. NOW.
VRRRM
!
HM?

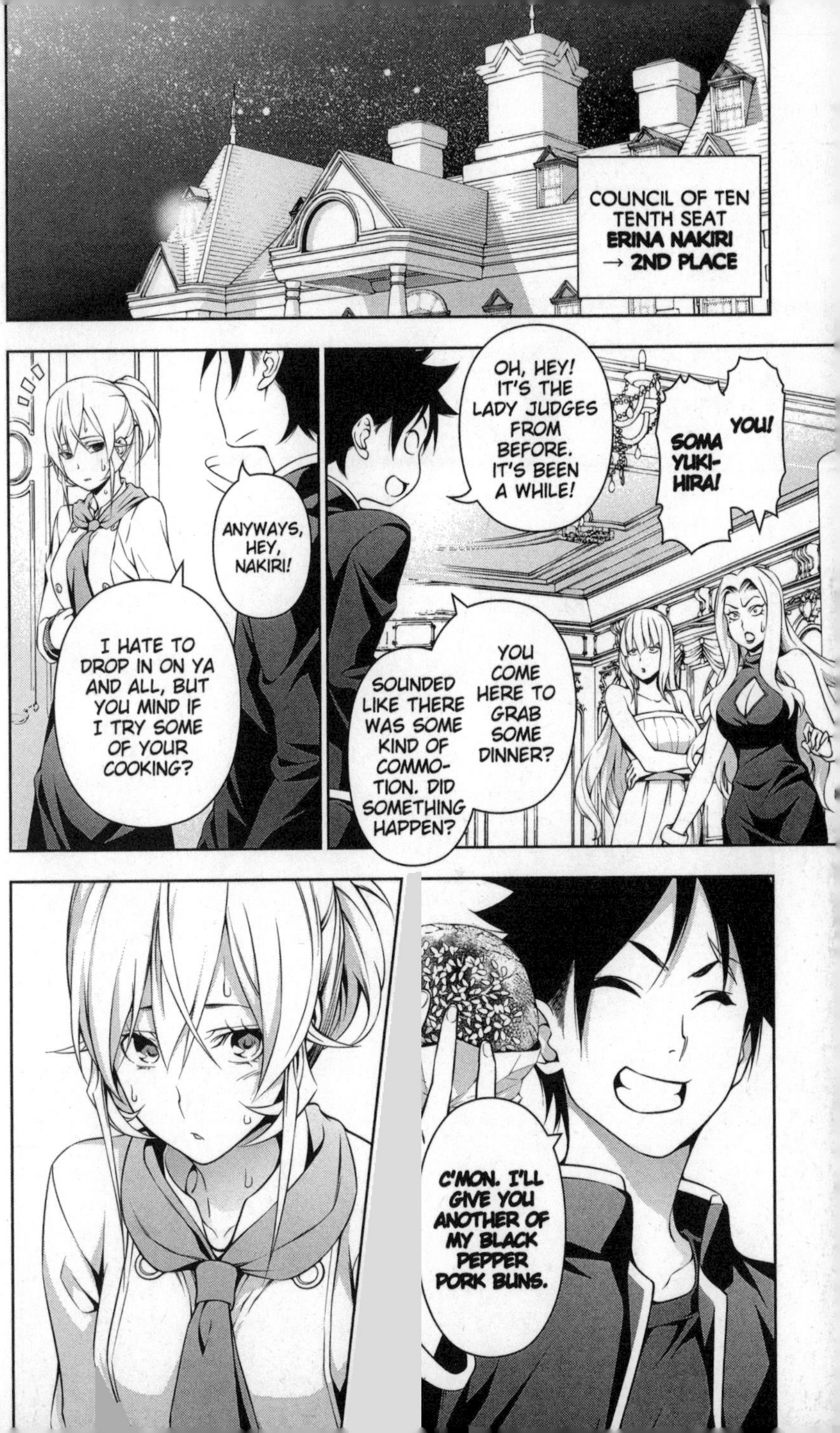
COUNCIL OF TEN TENTH SEAT **ERINA NAKIRI → 2ND PLACE**
YOU!
SOMA YUKIHIRA!
OH, HEY! IT'S THE LADY JUDGES FROM BEFORE. IT'S BEEN A WHILE!
YOU COME HERE TO GRAB SOME DINNER?
SOUNDED LIKE THERE WAS SOME KIND OF COMMOTION. DID SOMETHING HAPPEN?
ANYWAYS, HEY, NAKIRI!
I HATE TO DROP IN ON YA AND ALL, BUT YOU MIND IF I TRY SOME OF YOUR COOKING?
C'MON. I'LL GIVE YOU ANOTHER OF MY BLACK PEPPER PORK BUNS.

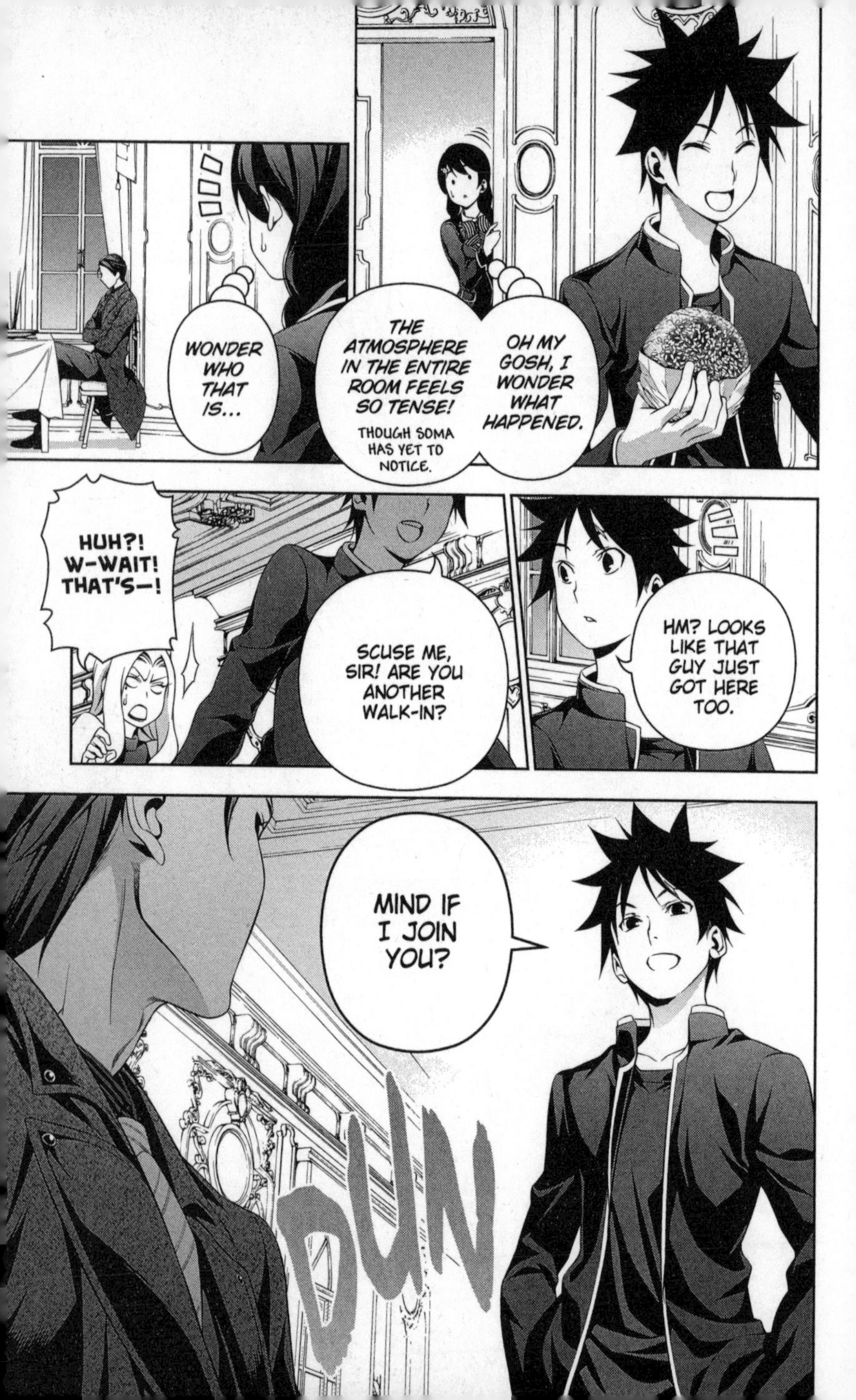
OH MY GOSH, I WONDER WHAT HAPPENED.
THE ATMOSPHERE IN THE ENTIRE ROOM FEELS SO TENSE!
THOUGH SOMA HAS YET TO NOTICE.
WONDER WHO THAT IS...
HM? LOOKS LIKE THAT GUY JUST GOT HERE TOO.
SCUSE ME, SIR! ARE YOU ANOTHER WALK-IN?
HUH?! W-WAIT! THAT'S—!
MIND IF I JOIN YOU?
DUN

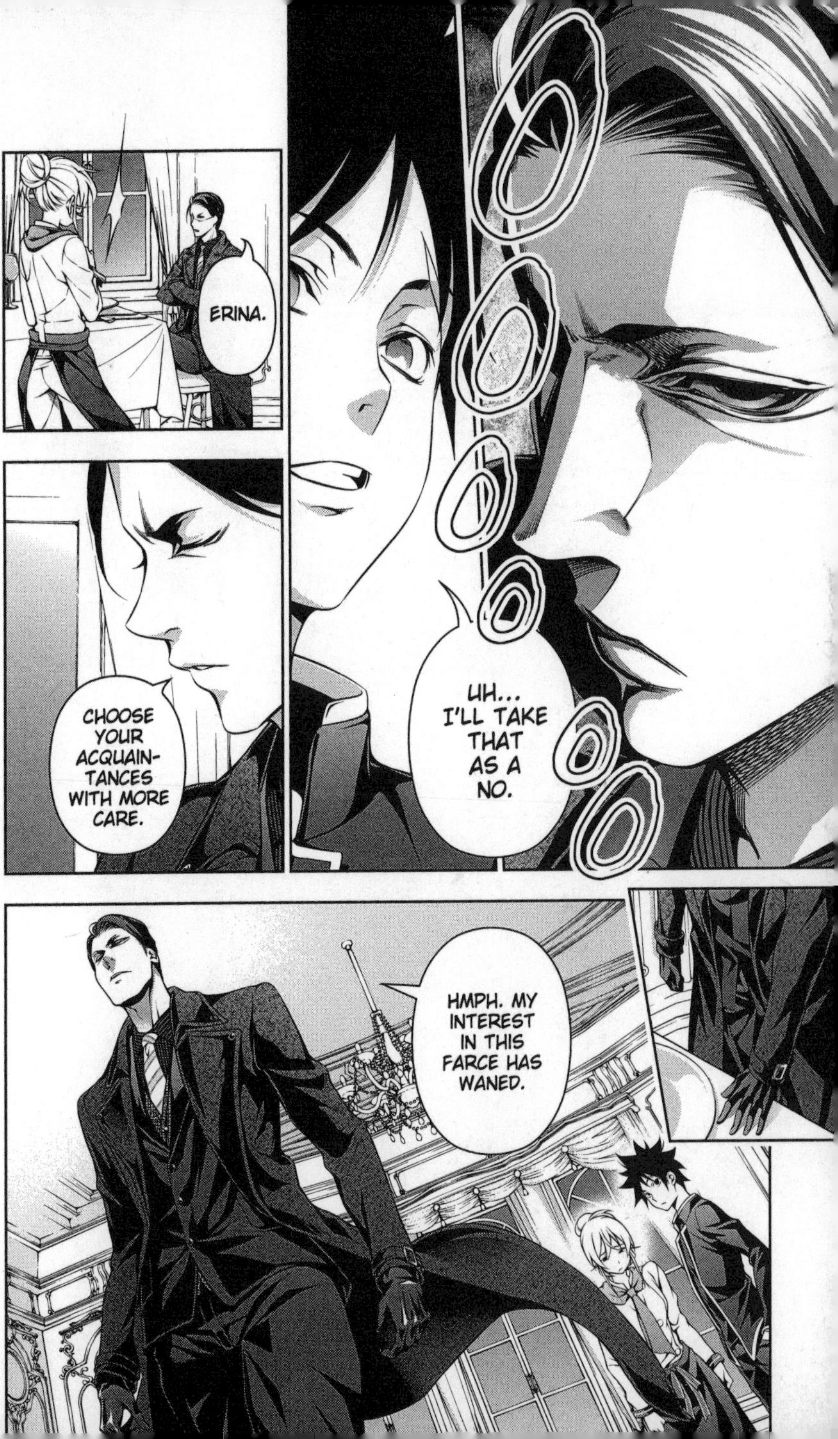
UH... I'LL TAKE THAT AS A NO.
ERINA.
CHOOSE YOUR ACQUAIN-TANCES WITH MORE CARE.
HMPH. MY INTEREST IN THIS FARCE HAS WANED.

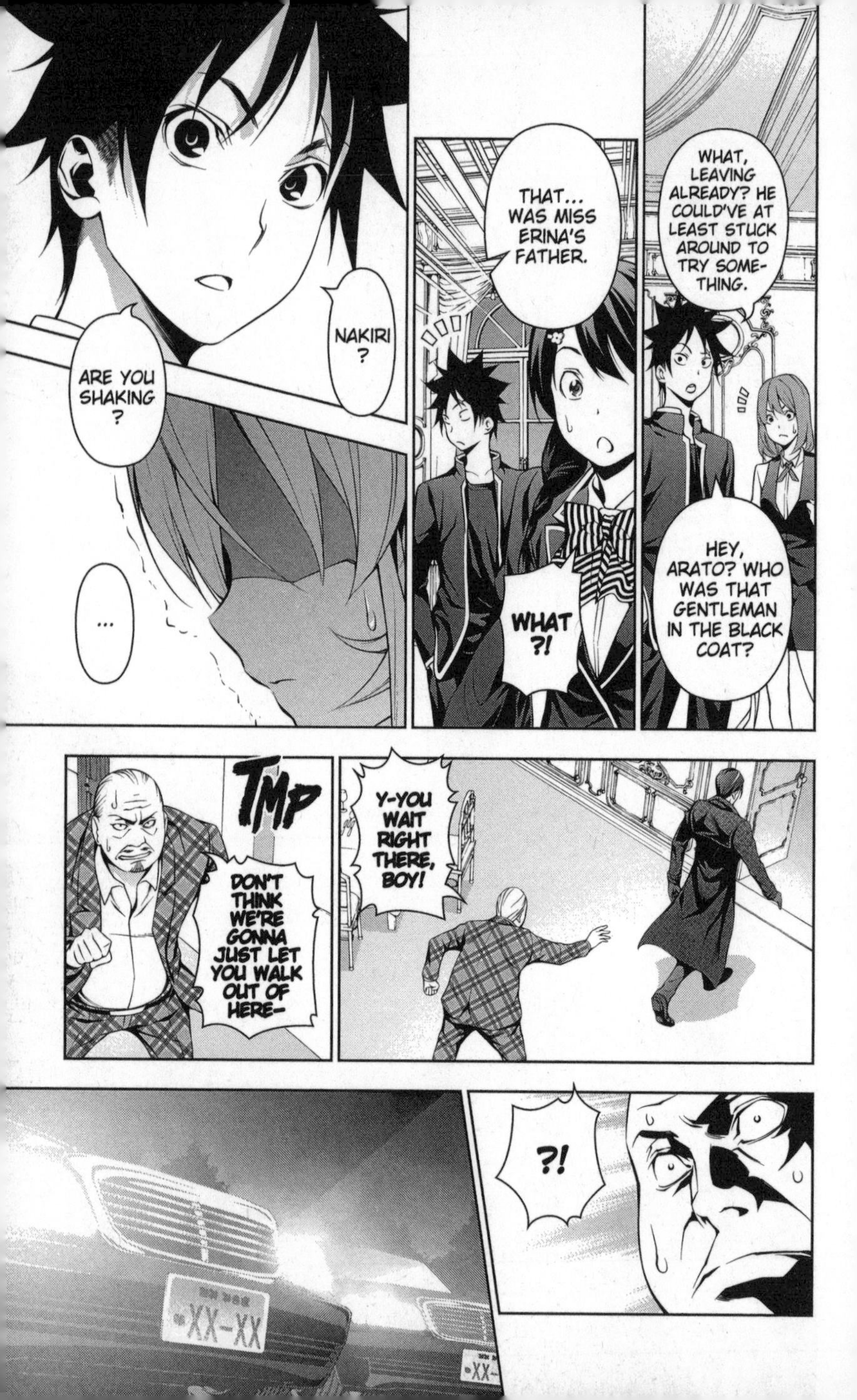
WHAT, LEAVING ALREADY? HE COULD'VE AT LEAST STUCK AROUND TO TRY SOME-THING.
HEY, ARATO? WHO WAS THAT GENTLEMAN IN THE BLACK COAT?
THAT... WAS MISS ERINA'S FATHER.
WHAT ?!
NAKIRI ?
ARE YOU SHAKING ?
...
Y-YOU WAIT RIGHT THERE, BOY!
TMP
DON'T THINK WE'RE GONNA JUST LET YOU WALK OUT OF HERE-
?!
XX-XX

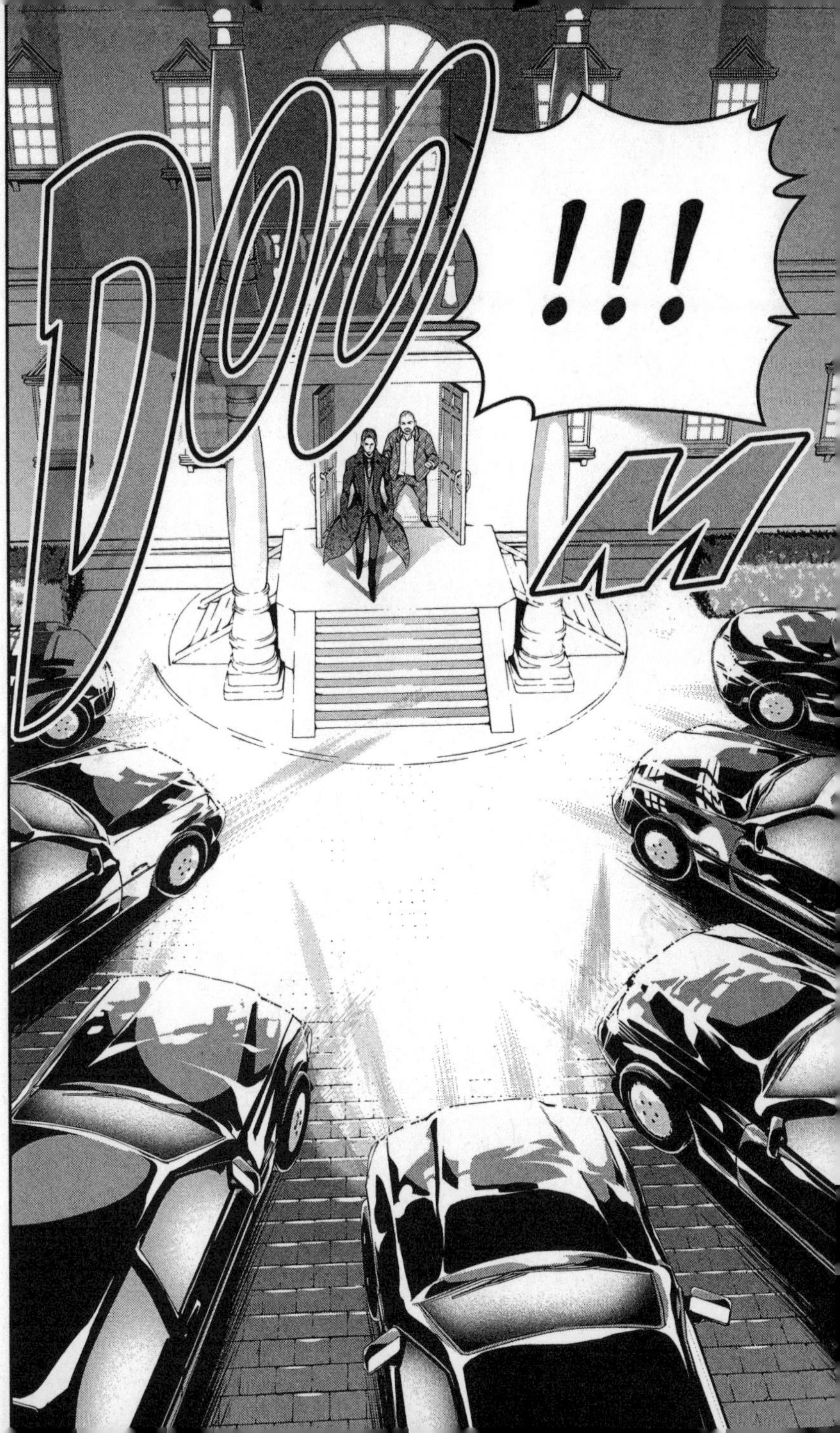
DOOOM!!!

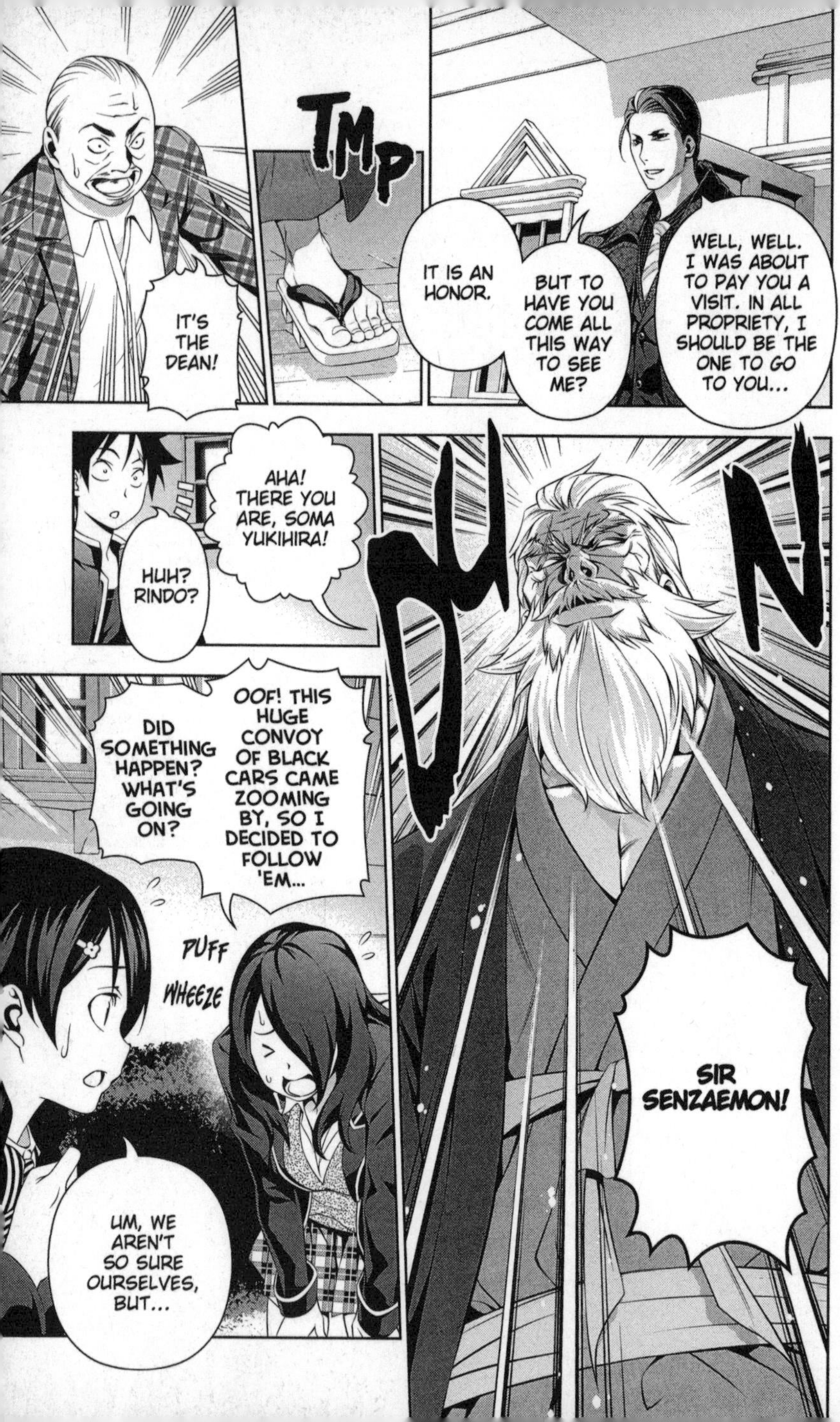
WELL, WELL. I WAS ABOUT TO PAY YOU A VISIT. IN ALL PROPRIETY, I SHOULD BE THE ONE TO GO TO YOU...
BUT TO HAVE YOU COME ALL THIS WAY TO SEE ME?
IT IS AN HONOR.
TMP
IT'S THE DEAN!
SIR SENZAEMON!
AHA! THERE YOU ARE, SOMA YUKIHIRA!
HUH? RINDO?
OOF! THIS HUGE CONVOY OF BLACK CARS CAME ZOOMING BY, SO I DECIDED TO FOLLOW 'EM...
DID SOMETHING HAPPEN? WHAT'S GOING ON?
PUFF
WHEEZE
UM, WE AREN'T SO SURE OURSELVES, BUT...

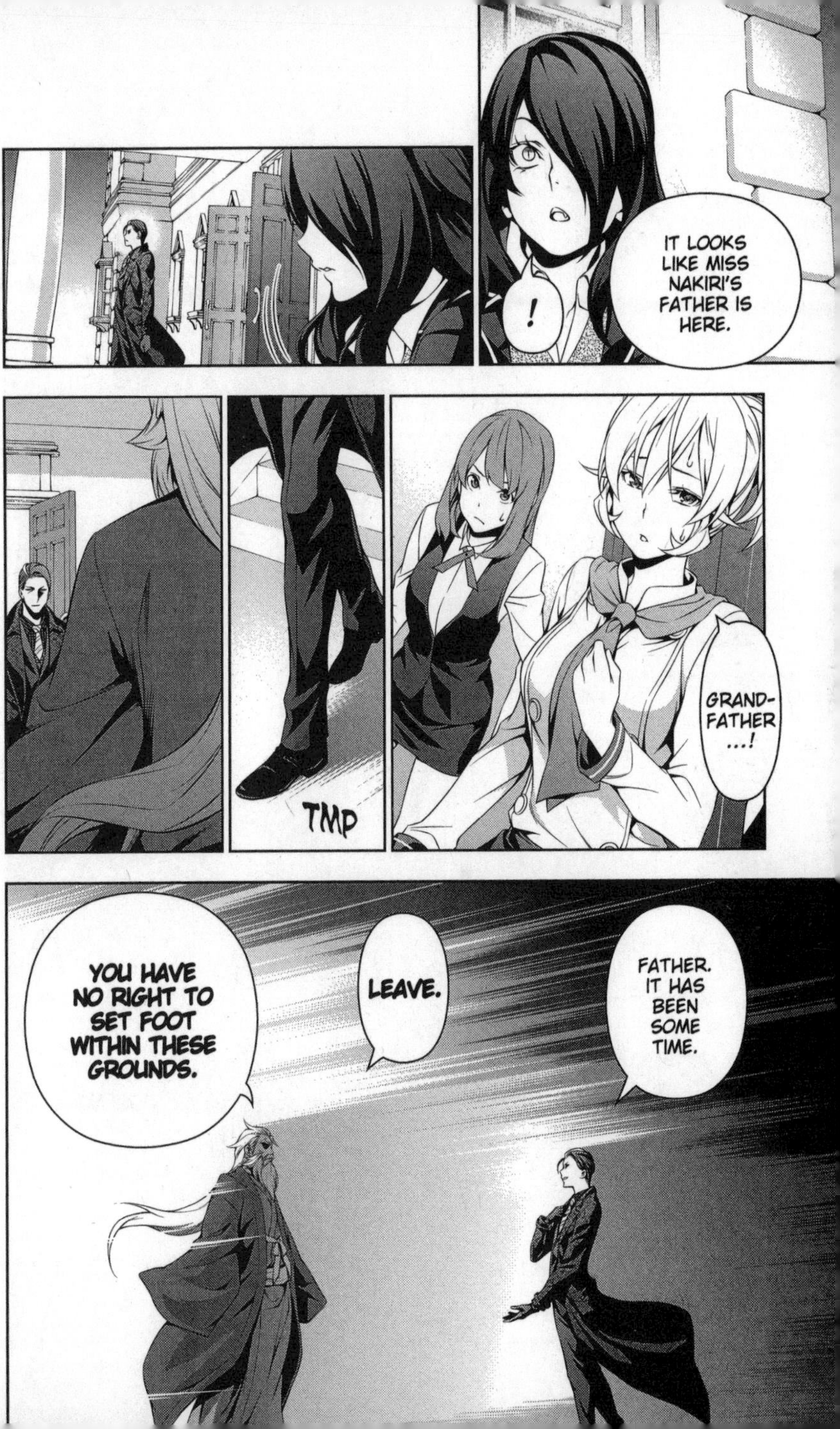
IT LOOKS LIKE MISS NAKIRI'S FATHER IS HERE.
!
GRAND-FATHER ...!
TMP
FATHER. IT HAS BEEN SOME TIME.
LEAVE.
YOU HAVE NO RIGHT TO SET FOOT WITHIN THESE GROUNDS.

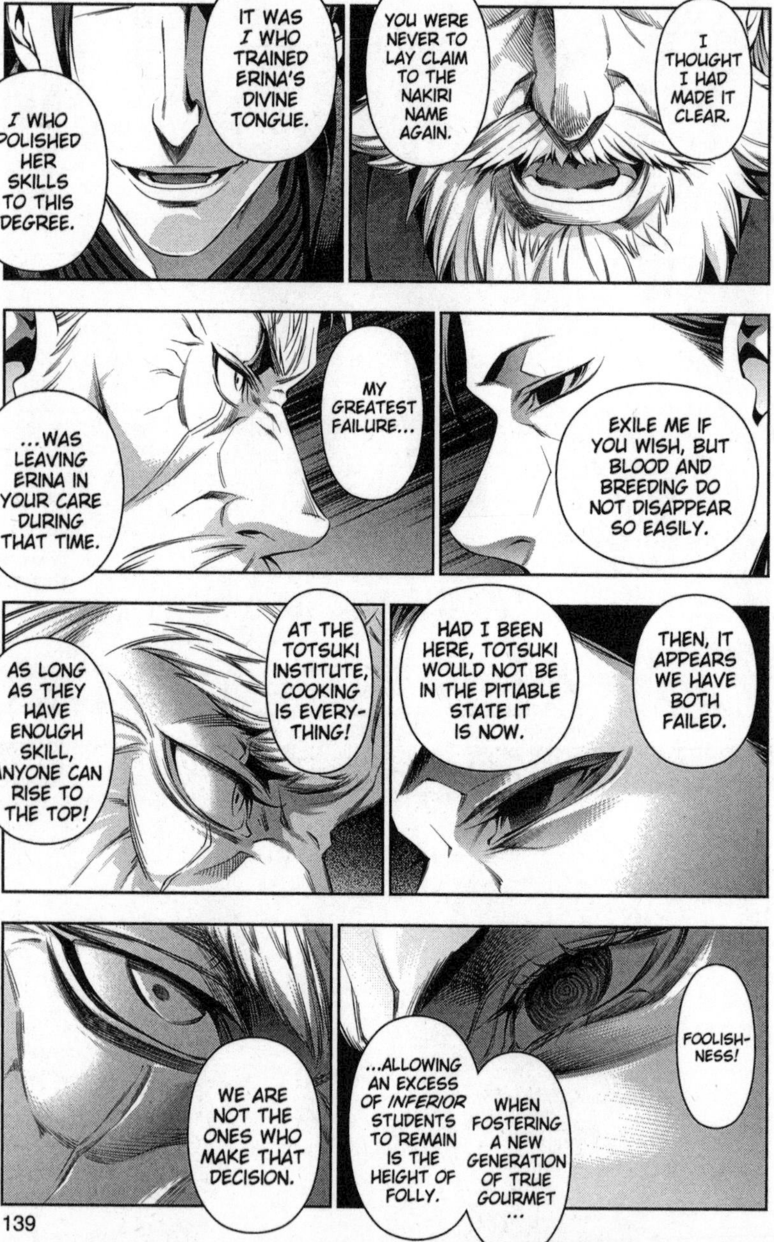
I THOUGHT I HAD MADE IT CLEAR.
YOU WERE NEVER TO LAY CLAIM TO THE NAKIRI NAME AGAIN.
IT WAS *I* WHO TRAINED ERINA'S DIVINE TONGUE.
I WHO POLISHED HER SKILLS TO THIS DEGREE.
EXILE ME IF YOU WISH, BUT BLOOD AND BREEDING DO NOT DISAPPEAR SO EASILY.
MY GREATEST FAILURE...
...WAS LEAVING ERINA IN YOUR CARE DURING THAT TIME.
THEN, IT APPEARS WE HAVE BOTH FAILED.
HAD I BEEN HERE, TOTSUKI WOULD NOT BE IN THE PITIABLE STATE IT IS NOW.
AT THE TOTSUKI INSTITUTE, COOKING IS EVERY-THING!
AS LONG AS THEY HAVE ENOUGH SKILL, ANYONE CAN RISE TO THE TOP!
FOOLISH-NESS!
WHEN FOSTERING A NEW GENERATION OF TRUE GOURMET...
...ALLOWING AN EXCESS OF *INFERIOR* STUDENTS TO REMAIN IS THE HEIGHT OF FOLLY.
WE ARE NOT THE ONES WHO MAKE THAT DECISION.

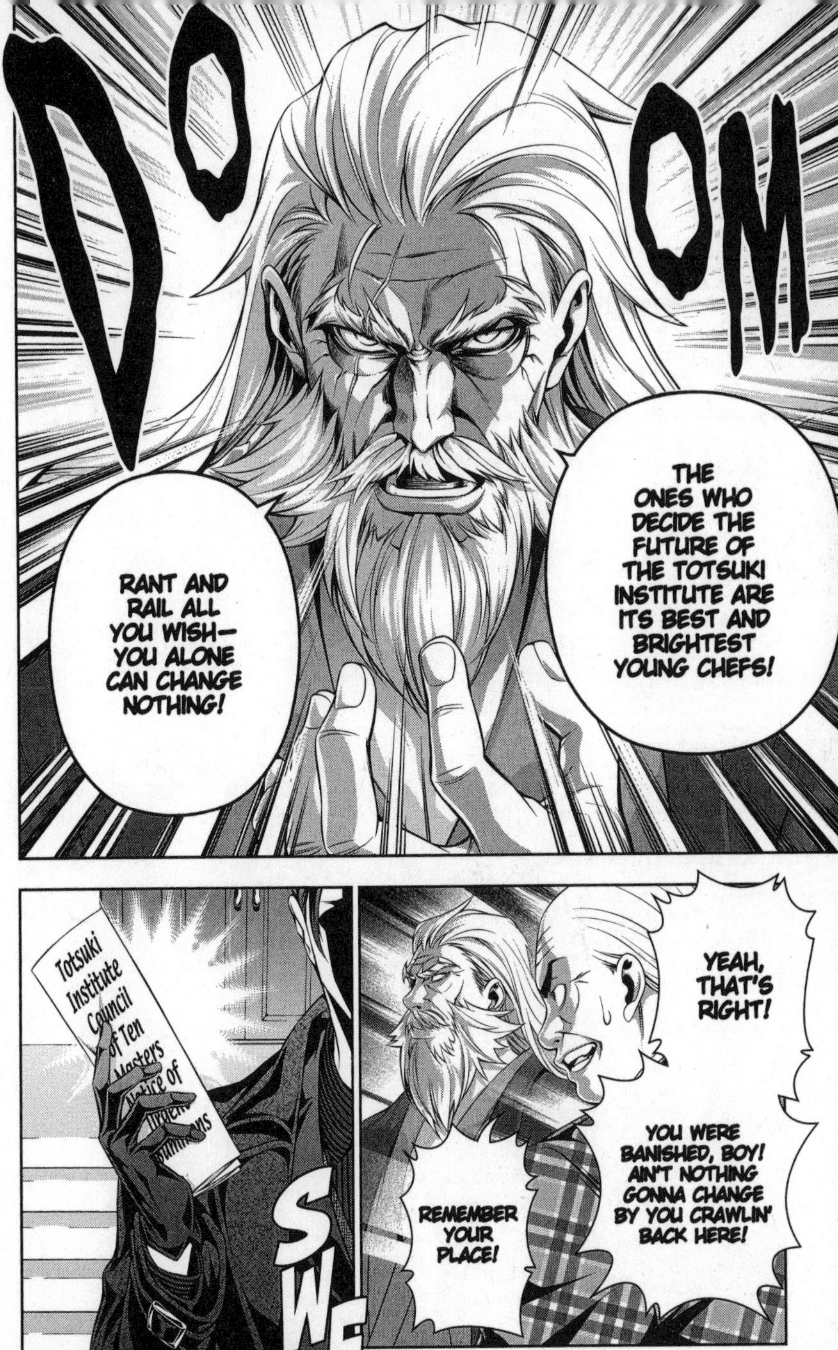
DOOM
THE ONES WHO DECIDE THE FUTURE OF THE TOTSUKI INSTITUTE ARE ITS BEST AND BRIGHTEST YOUNG CHEFS!
RANT AND RAIL ALL YOU WISH—YOU ALONE CAN CHANGE NOTHING!
YEAH, THAT'S RIGHT!
YOU WERE BANISHED, BOY! AIN'T NOTHING GONNA CHANGE BY YOU CRAWLIN' BACK HERE!
REMEMBER YOUR PLACE!
Totsuki Institute Council of Ten Masters Notice of
SWF

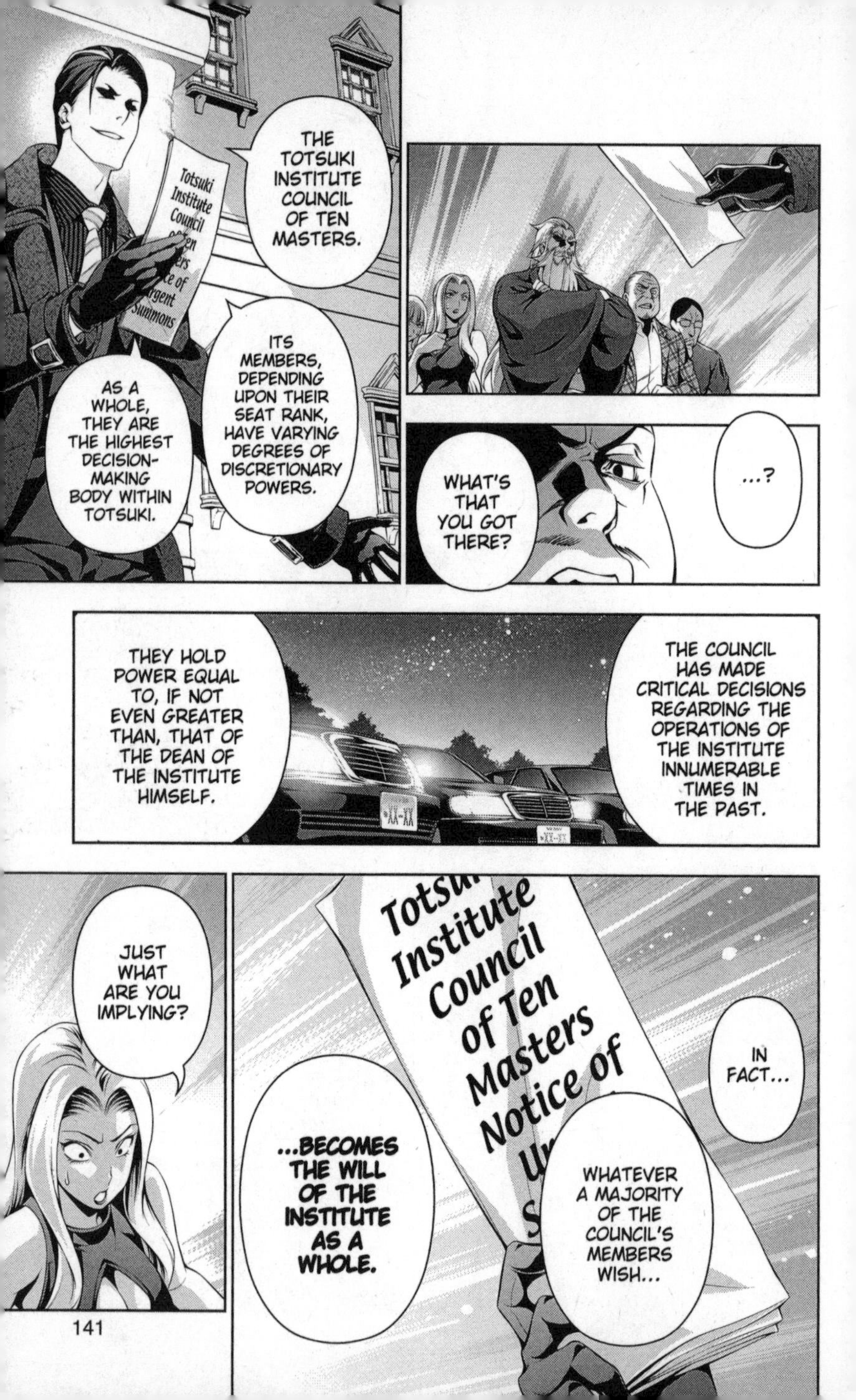
...?
WHAT'S THAT YOU GOT THERE?
THE TOTSUKI INSTITUTE COUNCIL OF TEN MASTERS.
ITS MEMBERS, DEPENDING UPON THEIR SEAT RANK, HAVE VARYING DEGREES OF DISCRETIONARY POWERS.
AS A WHOLE, THEY ARE THE HIGHEST DECISION-MAKING BODY WITHIN TOTSUKI.
THE COUNCIL HAS MADE CRITICAL DECISIONS REGARDING THE OPERATIONS OF THE INSTITUTE INNUMERABLE TIMES IN THE PAST.
THEY HOLD POWER EQUAL TO, IF NOT EVEN GREATER THAN, THAT OF THE DEAN OF THE INSTITUTE HIMSELF.
IN FACT...
WHATEVER A MAJORITY OF THE COUNCIL'S MEMBERS WISH...
...BECOMES THE WILL OF THE INSTITUTE AS A WHOLE.
JUST WHAT ARE YOU IMPLYING?

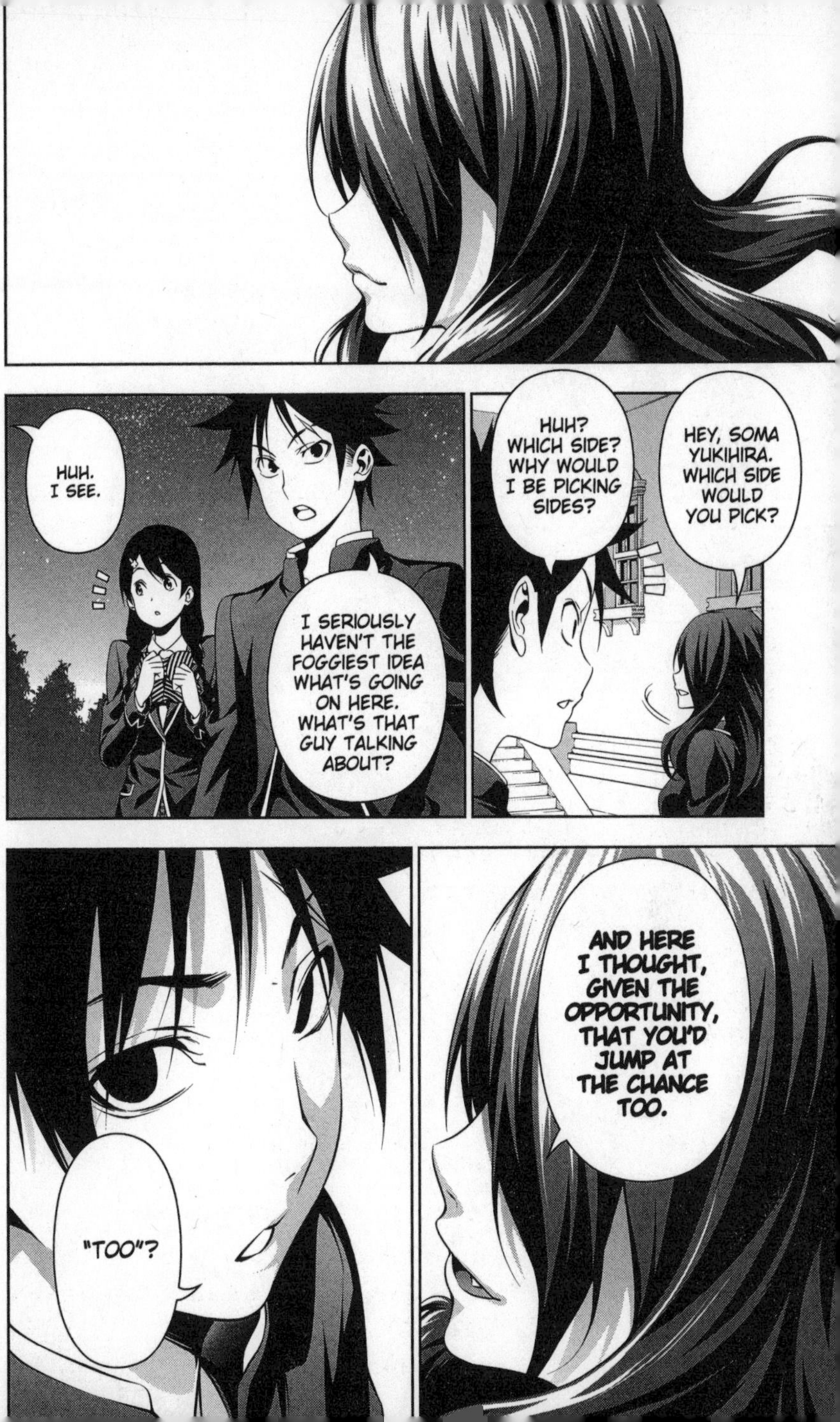
HEY, SOMA YUKIHIRA. WHICH SIDE WOULD YOU PICK?
HUH? WHICH SIDE? WHY WOULD I BE PICKING SIDES?
HUH. I SEE.
I SERIOUSLY HAVEN'T THE FOGGIEST IDEA WHAT'S GOING ON HERE. WHAT'S THAT GUY TALKING ABOUT?
AND HERE I THOUGHT, GIVEN THE OPPORTUNITY, THAT YOU'D JUMP AT THE CHANCE TOO.
"TOO"?

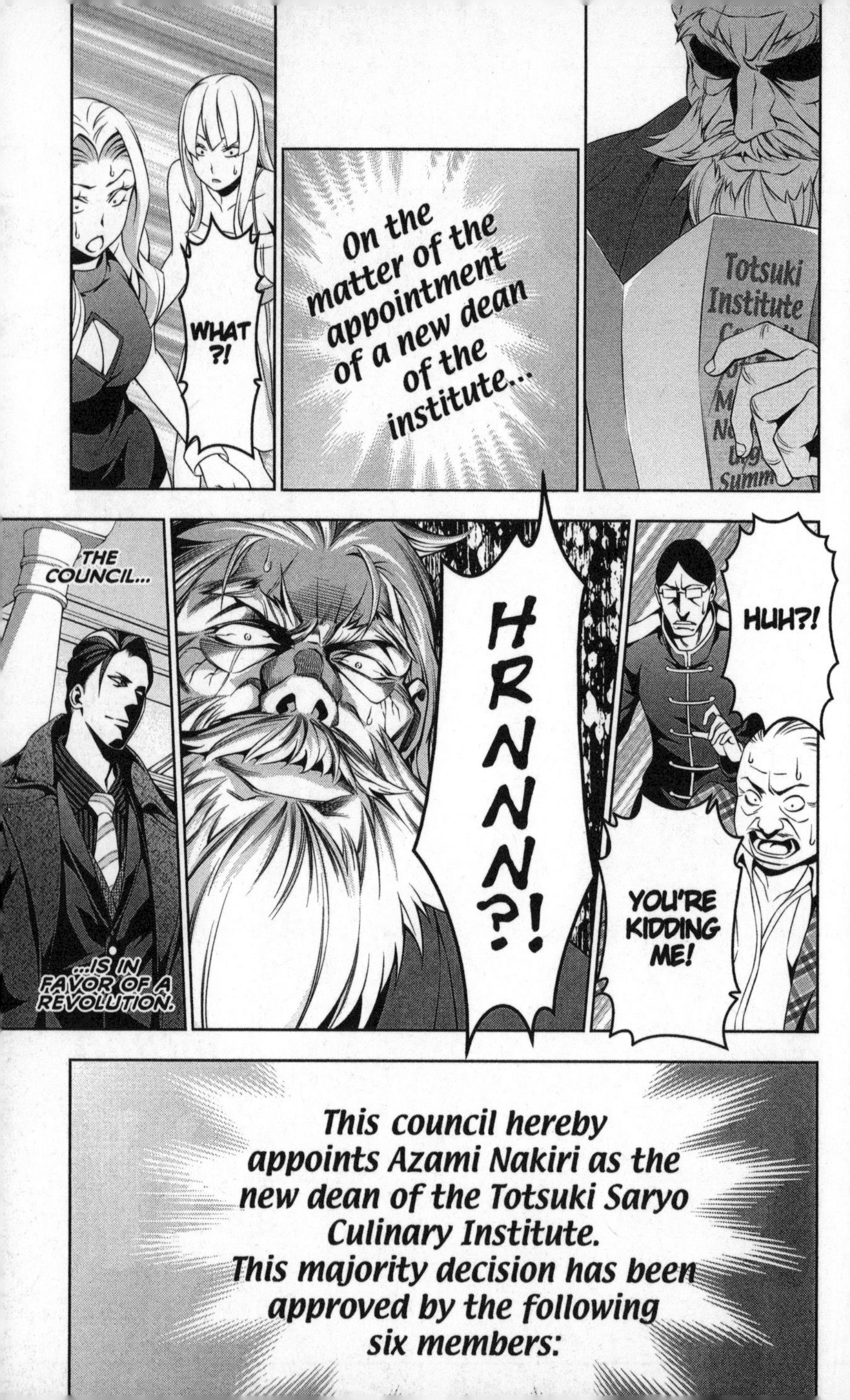
Totsuki Institute
On the matter of the appointment of a new dean of the institute...
WHAT ?!
HUH?!
YOU'RE KIDDING ME!
HRNNN?!
THE COUNCIL...
...IS IN FAVOR OF A REVOLUTION.
This council hereby appoints Azami Nakiri as the new dean of the Totsuki Saryo Culinary Institute.
This majority decision has been approved by the following six members:

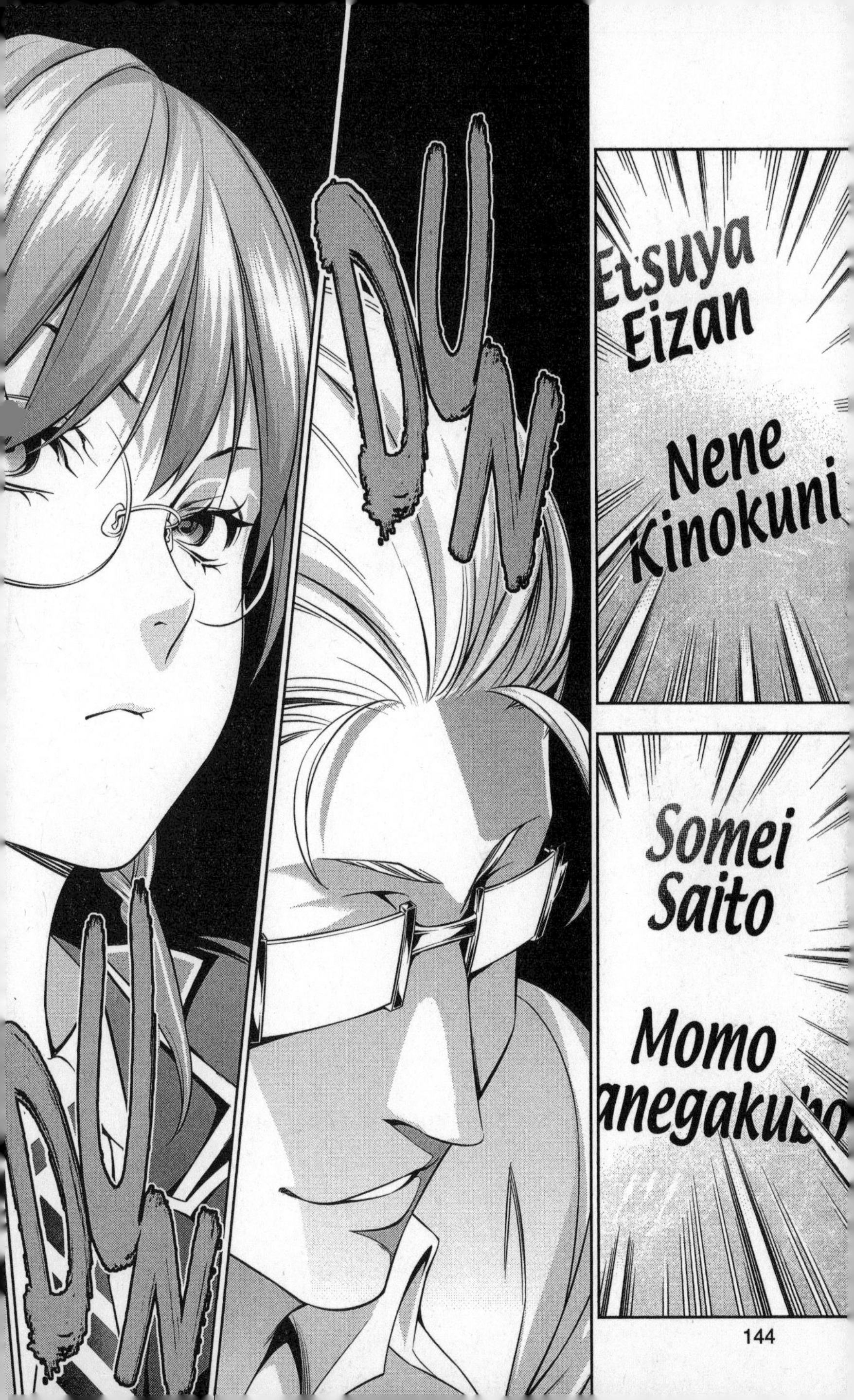
Etsuya Eizan
Nene Kinokuni
Somei Saito
Momo anegakubo
DUN
DUN

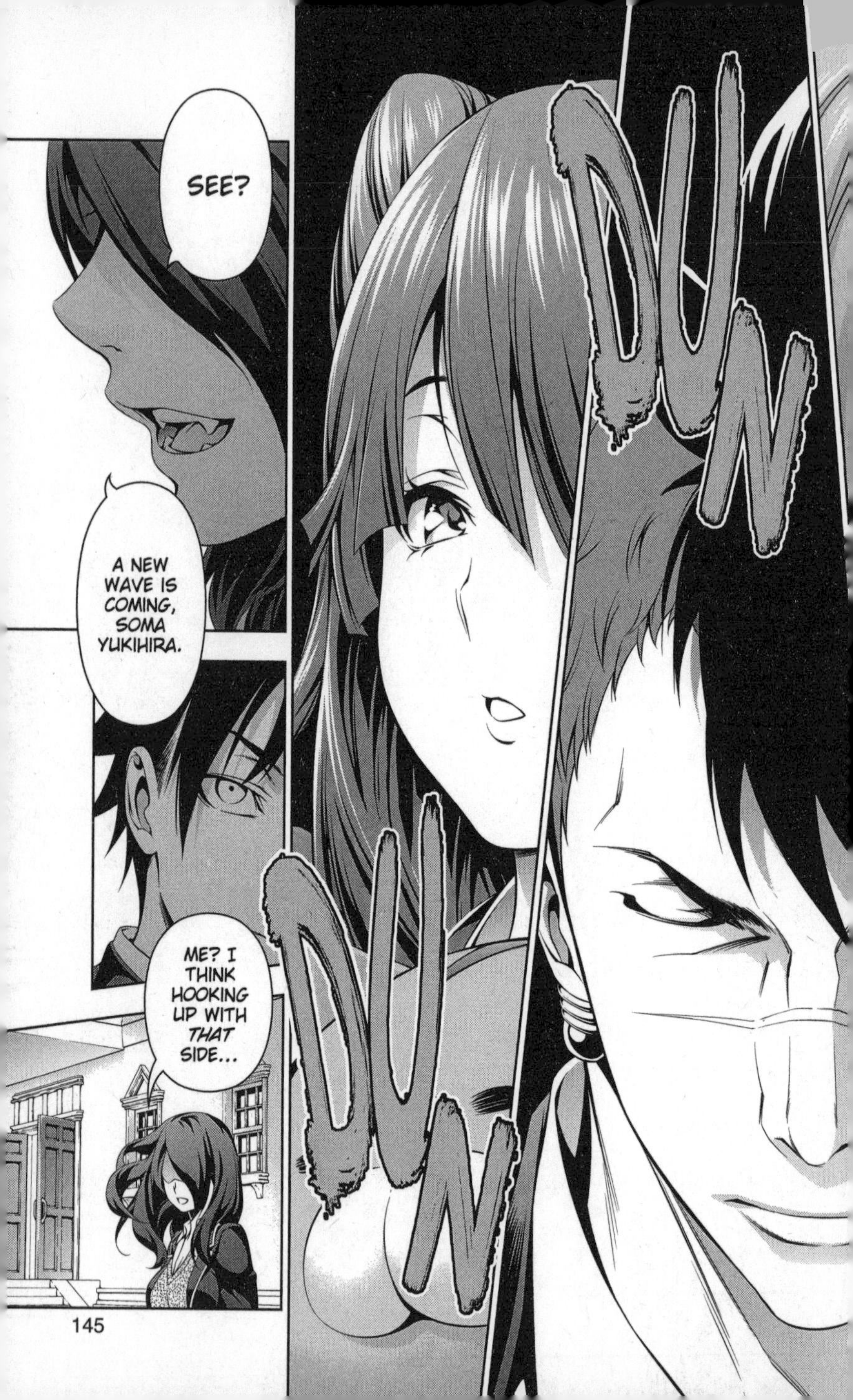
DUN
DUN
SEE?
A NEW WAVE IS COMING, SOMA YUKIHIRA.
ME? I THINK HOOKING UP WITH *THAT* SIDE...

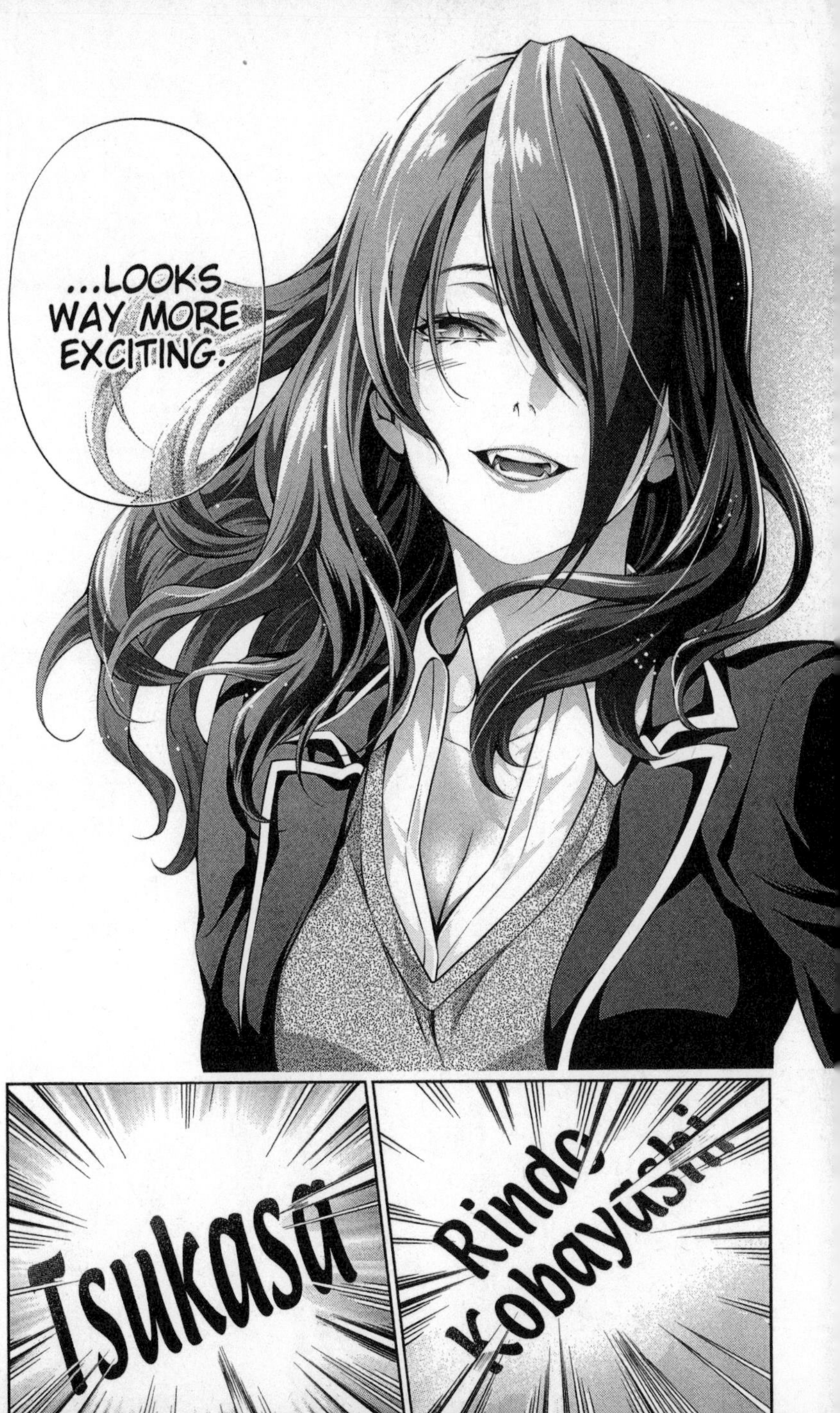
...LOOKS WAY MORE EXCITING.
Rindo Kobayashi
Tsukasa

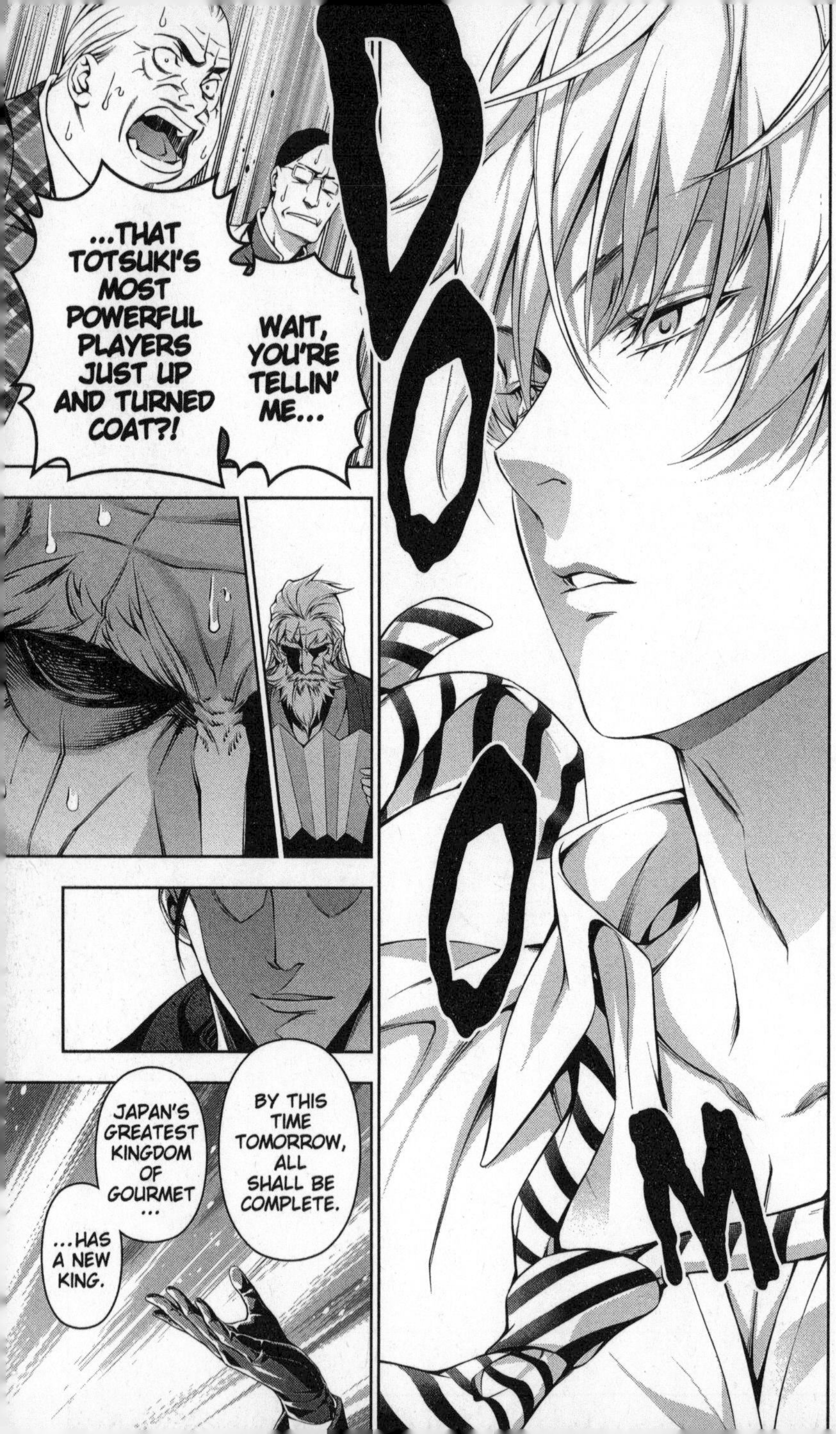
DOOOM
WAIT, YOU'RE TELLIN' ME...
...THAT TOTSUKI'S MOST POWERFUL PLAYERS JUST UP AND TURNED COAT?!
BY THIS TIME TOMORROW, ALL SHALL BE COMPLETE.
JAPAN'S GREATEST KINGDOM OF GOURMET ...
...HAS A NEW KING.

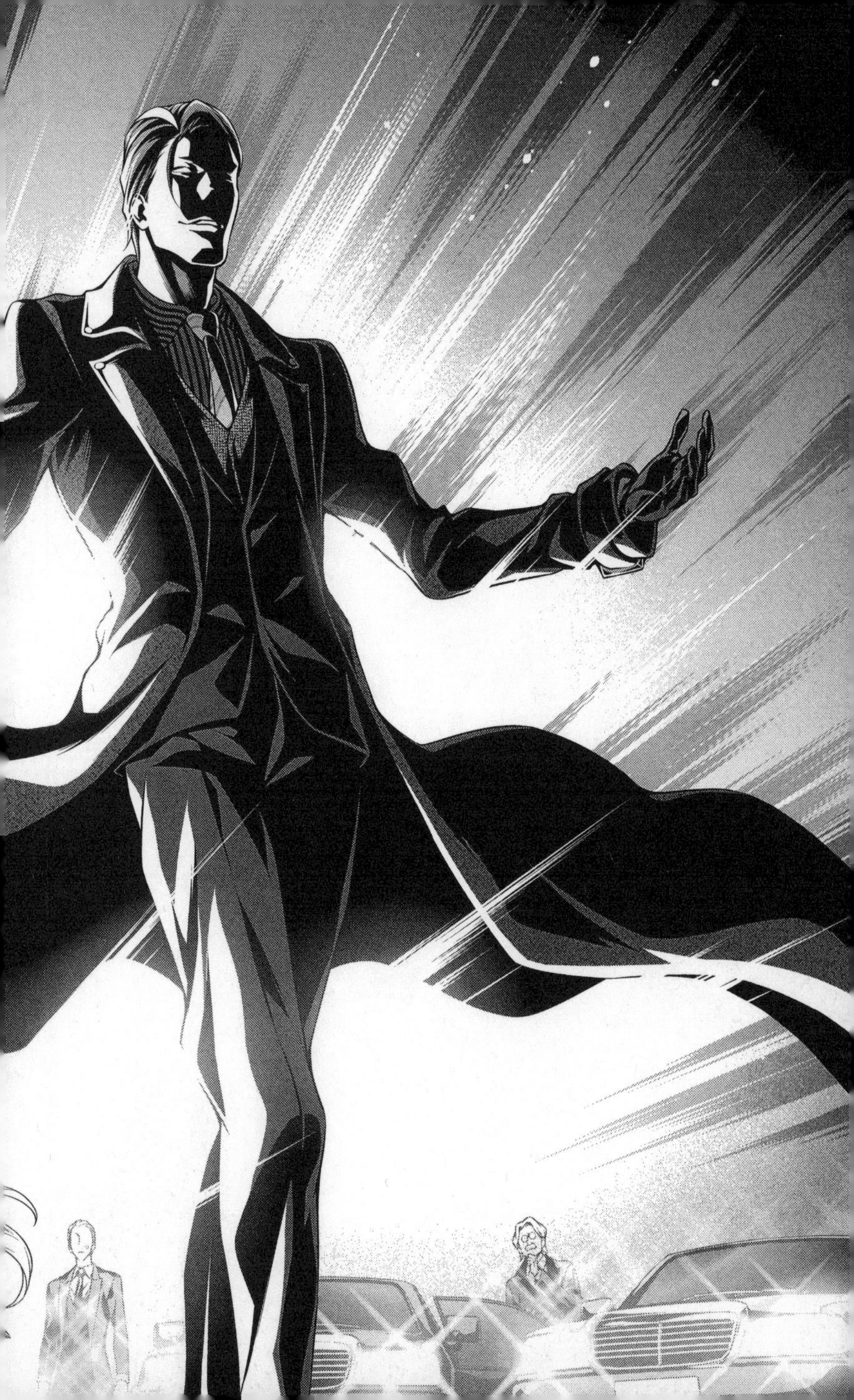

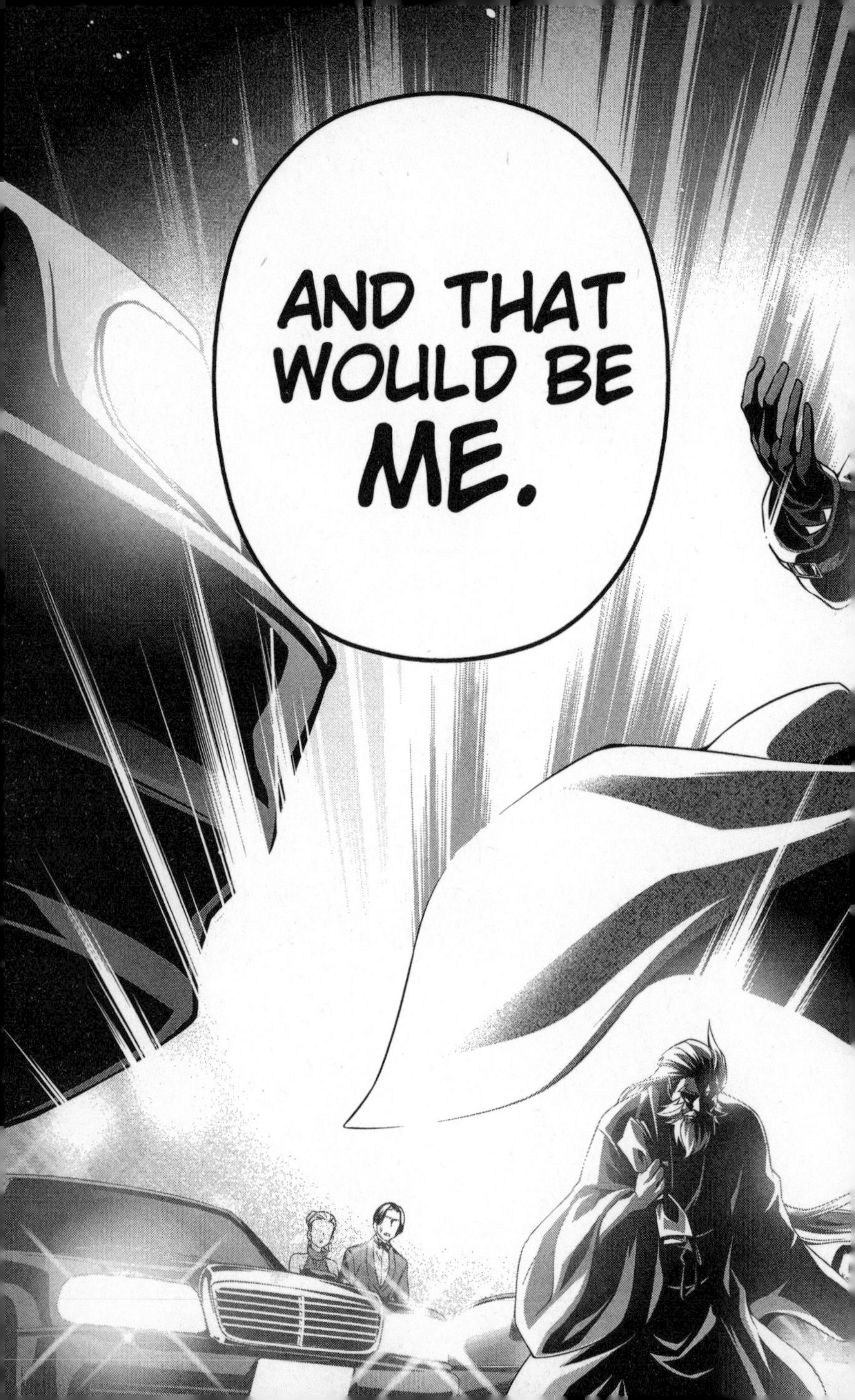
AND THAT WOULD BE ME.

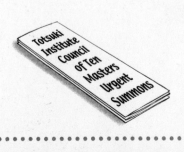

Totsuki
Institute
Council
of Ten
Masters
Urgent
Summons

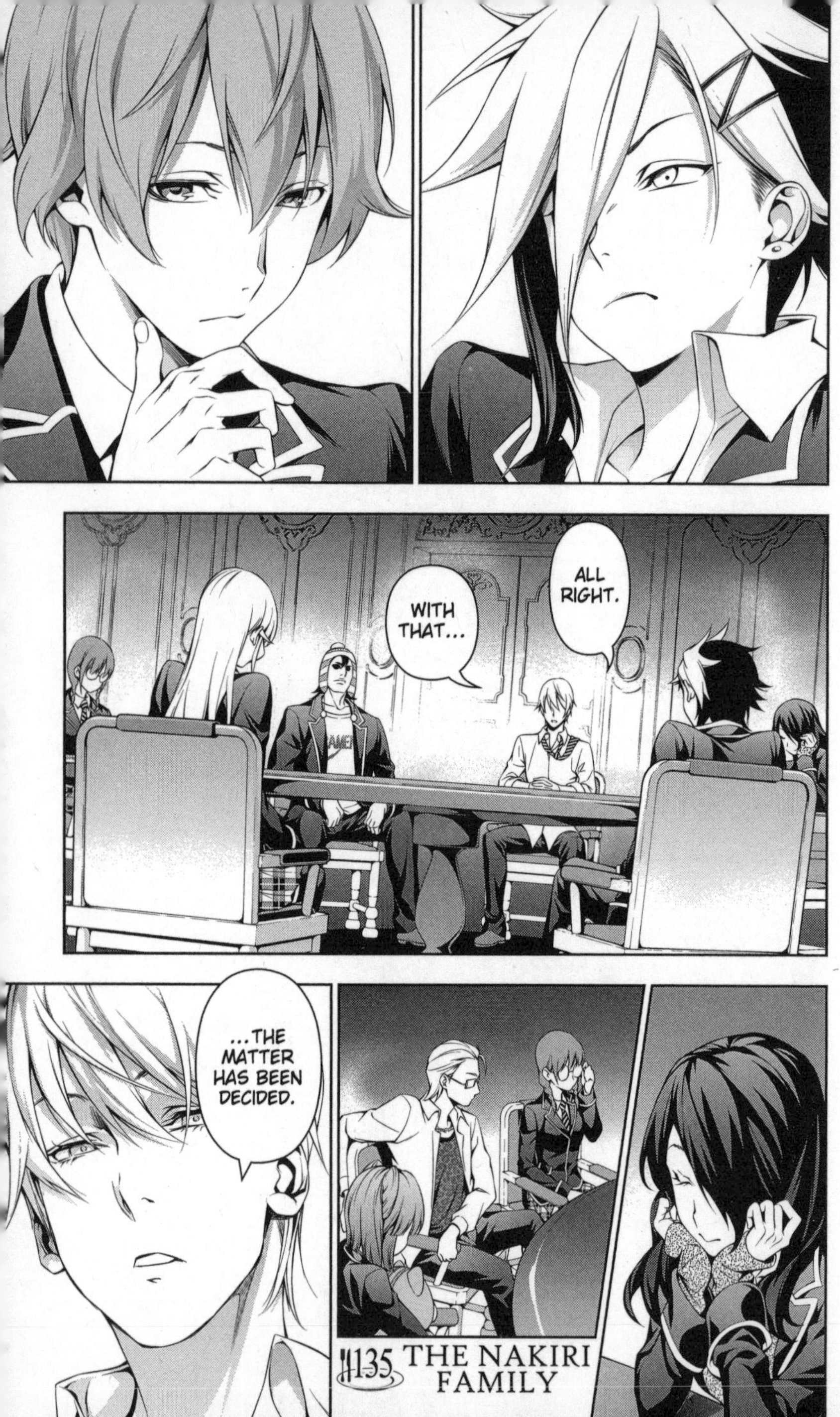
ALL RIGHT.
WITH THAT...
...THE MATTER HAS BEEN DECIDED.

135 THE NAKIRI FAMILY

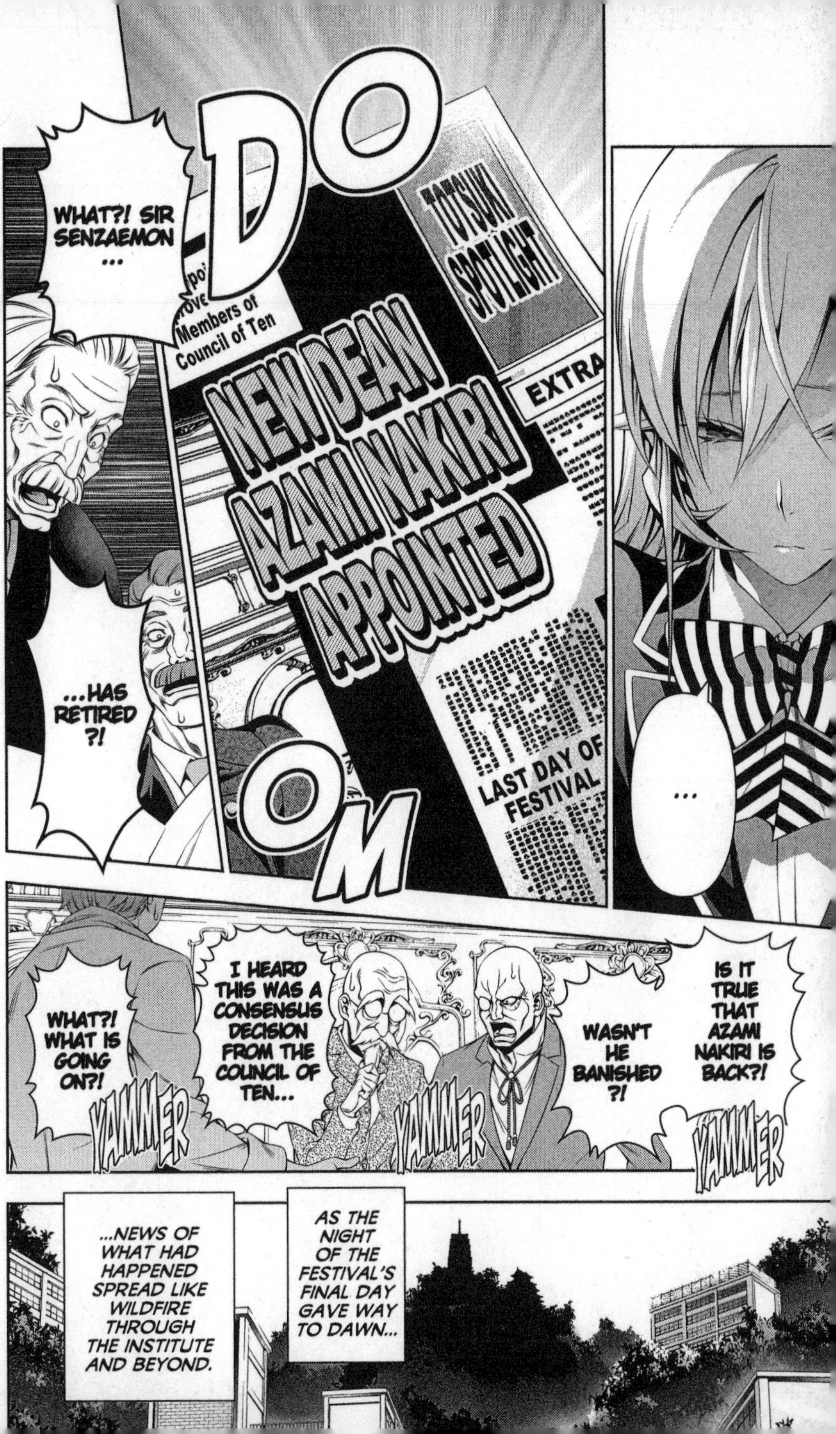
...
DO
TOTSUKI SPOTLIGHT
EXTRA
NEW DEAN AZAMI NAKIRI APPOINTED
Members of Council of Ten
LAST DAY OF FESTIVAL
OM
WHAT?! SIR SENZAEMON ...
...HAS RETIRED ?!
IS IT TRUE THAT AZAMI NAKIRI IS BACK?!
YAMMER
WASN'T HE BANISHED ?!
I HEARD THIS WAS A CONSENSUS DECISION FROM THE COUNCIL OF TEN...
YAMMER
WHAT?! WHAT IS GOING ON?!
YAMMER
AS THE NIGHT OF THE FESTIVAL'S FINAL DAY GAVE WAY TO DAWN...
...NEWS OF WHAT HAD HAPPENED SPREAD LIKE WILDFIRE THROUGH THE INSTITUTE AND BEYOND.

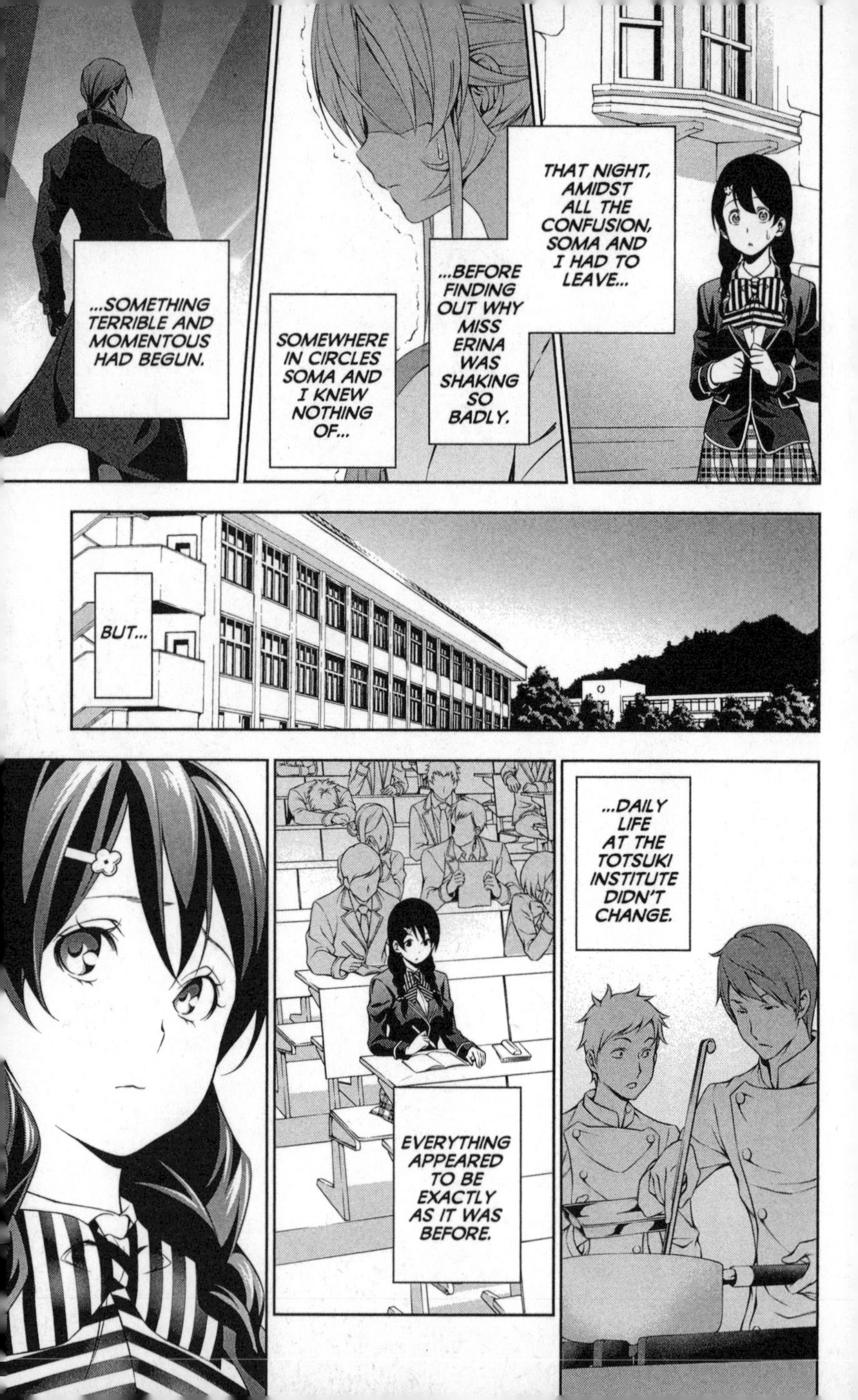
THAT NIGHT, AMIDST ALL THE CONFUSION, SOMA AND I HAD TO LEAVE...
...BEFORE FINDING OUT WHY MISS ERINA WAS SHAKING SO BADLY.
SOMEWHERE IN CIRCLES SOMA AND I KNEW NOTHING OF...
...SOMETHING TERRIBLE AND MOMENTOUS HAD BEGUN.
BUT...
...DAILY LIFE AT THE TOTSUKI INSTITUTE DIDN'T CHANGE.
EVERYTHING APPEARED TO BE EXACTLY AS IT WAS BEFORE.

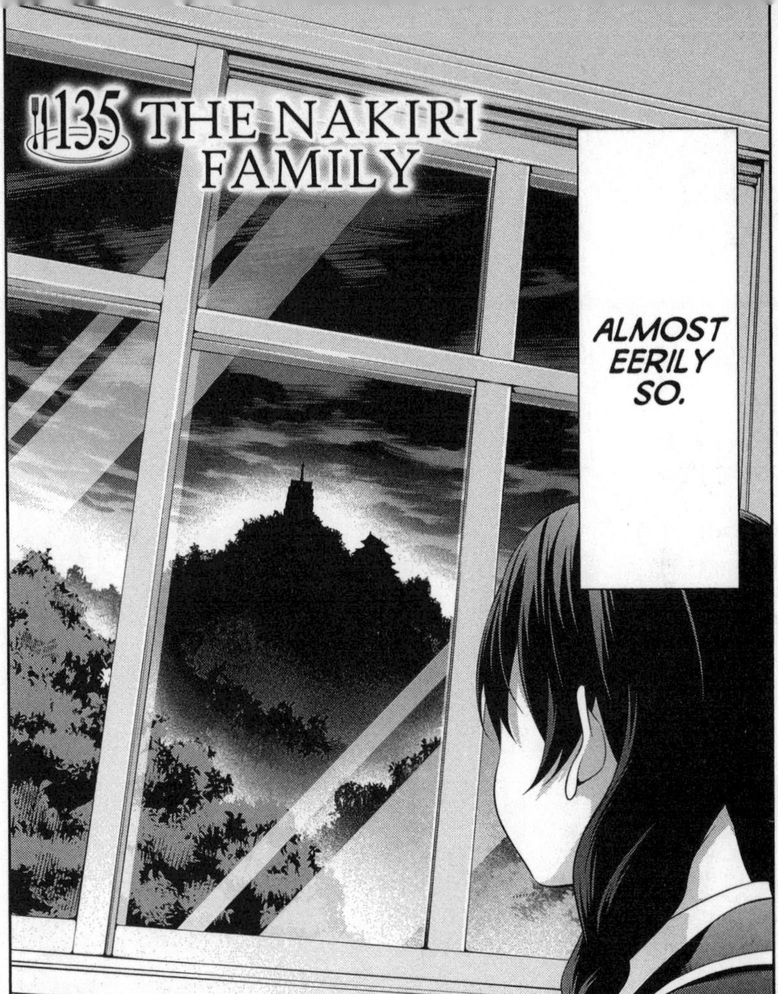
135 THE NAKIRI FAMILY
ALMOST EERILY SO.
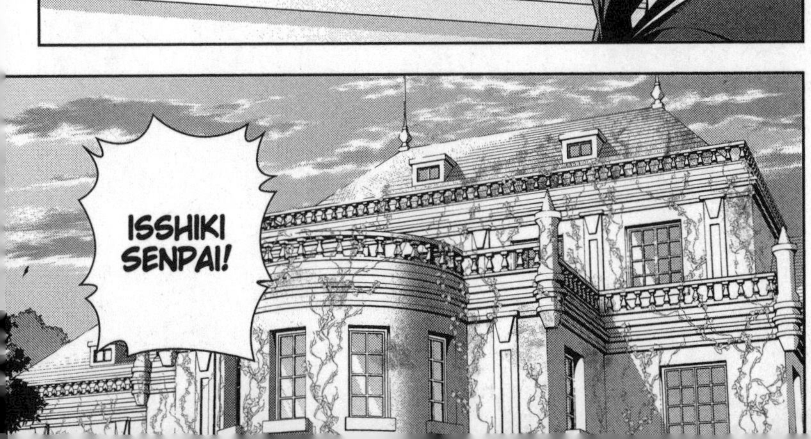
ISSHIKI SENPAI!

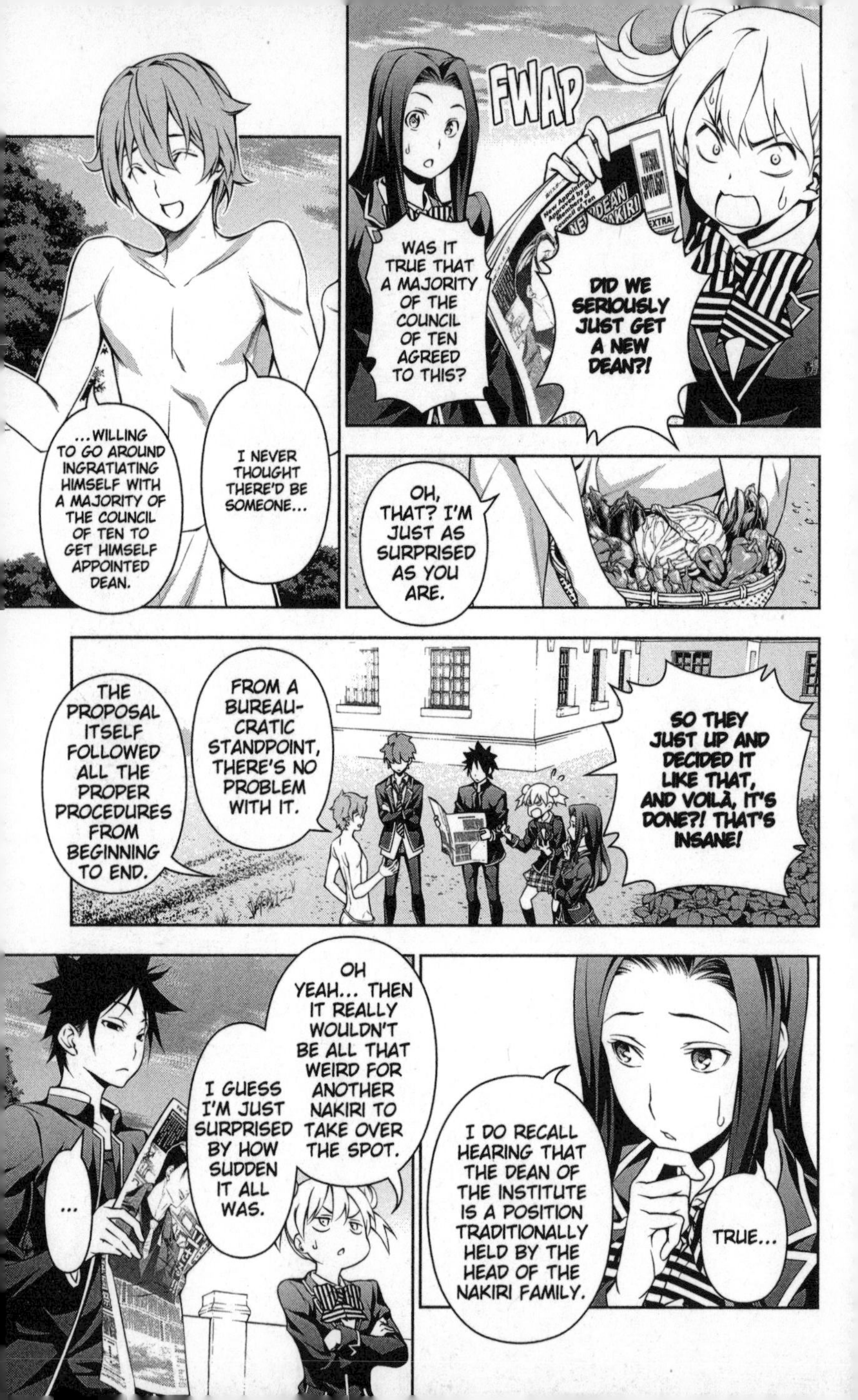
FWAP
TOTSUKI SPOTLIGHT
EXTRA
DID WE SERIOUSLY JUST GET A NEW DEAN?!
WAS IT TRUE THAT A MAJORITY OF THE COUNCIL OF TEN AGREED TO THIS?
OH, THAT? I'M JUST AS SURPRISED AS YOU ARE.
I NEVER THOUGHT THERE'D BE SOMEONE...
...WILLING TO GO AROUND INGRATIATING HIMSELF WITH A MAJORITY OF THE COUNCIL OF TEN TO GET HIMSELF APPOINTED DEAN.
SO THEY JUST UP AND DECIDED IT LIKE THAT, AND VOILÀ, IT'S DONE?! THAT'S INSANE!
FROM A BUREAU-CRATIC STANDPOINT, THERE'S NO PROBLEM WITH IT.
THE PROPOSAL ITSELF FOLLOWED ALL THE PROPER PROCEDURES FROM BEGINNING TO END.
I DO RECALL HEARING THAT THE DEAN OF THE INSTITUTE IS A POSITION TRADITIONALLY HELD BY THE HEAD OF THE NAKIRI FAMILY.
TRUE...
OH YEAH... THEN IT REALLY WOULDN'T BE ALL THAT WEIRD FOR ANOTHER NAKIRI TO TAKE OVER THE SPOT.
I GUESS I'M JUST SURPRISED BY HOW SUDDEN IT ALL WAS.
...

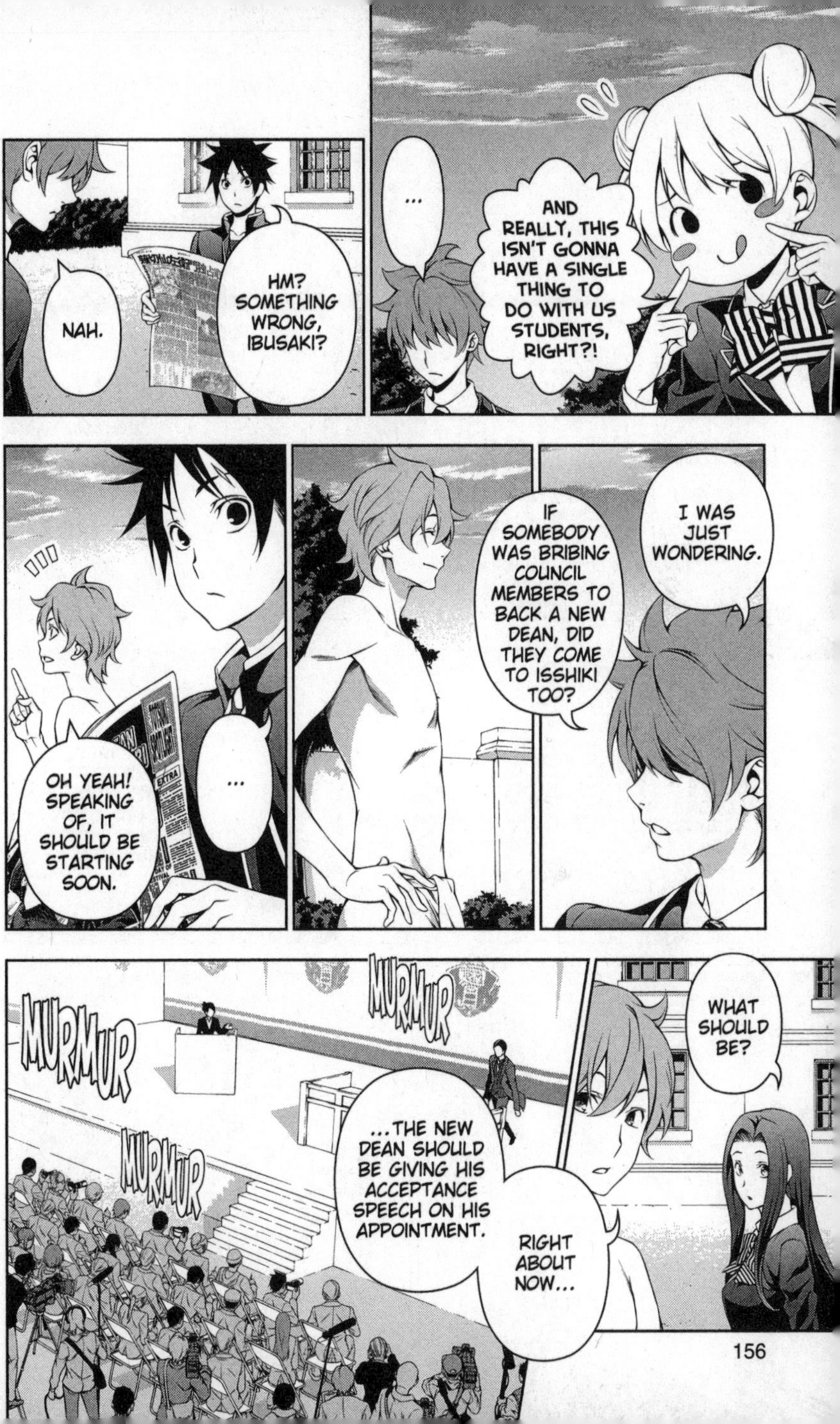

AND REALLY, THIS ISN'T GONNA HAVE A SINGLE THING TO DO WITH US STUDENTS, RIGHT?!
...
HM? SOMETHING WRONG, IBUSAKI?
NAH.
I WAS JUST WONDERING.
IF SOMEBODY WAS BRIBING COUNCIL MEMBERS TO BACK A NEW DEAN, DID THEY COME TO ISSHIKI TOO?
...
OH YEAH! SPEAKING OF, IT SHOULD BE STARTING SOON.
WHAT SHOULD BE?
...THE NEW DEAN SHOULD BE GIVING HIS ACCEPTANCE SPEECH ON HIS APPOINTMENT.
RIGHT ABOUT NOW...
MURMUR
MURMUR
MURMUR

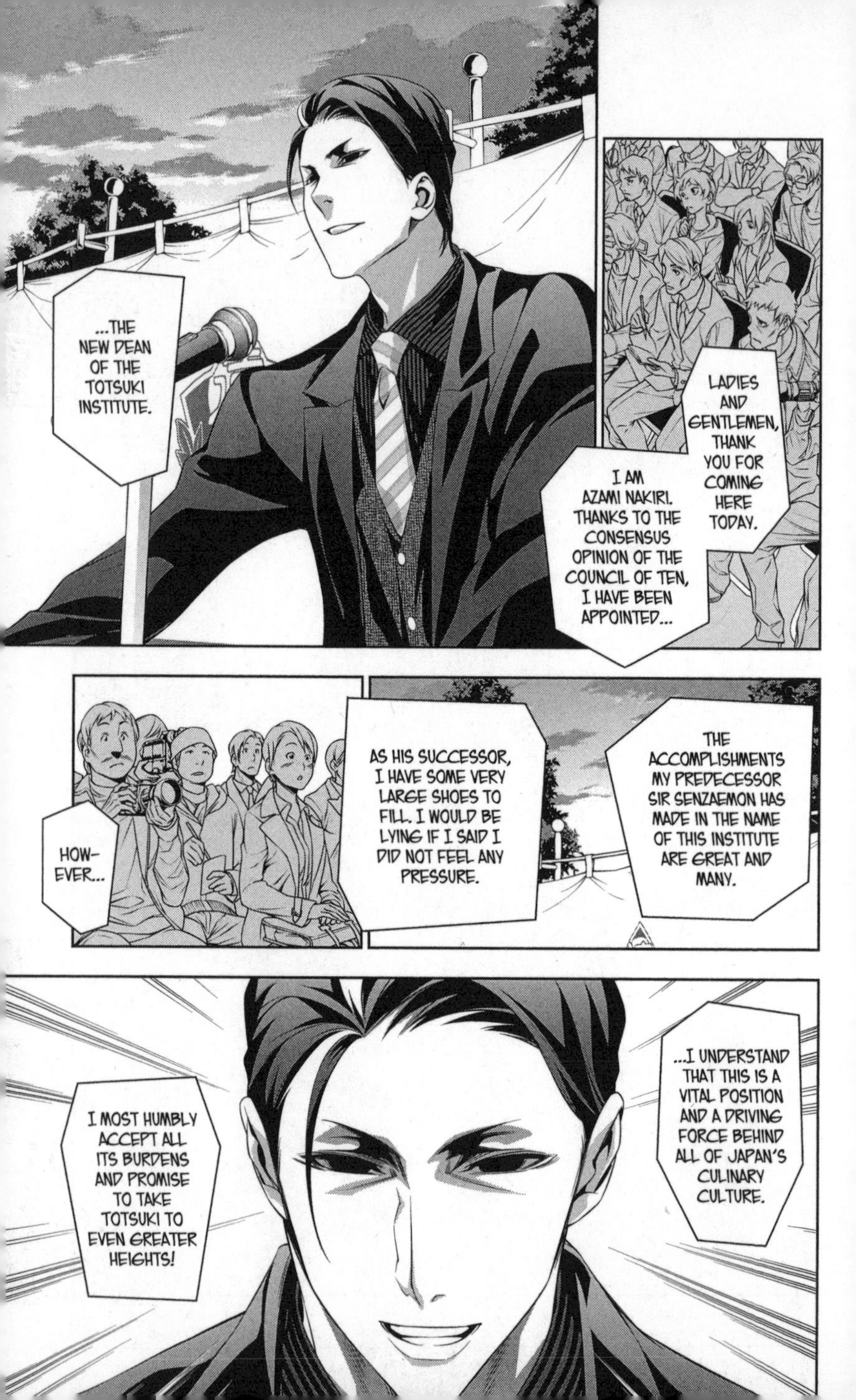
LADIES AND GENTLEMEN, THANK YOU FOR COMING HERE TODAY.
I AM AZAMI NAKIRI. THANKS TO THE CONSENSUS OPINION OF THE COUNCIL OF TEN, I HAVE BEEN APPOINTED...
...THE NEW DEAN OF THE TOTSUKI INSTITUTE.
THE ACCOMPLISHMENTS MY PREDECESSOR SIR SENZAEMON HAS MADE IN THE NAME OF THIS INSTITUTE ARE GREAT AND MANY.
AS HIS SUCCESSOR, I HAVE SOME VERY LARGE SHOES TO FILL. I WOULD BE LYING IF I SAID I DID NOT FEEL ANY PRESSURE.
HOW-EVER...
...I UNDERSTAND THAT THIS IS A VITAL POSITION AND A DRIVING FORCE BEHIND ALL OF JAPAN'S CULINARY CULTURE.
I MOST HUMBLY ACCEPT ALL ITS BURDENS AND PROMISE TO TAKE TOTSUKI TO EVEN GREATER HEIGHTS!

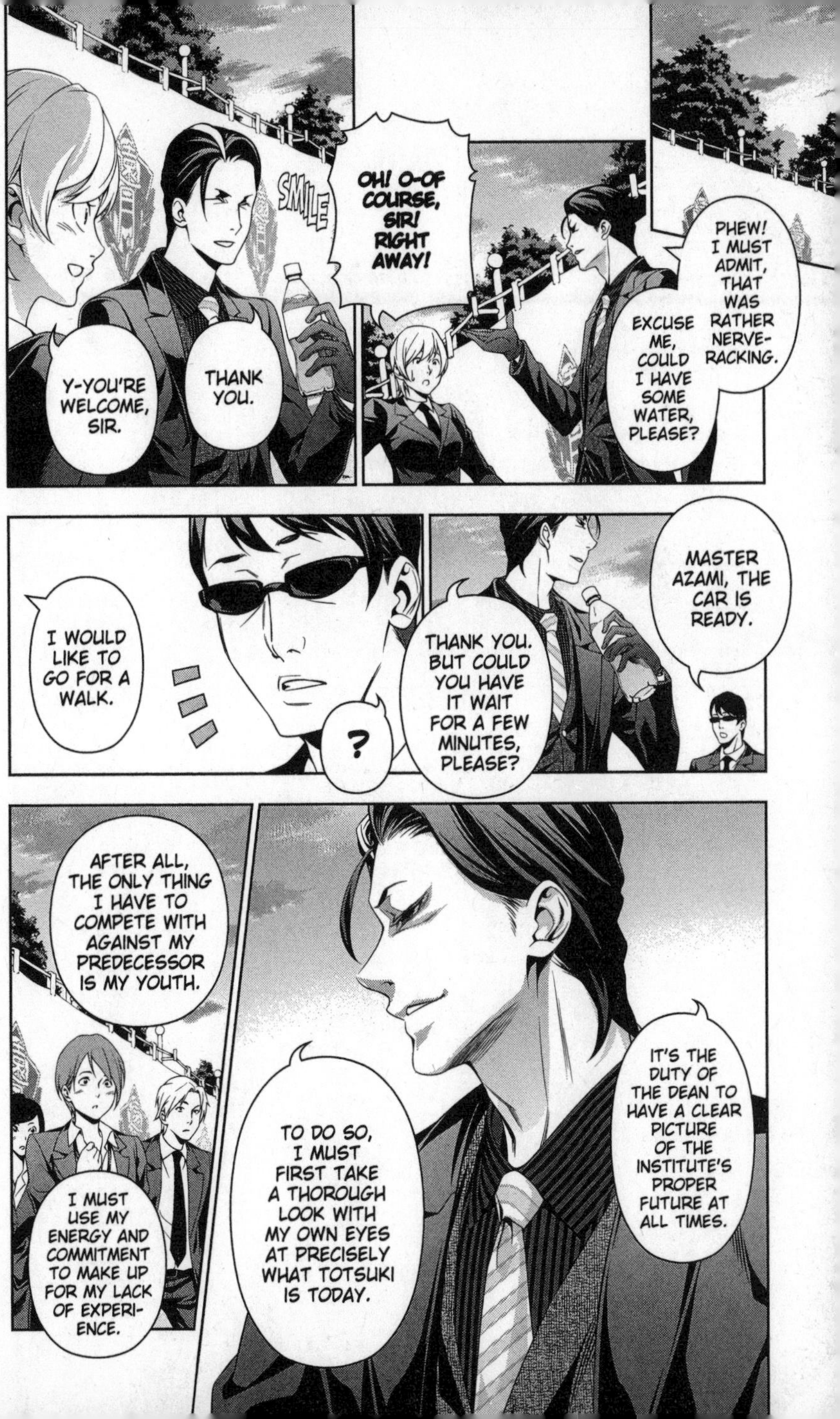
PHEW! I MUST ADMIT, THAT WAS RATHER NERVE-RACKING.
EXCUSE ME, COULD I HAVE SOME WATER, PLEASE?
OH! O-OF COURSE, SIR! RIGHT AWAY!
SMILE
THANK YOU.
Y-YOU'RE WELCOME, SIR.
MASTER AZAMI, THE CAR IS READY.
THANK YOU. BUT COULD YOU HAVE IT WAIT FOR A FEW MINUTES, PLEASE?
?
I WOULD LIKE TO GO FOR A WALK.
IT'S THE DUTY OF THE DEAN TO HAVE A CLEAR PICTURE OF THE INSTITUTE'S PROPER FUTURE AT ALL TIMES.
TO DO SO, I MUST FIRST TAKE A THOROUGH LOOK WITH MY OWN EYES AT PRECISELY WHAT TOTSUKI IS TODAY.
AFTER ALL, THE ONLY THING I HAVE TO COMPETE WITH AGAINST MY PREDECESSOR IS MY YOUTH.
I MUST USE MY ENERGY AND COMMITMENT TO MAKE UP FOR MY LACK OF EXPERI-ENCE.

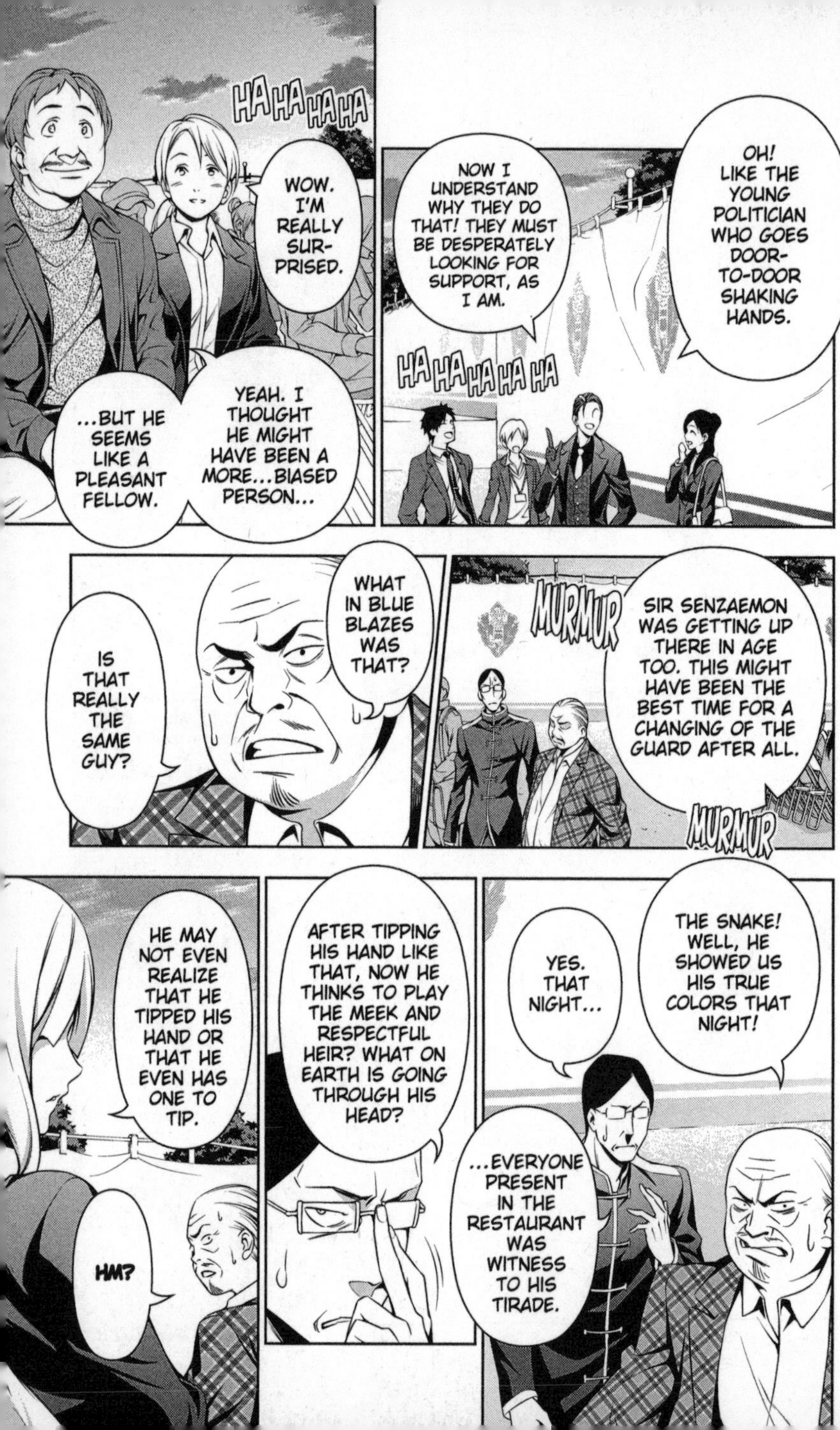
OH! LIKE THE YOUNG POLITICIAN WHO GOES DOOR-TO-DOOR SHAKING HANDS.
NOW I UNDERSTAND WHY THEY DO THAT! THEY MUST BE DESPERATELY LOOKING FOR SUPPORT, AS I AM.
HA HA HA HA HA
HA HA HA HA
WOW. I'M REALLY SUR-PRISED.
YEAH. I THOUGHT HE MIGHT HAVE BEEN A MORE...BIASED PERSON...
...BUT HE SEEMS LIKE A PLEASANT FELLOW.
MURMUR
SIR SENZAEMON WAS GETTING UP THERE IN AGE TOO. THIS MIGHT HAVE BEEN THE BEST TIME FOR A CHANGING OF THE GUARD AFTER ALL.
MURMUR
WHAT IN BLUE BLAZES WAS THAT?
IS THAT REALLY THE SAME GUY?
THE SNAKE! WELL, HE SHOWED US HIS TRUE COLORS THAT NIGHT!
YES. THAT NIGHT...
...EVERYONE PRESENT IN THE RESTAURANT WAS WITNESS TO HIS TIRADE.
AFTER TIPPING HIS HAND LIKE THAT, NOW HE THINKS TO PLAY THE MEEK AND RESPECTFUL HEIR? WHAT ON EARTH IS GOING THROUGH HIS HEAD?
HE MAY NOT EVEN REALIZE THAT HE TIPPED HIS HAND OR THAT HE EVEN HAS ONE TO TIP.
HM?

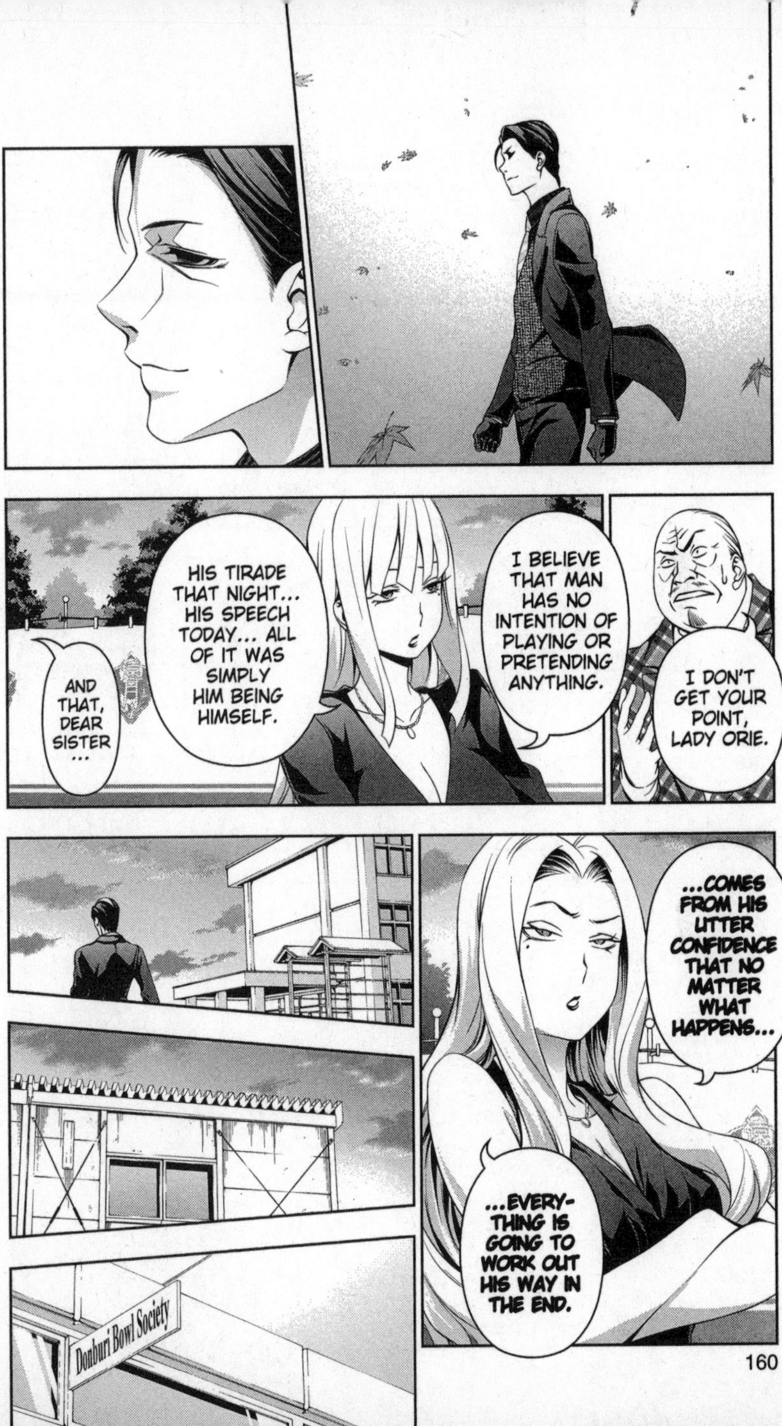
I DON'T GET YOUR POINT, LADY ORIE.
I BELIEVE THAT MAN HAS NO INTENTION OF PLAYING OR PRETENDING ANYTHING.
HIS TIRADE THAT NIGHT... HIS SPEECH TODAY... ALL OF IT WAS SIMPLY HIM BEING HIMSELF.
AND THAT, DEAR SISTER...
...COMES FROM HIS UTTER CONFIDENCE THAT NO MATTER WHAT HAPPENS...
...EVERY-THING IS GOING TO WORK OUT HIS WAY IN THE END.
Donburi Bowl Society

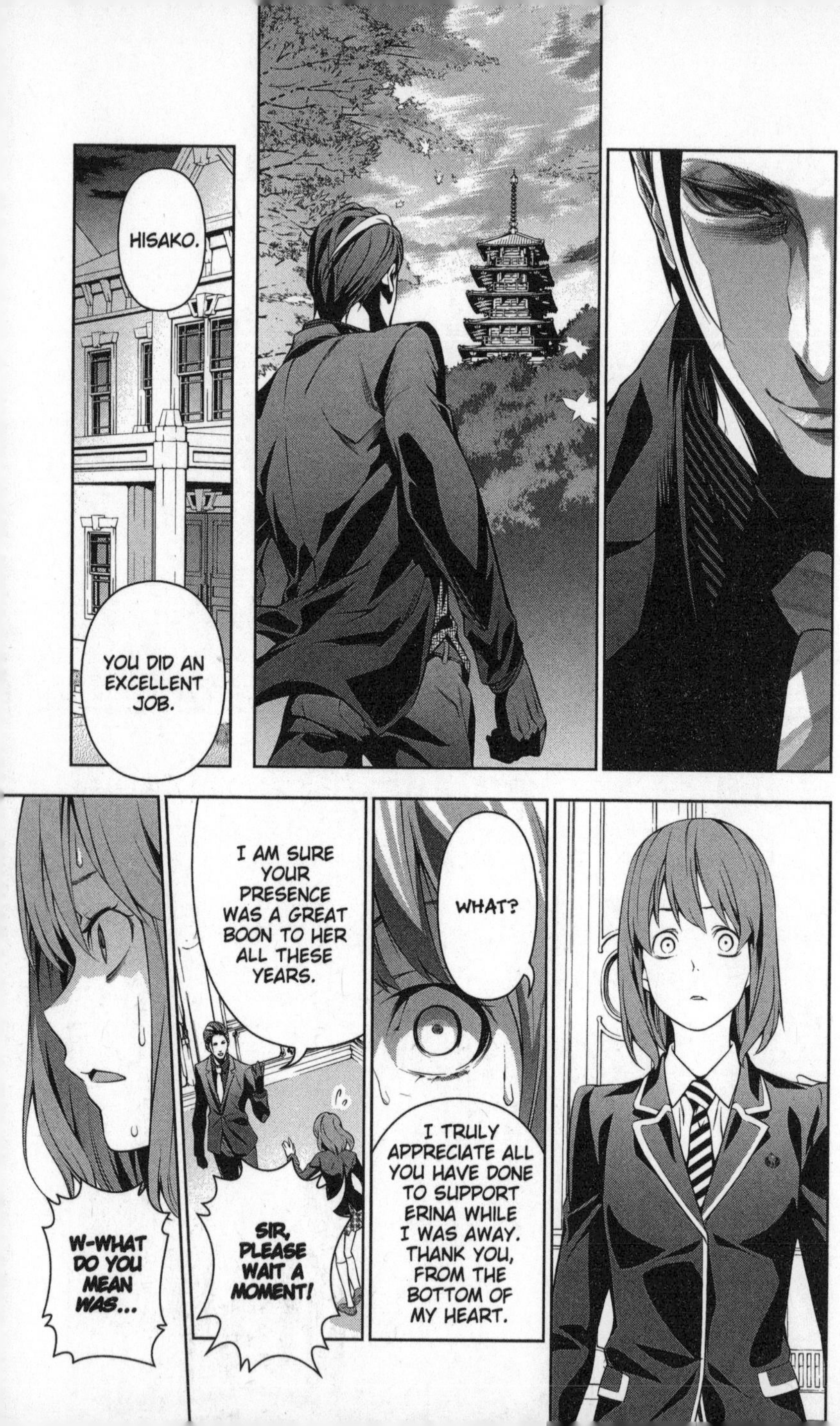

HISAKO.
YOU DID AN EXCELLENT JOB.
WHAT?
I TRULY APPRECIATE ALL YOU HAVE DONE TO SUPPORT ERINA WHILE I WAS AWAY. THANK YOU, FROM THE BOTTOM OF MY HEART.
I AM SURE YOUR PRESENCE WAS A GREAT BOON TO HER ALL THESE YEARS.
SIR, PLEASE WAIT A MOMENT!
W-WHAT DO YOU MEAN WAS...

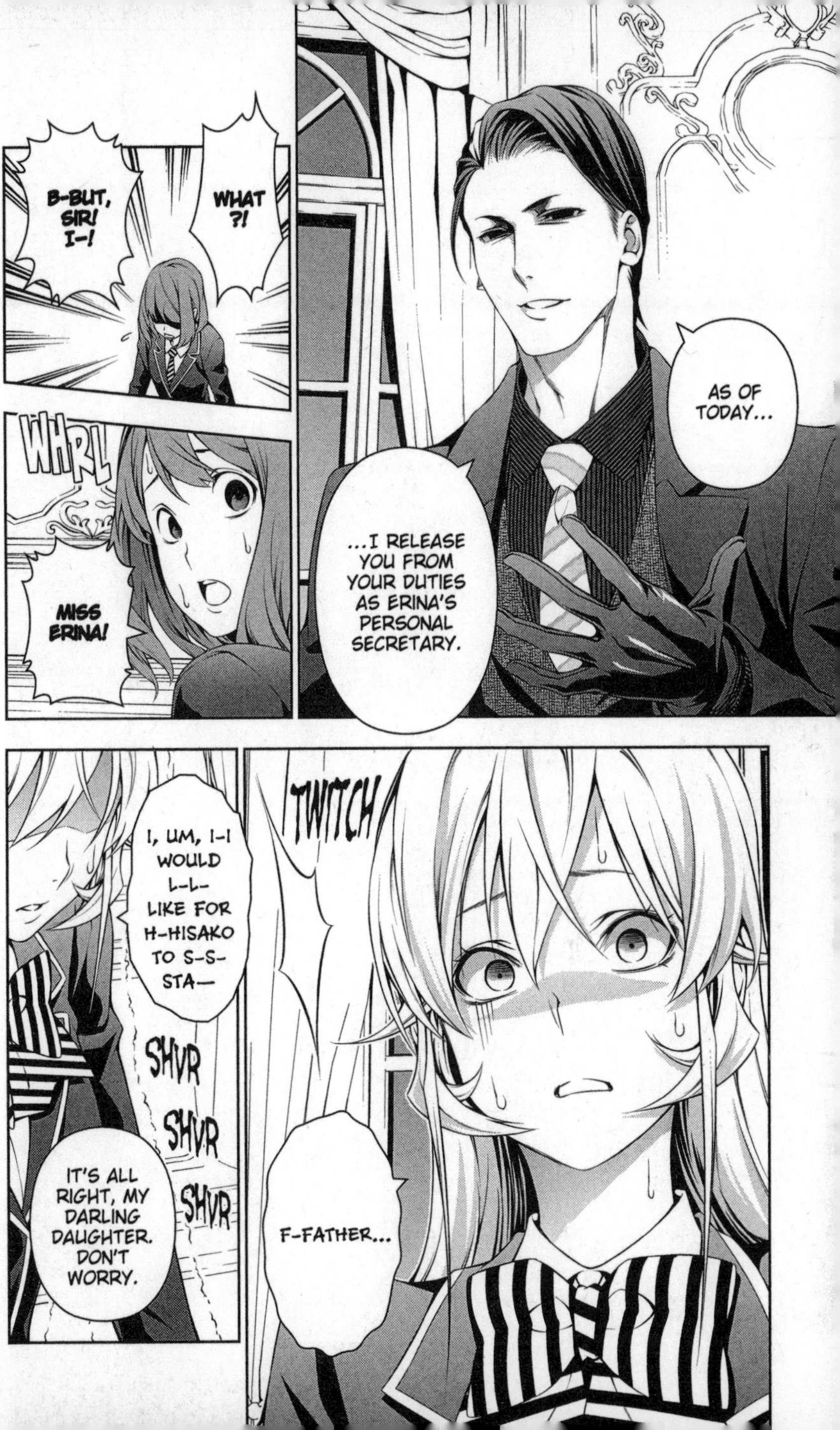
AS OF TODAY...
...I RELEASE YOU FROM YOUR DUTIES AS ERINA'S PERSONAL SECRETARY.
WHAT ?!
B-BUT, SIR! I-!
WHRL
MISS ERINA!
TWITCH
F-FATHER...
I, UM, I-I WOULD L-L- LIKE FOR H-HISAKO TO S-S- STA—
SHVR
SHVR
SHVR
IT'S ALL RIGHT, MY DARLING DAUGHTER. DON'T WORRY.

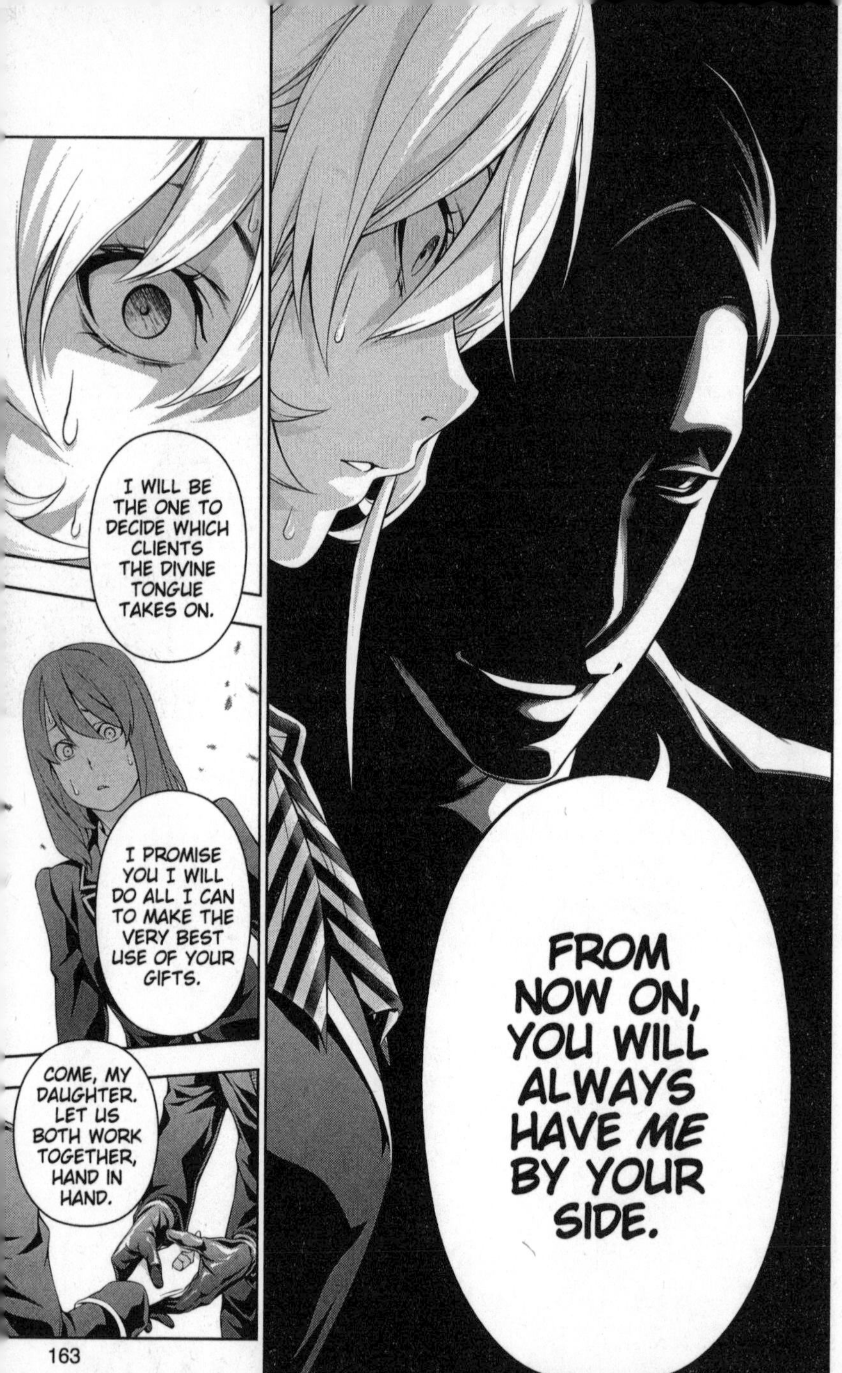
FROM NOW ON, YOU WILL ALWAYS HAVE ME BY YOUR SIDE.
I WILL BE THE ONE TO DECIDE WHICH CLIENTS THE DIVINE TONGUE TAKES ON.
I PROMISE YOU I WILL DO ALL I CAN TO MAKE THE VERY BEST USE OF YOUR GIFTS.
COME, MY DAUGHTER. LET US BOTH WORK TOGETHER, HAND IN HAND.

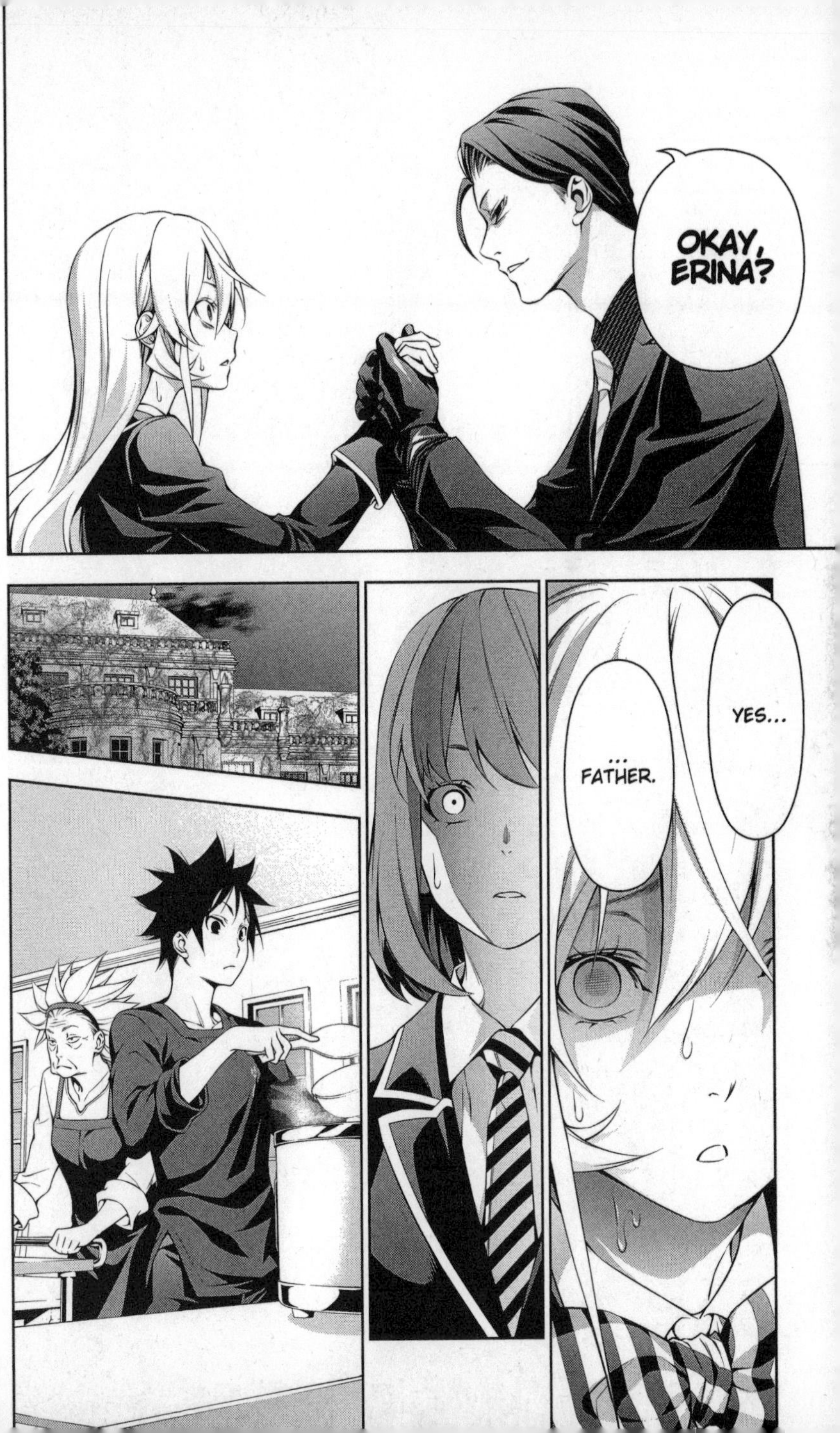
OKAY, ERINA?
YES...
...FATHER.

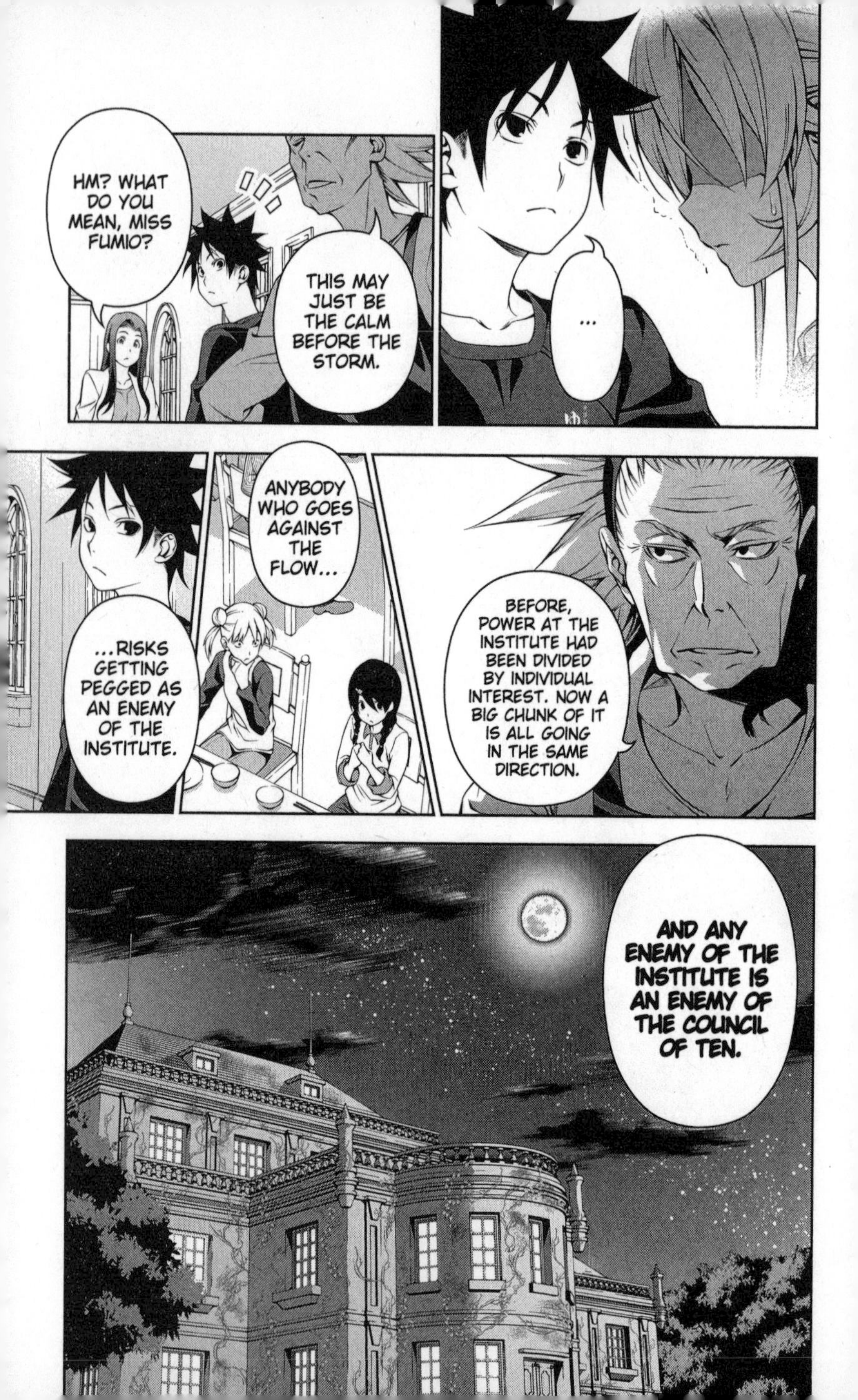
...
HM? WHAT DO YOU MEAN, MISS FUMIO?
THIS MAY JUST BE THE CALM BEFORE THE STORM.
BEFORE, POWER AT THE INSTITUTE HAD BEEN DIVIDED BY INDIVIDUAL INTEREST. NOW A BIG CHUNK OF IT IS ALL GOING IN THE SAME DIRECTION.
ANYBODY WHO GOES AGAINST THE FLOW...
...RISKS GETTING PEGGED AS AN ENEMY OF THE INSTITUTE.
AND ANY ENEMY OF THE INSTITUTE IS AN ENEMY OF THE COUNCIL OF TEN.

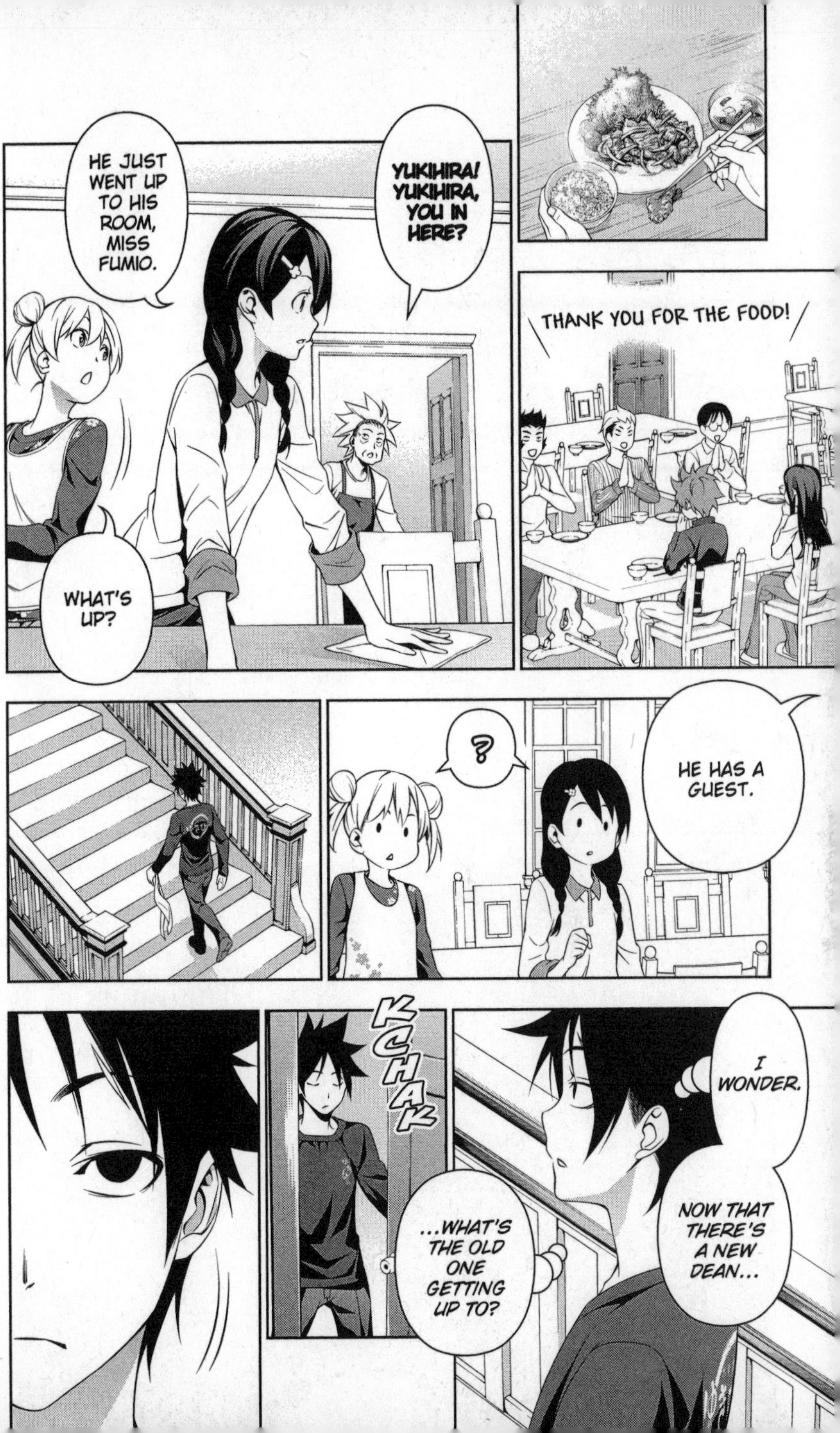
THANK YOU FOR THE FOOD!
YUKIHIRA! YUKIHIRA, YOU IN HERE?
HE JUST WENT UP TO HIS ROOM, MISS FUMIO.
WHAT'S UP?
HE HAS A GUEST.
?
I WONDER.
NOW THAT THERE'S A NEW DEAN...
KCHAK
...WHAT'S THE OLD ONE GETTING UP TO?

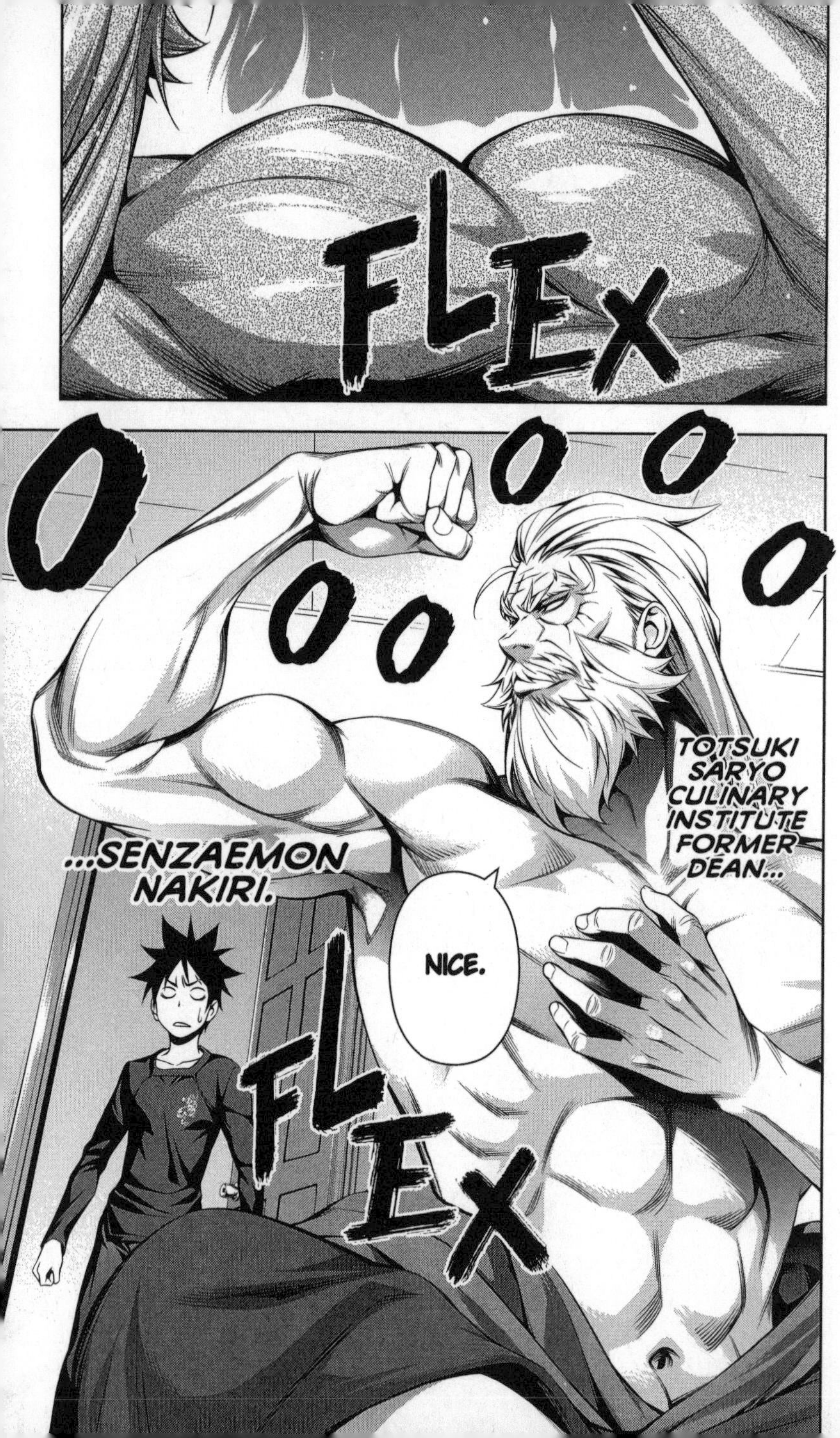
FLEX
OOOOOO
TOTSUKI SARYO CULINARY INSTITUTE FORMER DEAN...
...SENZAEMON NAKIRI.
NICE.
FLEX

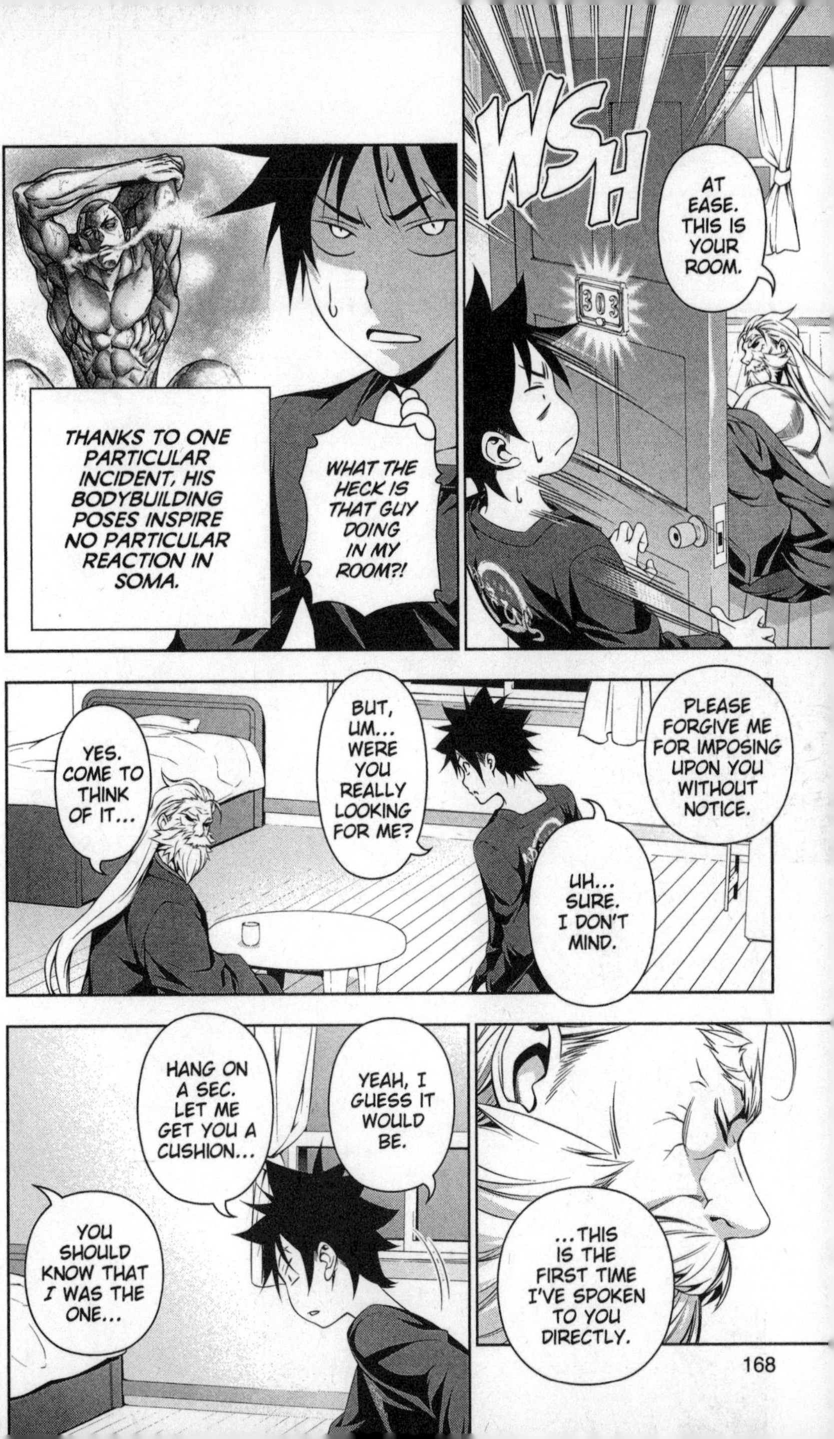
WSH
AT EASE. THIS IS YOUR ROOM.
303
WHAT THE HECK IS THAT GUY DOING IN MY ROOM?!
THANKS TO ONE PARTICULAR INCIDENT, HIS BODYBUILDING POSES INSPIRE NO PARTICULAR REACTION IN SOMA.
PLEASE FORGIVE ME FOR IMPOSING UPON YOU WITHOUT NOTICE.
UH... SURE. I DON'T MIND.
BUT, UM... WERE YOU REALLY LOOKING FOR ME?
YES. COME TO THINK OF IT...
...THIS IS THE FIRST TIME I'VE SPOKEN TO YOU DIRECTLY.
YEAH, I GUESS IT WOULD BE.
HANG ON A SEC. LET ME GET YOU A CUSHION...
YOU SHOULD KNOW THAT I WAS THE ONE...

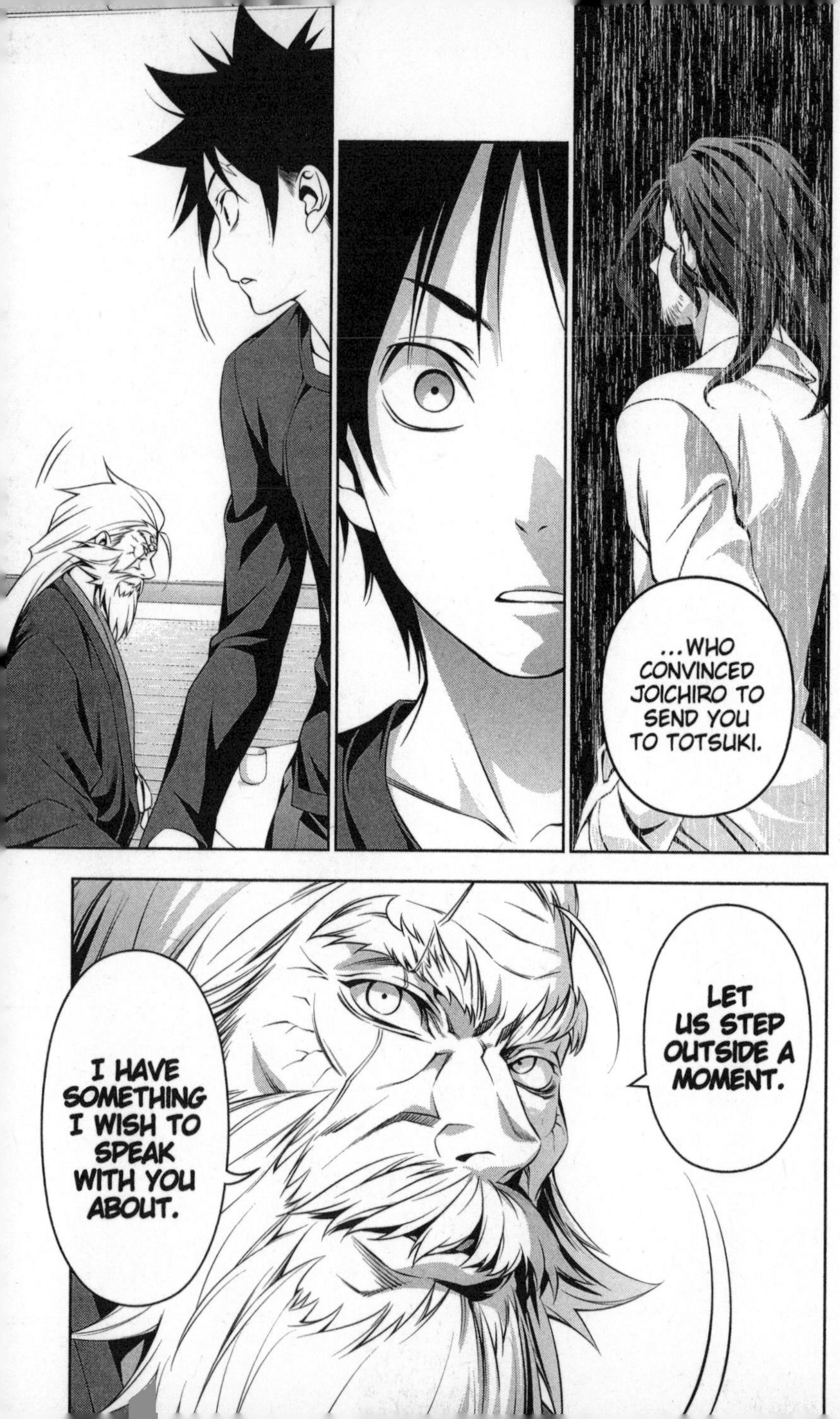
...WHO CONVINCED JOICHIRO TO SEND YOU TO TOTSUKI.
LET US STEP OUTSIDE A MOMENT.
I HAVE SOMETHING I WISH TO SPEAK WITH YOU ABOUT.

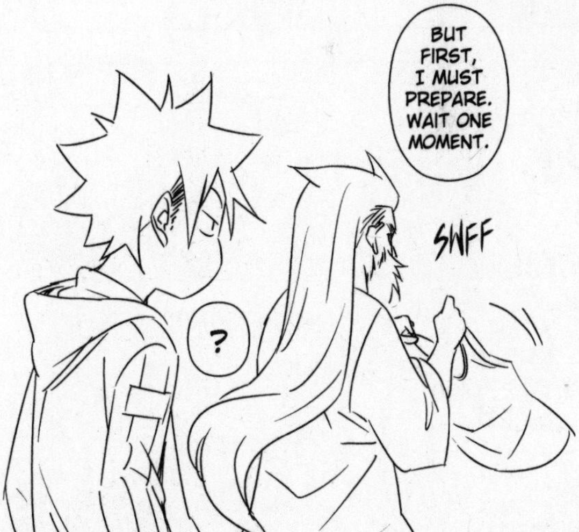
BUT FIRST, I MUST PREPARE. WAIT ONE MOMENT.
SWFF
?

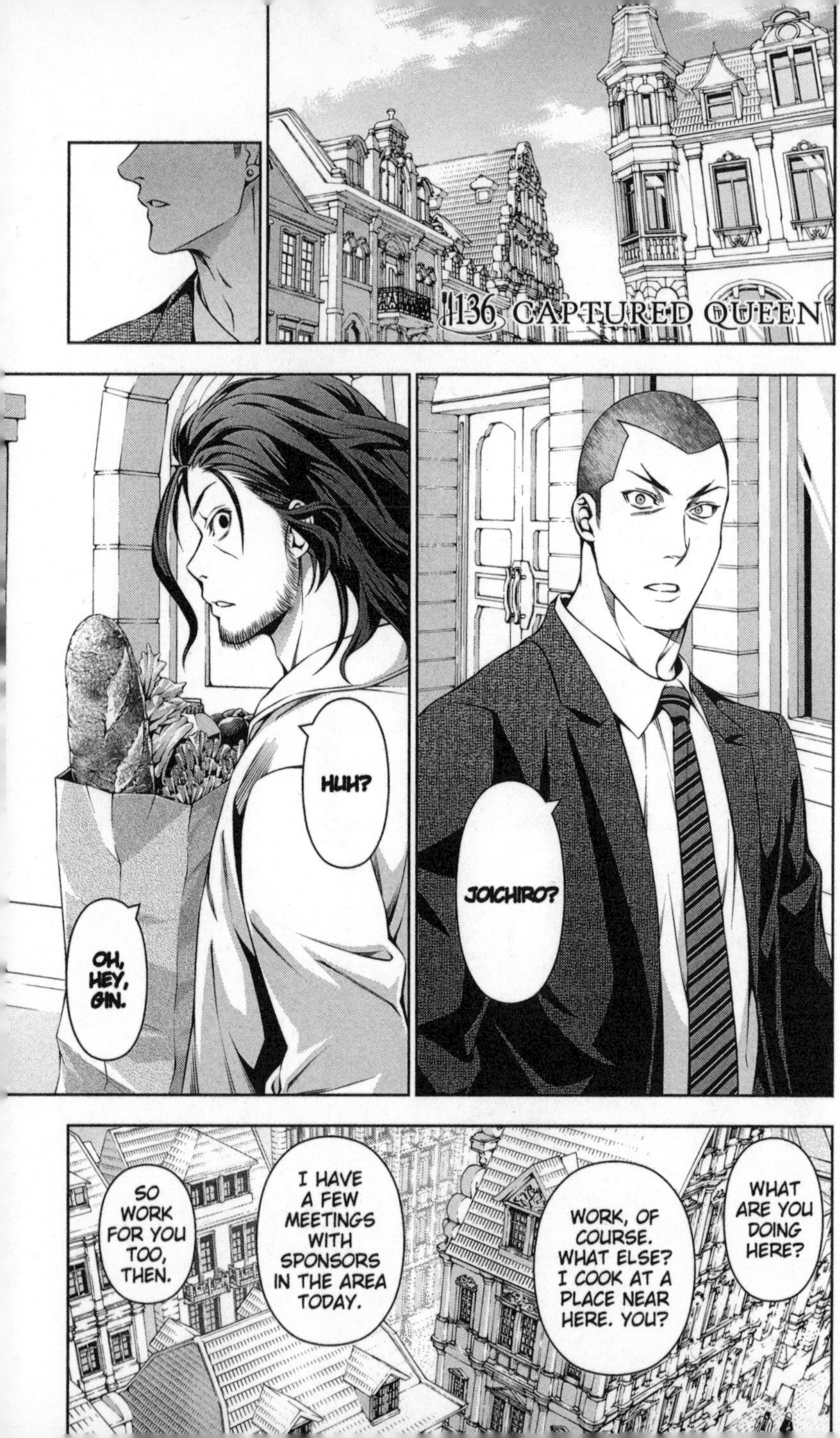
#136 CAPTURED QUEEN
JOICHIRO?
HUH?
OH, HEY, GIN.
WHAT ARE YOU DOING HERE?
WORK, OF COURSE. WHAT ELSE? I COOK AT A PLACE NEAR HERE. YOU?
I HAVE A FEW MEETINGS WITH SPONSORS IN THE AREA TODAY.
SO WORK FOR YOU TOO, THEN.

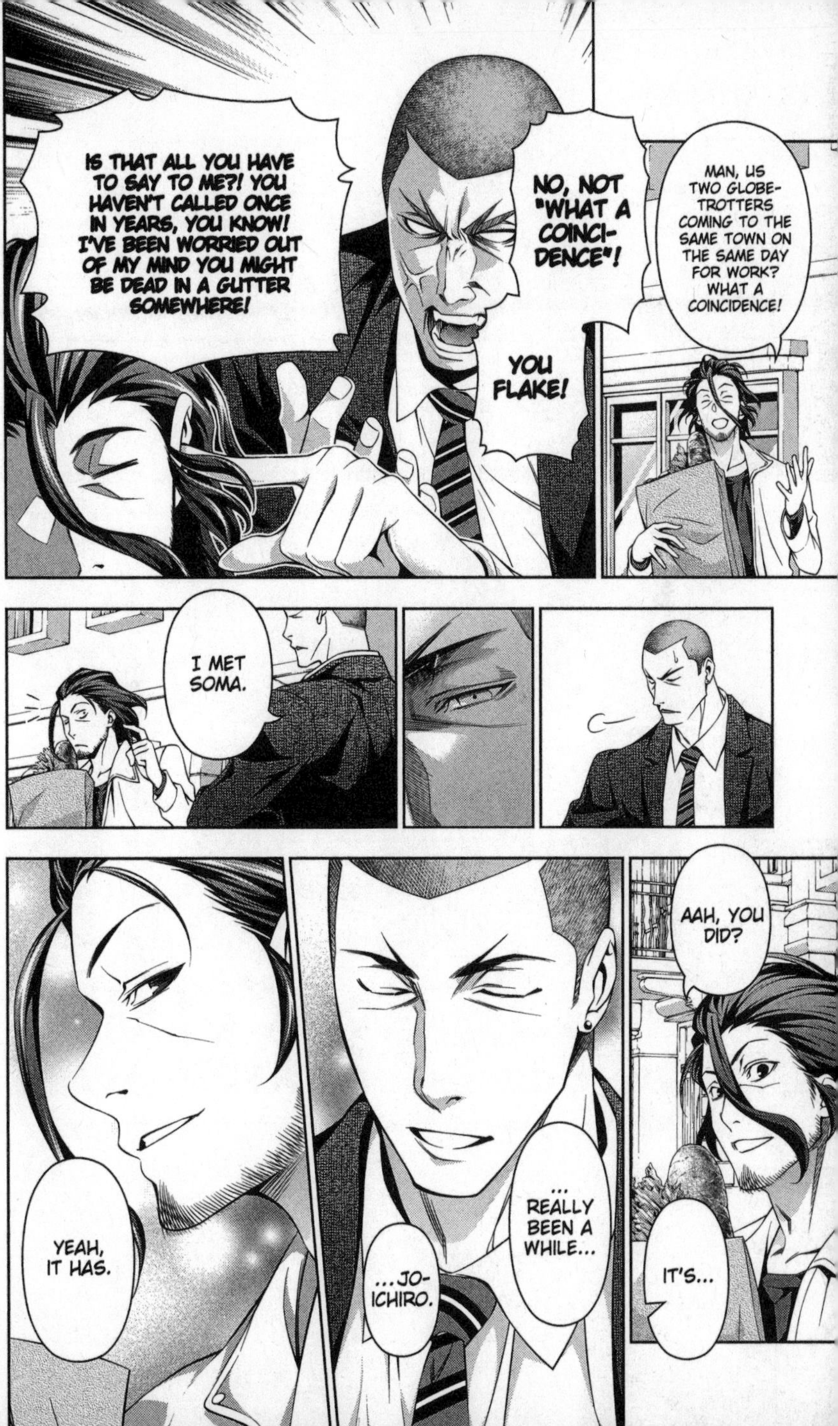
MAN, US TWO GLOBE-TROTTERS COMING TO THE SAME TOWN ON THE SAME DAY FOR WORK? WHAT A COINCIDENCE!
NO, NOT "WHAT A COINCI-DENCE"!
YOU FLAKE!
IS THAT ALL YOU HAVE TO SAY TO ME?! YOU HAVEN'T CALLED ONCE IN YEARS, YOU KNOW! I'VE BEEN WORRIED OUT OF MY MIND YOU MIGHT BE DEAD IN A GUTTER SOMEWHERE!
I MET SOMA.
AAH, YOU DID?
IT'S...
... REALLY BEEN A WHILE...
...JO-ICHIRO.
YEAH, IT HAS.

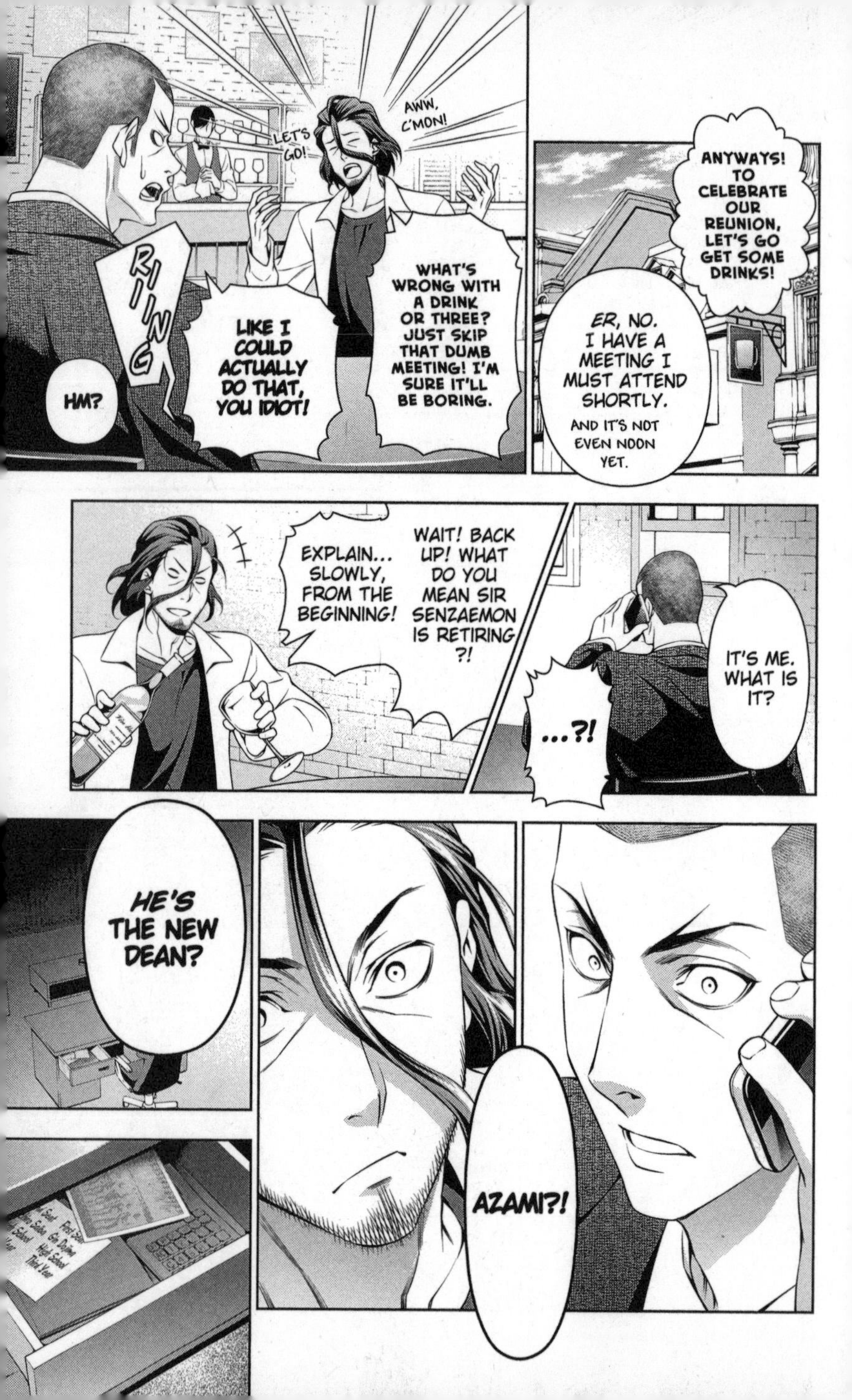
ANYWAYS! TO CELEBRATE OUR REUNION, LET'S GO GET SOME DRINKS!
ER, NO. I HAVE A MEETING I MUST ATTEND SHORTLY.
AND IT'S NOT EVEN NOON YET.
AWW, C'MON!
LET'S GO!
WHAT'S WRONG WITH A DRINK OR THREE? JUST SKIP THAT DUMB MEETING! I'M SURE IT'LL BE BORING.
LIKE I COULD ACTUALLY DO THAT, YOU IDIOT!
RIIING
HM?
IT'S ME. WHAT IS IT?
...?!
WAIT! BACK UP! WHAT DO YOU MEAN SIR SENZAEMON IS RETIRING?!
EXPLAIN... SLOWLY, FROM THE BEGINNING!
AZAMI?!
HE'S THE NEW DEAN?

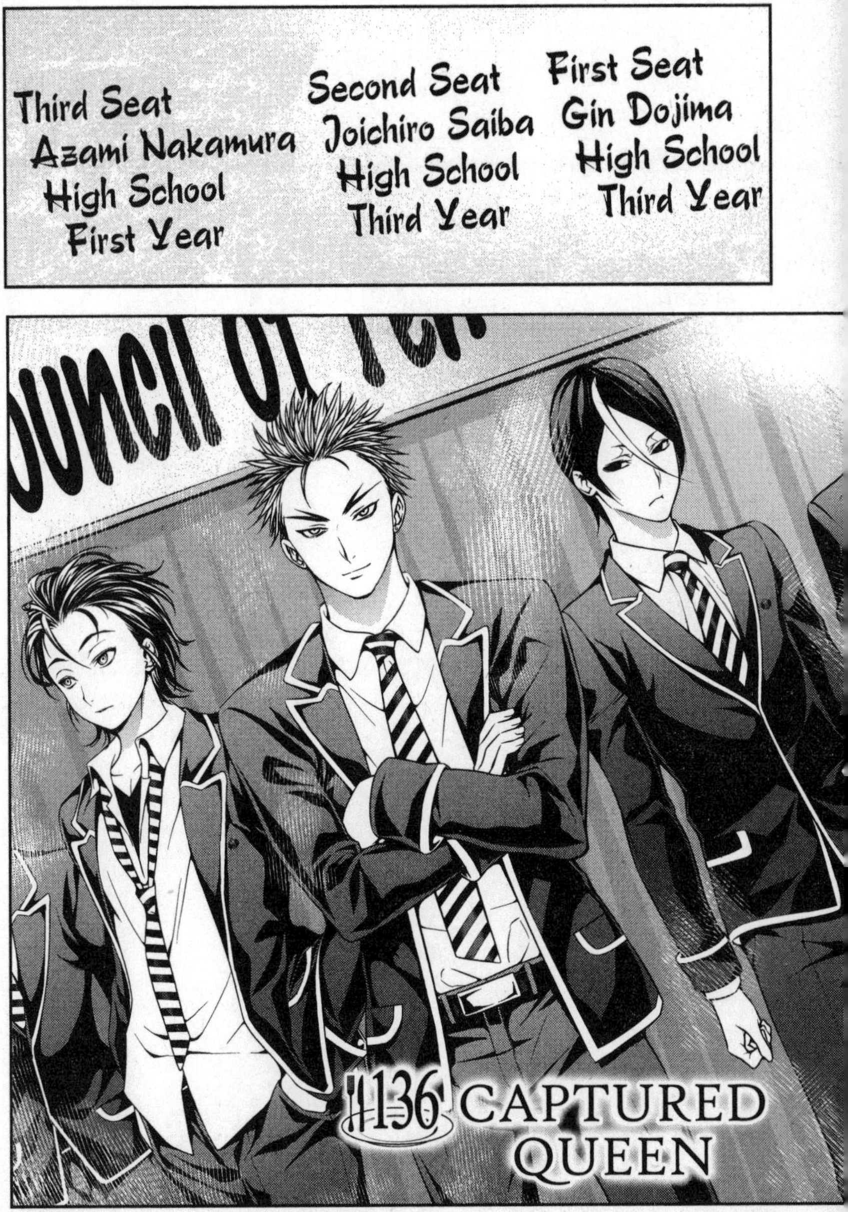
First Seat Gin Dojima High School Third Year
Second Seat Joichiro Saiba High School Third Year
Third Seat Azami Nakamura High School First Year
136 CAPTURED QUEEN

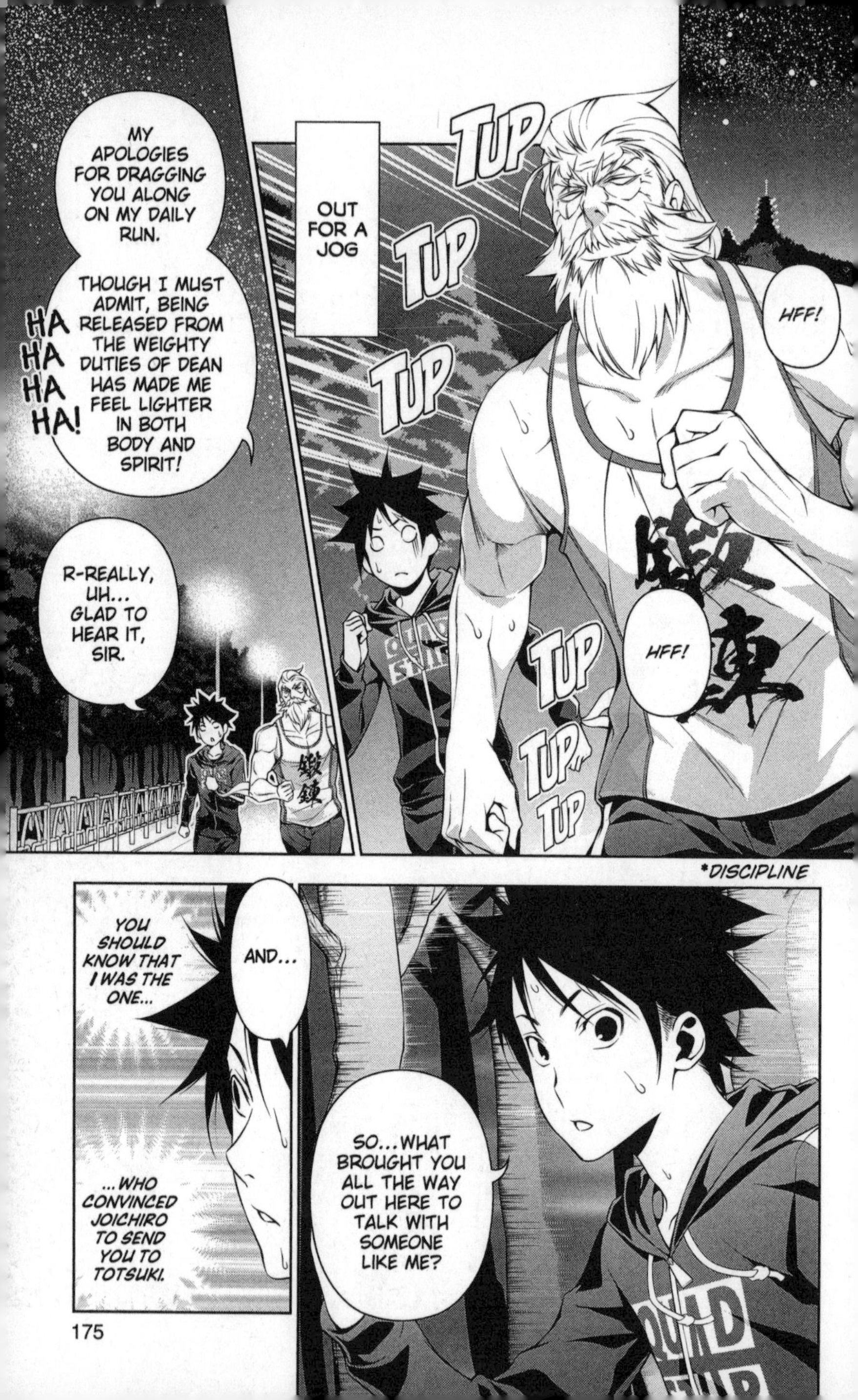
OUT FOR A JOG
TUP
TUP
TUP
HFF!
HFF!
TUP
TUP
TUP
MY APOLOGIES FOR DRAGGING YOU ALONG ON MY DAILY RUN.
THOUGH I MUST ADMIT, BEING RELEASED FROM THE WEIGHTY DUTIES OF DEAN HAS MADE ME FEEL LIGHTER IN BOTH BODY AND SPIRIT!
HA HA HA HA!
R-REALLY, UH... GLAD TO HEAR IT, SIR.
*DISCIPLINE
AND...
SO...WHAT BROUGHT YOU ALL THE WAY OUT HERE TO TALK WITH SOMEONE LIKE ME?
YOU SHOULD KNOW THAT I WAS THE ONE...
...WHO CONVINCED JOICHIRO TO SEND YOU TO TOTSUKI.

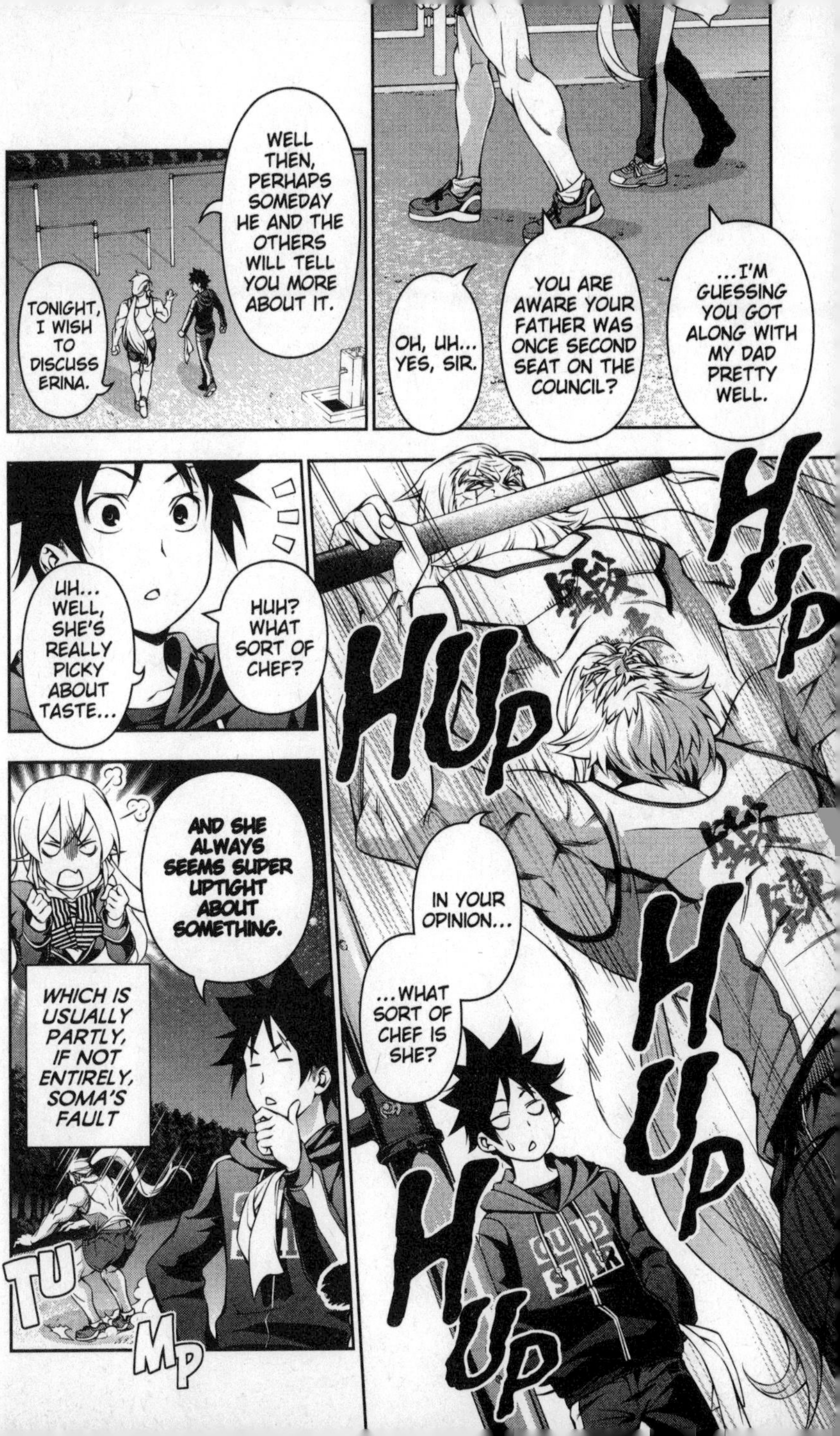
...I'M GUESSING YOU GOT ALONG WITH MY DAD PRETTY WELL.
YOU ARE AWARE YOUR FATHER WAS ONCE SECOND SEAT ON THE COUNCIL?
OH, UH... YES, SIR.
WELL THEN, PERHAPS SOMEDAY HE AND THE OTHERS WILL TELL YOU MORE ABOUT IT.
TONIGHT, I WISH TO DISCUSS ERINA.
HUP
HUP
IN YOUR OPINION...
...WHAT SORT OF CHEF IS SHE?
HUP
HUP
HUP
HUH? WHAT SORT OF CHEF?
UH... WELL, SHE'S REALLY PICKY ABOUT TASTE...
AND SHE ALWAYS SEEMS SUPER UPTIGHT ABOUT SOMETHING.
WHICH IS USUALLY PARTLY, IF NOT ENTIRELY, SOMA'S FAULT
TUMP

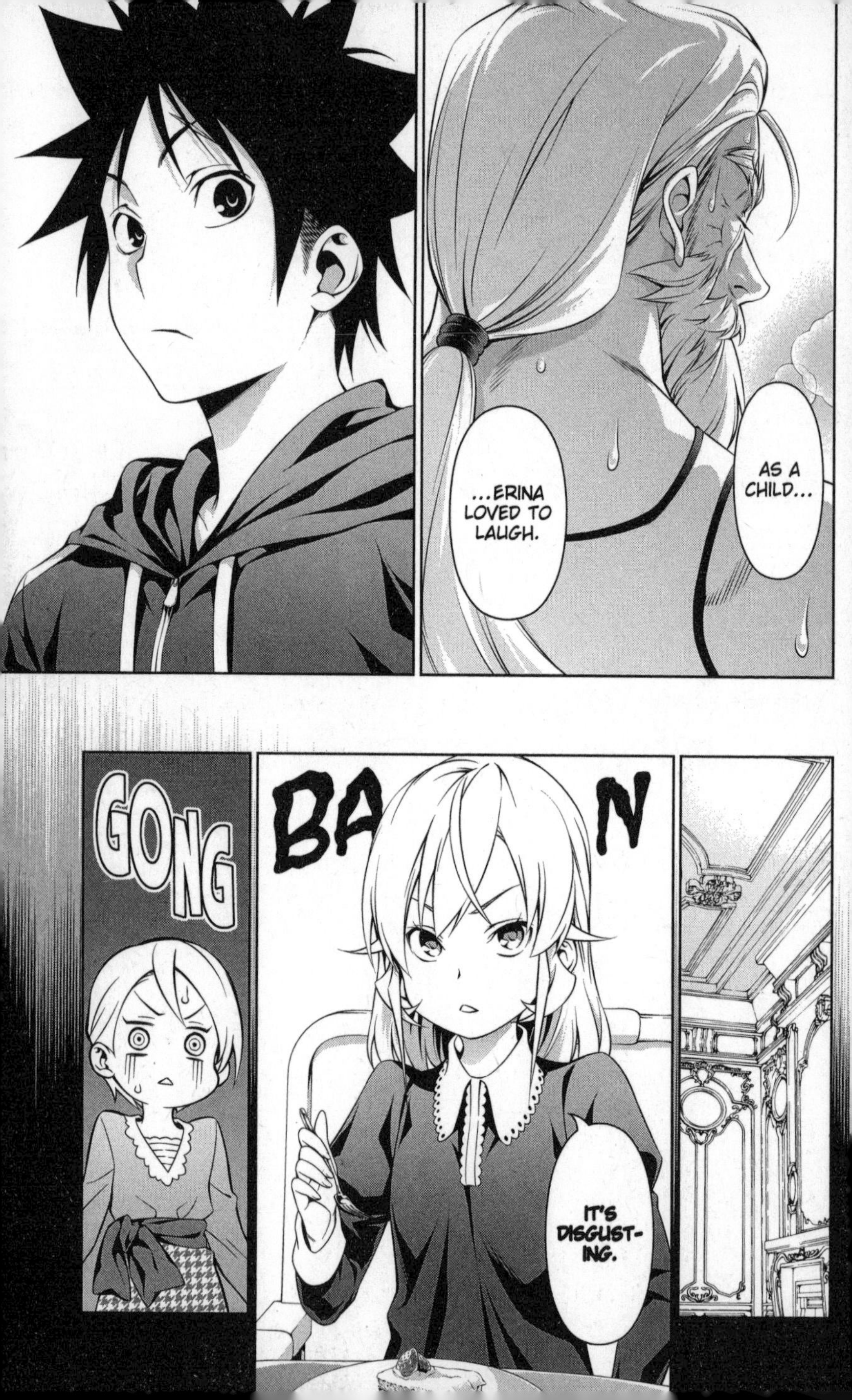
AS A CHILD...
...ERINA LOVED TO LAUGH.
BA N
IT'S DISGUST-ING.
GONG

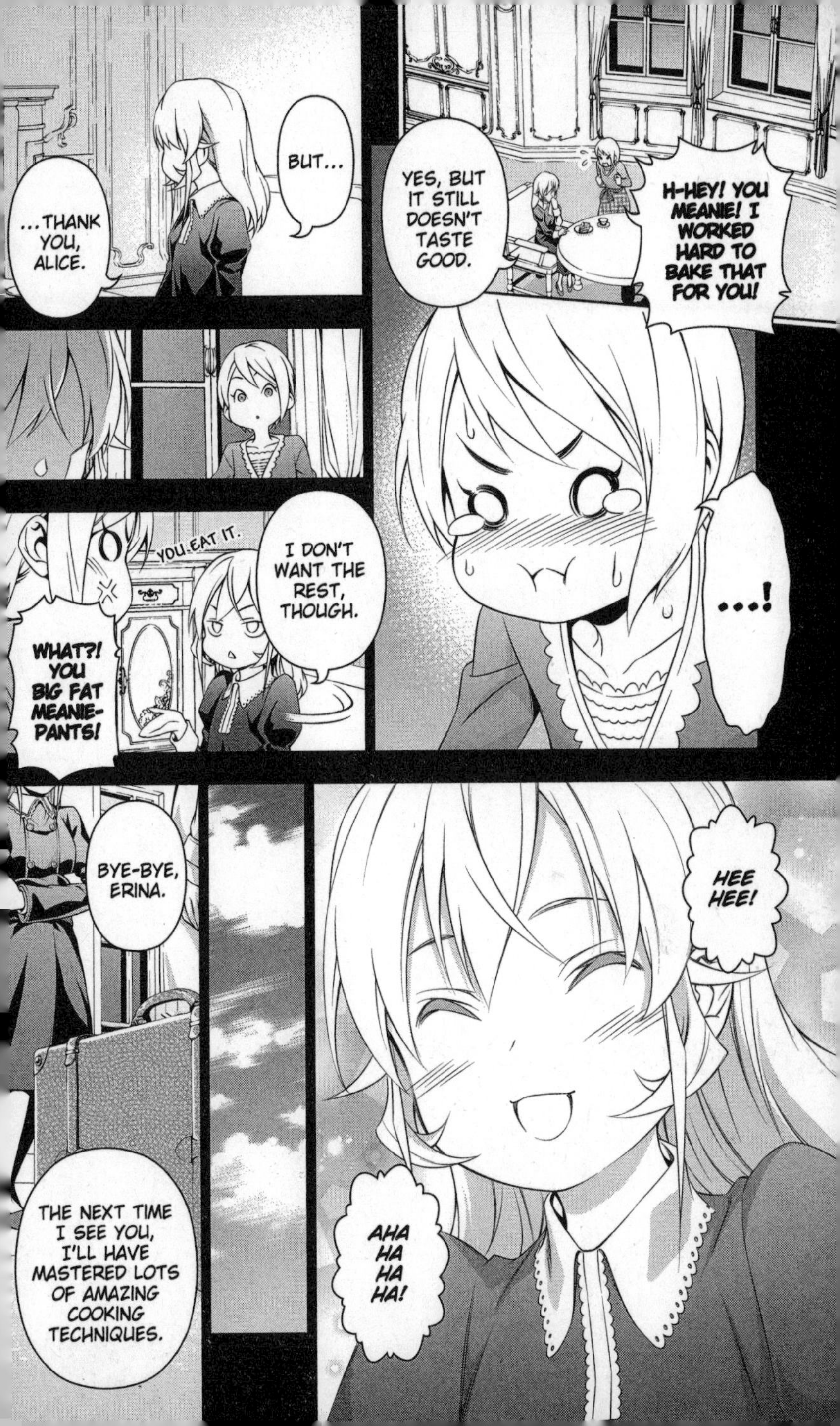
H-HEY! YOU MEANIE! I WORKED HARD TO BAKE THAT FOR YOU!
YES, BUT IT STILL DOESN'T TASTE GOOD.
BUT...
...THANK YOU, ALICE.
...!
I DON'T WANT THE REST, THOUGH.
YOU EAT IT.
WHAT?! YOU BIG FAT MEANIE-PANTS!
HEE HEE!
AHA HA HA HA!
BYE-BYE, ERINA.
THE NEXT TIME I SEE YOU, I'LL HAVE MASTERED LOTS OF AMAZING COOKING TECHNIQUES.

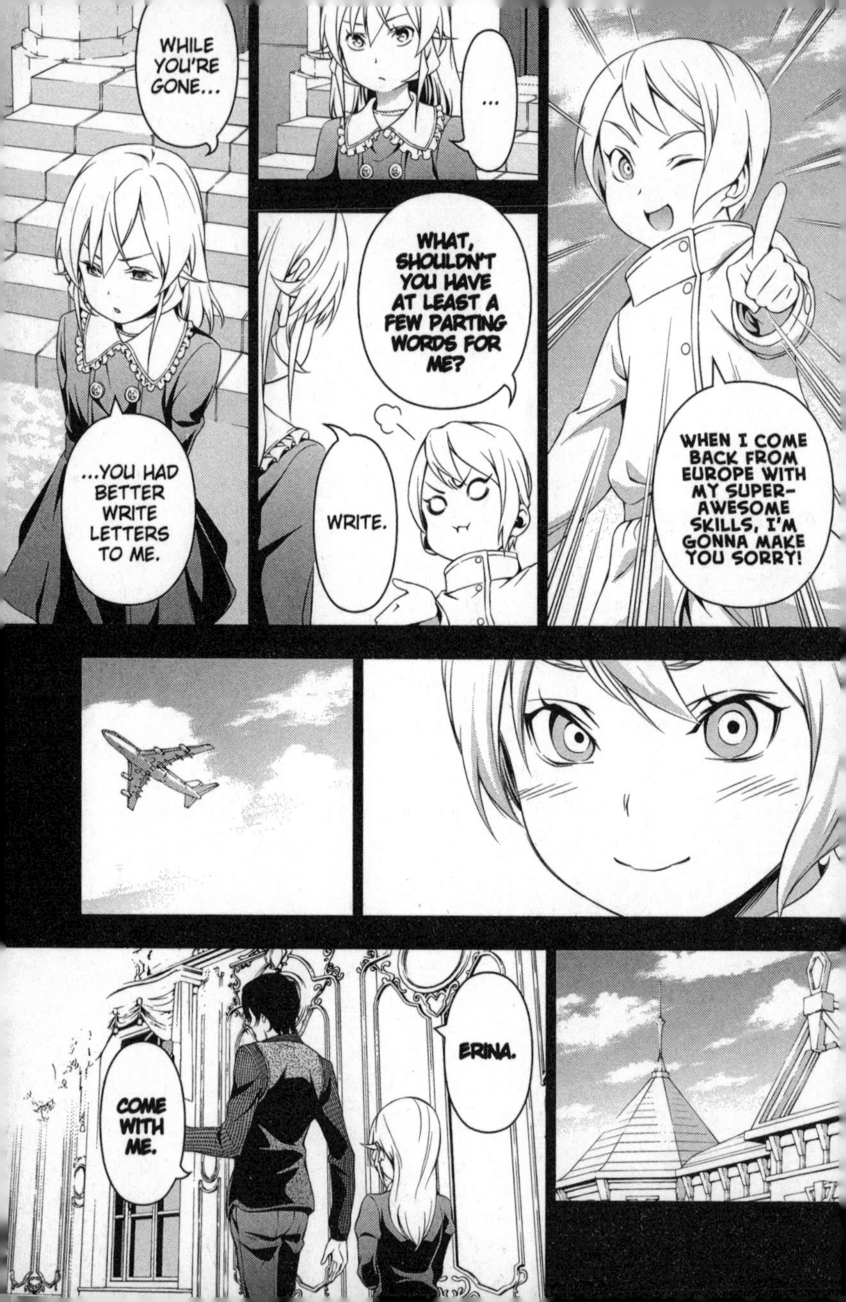
WHEN I COME BACK FROM EUROPE WITH MY SUPER-AWESOME SKILLS, I'M GONNA MAKE YOU SORRY!
...
WHAT, SHOULDN'T YOU HAVE AT LEAST A FEW PARTING WORDS FOR ME?
WRITE.
WHILE YOU'RE GONE...
...YOU HAD BETTER WRITE LETTERS TO ME.
ERINA.
COME WITH ME.

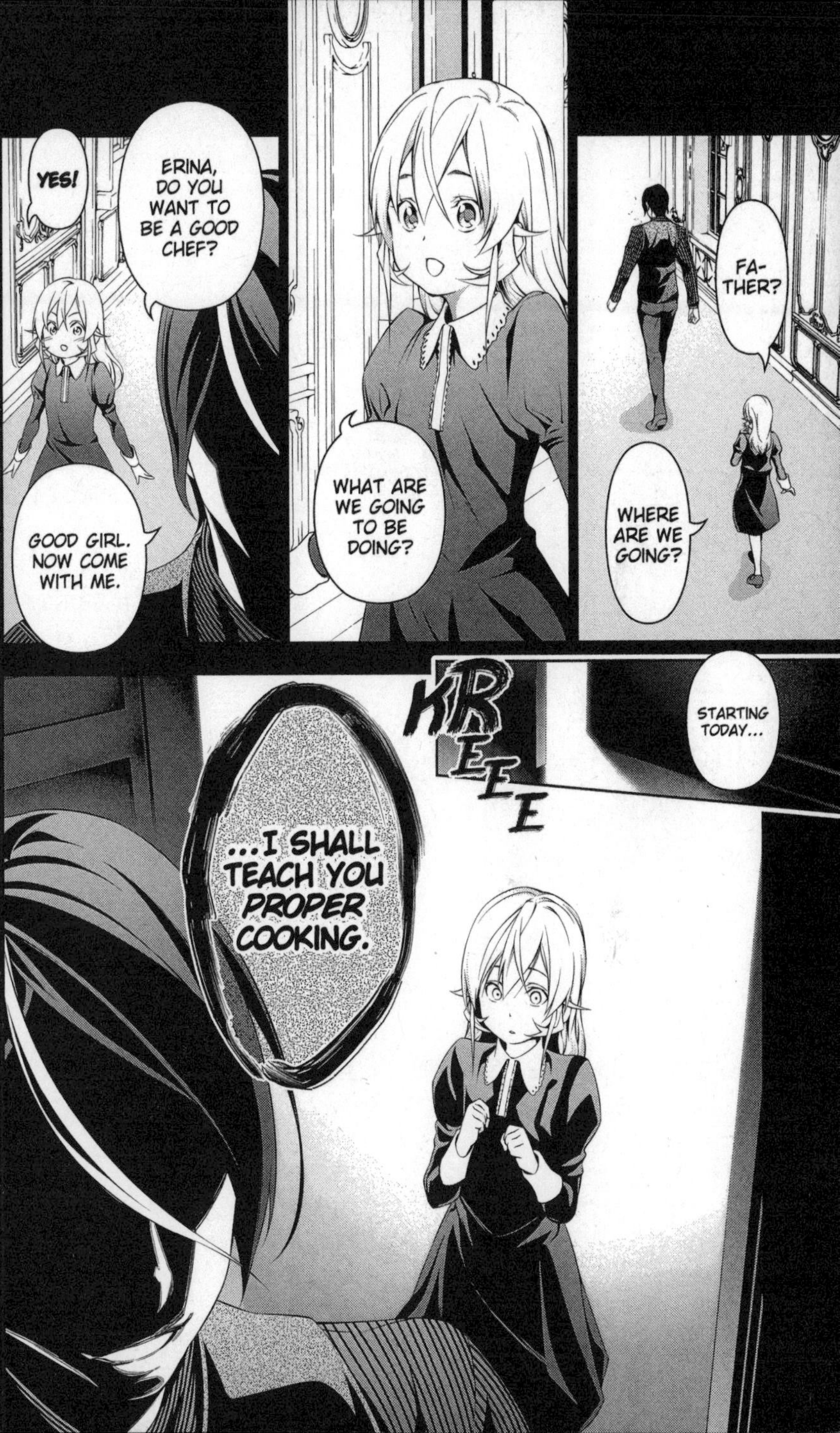
FA-
THER?
WHERE ARE WE GOING?
WHAT ARE WE GOING TO BE DOING?
ERINA, DO YOU WANT TO BE A GOOD CHEF?
YES!
GOOD GIRL. NOW COME WITH ME.
STARTING TODAY...
KREEE
...I SHALL TEACH YOU PROPER COOKING.

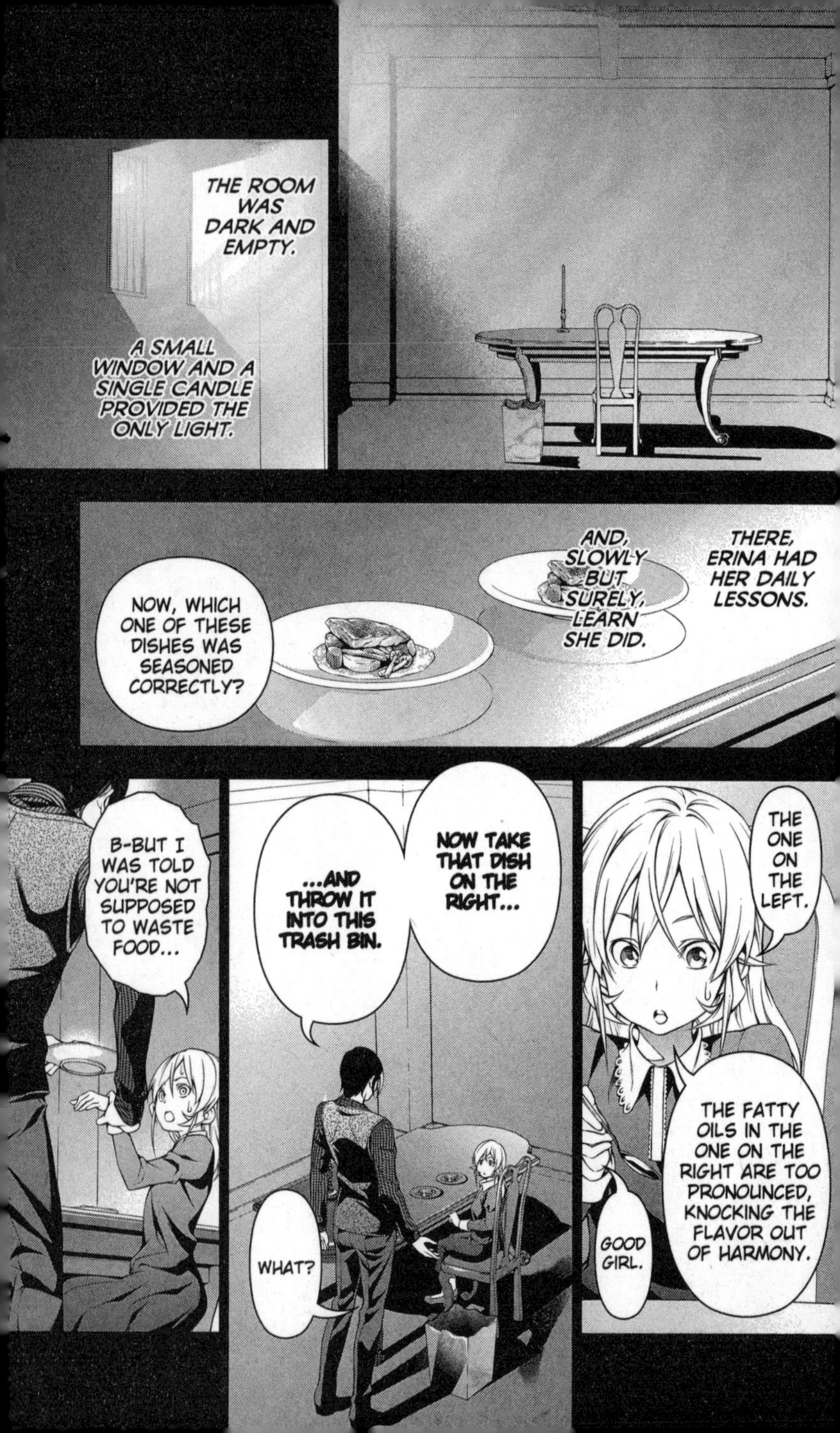
THE ROOM WAS DARK AND EMPTY.
A SMALL WINDOW AND A SINGLE CANDLE PROVIDED THE ONLY LIGHT.
THERE, ERINA HAD HER DAILY LESSONS.
AND, SLOWLY BUT SURELY, LEARN SHE DID.
NOW, WHICH ONE OF THESE DISHES WAS SEASONED CORRECTLY?
THE ONE ON THE LEFT.
THE FATTY OILS IN THE ONE ON THE RIGHT ARE TOO PRONOUNCED, KNOCKING THE FLAVOR OUT OF HARMONY.
GOOD GIRL.
NOW TAKE THAT DISH ON THE RIGHT...
...AND THROW IT INTO THIS TRASH BIN.
WHAT?
B-BUT I WAS TOLD YOU'RE NOT SUPPOSED TO WASTE FOOD...

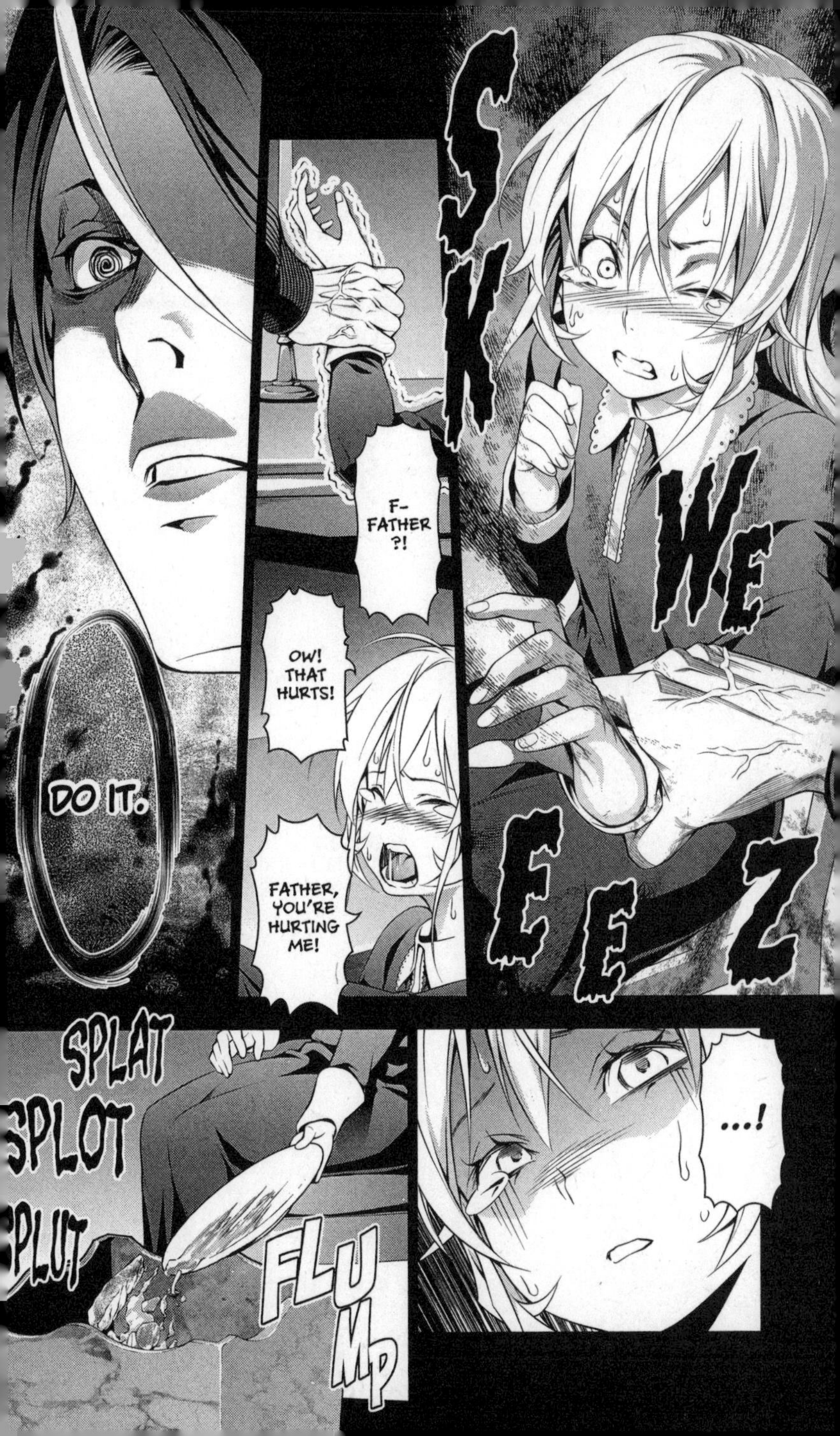
SKWEEEZ
F-FATHER?!
OW! THAT HURTS!
FATHER, YOU'RE HURTING ME!
DO IT.
...!
SPLAT
SPLOT
SPLUT
FLUMP

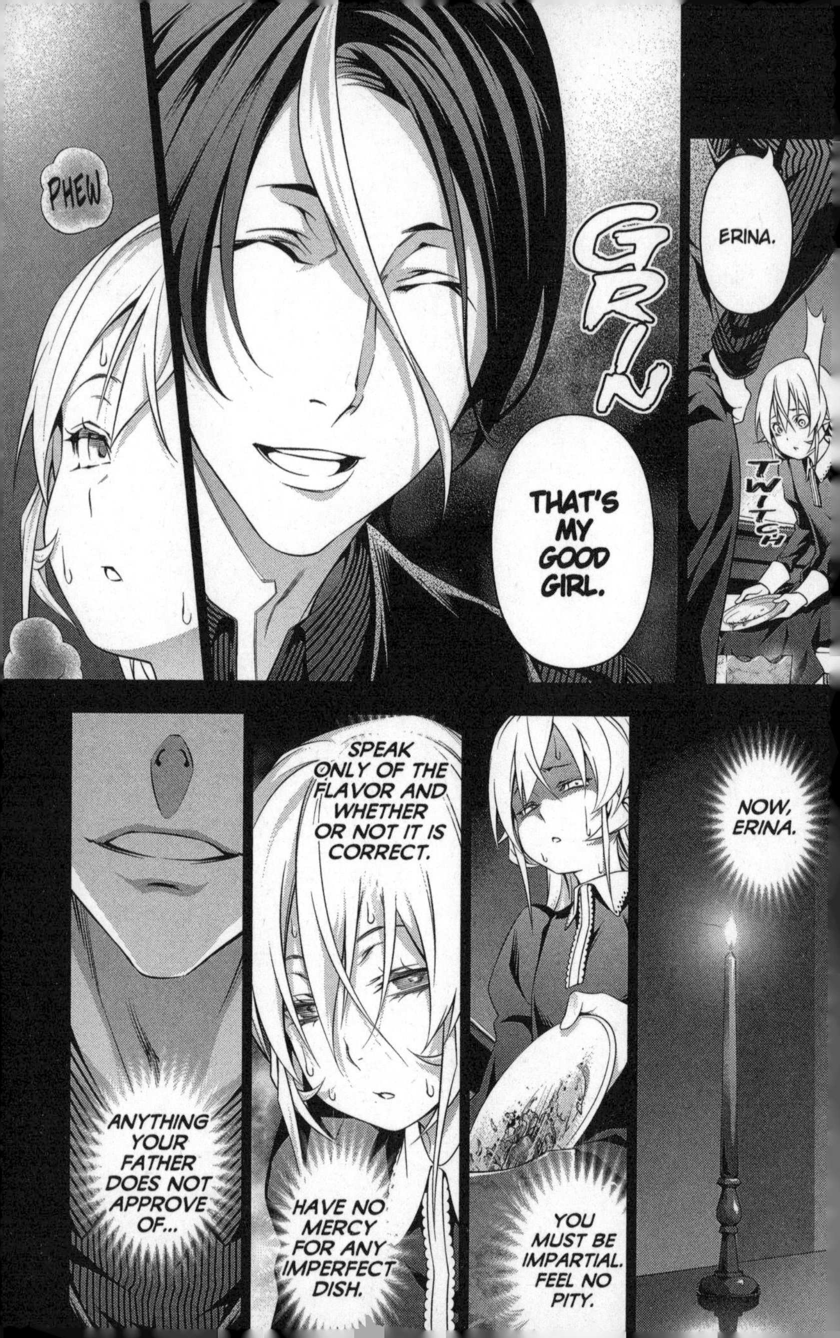
ERINA.
TWITCH
GRLL
THAT'S MY GOOD GIRL.
PHEW
NOW, ERINA.
YOU MUST BE IMPARTIAL. FEEL NO PITY.
SPEAK ONLY OF THE FLAVOR AND WHETHER OR NOT IT IS CORRECT.
HAVE NO MERCY FOR ANY IMPERFECT DISH.
ANYTHING YOUR FATHER DOES NOT APPROVE OF...

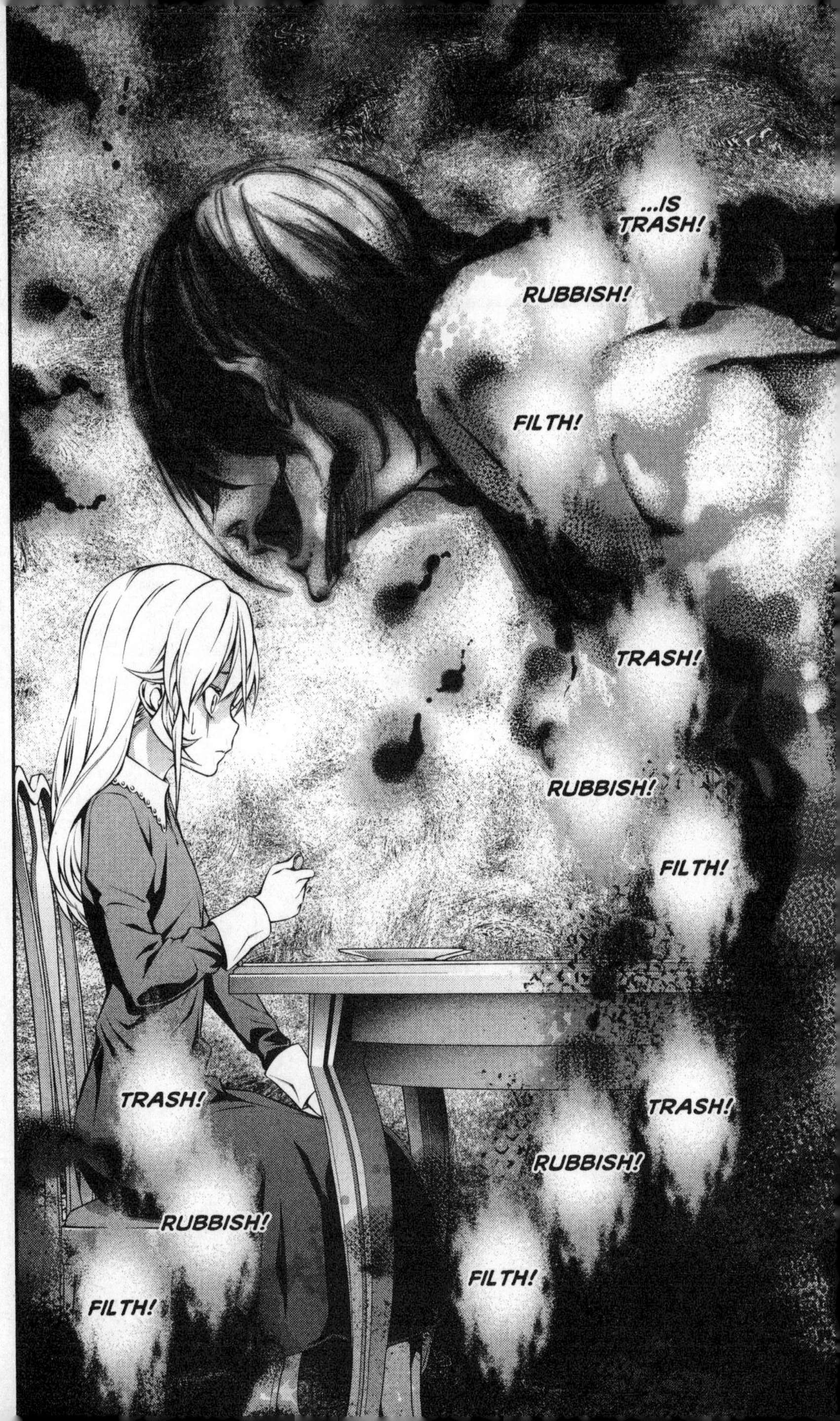
...IS TRASH!
RUBBISH!
FILTH!
TRASH!
RUBBISH!
FILTH!
TRASH!
RUBBISH!
TRASH!
RUBBISH!
FILTH!
FILTH!

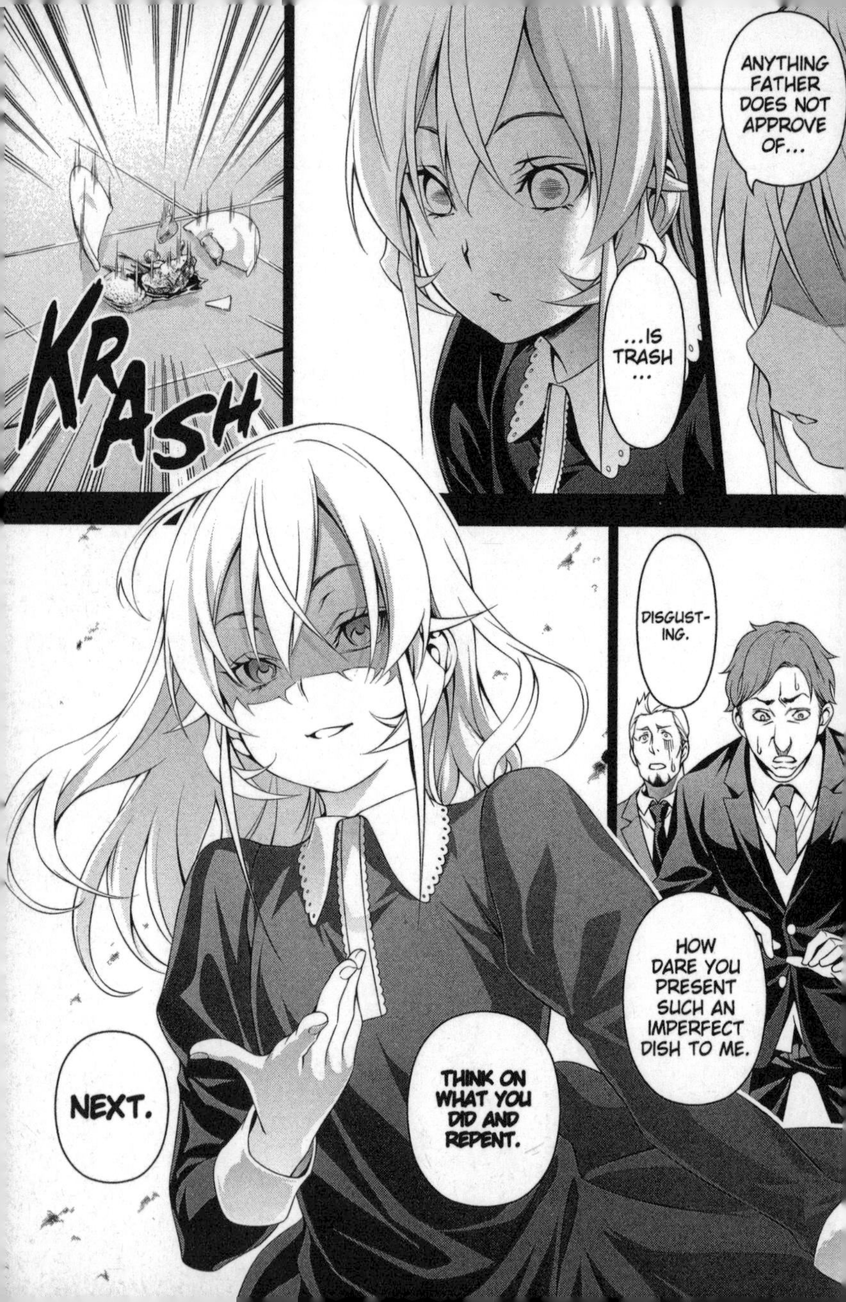
ANYTHING FATHER DOES NOT APPROVE OF...
...IS TRASH...
KRASH
DISGUST-ING.
HOW DARE YOU PRESENT SUCH AN IMPERFECT DISH TO ME.
THINK ON WHAT YOU DID AND REPENT.
NEXT.

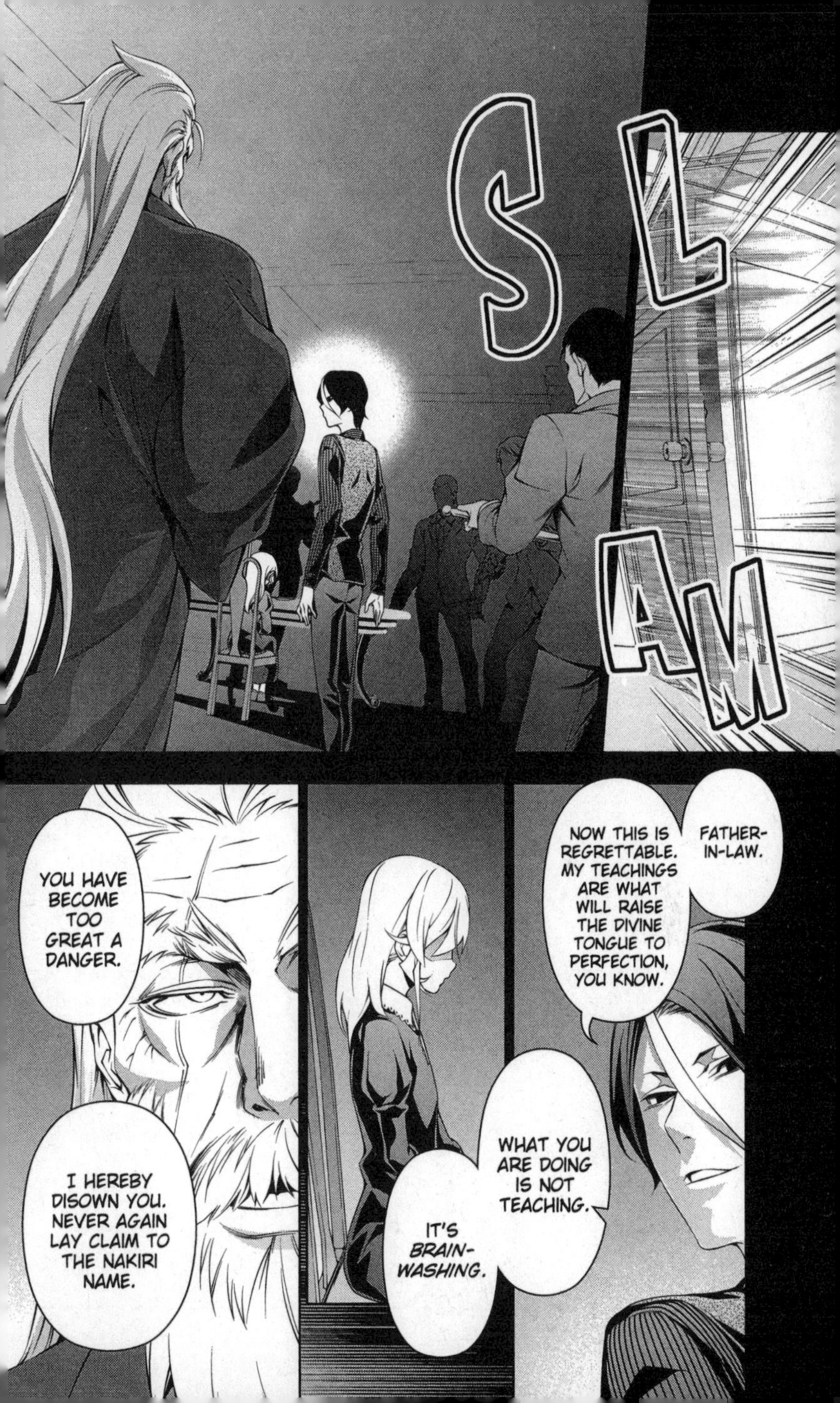
SLAM
FATHER-IN-LAW.
NOW THIS IS REGRETTABLE. MY TEACHINGS ARE WHAT WILL RAISE THE DIVINE TONGUE TO PERFECTION, YOU KNOW.
WHAT YOU ARE DOING IS NOT TEACHING.
IT'S BRAIN-WASHING.
YOU HAVE BECOME TOO GREAT A DANGER.
I HEREBY DISOWN YOU. NEVER AGAIN LAY CLAIM TO THE NAKIRI NAME.

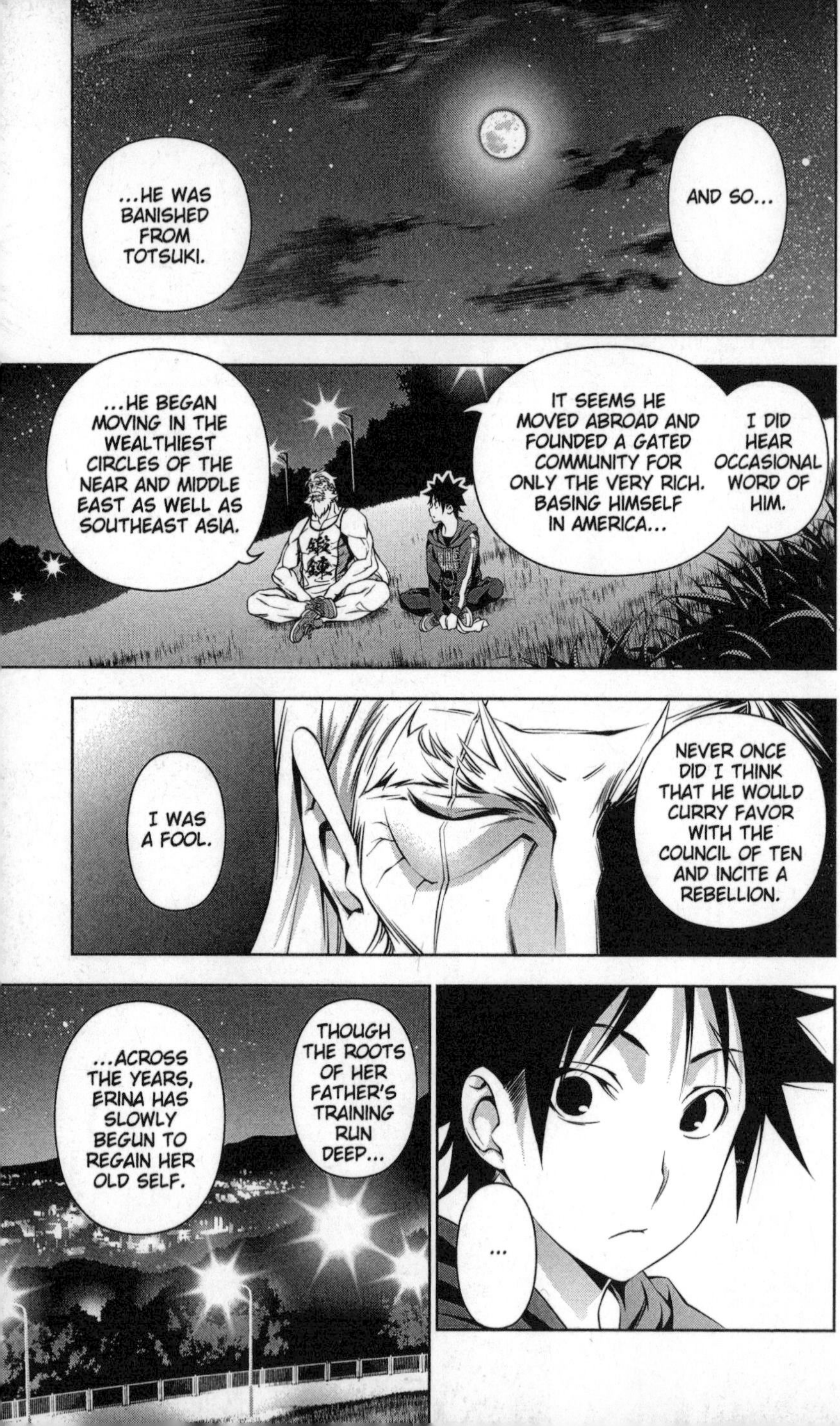
AND SO...
...HE WAS BANISHED FROM TOTSUKI.
I DID HEAR OCCASIONAL WORD OF HIM.
IT SEEMS HE MOVED ABROAD AND FOUNDED A GATED COMMUNITY FOR ONLY THE VERY RICH. BASING HIMSELF IN AMERICA...
...HE BEGAN MOVING IN THE WEALTHIEST CIRCLES OF THE NEAR AND MIDDLE EAST AS WELL AS SOUTHEAST ASIA.
NEVER ONCE DID I THINK THAT HE WOULD CURRY FAVOR WITH THE COUNCIL OF TEN AND INCITE A REBELLION.
I WAS A FOOL.
...
THOUGH THE ROOTS OF HER FATHER'S TRAINING RUN DEEP...
...ACROSS THE YEARS, ERINA HAS SLOWLY BEGUN TO REGAIN HER OLD SELF.

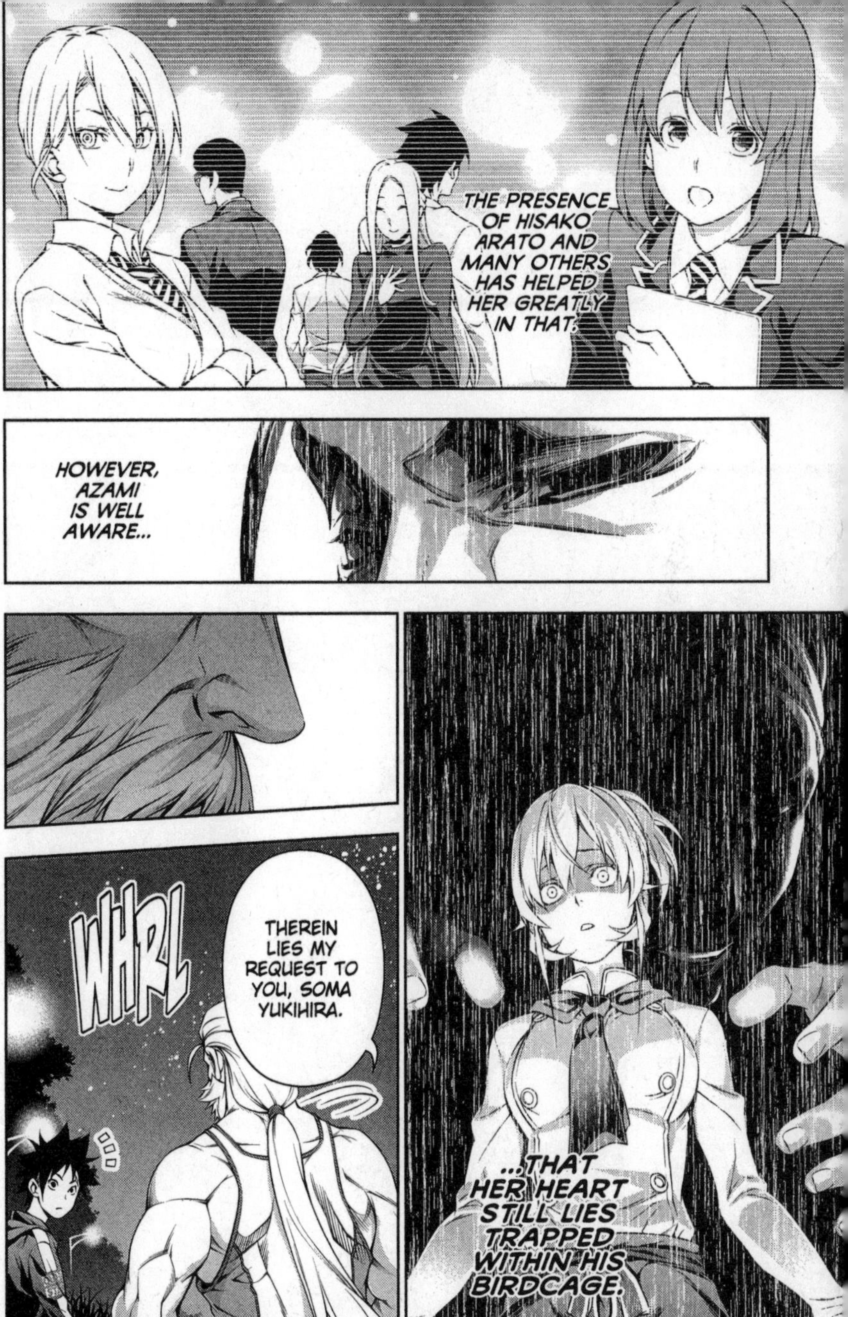
THE PRESENCE OF HISAKO ARATO AND MANY OTHERS HAS HELPED HER GREATLY IN THAT.
HOWEVER, AZAMI IS WELL AWARE...
...THAT HER HEART STILL LIES TRAPPED WITHIN HIS BIRDCAGE.
WHRL
THEREIN LIES MY REQUEST TO YOU, SOMA YUKIHIRA.

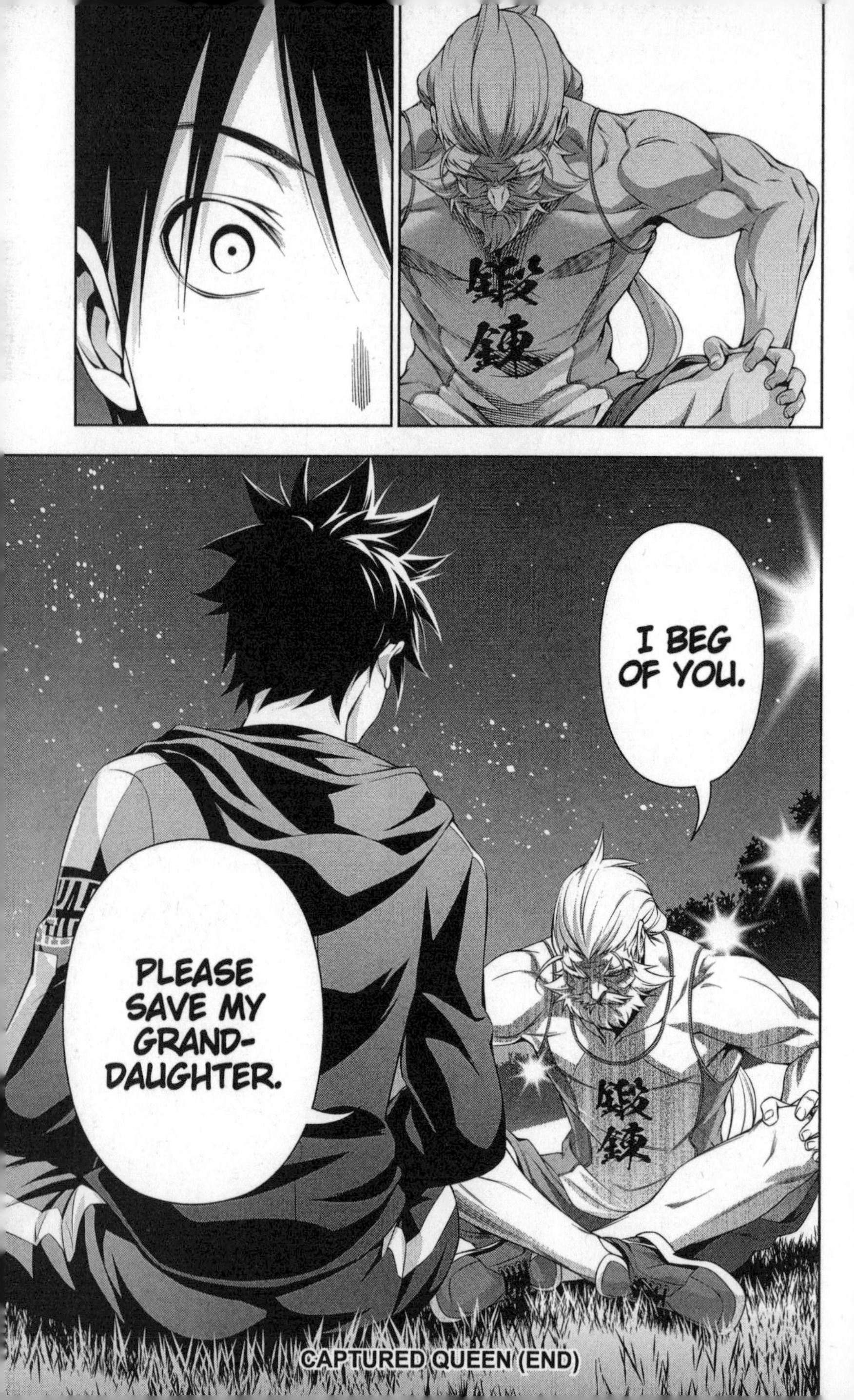
鍛錬
I BEG OF YOU.
PLEASE SAVE MY GRAND-DAUGHTER.
CAPTURED QUEEN (END)

EYESHIELD 21

STORY BY **RIICHIRO INAGAKI**
ART BY **YUSUKE MURATA**

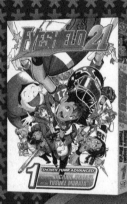

From the artist of *One-Punch Man!*

Wimpy Sena Kobayakawa has been running away from
bullies all his life. But when the football gear comes
on, things change—Sena's speed and uncanny ability
to elude big bullies just might give him what it takes to
become a great high school football hero! Catch all the
bone-crushing action and slapstick comedy of Japan's
hottest football manga!

You're Reading in the Wrong Direction!!

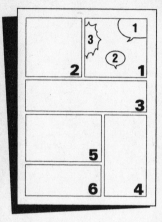

Whoops! Guess what? You're starting at the wrong end of the comic!

...It's true! In keeping with the original Japanese format, **Food Wars!** is meant to be read from right to left, starting in the upper-right corner.

Unlike English, which is read from left to right, Japanese is read from right to left, meaning that action, sound effects and word-balloon order are completely reversed... something which can make readers unfamiliar with Japanese feel pretty backwards themselves. For this reason, manga or Japanese comics published in the U.S. in English have sometimes been published "flopped"—that is, printed in exact reverse order, as though seen from the other side of a mirror.

By flopping pages, U.S. publishers can avoid confusing readers, but the compromise is not without its downside. For one thing, a character in a flopped manga series who once wore in the original Japanese version a T-shirt emblazoned with "M A Y" (as in "the merry month of") now wears one which reads "Y A M"! Additionally, many manga creators in Japan are themselves unhappy with the process, as some feel the mirror-imaging of their art skews their original intentions.

We are proud to bring you Yuto Tsukuda and Shun Saeki's **Food Wars!** in the original unflopped format.

For now, though, turn to the other side of the book and let the adventure begin...!

—Editor

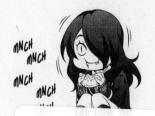

MNCH
MNCH
MNCH
MNCH

D0557530